Transforming Liberalism

The Theology of James Luther Adams

To Beeth, and Matt —

George Kimmich Beach

Geo. K Beach

SKINNER HOUSE BOOKS

BOSTON

Printed in the United States.

Cover design by Suzanne Morgan
Text design by Sandra Rigney

ISBN 1-55896-482-7

Library of Congress Cataloging-in-Publication Data

Beach, George K.
    Transforming liberalism: the theology of James Luther Adams / George Kimmich Beach.—1st ed.
        p. cm.
    Includes biobliographical references and index.
    ISBN 1-55896-482-7 (alk. paper)
    1. Adams, James Luther, 1901–   I. Title.

BX9869.A32B43 2004
230'.91—dc22   2004014926

5 4 3 2 1
07 06 05 04

We gratefully acknowledge permission for the following materials:

Excerpt from *Murder in the Cathedral* by T. S. Eliot, copyright 1935 by Harcourt, Inc. and renewed 1963 by T. S. Eliot, reprinted by permission of the publisher.

Excerpt from "East Coker" in *Four Quartets*, copyright 1940 by T. S. Eliot and renewed 1968 by Esme Valerie Eliot, reprinted by permission of Harcourt, Inc.

"For the Time Being," copyright 1944 and renewed 1972 by W. H. Auden, "September 1, 1939," copyright 1940 and renewed 1968 by W. H. Auden, from *Collected Poems* by W. H. Auden. Used by permission of Random House, Inc.

"This consciousness which is aware" reprinted by permission of the publishers and the Trustees of Amherst College from *The Poems of Emily Dickinson*, Thomas H. Johnson, ed., Cambridge, Mass.: The Belknap Press of Harvard University Press, copyright © 1951, 1955, 1979, 1983 by the President and Fellows of Harvard College.

To James Luther Adams,
masterful teacher, wise mentor, constant friend,
who spoke to us "not without a parable,"
that the community-forming and transforming power
be not hidden from the rising generation;

and to my dear grandchildren,
Alec, Elizabeth, Erick, and Elise.

Give ear, O my people, to my law: incline your ears to the words of my mouth. I will open my mouth in a parable: I will utter dark sayings of old: Which we have heard and known, and our fathers have told us. We will not hide them from their children, showing to the generation the praises of the LORD, and his strength, and his wonderful works that he hath done.

—Psalm 78:1-4

And he said unto them, Is a candle brought to be put under a bushel, or under a bed? And not to be set on a candlestick? For there is nothing hid which shall not be manifested; neither was there any thing kept secret, but that it should come abroad. If any man has ears to hear, let him hear. And he said unto them, Take heed what ye hear: with what measure ye mete, it shall be measured to you, and unto you that hear shall more be given. For he that hath, to him shall be given, and from him that hath not, from him shall be taken even that which he hath.... And with many such parables spake he the word unto them, as they were able to hear it. But without a parable spake he not unto them....

—Mark 4:21-25, 33

Contents

Introduction

JLA wears his vast learning gracefully.... As a theologian he is *sui generis*: his work is liberal in spirit while it respects and draws upon many traditions; it is catholic in its range of knowledge and insight; his canon includes much more than that drawn upon by traditionalist and parochial colleagues; it has the aroma of moral and intellectual passion.

—James M. Gustafson

PROFESSOR GUSTAFSON'S WORDS on the uniqueness and power of James Luther Adams as thinker and teacher testify to Adams's importance to the communities in which he worked. I would offer a more personal testimony. Jim Adams was a man of immense appreciations, a quality he would signal in his lectures by saying, "Now here is something remarkable!" An interpretive commentary would follow on such disparate matters as the emergence of contemporary sensibility in the "serial" music compositions of Anton Webern, or the ethical ethos reflected in television soaps (he had his own lunchtime favorite), or the imagery of spiritual transformation projected by the sixteenth-century revolutionary Thomas Münzer. Being vastly curious and enthusiastic, Adams sparked curiosity and enthusiasm in his auditors. In this way his "moral and intellectual passion" became a source of astonishment and delight.

Adams said that he had learned early on—from his college speech professor—that a good public speaker is one who "elicits involuntary attention"—a lesson he took to heart and learned well. With but little exaggeration we can say that he was interested in everything, tried to read everything, and spoke or wrote almost as broadly. Perhaps this is why he never did what many of his friends and students wished upon him, to present his theological thought in a comprehensive and unified way. In the end, the wish for his magnum opus reflected not his need but our own, for he never expressed the slightest regret or sense of unfulfilled promise in his lifework, which includes hundreds of published essays and addresses.

This book brings together Adams's numerous memorable and insightful words—including the stories for which he is justly famous—on the entire range of his religious, historical, cultural, and ethical interests. In fact, his thought does not fit into traditional categories. For anyone who would write about his thought as a unified whole, the challenge is to find a central, organizational principle that is inherent within his thought, not imposed from without.

Why undertake the effort to understand Adams? One of his students, Karen Smith, suggests an answer: "Adams belongs in the company of such artist-teachers as Andreas Segovia and Elisabeth Schwarzkopf," who performed as masterfully as they taught. I have found that "sitting at the feet" of Jim Adams was an educational experience unavailable elsewhere, and I am entirely certain that others will also.

The Impact of Adams's Thought

The influence of James Luther Adams can be gauged by the statements of his students and professional colleagues in the fields of theology and religious social ethics. James Gustafson and other academic colleagues—many of them his students at the University of Chicago and at Harvard—have spoken of the distinctive character and broad range of his thought. Often they speak not only of his intellectual creativity but also his generosity and personal interest. Paul Tillich, probably the most influential liberal theologian of the twentieth century, remarks on the blend of intellectual and personal qualities that he found in Adams, in a tribute published in the *Festscrift* presented to Adams when he retired from Harvard:

> Without my dear friend, Jim Adams, I would not be what I am, biographically as well as theologically. He received me graciously when I came to Chicago as a German refugee; he has studied my thought so thoroughly that I have sent to him all those who wanted to know about it, because he knows more about my writings than I do myself.... There is a humility in his attitude which I deeply admire. It is ultimately an expression of *agape*, which cares for the smallest, without itself becoming small. But there is another side of him that is equally astonishing: the largeness of interests and involvements in all sides of [humanity's] cultural creativity: in the arts as well as in the sciences. Again it is love, the *eros* toward the true and the beautiful, which makes it possible for him to unite intensive participation in these functions of the human spirit with his continuous concern for the practical problems of individuals as well as of the society. In theological terminology I could say that James Luther Adams is a living proof of the ultimate unity of *eros* and *agape* and for the possibility that this unity becomes manifest, however fragmentarily, in a human being.

Adams is associated with Paul Tillich as a translator of his early writings from the German and as an interpreter of his thought. During the latter part of his career, he and Tillich were colleagues at Harvard, where Adams was Edward Mallinckrodt Jr. Professor of Divinity and Tillich was University Professor.

In addition to his writings on Tillich, Adams's largest and most distinctive contribution to contemporary thought concerns voluntary associations as agencies of democracy and reform. The social and political significance of this work is noted by Professor Walter George Muelder, of Boston University School of Theology:

> No contemporary theologian has contributed more or stimulated as much thinking and research about voluntary associations as Prof. Adams has. Their origins, types, conflicts, pathologies, and promise have all engaged his attention.... For Adams the church ought to be a voluntary society and so conceived both theologically and socially. It has been a genuine historical paradigm for other voluntary associations since the days of the early church.... The struggle for religious liberty and the resultant separation of church and state, still incompletely realized, stand at the center of the human struggle for a humane and open society.... Voluntary associations profoundly affect the ethos and action-style of society. Adams's thesis that they are indispensable for genuine freedom is persuasive.

Another tribute to Adams's influence, showing how closely the intellectual and personal sides of his lifework were related, was recently given by David Little, formerly senior scholar of the United States Institute of Peace, now a professor at Harvard Divinity School. He comments on the effect Adams had on both his ideas and his sense of moral priorities.

> When I came to Harvard Divinity School some forty years ago, I was a resolute and committed Barthian, heavily influenced by neo-orthodox theology... which had taught me to be dismissive in my encounters with alien views. Naturally, I was deeply suspicious of liberal Protestantism, particularly that sort identified as Unitarianism, of which JLA [Adams] was a leading representative. May I say that, in this respect,

my experiences with JLA turned out to be life-transforming. It was a profoundly liberating experience to encounter a genuinely liberal spirit, a man who was tolerant in the very best sense of the word. He welcomed views he didn't accept or altogether share, and almost seemed happiest in the presence of people who disagreed with him. JLA ... greatly influenced my subsequent professional concern with human and natural rights, and in particular with the task of implementing religious freedom and equality around the world.

Little's words were spoken in an address—the 2003 James Luther Adams Lecture, in Cambridge, Massachusetts—on the importance of natural law theory in dealing with intercultural conflict in the contemporary world. While this book comments on natural law and on many other intellectual contributions of Adams, its focus is on our sense of Adams as a *mahatma*, a "great soul" who affects our understanding of what it means to be a moral and spiritual member of the human community.

Theology in a Prophetic Key

The core of Adams's thought is rooted in the idea of a prophetic theology. Paul Tillich, a one-time leader in the German "religious socialist" movement, says of Adams,

> He represents the prophetic element in Christianity that much [of the] teaching in the churches badly neglects. I even may confess that I feel him as a "thorn in my flesh," when "the flesh" tries to ignore the social implications of the Christian message! He represents in his whole being a warning against a theology that sacrifices the prophetic for the mystical element, though both of them, as he and I agree, are essential to religion.

Adams defines mysticism as "a sense and taste" for "the infinite, the ground of all meaningful existence." He gives mysticism a place within the context of a prophetic religion, but there is no doubt that his heart lies not with the private, inward, and "infinite" realms of life, but with the public realm, the realm of ethical commitments and socially formed identity. At the time that Tillich wrote those words, almost thirty years had passed since Adams published his remarkable "mid-life" autobiographical essay—in 1939, at age thirty-eight—titled "Taking Time Seriously." In this essay, he describes the intellectual, moral, and spiritual place to which his pilgrimage had brought him:

> In Tillich's view of the dialectical nature of reality, of revelation, of God, of the Kingdom, of human nature and history, I find an interpretation and an application of Christian doctrine which are far more relevant to the social and divine forces that determine the destiny of humanity than in any other theologian I happen to know about. Here, if ever, is a theologian who takes time seriously.

The dialectic that Adams finds central and illuminating in Tillich—a concept frequently referred to in his own writings—is not forbiddingly abstract. Unlike formal, deductive logic, dialectical logic is a way of thinking that describes oppositions and seeks unities. I learned at my artist-mother's knee that there are no pure blacks and whites in nature. So too there are no pure opposites in moral and spiritual life; oppositions are always found in shades of gray that, in time, give way to new realities. We can say that dialectic constantly moves from "either/or" to "both/and." For instance, Adams tells the story of two theological students, one keen on God and the other keen on ethical commitment. The first accuses the second of having "mere morality," and the second retorts that the first has "mere God." The argument is familiar and significant, of course, but for Adams it is finally a matter of "both/and." Theology and ethics are inextricably interrelated in his thought; each criticizes, enriches, and thus—in time—each decisively modifies the other. In short, they are dialectically related.

Further introductory comment will help the reader understand Adams's use of dialectic, including many places where it is implicit but not specifically named. *Dialectic* does not always have a precise meaning, as in the familiar notion of a movement of thought from thesis to antithesis to synthesis. The concept seems to have originated with the idea of *dialogue*: Plato proposed that thought progresses to reasoned conclusions through a conversational inquiry between two or more minds (see his *Theatetus*); thus most of his writings took the form of dialogues, especially between Socrates and others. Thinking itself, then, may be seen as "the dialogue of the mind with itself"—thought moving from question to answer, to further question and further answer. More generally stated, dialectic is a form reasoning through oppositions, toward unities. Adams does this constantly.

Adams's thought most clearly shows its dialectical bent when he counterposes two thinkers (for instance, Søren Kierkegaard and Karl Marx) or two ideas (for instance, natural law and creative novelty) and suggests that truth must synthesize elements of both. He often cites Pascal's advice, "Practice opposite virtues and occupy the distance between them," as a dictum that shows the kinship between dialectic and paradox. But is dialectic rooted in the dynamics of historical change as well as in human thinking? Adams implies that it is, as when he speaks of theories of the periodization of history (usually in triads, from Joachim of Fiore to Karl Marx) and of Tillich's sense of "the dialectical nature of reality." He enjoys noting that the "dispensational theology" that he learned as a child—the idea that the new and old Testaments, or Covenants, are linked historical epochs—prepared him to understand that the question of meaning and direction in history is a central theological issue.

Adams articulates theology "in a prophetic key" because he believes that social relevance and ethical commitment are the touchstones of authentic faith. Authentic faith is reliance upon that which, when we are faithful, will not betray us; he calls "spurious" faith our "ever-recurrent reliance upon the unreliable." His theological writings are an ongoing essay on the difference between authentic and spurious faith, and between reliable and unreliable faith. The dialectical relationship between faith and ethical com-mitment that Adams proposes leads to a conclusion that may seem surprising, given his thoroughly Biblical language. Ethical commit-ment is a clearer sign of authentic faith than is any particular lan-guage of religion, including God-language itself. He writes,

> An authentic prophet is one who prophesies in a fashion that does not comfort the people, but actually calls them to make some new sacrifices. That's an authentic prophet, whether one speaks in the name of God or whatever. A great deal of au-thentic prophetism in the modern world is to be found in non-religious terms and in non-church configurations, often even hostile to the church. The churches themselves have broadly failed the prophetic function. Therefore a good deal of atheism, from my point of view, is theologically significant.

Prophetic faith yields a theology of hope. It means proclaim-ing in the face of present injustice, a justice to come, and in the face of present hatred and fear, a peace to come—*both* as moral commitments *and* as articles of faith. It means knowing that the sin of religion is "cheap grace," offering spiritual comfort without "the call to make some new sacrifices."

With his liberal and in some respects radical perspective, Adams is able to communicate with the secular-minded and the frankly untheological. Nevertheless, he works within an explicitly Christian theological framework. When he speaks of prophetic theology, he is pointing to the creative edge within the religious currents of his time and our own. So doing, he seeks to take "lib-eral religion" out of an increasingly isolated and culturally mar-ginal status and transform it. Liberalism has accented divine immanence and benevolence, the point of identifying human ideas and ideals with God, and then noticing that our ideas and ideals are assumed to be self-authenticating, rendering God dis-pensable. The new liberalism that Adams seeks accents God's transcendence and power. Liberalism has tended to attenuate reli-

gion to the point where its own children have opted for straight-
forward secularism. The transformed liberalism that Adams seeks
knows that we are "incurably religious." In sum, his prophetic theology does not soften theological concepts but radicalizes them:

> Prophetic theology...rejects the notion that Christian faith
> can provide sanction for a culture-religion. It holds that his-
> tory and culture point beyond themselves to a commanding,
> judging, sustaining, and transforming reality. Confidence in
> and response to this reality is the nerve of prophetic faith.

Political ideologies such as fascism and communism provided
demonstrations of what Adams and his generation see as "culture-
religion" raised to its highest pitch. To the critical thrust of the
prophetic theology, Adams adds a creative thrust—again, it is
both/and:

> The Lord of history calls men and women into a community
> of faith. In response to the Lord of history this community
> of faith takes time and culture seriously, so seriously as to
> hold that political and social institutions, the arts and the
> sciences, as well as the individual believer, have a vocation
> from on high. Indeed, prophetic faith in its critical and
> formative power serves as the basis for a true and viable au-
> tonomy of these spheres. Redemption is for them as well as
> for individual persons. Accordingly, prophetic theology rec-
> ognizes the obligation to interpret the signs of the times in
> the light of the End, that is, of the Reign of God. It aims to
> speak to the concrete situations in which men and women
> find themselves.

This is vintage Adams, packing multiple themes into a single
paragraph— community of faith, political and social institutions,
the arts *and* the sciences, vocation, redemption, the interpretation
of history, eschatology, the concrete situation—leaving our minds
spinning. This book unpacks these same themes.

Biographical Sketch

Adams transcends denominational categories. It is not an exaggeration to say that he speaks to, and deeply affects, people of every faith tradition and of no definable faith. At the same time he has deep roots in Protestant Christianity and was actively engaged in Unitarian Universalist churches and associations throughout his adulthood. While intellectuals commonly disguise their religious roots and eschew "organized religion," Adams holds that historically formed and institutionally embodied commitments are essential to character formation and ethical responsibility. His byword, "taking time seriously," means at least this: Know your historical roots and participate fully in your present religious, professional, and civic communities. A significant instance of Adams's church involvement is his proposal, late in his career, of revised language for the Principles and Purposes statement of the Unitarian Universalist Association. Among several "sources of the living tradition we share," the statement, adopted in 1985, names the following: "Words and deeds of prophetic women and men which challenge us to confront powers and structures of evil with justice, compassion, and the transforming power of love." The words are redolent with Biblical language and Adams's own prophetic theology.

James Luther Adams was born in 1901 in the small farming community of Ritzville, Washington, the son of an itinerant fundamentalist minister and an equally devout mother. Soon his father shifted from the Baptist fold to the Plymouth Brethren, a sect that held to St. Paul's example of a "tent-making" rule of ministry: To accept pay for preaching the Gospel corrupts the faith, for a true preacher is beholden only to God. As a result his father worked at farming until physical disability threw responsibility for supporting the family onto young James and his two sisters. An astonishing array of enterprises followed, from his childhood to his youth, when Adams became the secretarial assistant to a regional superintendent on the Northern Pacific railroad. He chose the University of Minnesota because it was on the railroad line and he could continue to work full-time and study. He seldom slept—a persisting life pattern. While in college Adams rejected the otherworldly and rigidly fundamentalist Christianity of his youth, to his parents' chagrin, initially rebelling against all religion. Before graduation, however, he yielded to the calling that underlay all his protests against it: He enrolled in Harvard Divinity School, in Cambridge, Massachusetts, to study for the ministry.

From this time his mind was formed and reformed by his theological studies and, in his restless quest to "deprovincialize" himself, by reading and studying English and comparative literature. His liberal theological convictions led to pastorates in Boston-area Unitarian churches, first in Salem and later in Wellesley Hills, where he vividly remembers tangling with conservative patriarchs in his own congregations over social issues—in particular, unionization of cotton mills and flag-waving patriotism. He married Margaret Ann Young of Salem, a student at the New England Conservatory. He and Margaret had three daughters, raised largely during their years in Chicago, and were devoted to each other through fifty years of marriage.

A sense of disillusionment with the church led Adams to question his commitment to ministry. During his pastorates he taught English composition at Boston University part-time and could have become an English professor, just as earlier in his life, he could easily have become a railroad executive. What held him, he reflected, was his commitment to the Church as a community of faith, something the university could not embody for him. In the end, however, by preparing himself for teaching in a theological seminary, he was able to choose both worlds. Commitment to meaning-providing social institutions became the hallmark of his religious and moral vocation.

Besides the usual voracious diet of readings in history, sociology, the arts, and theology, he undertook two extended study trips to Europe in the 1920s and 1930s—visiting England, France, and especially Germany. This was the heyday of Karl Barth, Paul Tillich, Rudolf Bultmann, Karl Jaspers, Martin Heidegger, Rudolf

Otto, Dietrich Bonhoeffer, and many less famous figures in German theology and philosophy. He met or studied with all of them. This was also the time when Nazism overwhelmed Germany and infected virtually all its institutions. Resistance, Adams learned from several "palpitating" experiences, became increasingly risky and costly. Many of his most vivid stories come out of these encounters. The wider significance that he drew from these European experiences was the recognition that, in the face of fascist fanaticism, liberal institutions—church, state, university—generally met a crisis of integrity and courage.

He returned home to teach theology and social ethics at Meadville Theological School, the Unitarian seminary in Chicago, and subsequently, the Federated Theological Faculty of the University of Chicago. In Chicago, liberal social and political organizations engaged his energies (he founded, with others, the reformist Independent Voters of Illinois). In consequence, his doctoral studies and dissertation (on the political and cultural theology of Paul Tillich) were completed only several years afterward. In 1956 Adams was appointed to the faculty of Harvard Divinity School, where he taught Christian social ethics to ministerial and doctoral-degree students from the whole range of faith traditions. The homes of Jim and Margaret Adams, first in Chicago and later in Cambridge, became centers for discussion among students, academic colleagues, and community activists. Their weekly late-evening open house became an important part of my own theological education at Harvard. During this time Adams was publishing dozens of essays, book introductions, and addresses in the areas of historical and contemporary theology and religious social ethics. Late in his career, former students assembled and, with his collaboration, published several collections of his essays and addresses.

Following his Harvard retirement, Adams accepted teaching appointments, first in Boston and then in Chicago. After his third "retirement," he and Margaret returned to their home in Cambridge, and shortly afterward, in 1977, Margaret succumbed to cancer. They were devoted to each other; he had dedicated a book to her as "the beloved" and writes with deep feeling about the spiritual significance of marriage. The James Luther Adams Foundation was formed at this time to provide secretarial and publications support, helping him to continue lifelong passions—writing and speaking, religion and politics, conversation and ministry. In 1994, after years of intense discomfort due to disintegrating vertebra, still lucid and engaged with others until his last six months, James Luther Adams died at the home he and Margaret had built on the historic Shady Hill estate in Cambridge, Massachusetts.

"Liberalism Is Dead. Long Live Liberalism!"

During the midyears of his long and active life, Adams became a man with a mission, namely, to transform religious and political liberalism into a realistic, resilient, and indeed transforming cultural force. In this period (roughly 1935 to 1945) Adams undertook several life-changing initiatives, in addition to shifting from the parish to a teaching ministry. Seeing his adopted Unitarian denomination fall into incipient decline, he founded with several allies the Commission of Appraisal, which renewed institutional confidence and purposefulness within the Unitarian denomination in the ensuing years.

Seeing liberal religion caught in a "cultural lag," compared with the intellectual and social currents that he had experienced in Europe, Adams cofounded and edited a new quarterly, *The Journal of Liberal Religion*. At the same time, he threw himself into numerous social causes—civil liberties, urban community organization, fighting American isolationism, fighting racism, and other expressions of his ethics of engagement in voluntary associations. He also completed his doctoral dissertation for the University of Chicago, published as *Paul Tillich's Philosophy of Culture, Science, and Religion*. As the creator of a language of faith that was both innovative and historically rooted, Tillich provided the intellectual basis of the theological renewal that Adams sought.

Adams announced his intention to seek a transformed liberalism in an editorial titled "Why Liberal?", which was published in the second issue of *The Journal of Liberal Religion*, and continued in the third issue with the provocative title "The Liberalism That Is Dead." In the first of these, he identifies four "essential elements of liberalism." "First, liberalism holds that nothing is complete, and thus nothing is exempt from criticism"—including liberalism itself. "Second, liberalism holds that all relations between persons ought ideally to rest on mutual free consent and not on coercion"—but note the caveat, "ideally." "Third, being an ethical procedure ... liberalism involves the moral obligation to direct one's effort toward the establishment of democratic community." Thus liberalism is a philosophy with intrinsic social and political dimensions. It also has intrinsic spiritual consequences: "Fourth, liberalism holds that the resources (human and divine) which are available for the achievement of meaningful change justify an attitude of ultimate optimism"—a principle of hope that he combines with a proximate pessimism. Adams continues,

> Now we may return to the previous question: Why liberal? And we answer: Because confidence in the principles of liberalism is the only effective resistant to the ultimate skepticism and despair on the one side and to blasphemous claims to authority and suppressions of criticism on the other. These are the enemies of the human spirit whose dangers are threatening today.

In "The Liberalism That Is Dead" he returns to these same four elements and describes the way they have been distorted or trivialized. In consequence, liberalism is widely seen as ineffectual in the face of contemporary ideological and spiritual conflicts, and therefore passé. First, liberalism's dynamic sense of truth and its consequent insistence that "nothing is exempt from criticism" is turned into a relativism that thinks all beliefs equally true. Then no historically rooted faith is possible and spiritual fads rush in to fill the void. Second, liberalism's devotion to voluntary consent and rejection of coercion are distorted as an anti-institutional bias and a "fissiparous individualism." Announcing "individual freedom of belief," liberalism frustrates efforts to achieve consensus and shared commitment. Third, Adams finds liberalism infected with the biased belief of the middle class that "democratic community is already achieved," cutting the nerve of prophetic criticism, especially of economic and racial inequality. Believing that one's own culture and values are the most advanced and not conditioned by a social or psychological standpoint, Adams calls belief in "the immaculate conception of ideas." Finally, liberalism is distorted into a faith in progressive enlightenment, especially through education. Ignoring the tragic element in history and the "the evil that good men do," we ignore our own deepest spiritual and moral needs. He asserts,

> The liberalism that is dead is the liberalism that does not call for decision, that does not see that the divine spark in a person rises into flame only through the recognition of the need for a change of heart, a change which produces a skepticism concerning one's own self-sufficiency and "innate divinity"... Only where there is sincere recognition of incompleteness and failure, only there are the spirit of liberalism and true religion to be found. Hence the liberal expects to hear over and over again: Liberalism is dead. Long live liberalism!

We may say that "transforming liberalism" signifies both the task of liberalism willing to confront and change itself from within and the object of efforts, namely to be a liberalism that is genuinely transforming.

Adams's call for a transformed liberalism is as relevant today as it was when he first wrote these words more than sixty years ago. The historical situation and the intellectual climate of today are, of course, significantly different. Nevertheless, it is striking to see how our sense that we are living in a time of political and cultural crisis and our uncertainty about the ability of liberalism to respond effectively to the needs of the age have not abated but deepened. This is true in political, religious, and intellectual culture. The L-word is commonly shunned by politicians for a host of complex reasons, while *reform* is co-opted by conservatives in, for instance, systems of public welfare, the military, and education. The identity of liberal religion is contested between advocates of religious or secular Humanism, pagan or New Age spiritualities, and liberal Christian and other traditions, especially Buddhism. In consequence liberal religion labors under a disabling tentativeness and identity confusion.

In philosophical and cultural studies, including theology, the idea of postmodernism has arisen in response to the much-discussed and probably much-exaggerated "failure of the Enlightenment project"—the attempt to rationalize all realms of human life and to free people from all forms of "arbitrary authority." Since liberalism has been closely identified with the modern era, the emergence of a postmodern era suggests either an end to liberalism or, as Adams would have it, a radically transformed liberalism. In his seminal essay, "The Ages of Liberalism," Adams argues that liberalism should be understood as originating not in the Enlightenment (or modern) era of the eighteenth and nineteenth centuries, but in the Radical Reformation and Renaissance of the sixteenth and seventeenth centuries, when the idea of a free church separated from state control and the idea of returning to the cultural and religious sources of Western civilization took root. The present-day consequences of such an altered awareness of the origins of liberalism would be significant. The pathway to its renewal in our own postmodern era is not easy to chart, and Adams offers no prescriptions. But his twin claims, "by their groups you shall know them" and "by their roots you shall know them," reflect the associational and historical drives he finds in the Reformation and Renaissance eras and point the way forward. His conception of theology as a system of symbols or "root metaphors" that shape our beliefs about reality and our consequent value commitments is entirely contemporary. It recalls Wittgenstein's idea of religious belief as "a passionate commitment to a system of reference."

Since the idea of postmodernism is more clearly marked by what it is not than what it is, these comments are broad-brush and inherently indefinite. They indicate, however, the contemporary relevance of Adams's thought.

This is not so much a book *about* Adams's thought as it is a book *of* his thought. That is, it is not an academic study that seeks to analyze and evaluate Adams's writings. Rather, it is a synthesis of his thought, taking his own words and linking them within an interpretive structure. Understanding this may affect the way you read the book. Those who want to understand Adams's theological and ethical thought as an articulated whole will read it in the traditional way, from beginning to end.

Others may choose to open the book and read at any point or to turn to a particular subsection listed in the table of contents; a randomly selected citation or a story is likely to suggest meanings or associations in contexts beyond those provided here. This is in keeping with Adams's imaginative form of thought, one that opens outward to various meanings. In addition, there are innumerable interconnections between ideas and narratives found in disparate parts of the book, inviting you to reassemble it according to your own lights.

Adams does not characteristically use the abstract language of theory. For instance, although he was a professor of social ethics, he never discussed the classical theories of ethics. It is as if he took hold of the telescope from the other end and set out to describe social phenomena and our moral or immoral responses to them. In this process rules, ends, or qualities of character may be reflected, but theories such as deontology or teleology are not central to his ethics. What Adams does use, as others have also noted, is the concrete language of things and events, individuals and institutions. He does this to emphasize a point, making it vivid and memorable. Often, in addition, his words take on a symbolic or, in the case of his many stories, a parabolic meaning. Again, his method is in keeping with his content: He understands theology as the reinterpretation of central symbols of a religious tradition in the light of present history. Thus the Incarnation—speaking now in shorthand—is not about an event in the distant historical past but about a present embodiment of self-giving love to which we may give personal witness.

In the interest of presenting Adams's theological thought with the language of concrete things intact, the text includes hundreds of direct quotations from his writings, both the previously published and the unpublished. It also contains numerous citations that Adams drew from the works of others, making them his own in a secondary sense. Some citations are brief or aphoristic; others— especially the stories—are considerably longer. Still others are rhetorical expressions that display Adams's creative use of language, his own way of "eliciting involuntary attention."

Placing many quotations within new and sometimes enlarged contexts has the effect of making Adams an unwitting collaborator in a book he did not himself write. While I have called the book a synthesis of his theology, it could also be called a reading of his many-faceted moral and spiritual vision. (Adams liked Samuel Johnson's words on the art of writing; it is "the art of blotting," choosing this and omitting that.) The final result may sometimes blur the line between Adams's thought and my own—or more precisely, between what I have drawn from and what I have made of Adams's thought, forever blotting! The reader may wish for a more "immaculate conception of the truth" but is unlikely to find it.

How would Adams feel about this appropriation of his words to create this book? We cannot know for sure, but we do know what he said at his eighty-fifth birthday celebration in response to a series of speeches feting his lifetime achievements:

> I remember that Christopher Morley years ago said that after he had published a book he was anxious to read the reviews because he would then find out what he had been doing. And so today, I have been the recipient of many surprises.

With some such words drawing on his erudition and his uncanny wit, he would smile enigmatically. A few days later a letter might come noting omissions.

Adams gave broad latitude to the several editors who tracked down many of his "fugitive essays" and published them in several volumes. As editor of three books of his essays and addresses, the first two with his constant involvement and advice, I found Adams helpful but finally trusting, perhaps even eager to "find out what he had been doing." These publications, and those of Max Stackhouse, Herbert Vetter, and J. Ronald Engel, provide continuing access to his literary legacy. They display the immense range of Adams's interests, but they do not answer the question, What is the organizing principle that lends coherence to his thought? This book seeks the unity within its diversity, mindful that, unrepentant liberal that Adams was, he prized diversity over unity.

Adams is not a systematic thinker—not in the usual sense, or perhaps in any sense. (Thank goodness! many will say.) His student and editor, Max Stackhouse, comments on his elusive intellectual style:

> James Luther Adams is a critical and comparative, not a reflective and systematic thinker. He thinks vis-à-vis other minds, external evidence, or objective events. He seldom sets forth a point of view and works through the logical implications thereof, but continually engages one point of view with the historical alternatives.

The mode of thought that Stackhouse notes exemplifies the previously discussed dialectic that we often see at work in Adams. It is hardly surprising that recurrent ideas would be found in the thought of an inveterate storyteller, since stories have a common structure—a beginning situation, a middle disruption, and an end result.

One of Adams's rhetorical modes is the brief statement that encapsulates a complex whole, such as the following meta-narrative of Christian theology:

> "Creation" refers not only to the initial creation of the world in six days but also to the original innocence and balance of perfect mutuality in the Garden of Eden myth. It refers to the covenant of being, in nature and in the human person— primordial creativity or "original virtue" in contrast to "original sin." The "fall" is the fateful disturbance of "creation" and of mutuality, the separation from the original unity, the breaking of the covenant of being, through the use and abuse of freedom. The psyche turns against itself and others and surrenders to a destructive, demonic aggressiveness or despair; it violates mutuality. "Redemption" is not a return to the innocence of "creation," but rather an overcoming of the cleavage in a new and richer unity. This threefold pattern appears in the Bible, in early Christianity, in the Middle Ages, in the Reformation, and even in Marxism.

This passage not only encapsulates a complex whole in a few words, it also takes the form of a parable of human existence, with several levels of meaning.

When Adams speaks of *creation*, *fall*, and *redemption*, he is not thinking of historical or mythical events. He is thinking of ongoing, contemporary aspects of the spiritual reality within which we live and seek meaning. He is "doing theology," that is, thinking of the major symbols of a religious tradition and interpreting them in relation to the human condition in present history. The book reflects this threefold pattern. Its chapter headings transpose the traditional theological terms into the parallel terms *being, confronting,* and *renewing.* The reader will recognize in the triad the dialectical pattern *thesis, antithesis, synthesis.* The book views each of these aspects of spiritual reality on two levels, the ontological and the ethical; the resulting six chapters show the range and structure of Adams's thought. I do not take sides on the question of whether this pattern is only the author's heuristic device or is a "deep structure" in Adams himself. In any event, the organizational scheme yields a pattern into which the many pieces of his thought fit—more or less!

Reading Adams, it is easier to see (and enjoy!) all the trees than to see the forest they are in. The structure of this book is intended to provide the reader with a way of grasping the many-sided thought of Adams as a theologically coherent whole. This structure also serves as a way of lifting up the several dimensions of his argument about the transformation of liberalism— an argument *with* liberalism that is finally an argument *for* liberalism.

Liberalism is an historical movement, closely identified with the "modern age," comprised by ideas and attitudes that give centrality to personal and social freedom. As such, liberalism touches every area of human life—religion, economics, politics, social values, education, vocations, and the arts. The wide-ranging character of Adams's thought is rooted in the fact that he was interested in, and addressed *all* of these things, placing them within the context of basic religious and ethical ideas. Comments by Frederick S. Carney, one of Adams's doctoral students at the University of Chicago, illustrate the point. Carney recalls a lecture by Adams that he heard at a time when he was undecided about his field of study:

> The precise event that stood out for me, then, and still stands out today, was a highly animated and largely spontaneous lecture of forty minutes on, of all things, the religious experience of looking at a Cézanne apple. Imagine that! Teaching ethics by employing a a nineteenth-century artist to communicate to his hearers a sense of the metaphysical

reality of the world, of the divine mystery that undergirds it, and of the resulting serioiusness of the moral life! I decided before that day was over that my doctoral field would be Christian ethics.

The theology of James Luther Adams is centrally concerned with the "religious substance" that, Paul Tillich argued, lies within and animates all realms of culture. The great breadth and the argumentative edge of Adams's thought are in themselves expressions of the transformed liberalism that he seeks.

Adams speaks of theology as the re-interpretation of the major symbols of a religious tradition in the light of contemporary concerns. His intellectual energies ranged so widely because his concern was world-historical; characteristically, he advocated "epochal consciousness"—a mentality that asks what is happening today and what is the meaning of this age? His central contemporary concern was the transformation of liberalism, to enable it effectively to address the social and political crises of the present age. For he was afraid that liberalism, caught in a "cultural lag," was failing.

In these chapters Adams speaks, first, of religion as the fundamental source of meaning in human life; "being religious" is a matter of honoring both "the intimate" and "the ultimate" sides of human concern. A transformed liberalism will be more comfortable with religious feeling and expression, and more clear about the significance of religion in public life. In the second chapter Adams speaks of a new understanding of human nature and the human condition, for he sees intellectualism, rationalism, and scientism as dead ends for human self-understanding. Better that liberalism own its roots in voluntarism, a philosophical stance that recognizes the ways in which the mind follows the affections and understanding follows engagement and commitment; in brief, a stance that honors "the primacy of the will."

Power, Adams asserts in the third chapter, is not only the capacity to influence but also the capacity to be influenced. Liberalism's excessive optimism about human nature and progress in history have led it to misunderstand evil, often associating it with power. A transformed liberalism, he argues, will "venture a new beatitude: blessed are the powerful," recognizing that demonic abuses of power can only be confronted by authentic power. The fourth chapter concerns the moral imperative to confront injustice. A transformed liberalism will not oppose the individual to the group but will recognize that associational life, including religious and secular groups, is essential to the maintenance of democracy.

In the fifth chapter Adams lifts up the idea of covenant as a unifying social and spiritual process. Covenants operate significantly on the interpersonal and the societal levels; Adams goes on to suggest that reality itself can be understood as a "covenant of being." This ontological vision of reality as a web of internal relations both reflects and corrects our historical covenants. In this way, a transformed liberalism will understand the critical and creative role of theological reflection in human life.

In the final chapter, on the renewal of faith, Adams argues that the central religious question is what is the meaning of human history? And the central moral question is how shall we live and work in response to that meaning? He believes that if we lack any sense of a transcendent source of meaning and power, we will not be able to give reliable answers to these questions. Adams's own answer lies in his call for a faith that, in response to the divine, community-forming power, takes time seriously. Such a liberalism is transforming.

Being Religious:
The Intimate and the Ultimate

WHEN JAMES LUTHER ADAMS says, "The principal things that concern me are *intimacy* and *ultimacy*—the intimate and the ultimate," we are likely to think of the familiar distinction between divine imminence and divine transcendence. Liberalism has often accented the former and denigrated the idea of God's transcendence in traditional theism, but for Adams the two dimensions of religion are inseparable. Rather than discuss the question in abstract terms, he describes human experience in personal and metaphorical language that shows the connection between "the intimate" and "the ultimate," for instance, in these words:

> Love and justice can prevail only where they are supported
> by the fellowship, the friendliness, the concern of each for all
> and of all for each, and the sense of responsibility found in
> the community of primary relations. Those qualities of psy-
> chic relatedness are at the same time the working of the
> grace of God and the medium through which the divine
> power grows in history like the seed that grows in the earth
> "of itself," in Jesus' similie, for through them the active and
> the passive powers of sensitivity operate in mutuality.

Adams understands the intimate and the ultimate as *internally related*—a concept emphasized by process-relational philosophy—such that one is inconceivable without the other. By this alliterative, memorable language, he suggests that the meaning of life is to be found in the bond between our most personal feelings and an otherwise incomprehensible infinitude. This paradoxical awareness is reflected, for instance, in words that Adams cites from Martin Luther: "God is closer even to all his creatures than they are to themselves." Luther's statement contains the idea that divine power is persuasive and internally expressed, rather than coercive and externally imposed. But in the last analysis such ideas cannot be rationally explained, but only imaginatively felt. To be religious—to be "religiously musical," in Adams's phrase—is to have some sense of what this means.

When he calls himself "a theologian of grace," Adams invokes a particular form of religious consciousness. Consider this African proverb: "The whole body must bend down to remove a thorn from the foot." It evokes awareness of the intimate relationship between the great and the small or between the whole and the part, but it does so in a surprising way. We are accustomed to thinking of the humble service of the part to the whole, not the other way around. The idea of grace includes the idea of the whole serving the part, a reversal of worldly servitude. The reversal marks a transformation of consciousness; we inwardly smile for the "revelation" that is given. Such proverbs—small parables, in fact—repel full analysis as oil repels water; to "explain" them is reductive and falsifying. An instance of rhetorical genius is too elusive to be explained, such as the phrase from Dante that Howard Nemerov uses to describe the kind of fit that a poet seeks between a word and its object: It should be as close as "a beast running in its skin." In Adams's vision the intimate and the ultimate are *that close*.

Adams enjoyed telling the story of Martin Luther, who was asked what he would do if he knew that the world would come to an end the very next day. Luther replied, "I would go out and plant a tree." It is the story of the intimate, personal act carried out in the face of ultimate, imponderable facts, such as our own demise, and of responding in faith and hope. Adams told this story several times, in different contexts, but never to my knowledge paused to interpret it or to ask whether Luther really said it. Historians would probably label it apocryphal. But after all, how many good stories would there be if we had to stick to the facts?

An array of meanings may underlie this simple story. Was Luther expressing the attitude of blind faith and irrational hope? Was he also rejecting prognostication in principle, since in Christian vision God can work miracles? Was he perhaps hoping to substitute for apocalyptic terror a prophetic word potent enough to force a divine reprieve from the general destruction? Or was he saying that faith enables us to take control of our lives even in the face of catastrophe? Any of these reflections could follow from the story; their variety and significance attest to the power of a story or a parable that uses commonplace, personal experience to point to something transcendent, ultimate. Adams does not try to explain Luther's words, nor does he note the mythopoetic symmetry that often obtains between stories of the beginning and stories of the end, stories of planting and stories of uprooting. Neither does he note that we can speak of the end of time—of eschatology—only in mythic and personal terms.

Existentially, *eschatology* refers to our awareness of what Frank Kermode calls "the sense of an ending," something implicit in every story. Adams speaks of "eschatological consciousness," an awareness that the future weighs heavily upon the present by means of the decisions we can make *only* in the present. But faith can render the burden of responsibility light. Peter Steinke notes that "*escahtos* is the future influencing the present" and quotes Helmut Thielicke: "One who possesses the last hour need not be anxious about the next hour." In all these ways and more, awareness of the intimate and the ultimate meet.

In this chapter, Adams argues that "being religious" is an inescapable aspect of the human condition, although many seek to escape it. Religion arises from an awakened spiritual consciousness and an aroused moral conscience, and it is shaped by historically rooted symbols of meaning—symbols that link intimate experience and ideas of ultimate reality. Often this process begins, as it did in Adams's own life experience, with the recovery of feelings first experienced in childhood, leading to a re-valuation of the place of religion in one's life.

Mature religion does not remain at the level of felt experience, but undertakes critical and creative reflection; in Adams's words, "An unexamined faith is not worth having." Just as all people are "incurably religious," so too "all are theologians," Adams asserts; that is, all people make basic assumptions about meaning and values, whether they are deeply reflective about those assumptions or not. Liberalism has fostered a critical stance toward traditional religious faiths; when it does not equally foster self-criticism and its own spiritual sources, it loses a sense of sacred presence. To recover the sacred we must recover the sense of humility before that which transcends us, and, Adams accents, an accompanying readiness to be changed from within. He invites us to move from an unformed religious awareness to a crystallized religious self-understanding, recognizing points at which our ultimate concern is united with our intimate experience.

Religious Consciousness

Among the most joyful hymns arranged by Johann Sebastian Bach is *Wachet auf, ruft uns die Stimme*—"Sleepers, awake!" It bespeaks the consciousness that rises to the day with renewed confidence and strength:

> … No mortal eye hath seen,
> no mortal ear hath heard
> such wondrous things,
> therefore with joy our song shall soar
> in praise to God forevermore. Amen!

This Reformation-era hymn was one of many chorales that Adams and his young Turk friends succeeded in inserting into the new Unitarian hymnal, published in 1937, as part of their mission to bring the classics of Christian hymnody back into familiarity and use. Little of this hymnody has survived in subsequent Unitarian Universalist hymnals.

Renewed faith at the personal or the communal level will be rooted in an awakened religious consciousness. A substantial and potent religious consciousness is inseparable from "parabolic vision"—seeing what is hidden from ordinary view with the help of a saying, a story, an image, an allegory, or a parable. Life's endings and beginnings are matters of intense interest, emotionally freighted and veiled from sight. If wisdom is rooted in deep recollection, as philosophers since Plato have thought, then Adams's conscious beginnings will serve as a starting place for reflection on renewed consciousness and renewed faith:

> My earliest recollection goes back to the year 1906 when I was four years old. Our family was kneeling in prayer, all of us burying our heads in pillows. We could scarcely breathe, for the farmhouse was in the path of one of the worst dust storms of a decade in the Pacific Northwest, and we were praying for relief. A few minutes before, blinded by the dust, I had lost my way in the farmyard, and on rejoining the family circle my prayer may well have been one of thanksgiving for having found the path to the house as well as of petition for the quieting of the wind. I was told much later that my father, a Baptist country preacher of pre-millenarian persuasion, prayed then and there for the Second Coming.

Within these words we hear the pathos of the child's dawning recognition that the world contains forces beyond our control. Does God control them—using them against us or saving us from them? The child learns that we must cling to one another for such protection and comfort as we can get.

Religious consciousness seems to arise together with the consciousness of life itself—consciousness of life as something given, as something that is finite and indeed fragile. In time a person gains a self-conscious sense of who one is, a sense of identity and direction, sometimes thought of as one's "life purpose or destiny." Adams regards the achievement of personal identity as a central moral task of a person's life. In this vein he speaks of "the hound of our identity," an image he ascribes to Emily Dickinson. Apparently he is thinking of this mystery-laden poem:

> This consciousness that is aware
> Of Neighbors and the Sun
> Will be the one aware of Death
> And that itself alone
>
> Is traversing the interval
> Experience between
> And most profound experiment
> Appointed unto Men.
>
> How adequate unto itself
> Its properties shall be
> Itself unto itself and none
> Shall make discovery.
>
> Adventure most unto itself
> The Soul condemned to be—
> Attended by a single Hound
> Its own identity.

Religion is rooted in our earliest awareness of life as a contingent reality. We become aware at some point that life does not simply go on and on but achieves a final shape. Consciousness of our lives' finitude, Dickinson suggests, raises awareness of our life experience as a story with a beginning and an ending, a direction, and an inherent meaning and character. Such a story would also disclose our identity, first and foremost to ourselves.

Both personal and wider meanings that Adams may have seen in his earliest childhood memory remain in the background, without comment. Should we call it "The Whirlwind" or perhaps "The boy who found his way home"? The title depends on what we think the story is about, accepting Kenneth Burke's idea that a perfect title sums up the whole work. His story reminds us that the *intimate* experience of the child can raise *ultimate* issues, fundamental concerns of a person's life that are unresolved. The opposite effect can also be seen: Ultimate issues may bring the emergent person, even while still a small child, into awareness of intimate thoughts and feelings. Without subjectivity there is no sense of individual identity. For the child even temporary separation raises profound anxiety. Now the child wants to know, Is love here or only indifference? Is reunion possible, or does the separation foretell an eternal separation? We may think we outgrow these fears, but that child is always within us.

Religious questions are not abstract or speculative; they are existential questions calling for a yes-or-no answer. Speaking extemporaneously, Adams says, "The principal things that concern me are intimacy and ultimacy—the *intimate* and the *ultimate.*" The relationship between ultimate and intimate dimensions of life is dialectical; each side heightens consciousness of the other. If salvation signifies the spiritual wholeness of the person, then being religious is a way of being more fully human. Still, Adams is concerned that we may misunderstand his alliterative pair of terms, lest they encourage us to see religion only as focused on the spirituality or the inwardness of the individual. Reflecting on his terminology, he says,

> "The intimate" is not an adequate term because I am concerned not only with the interpersonal relationship, but with meaningful human fellowship, with the human drive for fellowship. Aristotle said that the human being is "an associating being." The quality of one's associations determines the character and the meaning of one's existence.

Usually Aristotle's term *zoion politikon* is translated "political animal." Adams draws fresh meaning from the term and proceeds to state one of the most characteristic accents of his thought: The quality, the character, and the meaning of our associations determine the quality, the character, and the meaning of our very existence. This conviction lies at the root of his critique of Emersonian individualism ("Whoso would be a man must be a nonconformist") and the semi-gnostic spiritualities of our time ("God is within us").

So what at first seems simple turns out to be complex. *Intimate* refers not just to a private and inward feeling but to a personal level of awareness that necessarily includes interpersonal experience. Like Aristotle, Adams suggests that an ultimate aim is inherent in intimate being, as the oak is inherent in the acorn. Inherent in the human being is a "drive for fellowship." He writes,

> Only in the city does high culture appear, including the arts and the sciences. The Horatian dictum *nil admirari* seems to have been an admonition to "gawk" at nothing, like a country bumpkin, an untutored rustic. This admonition was related to the virtue of urbanity, elegance of manners, that in principle belongs to the city. It connotes a sophistication not to be found among the pre-urbanites and the anti-urbanites. As against this sophistication, Oswald Spengler could say, "Urbanity killed Christianity." In pre-urban life the "elders" who had the obligation of resolving conflict did not consult the abstract axioms of law; they knew the parties to the conflict and all their relatives. They could attempt to bring about reconciliation in awareness of the wider and complex interpersonal context. Human relationships were predominantly personal.
>
> The re-personalization of urban life, where persons tend to become mere objects or commodities, where the "I-Thou relation" (Martin Buber) is lost, is precisely the goal of intentional communities. The criterion of such communities is adumbrated in a modern "psalm" by the English artist and social reformer William Morris. The first line reads: "Fellowship is life; lack of fellowship is death." Authentic and viable fellowship, however, must be a fellowship in self-criticism, a harbinger of the fellowship of renewal. The alternative is "fellowship" in routine, that is, in living death. The fellowship that is life is fellowship in growth.

As the term *intimate* must be qualified, so too must *ultimate*. Adams suggests *transcendent* as an alternative. He then adds that this term may also be unacceptable. Is he simply following the liberal theological tradition of Friedrich Schleiermacher, seeking to capture the ear of religion's "cultured despisers"? Perhaps. But the difficulty with God-language even in its abstract forms is real and profound. Almost any language we use objectifies what cannot in any ordinary sense be the object of our knowing.

St. Paul overcomes the inadequacy of prosaic language with eschatological and ecstatic utterance in his well-known "hymn to love"—*agape* in Greek, *caritas* in Latin—especially its climactic affirmation, "Then shall I know even as also I am known" (I Corinthians 13:12). That is, then we shall be known with the eyes of Love. Many reflections can follow from this intimate/ ultimate vision: We are capable of knowing and loving God because God first knows us and loves us. This may be stated: We, like all creatures, are included in God's love, and by virtue of this participation, we are capable of loving others. The "logic of faith" entailed in this proposition overcomes the problem of objectifying what cannot rightly be objectified. But many people will want more time for theological rumination before taking such a leap of faith.

Not to treat what is ultimate as at the same time intimate but rather to treat it as an object that can be impersonally regarded is to falsify it. Many philosophical theologians in the past century have recognized the problem of the falsifying tendency of ordinary language for the divine. They have reached for a new language of God; in fact, it is Paul Tillich's forging of a new language of theology that Adams identifies as a chief expression of his intellectual creativity.

Tillich rejects the God who is one being among many, "even the highest being"; he speaks of faith as ultimate concern and of God as "the ground of being." Karl Jaspers speaks of "the Encompassing," our sense of a surrounding and underlying reality without which existence could not be. Martin Buber seeks to bridge the gap between divine reality and human sensibility by speaking of the

"I-Thou relationship." The term evokes the intuitive sense of ulti-macy and sacredness as inherent in intimate human relationships. It then transfers this quality of interpersonal awareness to awareness of the relationship to God, "the Eternal Thou." Charles Hartshorne seeks to bridge the gap by speaking of "the divine relativity." God is not a frozen absolute, changeless and apart, Hartshorne says, but precisely that which enters into "internal relations" with all things and accordingly is changed by these relationships. God is known in temporal process, not static timelessness.

Here Adams seeks to bridge the gap between language and the Transcendent by telling a story that reflects the interplay of the in-timate and ultimate dimensions of existence:

> "The ultimate" is difficult to articulate in our day, for we live in a time when the ancient myths and the ancient vocabu-laries are anachronistic, or are not properly understood. I could call it the Transcendent, . . . but I'll tell a story about it.
>
> I was very influenced in my youth by reading the auto-biography of George Gordon. He was a miner's son who, without the normal prerequisites, was admitted to Harvard College as a special student. In fact, I believe he is the only person in the history of Harvard who was given a degree by acclamation after two years. He tells the story of studying Greek and coming in with his bluebook for the midterm exam. Professor William Goodwin said, "You're not permit-ted to take the exam—you're a special student." Gordon then said, "But I'd like to take it." "No, no, you're not getting credit," Dr. Goodwin said, "you don't need to take it." But Gordon protested, "You make me feel like an idiot—I'm not even worth being examined!" Finally Dr. Goodwin relented and let him take the exam. George Gordon concludes the story by saying, the meaning of human existence is to live in a community where there are standards, where there is judg-ment. For if you don't live in a community where there is a shared sense of judgment—and ultimately the judgment of God—then you're not on the way to becoming human.

It's the kind of story that begs for a triumphant George Gordon. We want him to ace that exam, and in our minds we even imagine it, like the Gestalt psychology experiment in which the eye closes the unclosed circle. What fills in the picture we tend to believe, in life generally and in religion particularly. Adams never tells us the outcome of the exam, but it does not matter.

The point of the story stands. Standards of achievement and judgment reflect a basic dynamic of human existence, for to be human is to be a member of a community, and our sense of worth as persons is rooted in our consent to (or else our dissent from) standards established by a community. We do not want to be an "idiot," a lesser sort of person to whom the standards do not apply. To be fully human is to recognize that there are cultural and moral standards of judgment and to want them to be applied to one's self.

We may find it surprising that, as a way to explain what he means by the *Transcendent*, Adams would use this story. Apparently, he means to assert that the Transcendent is not an abstract, metaphysical absolute, but a structure of *ultimate* being on the basis of which we have access to our full and authentic humanity—our *intimate* being. To deny the existence of ultimate standards to which we are personally, intimately responsible, or to be exempted from them, is to deny Transcendence and at the same time to deny our own dignity as persons. This is what makes the story a theological parable and not simply a story about psychology or one man's education.

Renewed religious consciousness will include concern for intimacy, for caring, for personal relationship and personal fulfillment, and also concern for ultimacy, for standards of excellence and standards of judgment, a mark of authentic humanity that we may either hit or miss. Adams tells the story of George Gordon in various contexts, sometimes in a way that accents the human virtue of having starch in the face of challenge, sometimes as a story of how standards of judgment and thus judgment itself is a humanizing element of human culture.

Genial soul though he usually was, Adams could deliver an unkind cut when he wanted. Commenting on Unitarian pride in being a "creedless" faith, he once said, "The trouble with being a Unitarian is, you can't flunk." If we have no measure and even no idea of a standard of achievement, then, as Jesus said in one of his dark sayings, our salt has lost its savor and we may as well cast it out of the house (Matthew 5:13).

Surely salt that has lost its savor cannot be salt. But how to keep our savor? In a memorial tribute to Samuel A. Miller, his friend and the former dean of Harvard Divinity School, Adams writes,

> Sam Miller admonishes that we must "keep in touch with the vast and wordless sea beneath us." We think immediately of that mysterious line in the Bible: "He hath established it upon the floods" [Psalm 24:2]. We cannot keep in touch with that vast and wordless sea if we are not given the light that enables us to lay hold of a unifying power beneath and beyond ourselves....

"Deep within the center of our house of clay," Dean Miller says, "there is an 'angel' yearning to communicate with the depths and with other such angels in many houses of clay." Adams comments,

> But the moment we recognize the angel within the center of our house, we are moved to repentance for our isolation from the source of creation and for our separation from each other. Such repentance prepares us to join "the inner church of the friends of God," the fellowship of forgiveness and costing love, the fellowship that remembers creation itself when the stars first sang together. When we have found this kind of comradeship we have been recipients of the inner light of grace. We see our darkness for what it is, and then we are blessed with the thrust of grace towards wholeness and action.

Adams often refers to Jesus' "figure of the seed," a symbol of the hidden workings of divine power and its effects. But not all seeds prosper. Frank Kermode, the literary critic, calls Jesus' parable of the sower (Mark 4:3-9 and parallels in Matthew and Luke), "a parable of parable-telling," since it concerns the basic issue of spiritual blindness and awareness, misunderstanding and understanding. Adams asks, rhetorically, "What was Jesus' view of the working of the kingdom of God?" and answers:

> Now we come to a mark of the genius of Jesus, the creator of the great parables, the employer of metaphor and simile. Here we see an independent young man who created parables of stunning simplicity which can be read with understanding by men and women of all times and places. He said: The kingdom is like unto a seed that grows of itself, even when people are sleeping. Or, it is like a tiny grain of mustard seed that people took and sowed in the fields. Or, it is like a pearl of great price sought by a merchant.

The parable of the seed growing secretly is transparent, yet points to something utterly obscure—the working of God in the world—and therefore something we must seek and discover ever again.

We dwell in mystery. Of some of the most important things in life we can only say, "Time will tell." Therefore we must "take time seriously" and live by imagination and by faith. Something fundamental to our being and essential to our well-being is obscure, hidden from our direct apprehension. In a seed, Howard Nemerov writes, "time to come has tensed / Itself, enciphering a script...." Prophetic visionaries in many traditions have cast up luminous symbols to enable us to foresee the future and dispel the mystery of existence. It is this casting up of symbols that I call *parabolic vision*. Sacred symbols illumine the way before us, inviting us to step into the light. Adams's best words are enciphered seeds. To him Jesus' "figure of the seed" expressed the essential meaning of "the kingdom of God"—the realm and community of God.

Adams reports and comments on the conversation of Mrs. Humphrey Ward with Walter Pater, the nineteenth-century English essayist and critic:

> In the enthusiasm of her youthful skepticism, Mrs. Ward one day said to Walter Pater that orthodox religion could not

hold out much longer against the assaults of science. To her surprise, Pater shook his head, "No, I don't think so. You think it is all plain, but I cannot. There are such mysterious things. Take that saying, 'Come unto me all you that are weary and heavy laden.' [Matthew 11:28] How can you explain that? There is a mystery in it—something supernatural." The quality of Jesus' words was matched only by the quality of his life. Indeed, if he had not possessed his power with words, we would not know about the quality of his life. There is much to ponder in this fact, so much that I venture a variation from the opening words of the Prologue of the Fourth Gospel, making them read, "In the beginning *is* the word" [John 1:1].

Words spoken in the past can exercise a creative power that is continuous and present. With this insight into the creative power of human language, our concept of God as Creator is transformed; creation is not an event in the distant past but a creative power operating in the present. Profound religious thinkers have always understood this. The prophet Isaiah speaks of the God "who stretches out the heavens like a curtain, and spreads them like a tent to dwell in" (Isaiah 40:22), suggesting to me the image of a cosmic circus tent, a structure upheld by poles and ropes, giving us all a place and a time, existence itself. Without the continuous "breath of God" inflating the whole, it would collapse into chaos and become nothing. Such fanciful images and metaphors can be demythologized, or perhaps must be, to be truly understood. Already in the thirteenth century, the theologian Thomas Aquinas says that creation is not a one-time event in the past, but must be the continuous, contemporaneous activity of God. Incarnation is likewise ubiquitous, or it is nowhere; such is the radical theological vision that uses stories to point beyond stories and myths in order to "demythologize" theological ideas.

Kenneth Burke, the poet and philosopher of rhetoric, says that there are three great wonders. First, that there is something, not nothing. Second, that some existent beings have the capacity to experience the pleasures and pains of sex and self-replication. Third, that among the latter, some existent, self-replicating beings have "the need and the capacity for symbolic action," in language and other symbol systems, for instance, money. We are here concerned mainly with the third of these great wonders; symbolic action, we may say, is our way of responding to, or coping with, the other two "great wonders." Stories (fictional or true), aphorisms, plays on words, proverbs, and other rhetorical devices all share in the parable-telling motive. These forms of symbolic action are not only prominent in Adams's verbal effusions; they are also intrinsic to the message he conveys.

All Are Theologians

What Paul Tillich calls "ultimate concern" is validated, in the thought of Adams, not by received doctrine or rational argument, but by the intimate concerns of our lives. When Adams speaks of the nature of theology, he regularly speaks of it as seeing the human condition in relation to transcendence. Theology is prophetic insofar as it challenges human purposes and projects in ways that are both creative and critical:

> Theology deals with meaning, with the meaning of life, with its nature and its resources, its perversions, its possibilities. It aims to deal with ultimate issues, with the perspectives in terms of which radical questions can be asked regarding life. Religious meaning is relatedness to the ultimate source and resource—to God. Therefore it is a relatedness to that which brings all of our believing and thinking and striving under question. To recognize this relationship or to refuse to recognize it is part of human freedom. God's divinity rests in the power to give rise to a creature who is free to turn against God.

> *Meaning* is not simply knowledge; more particularly, it is also the power to connect small and large things, hence the power to

create and to communicate. Once Adams told a group of new ac-
quaintances about mastering the Gregg system of shorthand as a
young assistant to a railroad superintendent. He commented that
he was taught that you must not deviate from the system by creating your own private system of notations, because others will
need to read what you have written. Why would he remember this
and relate it some sixty years later? To establish a point of personal
contact through a common interest and skill, and less obviously,
as an exemplification of the fact that all language communicates
meaning in "shorthand" ways.

In fact, the conscious use of this "compressive" capacity of
language is a key to linguistic creativity—yet with the limiting
condition that the "shorthand" not become a purely personal language. Words may contain hidden or deeply personal meanings,
but only up to a point, or "for the time being," if we are to enter
into a world of shared meaning. As Robert Frost says in
"Revelation," using the imagery of the children's game hide-and-
seek, "Those who hide too well away Must speak and tell us where
they are." Jesus the "latter-day prophet" said, "For there is nothing
hid, except to be made manifest; nor is anything secret, except to
come to light" (Mark 4:22), defining the prophetic task as both
pointing to and calling for an end to secrets. In prophetic theology, meaning has this structure and dynamic.

The intimate and the ultimate, taken as polar concepts, stand
in dialectical relationship to each other, providing both direction
and form to Adams's theological reflections. His words invite sustained reflection on our personal experience within its social and
historical contexts. We would all be theologians, he suggests, were
we all deeply reflective on our *intimate* (i.e., personal and interpersonal) experience and able to perceive the implications of
what we do or leave undone in *ultimate* (i.e., fully concerned and
committed) terms. Since "all are theologians" and to be a theologian is to think and speak prophetically, Adams speaks of "the
prophethood of all believers." The idea has Biblical warrant, as
when Moses declares, "Would that all of the Lord's people were

prophets, that the Lord would put his spirit upon them!"
(Numbers 11:29)

Stories are told in the declarative mood and in this respect are
framed as objective statements describing the character of reality,
as theology also intends. Theology may be seen as a particular way
of seeing, an "angle of vision" that is sometimes oblique. As Emily
Dickinson puts it, "Tell all the Truth but tell it Slant." What I have
called *parabolic vision* is a way of insight into the obscurity of
human existence, a way of uncovering an otherwise hidden truth.
Oddly, the language of indirection requires the most straightfor-
ward mood, the declarative. Adams recalls,

> Some years ago I was asked by the dean of the University of
> Chicago to give a series of radio talks on theology. I decided,
> possibly under the influence of [Alfred North] Whitehead, to
> articulate the series in terms of the five moods: the declara-
> tive, the imperative, the subjunctive, the interrogative, the ex-
> clamatory. That's a good way to suggest that theology begins
> with the recognition of some kind of fact: it begins with the
> declarative mood.... Even the first words in Genesis, "In the
> beginning God..."— are in the declarative mood.

A fact, however, is not always an objective, verifiable fact. It
may speak of something as obscure or variable as a state of human
consciousness. Paul Tillich says that the Biblical story of Adam
and Eve describes a state of "dreaming innocence," a state that is
shattered by the Fall, by which he means "a universal human
awareness" of separation from God. The brokenness of the original unity is symbolized by their expulsion from Eden. The dawn
of consciousness—a sense of identity and a sense of moral responsibility, in the individual or in the race—also signifies the
dawn of history. The Enlightenment heritage teaches us to see this
as pure gain, as if we only needed to see reality in the clear light of
reason and we would resolve our conflicts and act for the common
good. It passes over the elements of guilt and tragic loss.

Paul Tillich quotes G. W. F. Hegel in a lecture: "History is not the place of human happiness." In the darkened mood of our time, myriad willful and deadly conflicts have given history a sinister cast, for it is a realm of constant striving and strife. Stephen Daedalus says, "History is a nightmare from which I am trying to awake" in James Joyce's classic, *Ulysses*. Adams shares these pessimistic visions of history in part; he also transmutes them by way of the prophetic voice, calling us to rise to the spiritual and moral challenge of this day. For instance, in the rise of nationalist totalitarianism he sees the crisis of liberal democracy and the testing of liberalism itself. But he also believes that liberalism can transform itself. He speaks of liberal faith as justifying an "ultimate optimism," although tempered by a proximate pessimism.

The religious and moral response to this mixed sense of irretrievable loss and hope for a new beginning will be complex. Theological thought will become dialectical, reflecting the dynamic of separation and return that pervades existence itself and enters into the subconscious where it is sometimes reflected in dreams. To use oversimplified language, the movement runs from original unity, to present conflict, to final reunion, or in theological terms, from created goodness, to temporal brokenness, to eschatological hope. This pattern appears repeatedly in Adams's thought:

> One of the most striking things about dreams, according to Erich Fromm, is "the similarity between the products of our creativeness during sleep and the oldest creations of humanity— the myths." The myths are concerned even with the difference between waking and sleeping. For Buddhism deep sleep is a path to detachment, a symbol and anticipation of Nirvana. A similar dialectic between sleeping and waking appears in the notion of return from the tension of the day mind, to a lost unity latent in the night mind. The dimensions of the lost unity, the cleavage in the psyche, and the overcoming of the cleavage, are emphasized in the oldest

myth generally familiar to us: the Biblical myth of creation, fall, and redemption.

What is this Biblical myth about? Adams notes that religion is concerned with "the threats and supports to meaningful human existence." Threat and support are not purely oppositional; they are polarities, dialectically related, as when a false or anachronistic support gives way to threat, forcing us to find a new, more secure support.

Reflection on the phenomenon of dreams leads Adams to reflect on the basic structure of theology:

> Underlying the whole human enterprise are support and threat; but the support is primary, the indispensable dynamic of creative mutuality. Where this element of "creation" is completely absent, where the "fall" is complete and absolute, existence is no longer possible. The support is ultimately a "gift"—an expression of grace; the threat is a lurking temptation and insinuation. The sustaining, creative, commanding, judging, transforming power is a divine power, ultimately not of human making. The merely aggressive, self-serving, idolatrous perverter of freedom and mutuality is a demonic power that through excess can cause people and even whole communities to become "possessed." Yet, even this power depends in its way upon the support of being.

What basic confidence and faith remain in the face of all that seems to destroy morale or meaning? For Adams divine power, the support of our existence, is original and primary; demonic power, the threat, is derivative and secondary. That which threatens meaning and morale is a perversion of what is primary; it can sustain itself only in time and space because it participates in the created goodness of being. "Evil witnesses to the reality of the good, as the shadow points round to the sun," Adams says. Our need is to renew the creative good within our own, humanly made realm of being, so far as we are able, leaving the rest to powers and processes beyond our rational understanding or our morally competent control. Adams asserts,

> Everyone is a theologian, either conscious or unconscious, in the sense that everyone has some conception of the nature of reality, of the demands of reality, and of those elements in reality that support or threaten meaningful existence. Therefore, I would restate a doctrine of grace: we humans are dependent upon realities not of our own making, realities that oftentimes may destroy our own makings.

And if they do destroy our own makings, what then? Is judgment inextricably tied to grace, such that the threat itself serves the support, now more truly perceived? Ultimately, yes. Our ability to make this affirmation makes bearable the proximate reality—the world in which we judge as if our fallible judgments were the last word or even the Last Judgment. If anything has the power to move us to believe in God, it is these perceptions, especially seeing that grace operates even through the pain we both suffer and inflict, saving us from ourselves.

The point is central but easily missed, so perhaps another pass at it is in order. Adams barely completes his own thought in the foregoing sentences, namely, the recognition that destruction may save us from "relying on the unreliable," at least if we let go of the things of "our own making" that we idolize. In spite of his words about the tragic element in human existence, his assumptions are at root optimistic. A prophet may be one who, as he said, "prophesies doom," but it is always a conditional threat, never a sealed fate. A prophetic faith is rooted in a theology of hope. Christian, Jewish, and Islamic theologies have been both praised for their "realism" about human nature and criticized for playing upon fear—presenting God as a threat rather than as a support. Adams insists upon speaking of both threat and support, but he also insists that support is primary, that is, ontologically prior. Likewise, not the fear of God but the love of God is primary, because the latter requires the former while the former does not require the latter. This is also true, as lovers know, in our human experience of one another.

Bernard Lonergan, a Jesuit theologian in the Thomist intellectual tradition, says, "Faith is the knowledge born of religious love." Love precedes knowledge, in this view, just as faith precedes understanding. The fourteenth-century Franciscan theologian St. Bonaventura speaks in a similarly irenic and intellectually confident voice. Adams notes with his usual brevity and clarity,

> Theology is, in the language of Bonaventura, "an affective science," the science of the love of God, and the function of the church is to bring people into communion with a group wherein the divine power of transformation and the ethical standards rooted in it are operative.

Scientia, translated "science," from ancient times forward has referred to rational and systematic knowledge, as distinct from the knowledge of the household and the workplace, practical know-how. Since the Enlightenment we have increasingly severed faith from knowledge; knowledge of the real has been largely given over to the natural sciences, while faith has been relegated to the realms of subjective feeling and private opinion. Ever since this severing, giving us "value-free" science, economics, and even education, the soul of the age has been bleeding.

How then can we follow the inclinations of our hearts, when our hearts are seen, even by ourselves, as unreliable guides? In addition to Bonaventura, Adams appeals to two other theologians who place "the affections" at the center of their thought: Jonathan Edwards, who speaks of religion as a "cordial consent to being"— that is, gracious acceptance of reality as a whole—and Friedrich Schleiermacher, who speaks of religion as "the feeling of absolute dependence." Adams's understanding of faith as the attitude of ultimate reliance, and as the intellectual and moral discernment of that which is ultimately reliable, falls within this tradition. Religion remains, then, the inclination of the human heart—

toward peace, toward mercy, toward kindness. It is a passion, sub-
jecting the self to the reality of one's existence, and at the same
time, allowing oneself to be profoundly affected by it. The first
fruit of faith is to be able to trust these feelings and to go with
them. On this basis a reasoned understanding of the reality that
encompasses us, *scientia theologica*, can follow.

Adams speaks of the task of theology in several ways. He affirms the classical view that theology is "faith seeking understanding," first articulated by Anselm of Canterbury, a definition that
recognizes faith as an "original decision," that is, a commitment
that shapes one's whole outlook. In another context he offers a
working definition: "A way of defining theology is to say that its
function is to explicate the major symbols [of a religious tradi-
tion] in the light of the changing historical situation." More often
he speaks of theology in existential terms, as a description of "the
reality we confront and the reality we are":

> Theology is faith seeking understanding—understanding of
> yourself and understanding of reality. One of my favorite
> aphorisms is from Alfred North Whitehead: "Definition is
> the soul of actuality." That is the task of theology: to define
> reality, but also to define that capacity *in the human being*.
> Reality is not only that which we confront, but also that
> which is in the human being. There will always be an ele-
> ment of faith—unless you are in complete despair and say
> nothing has any meaning. If you don't go that far, you are in-
> volved in trying to define, to articulate, to locate meaning. So
> that is the search of faith for understanding—our under-
> standing of the reality we confront, and which we are.

For St. Anselm, writing in the twelfth century, faith is indubitable but not entirely comprehensible. In his tradition-driven
age, the received faith was a given; the task that Anselm marks out
for the theologian is to understand it by reason so far as possible;
revelation would complete the task. For every believer Christian
faith was a story you were securely in; what remained was to un-

derstand it and live out of it. This reverses the modern era's way of thinking, namely, the belief that, insofar as we are locked inside our own minds, only our discreet existences are indubitable. How do I know I exist? *I think*, according to Descartes, the man who seeks certainty in a world where everything can be doubted. Following Adams, we seek a way to return to Anselm's bold point of departure.

We tend to think that the quest for understanding by means of empirical knowledge, reason, common sense, or even esoteric wisdom is the only way to faith. We say to ourselves, "If and when it all makes sense, then I will believe." To the contrary, faith goes before understanding and enlarges it. "I believe in order that I may understand," is Anselm's formulation. And if I believe nothing, nothing at all will make sense. This is the logic of faith. The epistemological problem comes to a head in the fact that we cannot objectively view a reality that includes us; we cannot step outside of it, except in moments of ecstasy. *Ecstasy*, Paul Tillich likes to point out, literally means to stand outside oneself—or as we say, to be beside oneself. For Tillich faith and reason are reconciled in "the ecstasy of reason."

More soberly, the distinguished American poet Howard Nemerov comments on the close relationship between poetry and religion; the poet, he says, describes the human situation as precisely as he can, but it must be existential, that is, "a situation he is in." Recognizing the impossibility of scientific objectivity in the realm of existential or spiritual questions does not condemn us to pure subjectivity, leaving us with wholly personal or arbitrary understandings. The poet and the person of faith are still committed to truth—or perhaps we should say, to truth-telling. Truth-telling requires a certain humility, a renunciation of hubris. In protest against intellectual pride, Adams cites Oliver Wendell Holmes: "Man is in the belly of the universe, not the universe in the belly of man."

Adams defends the recently unpopular idea that philosophy is a partner to theology, but takes care to give priority to neither.

These views are articulated in response to Karl Barth's kerygmatic theology, which became the dominant, neoorthodox current in twentieth-century Protestant thought. Adams calls it *proclamationism*, since the Greek *kerygma* means "proclamation" and is used to signify the Biblical proclamation of the Word of God. Proclamationism, like the more recent "nonfoundational" theologies, claims that Christian faith is founded on divine revelation, which is independent of any philosophical foundations, leading Adams to observe that this stance is likely to invite unrecognized philosophical presuppositions. Against this blinkered view Adams paraphrases Socrates: "An unexamined faith is not worth having." In his view, the quest for a reasoned understanding has no less religious significance than faith and itself expresses an important form of faith, namely, fidelity to truth. In Adams's words,

> Christian faith is not able to avoid philosophy; faith seeks understanding and in doing so it turns to philosophy.... God moves in mysterious ways, and God's ways are not in human control through either faith or reason.
>
> Yet both faith and reason are God's gifts; each has its divine vocation. To deny its vocation to either of them is to indulge the striving for status—the original sin of the pecking order.... To isolate [theology and philosophy] from each other is to impair the community among those who live by the confession that the end of human existence is "to glorify God and to enjoy him forever."

By appealing to this luminous formulation from the Westminster Confession, a classical statement of Calvinist Christianity, Adams means to reject the anti-intellectualism that would isolate theology from philosophy. In the view of the medieval scholastics, he says,

> Human will follows the lead of the intellect, which grasps the world through the mediated forms of nature, society, doctrine, and sacrament. Salvation is mediated, it is not a mat-

ter of an immediate relationship between the isolated individual and God.

Adams does not contest this intellectualist viewpoint, although it contrasts with the voluntarism (a philosophy of will) often championed in his theological commentaries. He characteristically seeks to incorporate the insights of every great movement of thought into his own thought. Just so, he cites Thomas Aquinas ("The prime author and mover of the universe is intelligence") and honors the intellectual tradition he established. Thomism presupposes truths of faith established by divine revelation but seeks to illuminate them by reason. Adams notes that Thomas asserts that "being as such is good" and melds this philosophical foundation with modern perspectives:

> *Esse est bonum qua esse*; being is good as being. Reality is therefore norm-giving in this ontological-axiological minimum. Thus human beings find themselves, in Heidegger's term, "thrown into" the sort of existence that demands a minimum mutuality, with its concomitant threat of destruction if the demand is not met. But the reality of which human beings are part, and by which they are confronted, also offers the possibility of ever increasing mutuality and creativity.

Adams affirms the theological translation of stories, such as the Biblical creation myth, into rational principles. An example is Aquinas's assertion that "being as such" is good and his awareness that a moral imperative is inherent in this recognition. He affirms that it is our nature to increase mutuality and creativity in the world; therefore, to strive for these manifestly good ends is also morally imperative.

The Loss of the Sacred

Religious liberals have progressively lost a sense of being historically linked to a sacred tradition. The consequent loss of spiritual depth is not compensated by moral striving, individual freedom, and sheer variety. Adams repeatedly sounds this warning.

"Liberalism is dead. Long live liberalism!" he declared when the Second World War was just beginning and people committed to liberal democracy felt a profound sense of political and spiritual crisis. These are the words of a man deeply committed to liberalism in politics and religion alike, who for this very reason sees its need for transformation. Two points at which transformation is needed, Adams argues, are the understandings of historical tradition and human freedom. Adams tells of attending a lecture in a liberal church on religious education by a denominational representative:

> During the discussion that followed the address, one of the parents in the audience said, "I am puzzled by your exclusive emphasis on the present and the future. I have been in the habit of supposing that religious education in a liberal church should include a critical appreciation of our past and also...of the Bible." The "religious educator" replied, "I don't mean to say that the Bible has to be excluded. If you want it in the curriculum, I don't see why you should be prevented. We believe in freedom in the liberal church." This cavalier attitude...can only result in organized religious illiteracy.

The loss of a profound sense of being part of a tradition that forms us and claims us, long before we re-form or judge it, follows from a purely external conception of freedom. An unreflective liberalism sees values as matters of personal preference or, even more simplistically, as matters of individual choice, rather than as primary qualities of our personal and social lives, qualities requiring socialization and at the same time extending the freedom to make meaningful choices.

The troubling experience of a steady loss of sacred tradition among religious liberals was shared by many theological students of my generation—one of the things that made Adams so impor-

tant to us. My own experience is instructive. Growing up
Unitarian in the 1950s acquainted me with the power of a consciously counterculture religious ethos. The sense of standing
apart was also accompanied, with doubtful warrant, by a sense of
superiority. For instance, our generation was popularly labeled the
Silent Generation, and we young Unitarians were determined to
be *not that*—not the pious, narrow-minded, and conformist
young people we grew up with in the suburbs. We sang union
songs and indulged in other mild forms of radicalism; we sang
sacrilegious songs and delighted ourselves with other impieties. I
was astonished that a cute Catholic girl I dated thought the word
belly, which comes up in the picnic song in *Carousel*, too racy to
sing. Among the Unitarians, we could be so racy as to have a boy
impersonate pregnancy with a basketball and two grapefruits
under his sweatshirt. Today we may smile at all this, but back then
we found power in the spirit of dissent: We knew we were different, and the taste of freedom was heady.

Still, it was an empty identity insofar as we knew far better
who we were *not* than who we were, and the emptiness became
apparent as adolescence progressed and passed. So when Adams
came and spoke at one of our continental youth assemblies—an
example of how he put himself in touch with others, even
teenagers—he attracted my rapt attention. I knew then that I
would sit at his feet to study for the ministry—an expectation fulfilled a few years later when I chose Harvard Divinity School,
where Adams had joined the faculty.

In college I had toyed with religious humanism to fill my spiritual void, but I found that my sophisticated fellow Oberlinians
were uninterested in its pale negations and vague affirmations.
Then our Unitarian Channing Club brought Adams to speak at
Finney Chapel. Charles Grandison Finney himself might have
been delighted with his choice of a Biblical text, from the prophet
Joel and the Pentecost story: "I will pour out my spirit upon all
flesh" (Acts 2:17), but it baffled me, a "briar patch" Unitarian. The
Bible was such *terra incognita* to me that the very idea of the Holy

Spirit seemed foreign and laughable or perhaps threatening. Only
years later did I come to recognize that Pentecost, celebrating the
gift of divine law (Torah) in Judaism, and the gift of divine spirit
to the church in Christianity—in both cases, the miracles that create the religious community—is actually the myth of the Tower of
Babel turned inside out. Thus the gift of the spirit is the miracle of
"unity in diversity" and, as such, ought to be the holiest day in a
religious liberal's liturgical calendar rather than the almost unknown day it has become.

Max Stackhouse remarks that Adams is an unusual theologian
in that he takes the Holy Spirit, the third person of the Trinity, as
the focal point of his concept of God. But *diversity* can become a
buzzword signifying a purposeless variety. Adams voices discontent with liberal vagueness in sharp terms:

> We are asked, "What do you stand for?" and our loudest
> prophets respond, "Open-mindedness, the search for truth
> and freedom." We ask, "Is there God? Need we worship?"
> And the answer comes, "Why, that is for you to discover."
> "Well, then, what is religion?" "Why, that is religion—to re-
> main open-minded, be tolerant, have faith in man and
> progress." We are the spiritual descendants of those who
> have led the way through a century of intellectual and spiri-
> tual expansion. And now at long last we discover that our
> principal basis for unity is the right of private judgment. Our
> liberalism is in danger of dispersing itself into sheer variety.
> In the name of freedom we hail the Tower of Babel and its
> confusion of thought as an unmitigated blessing. Is it not
> time that our period of intellectual and spiritual expansion
> should be followed by one of concentration? The rejection of
> some brand of orthodoxy or a vague espousal on one kind
> or another of idealism is not enough to make a religious lib-
> eral. There must be a doctrine and a discipline.

These are hardly typical accents of liberalism, but they are
central Adamsean themes: discipline and doctrine. Disciplines

shape and nerve a way to depth. Doctrines render faith conceptual and explicit. These things he calls for and cajols for, rowing against the tide all the way. As often as it is an antitheological humanism, the tide is a lazy latitudinarianism. Adams tells this story about the laxity that leads to superficiality, adding that he "really shouldn't tell it," before proceeding to tell it, anyway:

> [A young minister] wanted to be examined by a congregational council before he was ordained. I was minister in Wellesley Hills at that time and I got three of my board members—all men of high professional skill—to serve. We gathered at this fellow's new parish for the congregational council to be held directly before the ordination service. He had managed to persuade Louis Cornish [president of the American Unitarian Association] to chair the council.
>
> On that Sunday there was a heavy snowstorm, which I knew would limit the attendance. One of the members from my board who had been selected wanted to go home. But I said, "No, if you please, we must go." So we plowed through the deep snow and got there but found very few others. And then Dr. Cornish didn't start at the appointed time. I finally said, "We've gathered here for a purpose, to examine this man and see if he's fit for ordination. I think we ought to start questioning him." Dr. Cornish said, "All right. Do you have a question?" I then said to the candidate, "You will be conducting public worship. Would you tell us, what is your conception of prayer, either private or public?"
>
> Dr. Cornish replied, "You don't think we get rain from prayer, do you?" I said, "Dr. Cornish, I thought *this* man was answering the questions. If you insist that I answer the question, I can tell you unambiguously, *No*." The laymen there were somewhat shocked by the superficiality of the exercise. The answers didn't give evidence of the candidate's having cerebrated on such matters. But as the time went on, we could hear the organ next door playing the prelude—so we finally voted him in!

The dissipation of professional standards in religious leadership had run apace since the previous century, roughly along with the rise of modern science and commerce. The marginalization of the church had begun, and the clergy mostly went along. Adams notes,

> The increasing complexity of the secular world has thrown the minister back into a separated world, a cloistered, protected environment. Ministers who have found seclusion and protection comfortable have gone to seed. Perhaps it was the uniformity of type produced by the limited environment of the minister that made Emerson remark, "The clergy are as like as peas; I cannot tell them apart."

If we who are clergy wince at Adams's words, we can console ourselves with the thought that self-derision is an old tradition. Emerson's unkind cut was carried a step further by his intellectual disciple, Theodore Parker, who had learned the effect on audiences of not mincing words. Adams comments that Parker "classed Meadville and Harvard together in familiar transcendentalist style," and cites his words:

> I was over at Cambridge the other day and I looked in at the Divinity School, and saw several of the bodies which were waiting their turn. The Egyptian embalmers took only seventy days, I think, to make a mummy out of a dead man. Unitarian embalmers use three years in making a mummy out of a live man. I think at Meadville they do it in less.

Theodore Parker wanted to radicalize Unitarianism, and it is not surprising that he saw the theological schools as the deadly enemies of such an attempt. But the urge to ethical relevance and social action beyond the ivory tower, which Adams shared with Parker, can yield an anti-intellectualism that denigrates theological learning.

Aware of the temptation, Adams quotes Abiel Abbot Livermore, who was president of Meadville Theological School from 1863 to

1890: "The saints that shine brightest in the American calendar are not the students of musty books, monks of ascetic devotion, the nuns of unnatural celibacy, the hair-splitters and logic grinders of dogmatic theology, but they who have sought to leave the world the better that they have lived in it." We do not miss the stale taste of anti-Catholicism, sugar-coated with righteousness, in Livermore's words. Adams comments, "Livermore virtually here betrays the intellectual disciplines with a kiss, the kiss of heroic activism."

Adams speaks of social ethics as a branch of theology. *Ethics*, he says, is "faith seeking understanding in the realm of moral action." Understanding will lead to the formulation of norms, but it is rooted in a vision of the good and a commitment to live in fidelity to that vision. The close relationship between the intimate and the ultimate, or between what Tillich calls the horizontal and the vertical dimensions of existence, also obtains between theology and ethics. He uses Arthur Koestler's typology—the yogi and the commissar—to enlighten the relationship:

> Kierkegaard and Marx are in complementary ways lop-sided. What Marx emphasizes in terms of social texture, Kierkegaard almost entirely ignores. What Kierkegaard stresses in terms of individual inwardness and integrity, Marx ignores. The contrast is that between the yogi and the commissar.

To marry the two—to find the true interrelation between theology and ethics, or to relate commitments of faith and commitments of moral value—is a chief spring of authentic religious reflection.

What we call *ethics* the Bible calls *works* or *good works*. According to the Epistle of James, faith without works is dead; according to Paul, works without faith is self-righteous striving. Adams could say, "Faith without ethics is spiritualism, ethics without faith is moralism, and both are hopelessly lopsided." He recalls,

> The late Dean William W. Fenn of Harvard Divinity School used to tell of a snatch of heated conversation between two

students he once overheard as he passed through the corridor of Andover Hall at the Divinity School. Attempting to bring an argument to a triumphant conclusion, the one student said, "All you have is *mere* morality." To this the other student replied scornfully, "And all you have is *mere* God!"

Adams often challenges fundamentalists, pietists, doctrinal purists, and religious existentialists—even Søren Kierkegaard—for their having "mere God," a God who does not require doing justice and loving mercy but is restricted to personal faith and inward spiritual "assurance." But the reduction of theological reflection to moral exhortation, leaving us with "mere morality," is equally deplorable. Reductive strategies, presumably intended to rescue religion from outmoded ideas, often serve to discredit it. "Mere morality" invariably slips into mere moralism. Adams notes this propensity in the history of liberal Christianity:

> Father George Tyrrell, the Catholic modernist of a generation ago, indicated cryptically the peril in modernizing the Gospel when he said that the liberal Christian looks down the deep well of higher criticism, sees his own image, and calls it "Jesus." The overweening confidence in the natural propensities of human nature and in the upward grain of history was a superficial view, and it could not be maintained before the facts of life.

Adams's close friend and mentor during his several trips to Germany in the 1920s and 1930s was Rudolf Otto, professor at Marburg University, best known for *The Idea of the Holy*, a seminal and influential work. Adams was especially affected by another work of Otto's, *Kingdom of God and Son of Man*, on account of its new interpretation of a concept that had largely been abandoned by liberal theology, the doctrine of last things (*eschatology*), due to its association with apocalyptic visions. Otto interprets the eschatology of Jesus, prominent in his words about the kingdom of God, as paradoxically both future and already present (sometimes called "realized"). For Adams, eschatology refers to an orientation to the future which motivates and directs us in the present, and as such is central to liberal thought.

Adams repeats a story told to him with great amusement by professor Otto:

> Otto recalled a distinguished and prolix American preacher speaking at an international conference. When he had delivered a long paragraph and paused for the translation, the interpreter said, *auf Deutsch*, "The speaker has spoken with great eloquence, and has declared that it is good to be good." With a nod from the interpreter, the man proceeded to another long paragraph. At the second pause for translation the interpreter said, "The speaker has again spoken eloquently, and declared that it is *indeed* good to be good." The man again proceeded to speak at length, and again paused for the translation. The interpreter said, "The speaker has declared, with great eloquence, that indeed, it is *very good* to be good."

Religion is reduced to it's-good-to-be-good moralism when we have no more than the airy eloquence of the speaker to stand on. In the slogan "Deeds, Not Creeds," some will hear a claim to moral superiority more clearly than they hear a commitment to risky, fallible, courageous moral action. Indeed, the spirit of Abiel Abbot Livermore is alive and well.

To be sure, Adams thumps the drum for good works, for deeds of justice: "Faith which is not the sister of justice will bring us to grief," he declares. But he also has his intellectual priorities straight:

> Religious commitment issues from the declarative into the imperative mood, from recognition of divine fact that defines and redefines and sustains virtue. This is the sense of Baron Friedrich von Hügel's assertion that "religion has primarily to do with is-ness and only secondarily with ought-ness."

"Is-ness" signifies the recognition, fundamental to faith, of a reality that is not only personal but also shared, and therefore public, a reality that is sacred—something we cannot manipulate or control, and for this very reason can give us to ourselves. Adams comments, "Without a recognition of a real Other, a religious object, there can be no religion, no prayer, no worship." He goes on to cite von Hügel's stricture against the moralism of liberals:

> Religion without God does not correspond to the specific religious sense, because no amount of Ought-ness can be made to take the place of Is-ness, to the given-ness of God—the recognition that everything is given. The moderns say: "Thank goodness we have got rid of the awful position of servant and master!" (Is it awful?) Canon S—— says God needs us to make the world. I must say I never heard Canon S—— helped God to make Saturn's rings. It sounds rather fusty somehow to me.

In a time when noted management consultants in the secular world promote religious and ethical conceptions of work and organizational leadership—for instance, Peter Block's *Stewardship: Choosing Service Over Self-Interest* (1993) and his recent *The Answer to How Is Yes* (2002) and Joseph Jaworski's *Synchronicity: The Inner Path to Leadership* (1996)—the churches look spiritually timid. When modern religious liberalism abandons the idea of servanthood as unworthy of human dignity or the idea of God's absolute transcendence as too otherworldly, it loses its sense of human proportion, the basis of a true humanism. If we are not servants of a higher will, then we are not ministers and are without vocation within the community of faith that Adams calls "the priesthood and the prophethood of all believers."

Being Born Anew

To be efficacious, ultimate meanings and values need to be manifested in our personal lives and in the common life of the community. This requires an inward and intimate change of heart, as Adams affirms:

In the Gospels we find that ministry is a call to servanthood. "Even the Son of man came not to be ministered unto," says Jesus, "but to minister" (Mark 10:45). The ministry is a proclamation of good news, the news that there is a sustaining, loving, creative, judging, forgiving, transforming power ushering in a new community. This power is not made with human hands and is not under human control. Again the message is to the individual, urging *metanoia*, "a change of heart, mind, and soul." It is also a call to a newly burgeoning community, transcending nation, race, sex, and class. In the first call to the individual the fundamental change is *intimate*; but in both the first and the second it is *ultimate*.

Those familiar with the history of liberal religion over the past half-century or more know that it has been curiously unchanged. Its antitheological bias and prickly individualism (Adams calls it "fissiparous individualism") have both been decried by critics for decades. But these same characteristics have also been stoutly defended; one Humanist leader declared that to be a true-believing Unitarian Universalist, you virtually had to be a "come-outer" from orthodoxy. How do we account for the static character of a movement that announces itself as radically open to change?

Religious liberals are not unlike Americans generally, a people largely untouched by the sense of historical crisis in the twentieth century and untouched by the accompanying turn toward existentialist thought in Europe. Americans have remained optimistic, individualistic, and idealistic in spite of the ravages of economic crisis, warfare, genocide, and totalitarianism. The liberal churches need to be seen in this historical context. Their character is in large measure a function of their sociological position, as gathering places for come-outers, people who come to these churches from an almost limitless reservoir of former churchgoers, anxious to work through the disintegrating remains of their childhood faiths. (In addition, the number of people who have been raised with virtually no religious involvement or identity, due to unreligious or anti-religious parents, is surprisingly large.) Many of these spiritual seekers (and many of their children after them) eventually proceed into secularism, while a smaller number turn back to more exacting forms and traditions of faith.

Adams is himself a come-outer, and for this reason can empathize with the experience of spiritual exile. But he is also one who ultimately affirms a neo-evangelical, politically radical, theologically unitarian and universalist Christianity. He does not put much stock in labels, however, and simply refers to himself as a liberal Christian. Reflecting on Adams's life against its historical background, a life that almost spanned the past century, the historian David Robinson observes, "Adams's spiritual odyssey incarnates much of the story of twentieth-century liberal religion." Presumably Robinson is thinking of Adams's journey from the fundamentalist Christianity of his childhood, to his seemingly complete rejection of Christianity in adolescent rebellion, to the liberal Christian Unitarianism of his mature years. It is a journey also followed by some others, not infrequently under Adams's influence. But it is a journey that remains atypical and controversial in an increasingly humanistic denomination.

Adams once recalled, "Once when a dozen of my friends and I got up a petition in a denominational meeting, Edwin Wilson (the leader of the humanist association) was heard to say, 'Here comes Adams and the Twelve.'" His smile, telling such stories, betrayed how much he enjoyed them. He loved being the center of attention and the burr under any too-comfortable saddle. For instance, in a denomination that defined itself against the very idea of born-again religion, Adams spoke of the centrality of religious conversion and told this story: "A matron, who was a proper Bostonian, exclaimed, 'Why should I be born again? I was born in Boston!'"

Adams is conscious of his own spiritual rebirths. His life displays conversions on several levels, in the pattern described by Bernard Lonergan—the intellectual, moral, and religious levels. These life changes are reflected in various autobiographical stories.

First, Adams's religious conversion entailed the reappropriation of the essential Christian faith of his upbringing, giving it
new form. In brief, the Biblical tradition generally and the words
and deeds of Jesus of Nazareth specifically provide the central
symbols for the interpretation of human existence in the face of
present history. Second, his moral conversion was occasioned especially by his encounter with Nazism and his sense of a cultural
and political crisis in Western democracy, requiring of him social-
ethical commitment and associational engagements. Third, his intellectual conversion was marked by his adoption of an existential
and voluntarist stance, that is, an outlook that accents decision
and will. In this he was especially influenced by Paul Tillich, whose
philosophical theology pairs existential questions with ontological, or theological, answers, and a dialectic driven by yes-and-no
decisions.

It is fascinating to observe the way in which elements of
Adams's childhood faith were transformed and preserved in new
form in his mature theology. The German philosophic tradition
calls it *Aufhebung*, the transformational process in which what is
negated is preserved in new form. Negation is never absolute in
this conception of dialectical movement. Adams is conscious of
this process in his own life experience. "Some of my friends think
I never got over being a Baptist," he says. "They should know, for
they, too, were raised in the Baptist fold."

How Adams managed the transition from his childhood piety
to his adolescent impiety to his renewed faith in young adulthood
is told, in significant part, in two stories from the autobiographical essay he wrote at midlife, a classic of the type:

> By the age of eleven I knew the whole plan of salvation ac-
> cording to the *Schofield Reference Bible*, and I testified for it
> in season and out. I even preached on the street and at the
> Salvation Army during my earlier years in college. The break
> came before I left college, but I did not give up religion. I
> simply changed my attitude; I decided that it was my mission
> to attack religion in season and out. I became a "campus rad-

ical" and joined with some other quondam fundamentalists to publish an undergraduate freelance sheet which we smugly called *The Angels' Revolt*. My new law was the scientific humanism of John Dietrich and my new prophecy was the anti-Rotarianism of H. L. Mencken.

His antireligious revolt is more than ideological; it marks a decisive break from his father and mother (a story he never fully told, probably because it was too painful).

Looking back at midlife (1939), Adams recognized that religion remained his ultimate concern in and through the "angels' revolt." In Jewish and Christian mythology the demons are rebellious angels, so we may say that Adams here recognized a demonic spirit in himself long before he encountered Paul Tillich's use of "the demonic" as a central concept of historical interpretation. He recalls a turning point in his life:

> One of the great surprises of my life came at the end of my senior year in college. I had been taking a course in public speaking and all my speeches had been vicious attacks on religion as I knew it—at least, they had been as vicious as I could make them. The shock came one day when on leaving the classroom I happened to say quite casually to the professor that I did not know what I was going to do after graduation. I was already profitably engaged in business, but I was thoroughly discontented. The professor replied in a flash, "You don't know what you are going to do? Why, I have known for months. Come around and talk to me some day." And then, right there in the presence of my enemies, the fundamentalists, he smote me. "There is no possible doubt about it," he said. "You are going to be a prr-eacher!" Later I went by night, like Nicodemus, to question this strange counselor. Within six weeks the arrangements were complete. I was to attend Harvard Divinity School.

True humanity is the ability to laugh not at but with another. It is the capacity to enjoy the idiosyncrasies and foibles of another person, and to see these quirks as intrinsic to their character. These partial truths of the self we tell as if they were the whole truth, until or unless we acknowledge the principle of humility— the willingness to say, "this I believe to be true, but I may be mistaken."

Renewed faith begins with a renewed sense of humility and a renewed willingness to eschew the substitution of simplistic formulas for complex realities. Renewed faith also brings with it a renewed sense of humor, as Adams reminds us,

> A reviewer in *The Times Literary Supplement* said, "Friedrich von Hügel is, we think, the most powerful apologist for the Roman Church now living." But von Hügel, in spite of what he called the "excessively handsome and resonantly sympathetic" attitude of the writer, expressed his reservations. In the next issue of *The Times* he wrote: "A dog who is quietly conscious of being but a dog, and of having long striven just to be a dog, and nothing more or other, may be allowed, perhaps, to feel some perplexity amidst his gratitude upon finding himself first prize among the cats."

The undergraduate professor who challenged Adams, Frank Rarig, was a beloved teacher at the University of Minnesota, where a building has been named for him. He happened also to be a Unitarian. Adams recalls that Rarig told him that his blanket rejection of religion, following his rebellion against fundamentalism, was due to his never having heard of "a self-critical religion." The comment constitutes a remarkable definition, for the capacity for self-criticism is the hallmark of human authenticity in *any* realm of thought and endeavor. Indeed, Adams never reverts to the uncritical stance of fundamentalism or accepts the dogmatic stance of neo-Reformation theology:

> If some people wish infallible guidance in religion, they are not going to find it in liberal religion. Of course, orthodox mentors will claim that this is the reason we need a divine guide, in a book or a church doctrine. Further, they some-

times tell us that the mortal sin of the liberal is the unwill-ingness to submit to divine authority and that this unwill-ingness grows out of intellectual pride. What the orthodox overlooks, however, is this: the most pretentious pride of all is that of those who think themselves capable of recognizing infallibility, for they must themselves claim to be infallible in order to recognize it.

The other side of this coin is the unconscious arrogance of re-ligious liberals who happily announce that they "do not possess all the truth," but only, they are sure, the most advanced truths avail-able. All of us tend to be adept at protecting our basic assumptions from serious questioning, when what we need are new and wider angles of vision that give us new eyes to see. Two intellectual men-tors for Adams are Friedrich von Hügel and Ernst Troeltsch—Catholic and Protestant theological liberals, respectively. He links them in two deeply insightful sentences—one on the nature of teaching and the other on the essence of religion:

> We may say with Friedrich von Hügel that it is the merit of Ernst Troeltsch to help us "grow in our very questions." In Troeltsch's view, precisely that process of growth should issue from "the specific kernel of religion," a unique and in-dependent source of "new life and power."

This is a penetrating definition of education itself and can be taken as a personal challenge—to grow in our very ques-tions, opening ourselves toward the mystery of existence, aware that the more we know of the mystery, the more it widens and deepens.

Adams's further comment on the process of growth likewise deserves continuing reflection: What is the kernel—the insight, the imperative, or the heart-searing recognition—that impels one to seek new life and power? I venture that for Adams himself, the central idea and recognition was never articulated as such. I call it *universal incarnation*, that is, the imperative to embody in time and history God's good intent. It can happen anywhere, at any time. Our best stories bear witness to it—or perhaps it requires our personal witness.

Donald W. Shriver Jr. comes close to saying this in a remarkable tribute to Adams as a teacher. In an essay written when he was president of Union Theological Seminary in New York, Shriver says,

> What did James Luther Adams teach us if not the indispensability of the story for the teaching art? ... [A colleague] told me how, for his generation of denominational leaders, Harvard was "neutral ecumenical turf." They come to Harvard as a place to acquire the technical intellectual tools for promoting their own highly fundamentalist versions of the Gospel. For some, however, Harvard comes as a surprise. The Gospel is potentially seductive, especially in the person of James Luther Adams. It's rather like going to war in another country and coming back with a foreign bride. With people like Ralph Lazzaro and Jim Adams around, Harvard introduced some of us to the possibility of a Unitarianism of the Second Person. That really was a surprise. ... It is hard to identify for a stranger what James Luther Adams taught us apart from telling that stranger who James Luther Adams is and who he became to us in our own idiosyncratic autobiographies. We all have our tales of how we were seduced. We are eager to tell these personal tales because our freedom to tell them is integral to what we have to tell. ... James Luther Adams resorts to [his stories] in glad abandon to historical concreteness ... exemplifying that art in the narrative form alone seems to embody both history and synthesis.

More simply, we may say, narratives embody both concrete fact and fundamental meaning. Shriver goes on to cite four of Adams's stories, including the following:

> One day a visitor at the University of Chicago was seeking for the office in Cobb Hall of the first President, William Rainey Harper. Encountering a scrub woman in the corri-

dor, he asked where to find the President. She replied, "I dunno. I jes' scrub here." When the visitor repeated the remark to the President, Harper replied, "We are beginning to specialize, you see."

Shriver comments, "Learning that has not lost its soul does not alienate itself from...the scrub woman," and adds a second thought:

> No, for the truth we have to learn has already united the scrub woman with the promise of the wholeness of us all. Truth finally bears a human likeness, is revealed in human shape, emptying itself and humbling itself to our condition, becoming our servant, colleague, teacher, friend. If this be not a Unitarianism of the Second Person, it is something equally remarkable.

Those familiar with the history of Protestant thought in the twentieth century cannot but feel an irony here. Theological liberals, Adams included, suggest that the archneoorthodox Protestant Karl Barth perpetrates a "unitarianism of the second person" due to his insistence that Jesus Christ represents the sole incarnation and revelation of God. The unitarianism of the second person that Shriver ascribes to Adams is, in an important sense, similar: Jesus in word and deed mediates "the specific kernel of religion," in Troeltsch's phrase, that takes root and grows in "new life and power." We enter into this faith tradition by witnessing to this life and this power in others, as Adams constantly did, and in ourselves.

Adams reflects on all three persons of the Holy Trinity—albeit one at a time. To read his masterful essay "Reason and the Religion of the Eighteenth Century" is to see his love of the first person, the Creator who presides over the Age of Reason. Nor can you read his essay "The Ages of Liberalism" and not see his love of the third person, the Holy Spirit who inaugurates an Age of the Spirit, an age already foreseen by Jeremiah (Jeremiah 31:31). More surprising and more elusive is Adams's Christological bent, which Dean Shriver perceives as the inner content of many of his stories.

Adams's emphasis on Jesus as a parable-teller and model of a contemporary ministry is pertinent, but Shriver's point has nothing to do with the figure of Jesus *per se*. Parables—stories that open awareness to hidden spiritual realities—are mediators of meaning, possibly sacred meaning. Told and retold through centuries, they enter into or form what I have called *sacred tradition*. Just as the story of Jesus as the Christ functions as a symbol, mediating the meaning of the divine in human terms, religious parables as such are functionally Christological. For in these ways meaning is given a lifelike embodiment, incarnation in human form and flesh. This is why Donald Shriver can find in Adams a "Unitarianism of the Second Person" and be delighted. Adams never commented on Shriver's shrewd observation but I can only imagine him absorbing it with a wry smile. He had an abundance of what Erik Erikson called *ego-strength*.

Adams commented several times upon the Trinitarian scheme for the three ages of Western history, espoused by Joachim of Fiore early in the thirteenth century, as the basis of subsequent philosophies of history. Karl Marx's "three ages" is a favorite example. Adams interprets "the three ages of liberalism" in the modern era of history, just as Joachim takes the three personae of the Holy Trinity as keys, but not in the usual order. The Age of the Spirit, marked by the rise of the Radical Reformation—roughly the sixteenth and seventeenth centuries—comes first. The Age of the Creator, the Enlightenment and Romantic periods of confidence in human reason and self-expression—roughly the eighteenth and nineteenth centuries—comes second. Our own postmodern age is difficult to characterize. Should we call it the age of information, the age of anxiety, or the age of the global struggle for justice? Adams calls it the Age of the Mediator—confirming Shriver's insight into the kernel from which his thought grew. As already suggested, parable-telling is essentially Christological because parables are concrete and personalized mediators of a meaning beyond appearances. They incarnate meaning in human form.

We could say: And it came to pass that Jesus of Nazareth invited us, in our own ways within our own personal and historical circumstances, to tell our own stories and to tell his story as a parable of self-giving love, the love that would save us and can empower us to surpass ourselves. Adams says,

> The Bible, like the classical literature of so many religious traditions, is a great work of art. The characteristic rhetoric of the Bible is indicated by the phrase, "And it came to pass...." What came to pass? Then you get a story! And these stories are among the great artistic presentations of humanity. I view God's incarnation in Jesus as partly manifest in his command of words and in his invention of parables. In the Gospels it is not conceivable that Jesus would have been able to elicit the loyalty of the disciples if he had not used magic words with the skill of a great artist.

He also remarks, "The fishermen saw in this man something of true religious affection and artistry." We could say it more simply, that they saw in him a supremely attractive figure—not for his insight, or righteousness, or piety, but for his passion and his imagination. For this reason the stories he told have often been rendered contemporaneous, remade as *stories we are in*. Adams cites a wonderful example:

> The "Cotton Patch" version of the book of Luke was written by Clarence Jordan, a Southerner who has been associated with Koinonia, the famous center in Georgia which for decades has tried to promote better race relations and in the course of time has been bombed and suffered many a protest against any change in race relations. The word *koinonia* in the New Testament refers to the fellowship, the living bond, that unites Christians. Consider a passage from the "Cotton Patch" preacher, the story of the Good Samaritan.
> "A man was going from Atlanta to Albany and some gangsters held him up...." (In Jordan's version, rather than a priest and a Levite "passing by on the other side," it is a

white preacher and a white gospel singer, and rather than a Samaritan who rescues him, it is a black man. The story concludes:) "So Jesus said, 'Well, then, you get goin' and start livin' like that.'" It is fascinating to observe the way in which certain stories figure in our lives. Often at moments of crisis or at moments when we see something essentially human, we think of these stories.

We could say that one who gives a good story to a people has opened something up for them, in this instance making available a transforming power that gives meaning and warmth to fellowship. What do we have, then, in this parable? Like a good many parables, there are many dimensions in it. I want to select only one dimension, the parable as an attack on stereotypes, stereotypes that conceal or distort reality. The question could be put to us, Who for us today is the Samaritan? Who for us today is imprisoned in stereotypes I mean our stereotypes, pinned wriggling on the wall?

Liberalism has been of two minds about Jesus, as the foregoing discussion of parable-telling may bring to mind. On the one hand liberalism has asked who the Jesus of history was, a quest recently renewed by The Jesus Seminar. Liberal Christians have long seen this as a way of distinguishing "the religion of Jesus" from "the religion about Jesus"—the Christological faith first articulated by St. Paul. Humanistic or secular liberals have seen this substituting a "Jesus-ology" for traditional Christology as a dubious compromise at best. Adams sometimes speaks of "the religion of Jesus," but at other times speaks of the meaning of Christian faith, as in his previous comment on Clarence Jordan's version of Jesus's parable of "the Good Samaritan," in Christological terms. He does not say that Jesus teaches us to be like the Good Samaritan. He says, rather, "One who gives a good story to people has opened up something for them, in this instance making available a transforming power that gives meaning and warmth to fellowship." In this view, Jesus exemplifies something that we can do in our own time and place,

embodying the same saving power that he embodied—just as
Clarence Jordan has done in his re-telling of the story. Both ver-
sions of the story have an artistry and both are courageous word-
acts, challenging local bigotries. The Christology of a transformed
liberalism affirms that anyone in any age can incarnate the redemptive power of God in some way, in some degree, by "giving a
good story to people," a story that speaks with artistry and courage
not only of redemptive deeds, but also for them.

From the earliest period of his mature thought forward,
Adams frequently pairs the concepts of *gift* and *task*. As in the fundamental pattern of the Covenant, a *task* (a moral duty freely accepted) is a response to a *gift* (an act of divine grace). In these
terms, Adams says, the Christ is both an embodiment of God's
love and our unsurpassed moral exemplar—both gift and task:

> Christ is the symbol and the realization in principle of the
> joining together of freedom and love. Jesus is both a gift and
> an indication of our task, a gift of the love of God that is at
> the heart of the universe and a call to all who would achieve
> the fulfillment of human freedom. He points us toward his
> Father; and his teachings and example furnish us with the
> supreme moral ideal, the fundamental principles of the good
> life which no coming time will transcend.

The ideas of divine love—often very hard to see—and human
freedom—often used for destructive, love-denying ends—are not
easily reconciled. Adams cites Quillen Shinn, the itinerate
Universalist preacher of a century ago, who sums up the
Universalist faith in these words: "Not a single atom, nor a single
soul can get beyond the reach of God's almighty force of love." This
immense claim, like Adams's own earlier assertion that "the love of
God...is at the heart of the universe," raises a tough question.
Does this "almighty force of love" overrule human freedom? Is it a
coercive power trumping our every decision? Adams's implicit answer is Yes, and yet he makes no attempt to resolve the apparent

contradiction between the sovereignty of divine love and the human freedom to fulfill or to trample, at will, what that love requires. He simply observes that the freedom of self-determination is fulfilled by the human capacity to respond to "the creative, sustaining, commanding, community-forming and transforming power of God"—in brief, the love of God. We may add the observation that it is precisely the reconciliation of love and freedom (like the lamb lying down with the lion) that, to the believer, is the miracle that confirms faith. That love liberates our best energies is a truth of human experience and overrides logic.

As a young boy, Adams recalls, he struggled with his fundamentalist parents over salvation and damnation, and in the process discovered his own ability to wound. He recounts his parents' worry that he was liable to end up in hellfire, since he had reached "the age of reason" and still had not been "saved," that is, had not attested to Christ as his personal savior. At this point young Luther, as he was known in the family, had a conversation with his parents that may represent his coming of age—with a vengeance:

> I said, "You say Heaven is perfect bliss and if I'm not saved I'll go to Hell?" "That's right," they replied. "And you're so concerned because you love me?" "Yes, of course." "Well"—now came the clincher—"if you love me and you're up in Heaven while I'm down in Hell, how can that be perfect bliss for you?"

To hold out as a child against your parents' will is to become conscious of your own free will and, ironically, of your power to inflict hurt, even on those who love you. So here again, the story has several dimensions. I'm not aware that Adams ever committed it to writing. Did he not do so because in his heart of hearts he suspected it was the sort of story a child might dream up but never act upon? He seems to have always been careful to honor his father and his mother, however difficult their relationships, especially with his father, may have become. In addition to great respect for his father as "a man of principle" and of deep faith, his attitude included large measures of forgiveness and compassion during his father's advanced years.

The story is further remarkable as an example of the way in which a strong religious idea, like "You must be born anew," deeply experienced in childhood and jettisoned as self-alienating in adolescence, may in our maturity return in new and powerful ways—or so Adams's story of himself teaches.

Crystallizing Religious Understanding

Adams is agitated by the loss of depth evident in the psychologizing and moralizing habits of much contemporary religious thought. It is not accidental that during Adams's theological development, Paul Tillich speaks of "the depth dimension" in theology. Tillich's God is never securely perched "in heaven above," but is "the ground of being" erupting from below. Adams draws significantly on Paul Tillich's work, especially his early "religious socialist" and "depth sociology" writings. These serve as antidotes to the flattening out of liberal theology, theology with an attenuated sense of historical roots and tragic loss. Tillich develops the New Testament term, *kairos*—meaning "time" in the sense of fulfilled or opportune time, hence a time open to transcendence. In the typical liberal view, history illustrates the past we have progressed beyond; it adopts the viewpoint of what it imagines is up-to-date and therefore superior. In an age marked by the sense of moral failure and tragic loss, deeper resources will be sought.

Adams holds a fundamentally liberal outlook on religion, namely, that it should serve to enlarge and not diminish our humanity. But it must do this, he asserts, on the basis of communally experienced and historically rooted faith, and it must bring people into the depths of life. The individualistic and ahistorical tendencies of liberal thought put him constantly in tension with his adopted religious and political liberalism. Adams holds that liberalism must no longer be confused with lax, uncritical, or mere broad-minded attitudes, least of all in an age of rising tyrannies of the Right and the Left. The aim of religious awareness, religious faith, religious community, and religious life must be radical change. Bringing together ultimate religious meaning and intimate personal experience, religion must effect a fundamental change in our personal and social lives. "There is no depth without a way to depth, according to Paul Tillich," Adams says, and cites Tillich's words:

> Something very tragic happens in all periods of humanity's spiritual life: truths, once deep and powerful, discovered by the great geniuses with profound suffering and incredible labor, become shallow and superficial. It can happen and unavoidably it does happen, because there is no depth where there is no way to depth. Truth without the way to truth is dead; and if it is still used, in detachment, it contributes only to the surface of things.

Every lover of ancient spiritual passion has felt this, in the face of the massive and deadening weight of modern secularity. There seems no way back, no bridge seems possible. The loss of depth in religious awareness vitiates, it seems, the attempt to renew faith among the liberal-minded. When we lose the very language of faith, "a way to depth," we lose the capacity to experience the depths. Symbolic language provides ways to mediate meanings, meanings that of necessity dwell beneath the hard, reflective surfaces of existence. In Tillich's intricate and subtle theological system, Adams finds a recasting of theological categories in the language of ontology and existentialism. Tillich's concepts of *being* and *existence* are dialectically related in a way that is analogous to Adams's pairing of *ultimate* and *intimate*.

Adams draws on the visionary language of the seventeenth-century Protestant mystic Jacob Böhme to recall the way Tillich invites us to plunge beneath the shimmering surface of

Existenz. Böhme's language, like Tillich's, is symbolic and ontological, but as Adams accents, it is also an ecstatic report of a
mystical experience:

> The style of [Tillich's] writing...reveals a luminous, nu-
> minous quality that is unique. A luminous style I have
> said. The metaphor is that of light. But the substance of his
> writing is numinous, for Tillich in principle intended it to
> be a reflected light, the light of eternity, the light of
> Numen...
>
> The luminous and numinous quality of Tillich's
> thought and intention is well illustrated by one of his
> mentors, the German theosophist of the seventeenth cen-
> tury, Jakob Böhme....As he was at work in his shop this
> shoemaker's glance was one day attracted by a polished
> pewter dish which with dazzling light reflected the sun. A
> strange feeling overpowered him, for it seemed as if he
> were looking into the very heart of reality and beholding
> its innermost mystery. Speaking of this experience Böhme
> said, "I fell into a great melancholy and sadness when I be-
> held the mighty deep of this world with its stars and
> clouds, rain and snow...for I saw evil and good, love and
> wrath in all things, in the earth and in its elements as well
> as in man and beast....In this Light I saw through all
> things and into all creatures....Then I had a great impulse
> to describe the Being of God." Here we see the great
> themes of Tillich, the darkness and the light, the coinci-
> dence of opposites.

In view of Adams's strictures against mystical "inwardness,"
the appeal to mystical vision and ecstatic union with the divine
in his interpretation of Tillich are surprising. He holds that mysticism is insufficiently subject to rational critique and excessively
subject to "inwardness," private feelings that divert attention
from social-ethical concerns. So his affirmation of mysticism as
a necessary element of authentic faith is significant. Kant writes

of "religion within the limits of reason alone"; Adams wants mysticism within the limits of an historical and prophetic faith alone:

> Mysticism is a sense and taste of the presence of or union with the ground of meaningful existence and purpose, the ground of everything finite, yet transcending everything finite. It is thus an indispensable element of all religion, but it is never properly a separate element. It must will-nilly obtain in relation to other aspects of religion, sacramental (meaning as mediated—made present—through finite, tangible vessels) and prophetic (meaning as personal, social-ethical demand), whether this relationship is positive or negative. When mysticism aims to remain separated it becomes demonic, inflating an "element" into identification with the whole. The hardest knife ill-used doth lose its edge. A religion that does not have the mystical element flattens out into mere sacramentalism—participation in socially accepted forms, a person who "just loves the liturgy." Air is indispensable for life but insufficient for nourishment. The mystical element is indispensable for religion but it must be accompanied by, indeed it must serve, sacramental and prophetic forces. The authentic mystical element is no anchorite. Let us not to the marriage of true members admit impediments.

In Shakespeare's *The Tempest*, Miranda asks, Were they benevolent or malevolent powers that brought us to this isle? Prospero answers, "Both, both, my girl!" From Adams we learn the necessity of saying "both, both"—both prophetic and mystical sensibilities, both eternity and temporality, both intimacy and ultimacy, both unity and diversity. He cites a both/and from Alfred North Whitehead: "I hazard the prophecy that that religion will conquer which can render clear to popular understanding some eternal greatness incarnate in the passage of temporal fact." He also cites Paul Tillich's strikingly similar prophesy: "The Word of God is any reality by means of which the eternal breaks with unconditional power into our contemporaneity." According to Adams, Tillich joins the immanent and the transcendent, the temporal and the eternal, the intuitive and the rational:

> In Paul Tillich's thought the concept of religion is derived from the concept of the Unconditional. Here Tillich shows himself to represent a special type of philosophy of religion, the type that relies on intuitive immediacy. The concept of the Unconditional has "turned off" many a reader. Karl Barth, who for the most part preferred Biblical language, spoke of the term as a "frozen monstrosity." It bears affinity to Anaximander's term, "the boundless." For Tillich the term aims to express the source of the unconditional claim expressed in the demand, "Thou shalt love the Lord thy God with all thy heart. . . ." It also points beyond the reality of finite differentiations. Tillich speaks of it as "our ultimate, unconditional concern, whether we call it 'God' or 'Being as such' or 'Truth as such' or 'Goodness as such' or whether we give it any other name." It is present even in distorted, though partially creative, form in demonic forces, for nothing can exist which is entirely separated from it. Thus the Unconditional is in various ways both affirming and negating; it is infinitely apprehensible, yet never comprehensible. Taking all of these ingredients into account, Tillich speaks of the relation between the Unconditional and the conditioned as "the paradoxical immanence of the transcendent."

Tillich does not abandon reason to rationalism, nor the reason that is inherent in the structures of reality, the *logos*, to what he calls the "calculating reason" of the natural sciences. Somewhat cautiously, Adams follows him. In this way Tillich maintains the distinction, drawn by German idealism and adopted by American transcendentalism, between *Vernunft* and *Verstand*, reason and understanding, the inward and intuitive faculty and the analytic and empirical faculty. Tillich calls revelation "the ecstasy of reason"— reason standing outside of itself without contradicting itself—

in his thought-transforming *Systematic Theology*, the first volume of which correlates and is subtitled, *Reason and Revelation*. Adams cites Tillich:

> Whenever we transcend the limits of our own being, moving towards union with another, something like ecstasy ("standing outside oneself") occurs.... Only through ecstasy can the ultimate power of being be experienced in ourselves, in things and persons, and in historical situations.

Adams notes that "venerable tradition demanded a systematic angelology of any full-fledged theologian." He tells a story about Paul Tillich reported to him by German theologian Helmut Thielicke, an instance in which Tillich's "ecstasy of reason" is in full flower:

> Professor Tillich was lecturing at Hamburg University when his seventieth birthday came, and accordingly Professor and Frau Thielicke arranged a birthday dinner. He had visited the Thielickes at home before, and preferred always to sit in a particular place in the study to be able to see through the window a beautiful tree that stands in the garden. Following the birthday dinner the two scholars enjoyed together a flask of wine in the study. After an hour of conversation Professor Thielicke in a jovial mood said to Paul Tillich, "I have always wanted to ask you a question about your theology. You have not yet set forth your doctrine of the angels. Paulus, what is your angelology?" The astonished Tillich replied, "Yes, yes, my angelology! My angelology? I must have a doctrine of the angels." After a brief pause, Tillich continued, "Well, here is my angelology. I say that the Greek gods, those wonderful Greek gods, are the angels." "Now, now, Paulus, surely you would not maintain that. Can you really imagine Pallas Athene was among those angels who at Bethlehem sang, 'Glory to God in the highest' at the birth of Christ?" "Yes, yes, that is difficult to believe, isn't it?" Tillich replied. Then, suddenly pointing out the window, Tillich said, "There they are,

the angels, in that tree out there! Don't you hear the angels singing there? They are in the branches of that gorgeous tree." Whereupon Professor Thielicke said, "Paulus, this is verily a miracle. You not only hear, you even see, angels in that tree. And this after we have drunk only one flask of wine!"

Adams reports this story with delight. He makes a related comment in another context:

> But it is not enough to speak of Tillich's dialectic as "ecstatic." The Tillichian dialectic is also an existential dialectic, in the sense of Schelling, namely, it aims to break through every intellectualist logism; it wishes to express the dialogue between the universal and the unique, between the necessary and the contingent.

To make this highly abstract reference to "the necessary and the contingent" more concrete, consider the familiar judgment: "Not to act is itself an action." The contradiction means that acting one way or another is inevitable, that is, *necessary*, and so that even "sitting on your hands," is a chosen action, that is, *contingent*.

Reduced to simpler terms, as nature abhors a vacuum, the "existential dialectic" of the German philosopher Friedrich Schelling abhors an abstraction. It deals with the contradictions not simply between ideas but more fundamentally, the contradictions in human existence and the way the conflicts that are generated by these contradictions reshape our personal and social existence. The dialectic of Tillich and Schelling does not deal with *ideas* in isolation from the *forces* that render reality dynamic; in this perspective, ideas can be seen to be unavoidably ideological, that is, inextricably tinged with self-interest. (This is the root of the Marxist concept of ideology too, but Marx focuses on the way social class interests shape thought.)

There is no way to evade the distorting effects of human self-interest—an aspect, we may say, of original sin. This may be the root of the human propensity to cling to false gods—the root

cause of the vast human misery of the Second World War, in
Adams's view:

> The axiom "Nature abhors a vacuum" has its spiritual
> analogue: human nature abhors an empty altar—it is incur-
> ably religious. Humanity is always "open to the infinite,"
> whether to the true infinite or to a false infinite. This is our
> greatness and our misery. Our greatest loyalties have been to
> false gods, to Mammon and Caesar and "the superior race."
> The War is revealing that human nature requires a great deal
> of suffering before it will abandon false gods.

To a group of early essays on the interpretation of history,
Tillich added a new essay, "The Storms of Our Times," in reference to the Second World War, then in progress. It was included
in the collection of Tillich's essays that Adams translated from
German and published in *The Protestant Era*. Adams himself suggested the title and years later titled his own final (and most definitive) interpretation of Tillich's thought, "The Storms of Our
Times and *Starry Night*." The former—the disruptions in the
twentieth century—are reflected in the latter—a religious consciousness that is profoundly unsettling and at the same time pacific, like van Gogh's famous painting. Citing Paul Tillich's words,
Adams says,

> Insofar as religion is a "superfluous consecration" of the forces
> that have given rise to disruptions, "the first word to be spo-
> ken by religion must be a word spoken against religion." But
> this word must be also a transforming word that transcends,
> or rather goes deeper than, the surface realities.
> Characteristically, Tillich finds transforming elements repre-
> sented...especially in the visual arts....Van Gogh's *Starry
> Night*, says Tillich, reveals a "disruption of the creative powers
> of nature." It plumbs below the surfaces where the forms are
> dynamically created." For Tillich, van Gogh's *Starry Night* un-
> veils something below the surface—potent...unconditional.
> The "storms of our times" are not to be endured without a

supportive and creative element. He refers to this "coincidence of opposites" as a "belief-ful realism . . ."

"Belief-ful realism" seeks a way beyond the impasse of traditional-
ism and idealism, by attending to the perceived workings of divine
and demonic forces in nature and history.

Those of us privileged to hear Paul Tillich lecture at Harvard
in the late 1950s know the magnetism of his persona. He had
learned English, reportedly with difficulty, only after coming to
the United States in adulthood as a political refugee from
Germany. His heavily accented English and his boldly abstruse
thought, in marked contrast to the then-current Anglo-American
philosophy, lent a fascination to his words. Tillich was the only
Harvard professor I ever heard roundly applauded after each lecture by a large hall of undergraduates and a smattering of graduate students—a gathering not easily impressed. Adams, too, notes
Tillich's impact:

> Wilhelm and Marion Pauck . . . writing of opposition at
> Harvard to Paul Tillich's ideas and vocabulary, report that
> "one philosopher went so far as to call Tillich's thought 'un-
> intelligible nonsense.'" Nevertheless, the response of stu-
> dents to his magnetic power was enormous. . . .
>
> Tillich himself was aware of the difficulty of his theo-
> logical language and could rise to humor about it. Once,
> when we were preparing essays in *The Protestant Era* for
> publication, I could not fully understand the intended
> meaning of several paragraphs in his text. When I consulted
> him about the problem, he looked at the passages for some
> time and then said, "I haven't the slightest idea what I in-
> tended there. Leave them out."

He also reports Tillich's comment that, since coming to America
and struggling with a new language, he had learned that "you
don't have to be obscure to be profound."

Adams notes that in a contemporary translation of the Bible
Jesus' command to be "perfect" is rendered: "Be ye all-inclusive,

even as your Father in heaven is all-inclusive." The verb *perfect* means "to complete." Adams wants to include also untheological (if not anti-theological) humanism:

> Among liberals no formulation is definitive and mandatory. Indeed, the word *God* may be replaced by the phrase "that which ultimately concerns humankind," or "that in which we should place our confidence."

Yes, but a qualification is in order. God-terms other than *God* are needed, and even religiously necessary, so long as we do not lose sight of what we are doing. I think this is why Martin Buber insists that *God* is one of those "hallowed words," an *Ur-worte* ("original word"), that is neither translatable nor replaceable. Tillich speaks of *God* as a symbol, a word that points beyond itself to an ontological reality, being itself, in which it participates. Similarly, we might think of *God* as the sign of a hidden reality that is known by the stories we tell of a sacred and finally unnamable presence. Adams speaks of God in these terms:

> God, or that in which we may have faith, is the inescapable, commanding reality that sustains and transforms all meaningful existence. It is inescapable, for no one lives without somehow coming to terms with it. It is commanding, for it provides the structure or the process through which existence is maintained and by which any meaningful achievement is realized. Indeed, every meaning in life is related to this commanding meaning, which no one can manipulate and which stands beyond every merely personal preference or whim. It is transforming, for it breaks through any given achievement. It is a self-surpassing reality. God is the reality that works upon us and through us and in accord with which we can discern truth, beauty, or goodness. It is that reality which works in nature, history, and thought and under certain conditions creates human good in human community. Where these conditions are not met, the human good, as sure as the night follows the day, will be frustrated or per-

verted. True freedom and individual or social health will be impaired.

The word *God* may be defined, but God remains undefined. Such a God is not only a philosophical idea; it is a living reality. But to maintain this affirmation, I believe that we inevitably feel tension with the impersonal language for God. An *It* will not do, as Martin Buber points out; we want a *Thou*. To be a person is to be a *Thou*, made in the image of—somehow reflecting—the Sacred Thou. Adams once said in a group discussion that a God conceived and spoken of as *impersonal* is soon felt to be *sub-personal* and beneath our fully personal level of concern, feeling, and relatedness. As he could have said, an *ultimate* that is not also *intimate* will always be something less than our "ultimate concern." The Psalmist said it long ago: Those who worship lifeless idols become like them; they render themselves insensate and are spiritually deadened (Psalm 115:4-7). And just this is the answer to the question Jesus' disciples asked (Mark 4), namely the reason for "speaking in parables." The reason is that literalism is an idol, a deadening fake.

Adams cites Tillich's citation from Martin Luther—words that sound virtually contemporary:

> Nothing is so small but that God is even smaller; nothing is so large but that God is even larger. He is an ineffable Being, above and outside everything we can name or imagine. God is nearer to all his creatures than they are to themselves. He has found the way for all his own divine essence to be completely in all creatures, and in man especially, in a deeper and more internal and more present manner than the creature is to itself. Thus he embraces all things and is within them; and at the same time he is nowhere. He cannot be comprehended by anyone.

Luther's words recall Pascal's impractical advice, often cited by Adams: "Practice opposite virtues and occupy the distance between them." Being religious, we may say, practice the "opposite" virtues of intimacy and ultimacy, all the while, with Emily Dickinson, "traversing the interval between." Adams tells a confessional story about his sense of being personally embedded in a sacred tradition:

> Kermit Eby of the C.I.O. and I taught courses every two or three years on Protestantism and trade unions, or on Protestantism and voluntary associations, or Protestantism and the theory of politics. Eby was at an earlier time the first executive director of the Independent Voters of Illinois.
>
> The association with Eby was a heartening experience. He was reared in the Church of the Brethren and I in the Plymouth Brethren. It is interesting to observe how the meaning of experiences of one's youth will at certain moments, become crystallized. On one occasion I went with Eby to participate in the foot-washing ceremony at the Church of the Brethren. What a unique experience! You participate in the Lord's Supper, and then you take turns washing each other's feet and drying them. Then after that the kiss of peace. Eby and I shared this kind of background, so we had strong motives in common, growing out of this earliest tradition of intimacy and ultimacy.

The experience is powerful, and Adams names the phenomenon in a way that no one, to my knowledge, has before. The *crystallizing* of religious understanding, through the coming together of ultimate meaning and intimate experience, effects a fundamental change in the person. Stated in the concrete terms of this experience, the foot-washing ritual becomes for him a parabolic experience of the intimate and humble service that defines the ultimate meaning of life.

    O thou great mover of the globe whereon we speed
    through space and time, thou who art higher than our
    highest thought, the ground of all that gives us breath

and life, we know thee as nearer to us than breathing.
We know thee as both intimate and ultimate, as
more deeply moving in the contrite heart than in the
paths of suns and stars, as more powerfully creative
in love and justice than in the might of atoms. Amen.

—JLA

Being Human:
Primacy of the Will

JOHANN WOLFGANG VON GOETHE amends the famous sacred text that opens the Gospel of John, "In the beginning was the Word," in these lines from *Faust*:

> The spirit aids! From anxious scruples freed
> I write, "In the beginning was the deed."

John's Gospel follows Genesis in speaking of the divine Word (*logos*) as the originating agency of creation. Goethe's revision, which Adams cites, gives primacy to the will—precisely the sort of bold departure, freed from "anxious scruples," that Goethe often advocates. To be sure, whatever is spoken is preceded by the will to speak, but Goethe suggests more than this. Words are not simply expressions of a preexisting idea. They are "speech acts," assertions of will. To be human is to reflect the creative and perhaps also the destructive power of God.

It is fashionable to speak of ours as a post-Enlightenment age, but Adams celebrates Immanuel Kant's pronouncement, which stands as a reminder that we are all children of the Enlightenment:

> Recognition of the contingency of human existence is pre-
> requisite to exercising human creativity. For it is liberating to
> see that "I happen to be such and such, and therefore, in free-
> dom of the will, can be other than I am—I can choose." The

motto of the Enlightenment, said Kant, is *Sapere aude!* Dare
to think!

The stereotypic idea of the Enlightenment is that it was an age
of reason, with Immanuel Kant as a chief progenitor. But as
Adams reminds us, the Enlightenment first and foremost accented
a radical freedom of will and represented a revolutionary human-
ization of every realm of thought.

What kind of a "liberal" is Adams? He reaches back beyond
the rationalism and scientism that grew from the Enlightenment
to its sources in the Renaissance and earlier humanizing strands of
thought. Adams's thought is consonant with the tradition of
"rhetorical theology" discussed by Marjorie O'Rourke Boyle. She
focuses on Erasmus' Renaissance humanism in contrast to
Medieval scholastic theology, noting these defining features of
rhetorical theology: the centrality of love (*caritas*), the primacy of
the will, and the vocation of theology to seek religious conversion.
Precisely these features are prominent in Adams's theology, although he never uses the term *rhetorical theology*. Boyle writes,

> The scholastic definition of theology was the formulation of
> Anselm: "faith seeking understanding." Faith is a theological
> virtue and it resides in the intellect. In scholasticism it seeks
> a virtue of the speculative intellect, understanding, and also
> understanding as a charismatic gift.... In the humanistic
> definition of theology, however, a theological virtue seeks a
> theological virtue, its proper perfection. Rhetoric seeks an
> act of the will, assent, and secures its religious end in con-
> version. Conversion involves charity alone. Charity [*caritas*]
> is a theological virtue and it resides in its own increase. Here
> is the definitional shift from scholasticism to humanism in
> theology: from faith seeking understanding to charity seek-
> ing charity. It is paralleled by a psychological shift from the
> intellectual to the volitional, from the speculative to the ex-
> periential. The humanistic reform in theology was... [in]
> continuity with the medieval tradition of those mystical the-

ologians from Bernard to Bonaventure and beyond who identified human excellence with will rather than the intellect, and who, not fortuitously, wrote rhetorically rather than dialectically about God.

Adams would have enjoyed Boyle's analysis as a thoroughgoing confirmation of his theological voluntarism. While he affirms Anselm's scholastic definition of theology as "faith seeking understanding," he does so as a matter of reordering modernist thought, that is, as a principle of understanding existence on the basis of faith, rather than of attaining faith on the basis of what we can understand. His theology is rhetorical not just in the sense that he frequently uses stories and other rhetorical devices, but in the basic sense that the chief aim of theology is to effect a change of heart and mind and will, that is, to raise affections, to provide interpretive images and root metaphors, and to motivate life transformation.

Adams's personal line of intellectual development carried him from the Minotaur of fundamentalist literalism, which he slew, to the enduring Christian insight that we must be born anew—that is, undergo a fundamental reorientation of the will—which he preserved in new form. Reflecting on his labyrinthine path to theological reconstruction, he is conscious of his intellectual and spiritual lineage, called *voluntarism*—in many respects an unexpected lineage for a religious liberal! He wrote in a letter to me,

> A thread in my development may be traced from my early fundamentalism, to my studies under Irving Babbitt at Harvard, through the experience of Nazism on to the study of Tillich. Babbitt, with his emphasis on the "higher will," defends the primacy of will over intellect, and then Tillich does the same. One can trace this heritage primarily from the Bible, for instance early in the idea of the will of God, in Jesus' conception of *metanoia*, in the Pauline war among the members, and in Augustine where the authentic will is love,

where "two cities" represent on the one hand the authentic will and on the other the perverted will, and on through Duns Scotus, Luther, and Calvin, and perhaps to Jonathan Edwards.... I think I now understand why I went from fundamentalism (through "scientific humanism") to Babbitt to Tillich. This thread of development, to be sure, takes on its own special character by reason of my reactions to the world about me. My first sermon after my return from Germany in 1936 was on the theme of "conversion."

His "reactions to the world about me" alludes especially to extensive periods of study in Germany, where he witnessed at first hand a nation descending into the demonic depths of Nazism. He came to feel that such events are hardly to be answered with liberal-minded reason or moral earnestness, but only with passion and steel-willed determination. Liberalism itself, he declares, must undergo a radical change of heart, mind, and will. He accents this idea in his inaugural sermon at Meadville Theological School in Chicago in 1937. The faculty and students of the Unitarian seminary, he tells us, were shocked that their newest professor would use such language, for the very idea of "conversion" was anathema among liberal-minded intellectuals. "Born again" religion, equated with fundamentalist revivalism and anti-intellectualism, was precisely that to which liberal religion sought to offer an alternative!

An intellectual who sought the power of deeply felt commitment, Adams—like Jonathan Edwards, the brilliant eighteenth-century philosophical theologian and preacher who seeks to "raise affections"—does not fit the expected pattern. Although Adams is often honored by his adopted denomination as a spokesman for liberal social causes, the tension arising from his philosophical and theological stance has never been resolved. He sees that conversion is not a question of emotional irrationality, the "enthusiasm" that the eighteenth-century divine Charles Chauncy excoriates. It is a question of spiritual power, the "enthusiasm" that Ralph Waldo Emerson praises when he says, "Nothing great was ever achieved

without enthusiasm." Rather than qualities of mind, moral recti-
tude, and critical distance, he again echoes Goethe, praising qualities of will: commitment, humility, boldness, and affection.

This chapter develops Adams's understanding of human nature and human existence under the conditions of time and history. He sees freedom both as a defining mark of humanity and as
an ideal condition of society. Thus human freedom is a wonderful
and often fearsome gift; it eludes definition, for to define it fully
would be to falsify it. Adams argues that "angelism"—imagining
that we can be free without the constraints of social and historical existence—is a dangerous illusion, one that religious other-
worldliness has often promoted. A renewed liberalism must
understand the tragic element in history—the destruction that
comes with creation, the loss that comes with gain. To the mind
and the heart of faith, tragedy is not the last word, for there is also
the possibility of metanoia, a radical change of heart and mind.
Finally, Adams affirms the spiritual freedom of persons, seen in
the human capacity to achieve a distinctive identity within an underlying sense of human vocation.

The Mystery of Human Freedom

We dwell within the mystery of human freedom: "In the beginning was the deed." Being "fated to be free"—as Adams is wont to
say—we cannot not choose and act, for not to act is itself a chosen action. We may often choose badly, and yet by acting freely we
can nevertheless transcend the determination wrought by antecedents or perhaps by fate itself. We can exercise our God-given
spiritual freedom. Adams recites the pontificating clergyman in
Henry Fielding's novel *Tom Jones*: "When I mention religion, I
mean the Christian religion; and not only the Christian religion
but the Protestant religion; and not only the Protestant religion,
but the Church of England." Adams's deadpan comment: "If his
words reflect a certain provincialism, they also exhibit some precision of definition." Clerical provincialism provides the humor,

but the use Adams makes of this satirical moment surprises us; it calls attention to something deeper, namely, recognition that the power to define is the power to affect and reshape the way we look at things and, in consequence, the way we act.

Consider the process of naming things. Names identify and call to mind objects that are not immediately before us. Further, by conceptualizing, they literally create a universe of mental objects that were inaccessible, if not nonexistent, before. Many philosophical puzzles are entailed in these propositions. For instance, is a name an arbitrary tag as the "nominalists" of the Middle Ages argue and as Shakespeare's Juliet suggests?

> What's in a name? That by which we call a rose
> By any other name would smell as sweet.

Or does the act of naming of itself invest reality, since what has not been identified does not enter into our mental world? So philosophical realists tend to think.

Genesis tells us that, along with its creation, God names light and then, no doubt thinking dialectically, names its absence: "God called the light Day, and the darkness he called Night." The Biblical creation story goes on to suggest that the original man and woman, called Adam and Eve, significantly participate in the creation of the natural order by conferring names on the animals (Genesis 2:19-20). It's as if truth requires a witness or prophet, one who sees, names, and truthfully announces.

Naming is a rudimentary form of conceptualizing, for concepts identify and label distinct realities—phenomena—that may or may not be visible. As named or as conceptualized phenomena, these "realities" become part of our mental and social homeland. Defining is a further specialization in the art of naming. Adams frequently cites Whitehead's aphorism: "Definition is the soul of actuality." But which comes first, we wonder, the definition or the actual object? *Naïve realists* will insist perception should simply conform to objective fact. *Subjectivists* will insist that since objective fact is unknowable, perception of fact decides "truth." *Voluntarists* insist that the creative (or perhaps the destructive) will of the individual determines what is the case and what is not. They are like the third baseball umpire in the story of the three umpires and the ways they call—that is, name—balls and strikes: The first umpire says, "I calls 'em as they is." The second says, "I calls 'em as I sees 'em." But the third umpire says, "They ain't nothin' till I calls 'em." The first two speak in the realist and subjectivist voices, respectively. The third speaks in what Adams calls the *voluntarist voice*, a synthesis of the first two and also the voice of faith—as if to say, "I am a witness to what is and thereby participate in its truth." Just so, religious truth is primarily a matter of personal witness, including trust in the testimony of others.

Adams holds that those who are linguistically creative render previously unseen realities visible by naming them; they "legislate"consciousness for the rest of us. For instance, T. S. Eliot "legislated" our consciousness of April when he called it "the cruelest month," since we all experience April as a time when warmth and growth return and then, if only temporarily, are snatched away by cold and even frost damage. In the Northern Hemisphere, by poetic extension, Eliot helps us understand that sometimes life is like that—a new hope snatched away. Adams is drawn to Shelley's bold claim for poetry, even as he is also drawn to Auden's hard-bitten realism about political power:

> In the last line of Shelley's "A Defense of Poetry"we read, "the poets are the unacknowledged legislators of the world." We might say with Shelley that they are the great legislators, guiding the mind toward or away from reality, actual or possible. I once heard the theologian-poet W. H. Auden answer a question about Shelley's dictum. He was asked, "Do you agree that the poets are the unacknowledged legislators of the world?" He pondered for a moment and then in his typically gruff manner said, "The poets? Certainly not. Who are these legislators? I would say—the secret police."

The history of our times favors Auden over Shelley. Nevertheless, Adams can enjoy Auden's show of gruff stuff and remain idealistic and perhaps romantic enough to agree with

Shelley. Auden, too, he would say, legislates our consciousness by his own insightful acts of theological naming, for instance, his definitions of *idolatry* ("taking what is frivolous seriously"), *space and time* ("Space is whom our loves are needed by, Time is our choice of How to love and Why"), and *faith* ("To choose what is difficult all one's days As if it were easy, that is faith, Joseph praise.") It is notable that each of these "definitions" involves not just keen observation but more particularly, spiritual decision.

We dwell within meaning-giving forms that transcend us, even while we have part in naming and creating them. This fact does not preclude critical thought; recognition of the mystery of transcendence need not lead to mystification and authoritarianism. It can lead to one of the most fundamental of all religious recognitions, namely, the necessity of an original decision, an existential commitment of the self. Such a leap of faith is not blind insofar as it arises from a conviction and serves not as a terminus but as a starting point for reflective thought.

Reflection on human nature also leads to reflection on ultimate reality. What is the meaning of God—that ultimate reality in whom "we live and move and have our being"? (Acts 17:28). Adams suggests that humans are those beings who ask: What may we truly rely on? What may we believe in? To seek what is ultimately reliable amid the plethora of things that are only relatively reliable and therefore, also, relatively unreliable, requires not blind faith but critical thought.

Plato envisions philosophical inquiry as dialogue between two voices and sees thought itself as a dialogue of the mind with itself. In *Sophist* he describes dialectic, by which he means the process of philosophic thought itself:

> Dividing according to Kinds, not taking the same Form for a different one or a different one for the same—is that not the business of Dialectic?...And the man who can do that discerns clearly one Form everywhere extended...and one Form connected in a unity through many wholes.... And the only person, I imagine, to whom you would allow this mastery of Dialectic is the pure and rightful lover of wisdom.

Adams's own thought is thoroughly dialectical. It takes this form because his attention is drawn to the dynamic that is inherent in the human life cycle and in the succession of historical events. Dialectic describes the forward movement of things in time, through conflict and reconciliation, through contest and communion. Both as moral and as metaphysical dynamic, a directive runs from analysis to synthesis. To synthesize is to combine and unify what is disparate and divided. Plato calls the process "participation" (*methexis*). The task of the philosopher is to discern the One within the Many, and the Many within the One. Adams cites Plato, here speaking for Socrates: "Show me the man who can combine the One and the Many and I will follow in his footsteps, even as in those of a god."

The theologian in us wants to see Plato's "One" as a God term and his "Many" as shorthand for the multiplicity of created beings. The process that links them and gives the Many their actuality, participation, thereby incorporates constituent elements within a whole. This is the root from which the imagination bears fruit, in the form of religious symbols, and without which it withers. Adams cites Emerson: "Man is a symbol-bearing tree."

F. M. Cornford observes that Plato's ideas, as eternal forms, are descended from the gods; being no mere abstractions, but divine powers, they are capable of effecting participation. The demythologizing of Plato's godlike ideas renders them more rational but also saps their potency. Ultimately, it undermines Platonism itself and paves the way for Aristotle's empirical and rational thought. We learn from this wrinkle in intellectual history a great deal about the limits of intellectualism as a philosophy of life, as compared to voluntarism, in which rational understanding follows from the decision made in good will. We need, we may say, One who lies beyond mythologizing and demythologizing, who can say, "I am that I am" and "Thou shalt have no other gods before me" (Exodus 3:14 and 20:3). This Yahweh, in himself unknown—personalized as male in a patriarchal culture—comes to be known primarily in the faithfulness of a people to his word and will.

In this light philosophical ideas are recognized as created in time with human participation, rather than as "eternal ideas" standing apart from human need and imagination and will. Nevertheless, in the face of historical change and deeply rooted cultural diversity, it has been felt essential to establish a rational and universal law; hence the idea of natural law. Adams says,

> The perennial problem of the One and the Many is the problem of discovering something that abides in the midst of change and serves to measure it, the problem of establishing and justifying ethical standards in their relation to the essential nature of humans and of things. The ancient philosophical concept of natural law purports to formulate a rational ideal of justice which, resting in the nature of things, proceeds from a principle valid for all humanity and provides a "higher law" to which changing laws and customs should somehow conform. However, in face of complex human situations, no universal definition will ever be adequate or wholly valid. We must always answer questions of justice within finite perspectives, and finite perspectives should be tentative perspectives. To make the "natural" or the rational immutable is to make the novel unnatural and irrational. It is to hold the Gorgon's freezing eye up to creation, and even into the face of God.

Adams could declare, "Natural law is dead! Long live natural law!" We cannot, it seems, live without the conviction that there is an unchanging higher law, and yet, neither can we live unequivocally *with* it. The arts and the sciences constantly remind us of the partiality of our vision and the relativity of our judgments. We live under the transcendental imperative to be reasonable; just so, not to recognize the limits of rationalism is unreasonable. In the end Adams gives a highly qualified endorsement of the idea of natural law:

> The Spanish Cardinal Merry del Val once said that for the Protestant the Bible is a wax nose to be twisted any way you please. Something similar could be said of the concept of natural law.... The legal realists assert that law is what the judges decide it is. In this view the positing of natural law is only a sign

of human vanity. As a protest against this vanity Justice Oliver Wendell Holmes Jr. reminded his students that "man is in the belly of the universe, the universe is not in the belly of man."

Seeing the relativity and the potential misuse of natural law does not move Adams to repudiate the idea itself. Rather, it moves him to recognize that all our perceptions of "the law of nature" are fallible and malleable. An element of subjectivity and bias will always cling to them. It invariably turns out that existence is more complex than we imagine or than we wish it might be. With Socrates we must continue to look for the true philosopher, one who can combine the One and the Many, that is, discern the unifying elements within diverse phenomena. Once again we are led to conclude that the One cannot be rationally delineated but only symbolically represented. We must finally "speak in parables."

Adams's thought is nuanced; ideas are presented and then qualified. He suggests that we may affirm the human drive for power and knowledge, but knowing the parable of Faust, we are not so easily influenced by those who claim to possess them and are the more attentive to the moral quality of their visions:

> The human being may be a reasoning being, but caught in history, our reason betrays its earthly attachments and its partial dependence upon the prevailing climates of opinion. But these difficulties cannot properly exempt us from concern with the problem of natural law. They only make it more complicated than many of the proponents of natural law have been willing to admit. Moreover, if the idea of natural law has been constrained and perverted by a demonic desire for power and for a knowledge that is immutable and infallible, by the *libido dominandi* and the *libido sciendi*, so also have the ideas of God, the holy, and the good. In all candor one must say to natural law in its distress what Mephistopheles said of Margaret, "She is not the first."

That is, Margaret (Goethe also calls her Gretchen) is not the first innocent to be betrayed by a false hope and brought to grief. The

"desire for power and a knowledge that is immutable and infallible" is a false hope and readily becomes a demonic longing for absolute control. Illusions sooner or later bring us to grief. Adams
teaches us to be reasonable but not rationalistic.

Wishful thinking is the Achilles' heel of religion. No longer
can we take human good will for granted—as if we ever truly
could!—for that is "the liberalism that is dead." In the face of a
death-dealing century, Adams renews his childhood acquaintance
with the apostle Paul's words about "the war within the members,"
and his later acquaintance with Augustine's idea of a struggle
within the person between two contending wills. He notes, "Both
the Old and the New Testaments are oriented to the will and the
love of God." In his epistle to the Romans, "Saint Paul finds within
himself two wills struggling with one another":

> For I delight in the law of God, in my inmost self, but I see
> in my members another law at war with the law of my mind
> and making me captive to the law of sin which dwells in my
> members. Wretched man that I am! Who will deliver me
> from the body of death? (Rom. 7:23)

Our will must be healed if our love is to be freed to do its
proper work of cherishing, nurturing, healing. In the perhaps surprising link between will and love, Adams finds St. Augustine in
the tradition of St. Paul:

> Augustine is a key figure for all later voluntarism, for he sees
> the human venture as an epic in which the drama of con-
> flicting wills exhibits on the one side an estranged humanity,
> perverted in will and misdirected in love, and on the other
> a restoring, reconciling power that redeems humanity and
> history.

Philosophical voluntarism becomes central in Adams's
thought about human nature virtually from the beginning of his
mature thought. In his view we turn out to be neither the rational
animal that Aristotle sees nor the irrational animal that Freud

sees, but rather the faithful or the faithless animal, the true or the loveless animal, depending on our "first love."

W. H. Auden cites Simone Weil's assertion, "Attention is an acceptable form of prayer," and relates it to free will. He says, "To attend to this and to ignore that" is a matter of choice, a matter of will. Adams also notes the importance of "attention," the capacity to be attentive and responsive to something of value outside one's self, the capacity to love:

> Augustine asks: What determines what individuals give attention to? He answers: We give attention in accord with our basic will, with our basic desire, our basic orientation or our love. Ultimately our love determines what we give our attention to. Augustine's psychology is a psychology of love: what one is committed to determines what one gives attention to.

We are accustomed to thinking of love as an emotion, not a decision—as an intense feeling, not an act of will. Will itself is often reduced to "willfulness," pure self-assertion. But Adams associates will with love—the mysterious sense of being irresistibly drawn and yet of freely choosing, hence of fulfilling, our will. Paul Tillich says directly in his Harvard lectures, Love is an act of will.

In Adams's own judgment his most significant contribution to the interpretation of Tillich—and he made many contributions over many years—was discerning the central role of will in his thought. An aspect of Tillich's theological creativity to which Adams calls attention is his invention of "a new language" of religion; for instance, he speaks of faith as "ultimate concern." The term reflects Tillich's voluntarism, for it suggests that faith is a basic orientation of heart and mind before it is assent to any propositions of faith. Deciding one's basic orientation often entails a reorientation of the self, called *metanoia*, an act of changing one's mind, or "turning one's face"—as in sacred history Abraham turns from Haran and Jesus turns toward Jerusalem.

Adams is drawn to the thought of Tillich for many reasons: his insistence that theology be politically engaged (preferably on the

Left); his magisterial interpretations of Western philosophy, theology, and art; and his identification with existential philosophy—a contemporary form of philosophical voluntarism. For the voluntarist the chief problem of human existence is not to know the good but to do the good that we know. To do the good that we know, at a minimum, our lives must be pointed in the right direction. We must be in love with what is great and good and with the divine, the ground and source of all being. Our capacity to live in spiritual freedom depends on it.

Love and *will* are usually understood as psychological terms only; in the thought of Tillich they become ontological terms primarily and psychological terms only secondarily. That is, they are understood as necessary forms of being. Even to call will a "form of being"seems misleading, for will is a power of being in the sense of *that which enables being to be.* Tillich says will does not merely fill a given form, it creates form. This is philosophical voluntarism, a way of thinking that gives primacy to will over intellect. *Intellect* here means the reasoning or any purely regulative mental function, for instance, assent or doubt. Adams comments that Tillich liked Nietzsche's statement that "will is the power of being in Being."

> Augustine is the philosopher of will, and he cites Tillich's words: and especially of the will which is love.... Love is original being; the power of love is the substance in everything that is.

Such is the image of God in which the human being *is* made—that is, is continually made, not *was* made in a mythic event in time past. Creation is continuous and contemporaneous, as the religious imagination intuits, or else it is only myth, a story about something that "never really happened," as skeptics say. We too do not merely fill but create and re-create the forms of our existence.

The idea of the primacy of the will is also prominent in American pragmatism, the movement of thought stemming from William James and C. S. Peirce. Peirce's "pragmatic theory of meaning," Adams notes, is concerned with the link between symbols and action. The nature of this linkage is a central theme in Adams's body of thought, as reflected in his keen interest in root metaphors, religious symbols, the arts (music, visual art, dance, fiction, poetry), and storytelling. These are not so much *what we see* as the means *by which we see*. They shape the way we see the world and therefore also the way we act. All of these are, in the broadest sense, parables, that is, forms of human expression and communication that reveal an otherwise hidden, obscure, "unstoried" meaning of existence. They exemplify the ways in which language is a form of *symbolic action*, in Kenneth Burke's term, for action follows from conception.

According to Adams, C. S. Peirce's pragmatic theory of meaning understands all language as motivated language—language that imposes meaning or intention upon reality:

> C. S. Peirce wants to leave no uncertainty about this: "Our idea of anything is our idea of its sensible effects; and if we fancy that we have any other, we deceive ourselves." The rule for attaining clarity of apprehension of meaning is this: "Consider what effects... we conceive the object of our conception to have. Then, our conception of these effects is the whole of our conception of the object."

The word *effects* may suggest mechanical or purely empirical causation. The term *consequences* retains the sense of effects for which we are morally responsible. The *meaning* of an act is its consequences, whether or not they are consciously or rationally intended. Just so, Adams's *ethics* is an ethics of consequences; that is, the moral person is not simply one who acts conscientiously or with good intentions, but one who takes responsibility for the consequences of his or her actions.

Peirce's pragmatic theory may seem excessively self-conscious, for it requires us constantly to think back from effects to an originating conception. On reflection, however, it seems intuitively obvious; the meaning of an idea or a belief is found in the conse-

quences that flow from it. A good tree is one that bears good fruit.
Adams recognizes that religious ideas, especially—conceptions of
the basic nature of the church, for example—reflect ideas of how
social or political institutions should be organized or, as reformers are wont to advocate, reorganized. Ernst Troeltsch's magisterial
work *The Social Teachings of the Christian Churches*, with its ideal
types of religious organization—the church, sect, and mystical
types—exemplifies Peirce's pragmatic theory of meaning: The
meaning of these typological terms is seen in the organizational
forms and ethical ideals that flow from them. Just this connection
between "ideal type," social organization, and ethical commitment
shows the intellectual kinship between Adams and Troeltsch.
Adams suggests that Peirce's idea is not so novel, after all:

> We may say that C. S. Peirce's pragmatic theory of meaning
> is already implied in the New Testament saying, "... by their
> fruits ye shall know them." The theology that does not ex-
> amine the social consequences of belief is in this respect
> meaningless from the point of view of the pragmatic theory
> of meaning.

What we may call Jesus' principle of moral discernment—"by
their fruits you shall know them" (Matthew 7:20)—turns out to be
a central tenet of pragmatism, as well.

The emergence of pragmatism in the modern era marked a
swing from idealism to instrumentalism, from speculative to practical considerations, from moralizing to psychoanalysis. From the
viewpoint of theological integrity, Adams accents the fatal flaw of
reducing religion to ethics—settling for "mere morality." From the
viewpoint of social ethics, he now accents the inadequacy of an
otherworldly spirituality, or "mere God," for the meaning of an
idea of God will depend on the real-world consequences that flow
from that belief.

Adams cites another pragmatist, William James, who once
was asked, "Is life worth living?"and answered, "Well, it all depends on the liver." As a psychologist, James observes that judg-

ment is not reserved for some ultimate Judgment Day but is continuous. "William James vividly reminds us of the element of judgment in life in his study of habit," Adams says, and quotes James:

> Every smallest stroke of virtue or vice leaves its never-so-little scar. The drunken Rip Van Winkle vows he will reform his habit, but he excuses himself for every fresh dereliction by saying, "I won't count this time." Well, he may not count it, and a kind Heaven may not count it; but it is being counted none the less. Down among the nerve cells and fibers, the molecules are counting it, registering and storing it up to be used against him when the next temptation comes.

Significant ethical ideas are implied here. Even our smallest choices have important consequences, although we commonly refuse to recognize moral consequences by self-deception: "I won't count this time." Adams cites Emerson: "The world is full of judgment days."

Judgment days—the recognition that we must choose among limited options and choose in timely fashion—are not bad in themselves. They are only bad, Adams says, if we fail to awaken to them and make a better decision:

> The human being is created in the image of God, endowed with freedom and power, with a freedom that is "open to infinity" and with a power of creativity that no other creature possesses. "There is surely something within us," says Sir Thomas Browne, "something that was before the elements and owes no homage unto the sun." But we can abuse this freedom and power. We can use them to turn against our Creator even to destroy ourselves and our fellows.

Yes, we reflect an absolute transcendence with our very being, but this affirmation is radical, for our freedom includes destructive fury against the creation and even against ourselves. Paradoxical recognitions of this sort arise frequently in the thought of Adams.

He asks us to look at two sides of a question, almost simultaneously. But just this is the reflective position of the person of faith,
one who lives within the mystery of freedom.

Against Angelism

Having our freedom under the conditions of finitude—having
to decide for this is to cut off the possibility of that—our lives
are shaped by our perceptions and our choices. The question,
then, comes to the fore: What will shape our perceptions and
our choices? Will it be the values that are rooted in a community and its spiritual and cultural traditions? The struggle for
survival in a poverty-stricken and shattered culture? The flashy
appeal of contemporary mass culture? These questions of social
and cultural context bear significantly upon ethics. They lead us
to ask, How do we become moral agents? What are the conditions that enable us to exercise our moral agency for the common good? Here Adams answers with one of his most
memorable aphorisms:

> Andre Malraux said, "Style-less pictures no more exist than
> do wordless thoughts." As Cardinal John Henry Newman
> put it, "Religion must express itself in particular acts. We
> cannot respect religion and insult its forms of expression." A
> purely spiritual religion is a purely spurious religion.

Recognizing the contingency of human existence and the risk
involved in any achievement, we must commit ourselves to particulars, as an artist commits to particular realizations of creative
imagination. Adams affirms the moral realism that begins with
acknowledgment of one's own biases and our need to overcome
them, against the prevalent "angelism" of much contemporary
spirituality:

> There is no such thing as poetry without poems, art without
> paintings, architecture without buildings, and there is no

such thing as an enduring faith without beliefs. The living spirit, says Schiller, creates and molds.

Adams is also aware of the staying-power of language from which "the living spirit" has fled. He alludes to the words of Robert Louis Stevenson: "Man is a creature who lives not upon bread alone but principally by catchwords."

Adams is especially interested in what Whitehead calls *root metaphors*, systemic images that shape an entire way of thinking about the world and human life. Certain root metaphors guide and shape consciousness: organism, mechanism, hierarchy, ecology—ideas abstracted from our images of nature (the body, the tree, the river, the rock, the seed, the fire, the mountain, etc.) or human artifice (the clock, the train, the pyramid, the garden, the city, etc.). Meanings branch out from and are sustained by each root or metaphorical system; the imagination lends to them a sense of profundity and spiritual power. Rational and scientific thought has sought to excise the metaphorical element in thought and put in its place objective observation and numerical measurement, in its quest for exactitude, but in Whitehead's judgment, in *Science and the Modern World*, "the exactness is a fake." Adams defines science with a story—or, rather, two stories:

> Science grows out of wonder, Aristotle tells us. The primordial scientist, let us say, was the first tadpole that raised its head above the surface of the water and asked, What's going on here, anyway? The pure scientist is not a utilitarian, one primarily concerned with use. The desire of science is simply to satisfy curiosity, as Whitehead used to say.
>
> One day the British Prime Minister, William Gladstone, visited Michael Faraday, to see his laboratory. After Faraday had spent an hour showing Gladstone his scientific apparatus, his drums and batteries, and his instruments for measuring electro-magnetism, the Prime Minister drew himself up and in pontifical condescension asked, "But what good is it all?" In a fashion calculated to be intelligible to the utili-

tarian politician, Faraday replied, "Well, Sir, some day you will be able to tax it."

The gods of ancient paganism are imaginative embodiments of spiritual power. As noted above, Francis Cornford observes that to the extent that the ancient gods became objects of "pure thought," abstracted from the gods as living beings, they were shorn of archaic power. To this extent rationalization makes the world incomprehensible. It represents not progress pure and simple but a trade-off, a loss that must be subtracted from the gain. Adams calls attention to Nietzsche's typology of philosophical outlooks, the calm, rational *Apollonian* and the passionate, irrational *Dionysian*. In these terms we may say that as the Apollonian world of clarity and order emerged, the Dionysian world of vitality and disorder fell into obscurity—but it would re-emerge in diverse creative and destructive forms.

Adams cites Oswald Spengler's saying, "Urbanity killed Christianity." He might also say that an excessively intellectual Platonism becomes an unbelievable Platonism, for a god who is only the idea of the good—that is, an ideal form—is incapable of effectuating actual goodness—that is, of embodying vitality and passion. Is it because the god-become-ideal loses the power to fight evil, or what may be worse, lost the will to fight evil?

Still, some ideas—ideas eluding strict definition—retain the power of fundamental symbols. "One must take into account," Adams says, "what Schelling called 'the infinity of the idea,' the fact that any fundamental symbol is pregnant with, latent with, a variety of implications or connotations." Following Friedrich Schelling, we empower ideas by converting them back into symbols: the Ganges, the Cross, the Two Tablets of the Law, the Lotus. This also means letting ourselves be changed by the symbol; it means learning "second naïvete," becoming like little children once again (see Matthew 18:3). A story that Adams tells illustrates the point:

> The nuclear physicist Leo Szilard, when he was age six, was asked by his teacher what a mother should do when she goes to the shoe store with her four children to buy shoes for each

at two pengo, but only has a ten-pengo bill. Leo replied, "She
needs another child."

Imagination has to do with the capacity to look at things in different and perhaps unexpected ways and functions in science and
mathematics at least as significantly as in art or everyday life.

As symbols, ideas need not have singular meanings or precisely defined import. Their power lies precisely in their inexacti-
tude, that is, their multi-valent meanings and ways of altering
perception. Nowhere is "the infinity of the idea" more evident,
Adams holds, than in great art—for instance, the work of Giotto
di Bondone (c. 1266–1337):

> The Arena Chapel in Padua is a brick box, barrel-vaulted
> within. Over the chancel Giotto painted the Eternal, sur-
> rounded by swaying angels, and listening to the counter-
> pleas of Justice and Mercy concerning doomed humankind.
> The Archangel Gabriel is serenely awaiting the message that
> would bring Christ to Mary's womb and salvation to earth.
> This is the Prologue. Opposite, on the entrance wall, is the
> Epilogue—a Last Judgment, with Christ enthroned as
> Supreme Judge and Redeemer amid the Apostles. These ten-
> sions within the divine economy bespeak the tensions and
> contrarieties that belong to the human condition as well.
> Without them religious belief and the consequences of reli-
> gious belief are doomed to degenerate into deformity, disil-
> lusion, and destruction, and to call forth from the Stygian
> depths both *hubris* and *nemesis*. Ultimately, the conse-
> quences of religious belief are not in our hands

The arts are a rich source of religious awareness, for as Tillich
says, they bring the substance of religion into the forms of culture.
Art is not sacred by virtue of its traditionally religious subject
matter, nor is all art with religious subject matter authentically sacred. Still less authentic is the sentimentally otherworldly art—
often adorned with angels—associated with New Age spirituality.
On the other hand, any artistic expression that calls up the ulti-

mate concerns of human existence and heightens awareness of them is sacred. Adams speaks of the work and thought of the dancer-choreographer Doris Humphrey, who when asked "What shall we dance about?"answered that the choreographer must identify "what is missing in the major voice of our time, the graceless voice of the right angle." Speaking of religion, she quotes P. W. Martin as saying, "The creative process is not constructive only, but has its destructive side, the nay no less than the yea. There is the dark and terrible aspect of God, the volcano as well as the Rock; creation comes from conflict."

Adams believes that the artist gives voice to an otherwise voiceless human need for what transcends rational calculation; authentic art is prophetic art insofar as it does not sanctify the present but prophesies against it in the name of the true infinite.

For Adams the idea of resistance to what has become culturally comfortable or acceptable is central to the struggle to recover authentic spiritual and moral conceptions of transcendence:

> Yale professor Charles Bennett was walking in the country near New Haven when, coming over a hillock, he observed in the distance a billboard, which he misread to say, "Gorton's God, No Bones." Drawing closer he realized that it announced, "Gorton's Cod, No Bones." Perhaps his misreading was conditioned by his own often-expressed suspicion that the God of many people is a God with no bones, a flabby, spineless non-entity, a God who exudes only a warm sentimental glow of indiscriminate indulgence.

The characteristic liberal turn in theology has been away from transcendence and toward immanence, away from a God with bones, a structure not readily pliable, and toward the God within, a subjectively known God made familiar by popular spirituality, a God that accommodates our feelings and desires. The alternative is a divine reality that stands over against us; in current psychological language, such a God is self-differentiated.

The Biblical God eludes definition and even defies being named but is shrouded in mystery and says, "I am who I am."

(Exodus 3:14) An alternative translation of this notoriously obscure sentence suggests absolute self-definition: "I shall be what I shall be." Such is Martin Luther's concept of God, cited by Adams:

> I call the omnipotence of God not that power by which he does not make many things he could make, but the actual power by which powerfully he makes everything in everything....God acts in everything and through everything....God is heroic and without rule. God is he for whose will there is no reason or cause, for he does not will something because it is good, but conversely, it is good because he wills it.

Adams comments, "This is Luther's conception of the 'naked absolute.'" Does this mean that Luther pushes the anti-rational swing of the pendulum too far? Such language has a dangerous ring, for it gives divine power priority over divine benevolence and divine will priority over divine reason. Without wholly endorsing these reversals, Adams commends them as needed correctives to the benevolent but boneless God usually encountered in liberal theology. Again he cites Luther:

> The creatures are so to speak the masks of God. God makes them work and helps them. Even the Goths, the Vandals, and the Turks are driven by him to attack and to destroy; and in this sense he speaks to us through them. They are God's word, although they destroy.

This astonishing idea may seem to imply an immoral God; but consider the ethical consequences that flow from this turn of thought. Three consequences, not insignificant and perhaps surprising, come to mind: First, we must hold all creatures—human and non-human—in respect, even in awe, and especially those who oppose us or oppress us; second, humility is in order because God may not be entirely "on our side," even though we imagine ourselves highly enlightened and entirely virtuous, as most people do; and third, so too, we should recognize the ways we create our own enemies and the way the enemy is also lodged within ourselves.

As a defender of the absolute authority of the crown, Thomas Hobbes is hardly Adams's favorite intellectual. Hobbes champions unquestioning belief apparently without being himself a religious believer. Still, Hobbes's unsentimental, positivistic cast of thought teaches something important about the role of will in faith, about faith as an original decision. "Without sharing its cynicism," Adams says, "the authoritarian in religion at times seems to adopt the sentiment of Thomas Hobbes," who says,

> It is with the mysteries of our religion as with wholesome pills for the sick, which swallowed whole have the virtue to cure, but chewed are for the most part cast up again without effect.

What seems scandalous to the moralist or the rationalist is a source of insight to the realist and the believer. Religious groups differentiate themselves from others by asserting some distinguishing dogma—for example, baptism by full immersion for serious Baptists, or the Transubstantiation of the elements in the Catholic mass—that outsiders find absurd but insiders, the "true believers," embrace the more tightly in the face of doubt and derision. Or is your one dogma this—that because you believe in individual freedom of belief, you think you have no dogma?

Among religious denominations with boundaries dividing "us" from "them" to defend, more Hobbesean bitter pills are swallowed whole than are chewed. In lighter vein, the following story told by Adams suggests as much:

> Two laymen, a Baptist and a Methodist, were always arguing over the rite of baptism. The Baptist was proud of his minister, for he had the reputation of being able to prove immersion from any text chosen for a sermon. One week the forthcoming sermon text was announced as, "The voice of the turtle is heard in the meadow" [Song of Songs 2:12]. "Now," said the Methodist, "he certainly cannot make out immersion from that text." The Baptist assured him that he could, and placed a bet on it. So they went to the Baptist

church together to hear the sermon. In the midst of the sermon the preacher said that in the previous week he had been walking in the woods. On becoming tired he decided to take rest on a log at the edge of a stream. But when he approached the log he noticed a turtle sitting on the end of it. So he tried to step quietly, in order not to frighten the turtle. But when he sat cautiously on the log the turtle jumped "bap" down into the creek. The preacher thought that if he remained very quiet the turtle might come back, and sure enough, a few minutes later it crawled up out of the water: "tism, tism, tism." The Methodist lost the bet.

Is the moral of this story the foolishness of proof-texting with full-blown fundamentalist assumptions about the Scripture? Or is it perhaps the admirable *chutzpah* of the Baptist, who believes so absolutely in his own particular version of the Gospel that he bets his faith on it? Or is it the creative ingenuity that a believer uses to vindicate his faith, going to extremes that we may think absurd and laughable, but that he finds intellectually and emotionally satisfying?

Reflection on human nature leads directly to reflection on human will—on the freedom to choose and the ways in which freedom is either secured or lost, on the ways human freedom is either authentic and turned toward good or else perverted and turned toward evil. For Adams these reflections come before rational questions and questions of the meaning of good and evil. They are recognitions of a given, the human condition. He works under the influence of the existentialist turn of thought. Existentialism flooded European thought in the "century of total war," as Raymond Aron named the twentieth century, or the "age of anxiety," as W. H. Auden named it. Gradually thereafter existentialism spilled over into American thought.

To assert "the primacy of the will" sounds sterile if we cannot say what its existential-experiential-personal-and-concrete meaning is. Perhaps it means this: No rules and no reasons will lead us to a safe haven; we actualize our creative freedom by courageous decision in the face of the contingency of human existence. In spite of his aversion to individualistic forms of existentialism, Adams draws deeply on its themes:

> The story of Little Red Riding Hood may be an incredible story, with its claim that a little girl capable of walking alone through the woods could mistake a wolf for her grandmother. But the story is more than just a tale that is told. As immemorial folklore it reflects emotional needs, anxieties, and hopes that everyone has. It implies an interpretation of human nature and of the human situation. In short the story belongs to the existentialist tradition. If one thinks of the happy ending of the story, one may say that it serves in its way the purpose of primitive magic, of effective ritual, and even of philosophizing: it gives a sense of ultimate confidence before the uncertainties of human existence. If one considers the identification of the grandmother with the wolf, then one may surmise that the story expresses the child's unconscious fear of the grandmother, fear in the face of the ambivalence she feels toward parental figures; or one may see in the story an expression of the child's ambivalent attitudes toward herself. Here we have the characteristic themes of existentialism: the ambiguity of human nature, the sense of the threats and demands of the human situation, the complex of guilt and anxiety or of fate and freedom, the merging of subject and object, the inevitable involvement of the total person in the decisions of existence, the lack of a neat and tidy system.

In the past century we have learned, if haltingly, to speak of human existence and the human condition rather than of human nature, which implies that people are the same everywhere and always, for there is an invariant and universal human essence. *Human existence* is embodied in history, implying that finitude is part of self awareness. *Human nature* is abstracted from history, a pattern of thought that makes it acceptable, for instance, to speak of *man* as if the word stands for a generic human being. Feminist theologies assert that this "disembodies" the male and renders the female invisible.

Existence is always located in a particular time and a particular place. Liberation theologies use the language of existence because they ask for personal engagement and commitment, and they insist that we forego claims to truth and right abstracted from social position and condition. Jacques Maritain names the attempt to transcend the limitations of the human condition *angelism*, a pejorative term adopted by Adams:

> According to Thomas Aquinas, three major attributes characterize the angels. *First*, they have not bodies; they exist independently of things; they are disembodied spirits or intelligences; consequently, they do not live in history. *Second*, all of their knowledge is innate; by divine illumination the innate knowledge is given them directly by God at the time of creation. Therefore, the angels cannot reason; they do not need to draw conclusions from premises or from experience; they have angelic knowledge by divine fiat. *Third*, there exist no two angels of the same species; each individual angel constitutes a separate species; every angel is an island unto itself. By means of these characterizations, the medieval thinker intended to bring into bold relief what a human being is not, and thus by implication he grasped the more clearly what one is. The human being has a body, lives in history and ideally can learn from experience, and lives with other members of the same species.

We proud humans are forever tempted to ignore these facts— our physicality, our temporality, and our sociality—imagining that through "spirituality" we can escape the limitations of human existence. So doing, we put our souls in peril, as Adams notes:

> John Calvin in preaching the Eighth Psalm asserted that God created man a little lower than the angels, but that man fell from grace and is now little higher than the devils.... Pascal

asserted that a person who sets out to be an angel will end only in becoming a brute.

No doubt in the ancient world atheism was virtually impossible. So there was no difficulty seeing that the problem was not God, gods, or no god, but rather, idolatry or authentic faith. But atheism in the sense of believing nothing, being devoted to nothing, is almost as impossible today. We are incurably religious. So the Biblical prophets, starting with Elijah, have renewed relevance.

The classic case of prophetic criticism of "the powers that be" is found in the Hebrew scriptures: "When Ahab saw Elijah, Ahab said to him, 'Is it you, you troubler of Israel?' And he answered, 'I have not troubled Israel, but you have...because you have forsaken the commandments of the Lord and followed the Baals'" (I Kings 18:17-18), that is, the Canaanite gods. Martin Luther King Jr. was similarly attacked as a disturber of the peace, as he notes and answers in his famous "Letter From the Birmingham Jail." Prophets have always been troublers of their age, questioning accepted wisdom and accepted authority. Adams sees a prophetic edge in existentialism:

> The significance of existentialism rests in its calling the human being back to Reality as immediately experienced and in its power to disclose again the questionable character of human existence, to see it in its contradictions, especially as they are manifest in our time, and thus to see it in its disrupted-ness, its abyss, its sense of meaninglessness and despair.

Guardians of modern culture have been similarly challenged by Marx and Nietzsche, "troublers" who trouble us all the more because of the anti-religious forms their prophesying takes. Adams goes on to cite Paul Tillich:

> In Marx we find by word and deed the spirit of the old Jewish prophecy, and in Nietzsche the spirit of Luther. Although their battle, in the one case for justice and in the other for the

creative life, took its form as a drive against God, it was an attack against a God who had been bound to a standpoint, that is, of bourgeois society.

The original freedom and goodness of human nature—a nature we imagine we share with the creative good will of God—includes the possibility, on the darker side of our imagination, of turning toward destructive ill-will. This logical possibility has paradoxical consequences, for evil is no simple or rational choice, but is ensnaring, addictive, irrational, unbounded. This is why Luther, arguing against the Renaissance humanist Erasmus, speaks of the human condition as one of "the bondage of the will" and why salvation is not simply enlightenment from darkness and confusion but must include liberation from inner conflict and bondage. Modern depth psychology makes the latter outlook newly relevant: We are a "force field," Adams suggests, in which contradictory urges and energies are displayed:

> The freedom to destroy and pervert is only the reverse side of the freedom that is the very basis of meaningful existence. As both Milton and Dostoyevsky perceived, freedom would not be freedom if it did not allow liberty to "the spirit that denies." Thus the meaning of human existence is bound up with a radical contradiction in human nature. And the contradiction is not merely human in dimension. As Martin Luther suggests, we are the *Schauplatz* of opposing cosmic forces—the forces of love and power, of mutuality and self-assertion. This opposition pervades the whole of human life, inner and outer. Our freedom has to be achieved in the teeth of this basic metaphysical and psychological tension, it has to be achieved through an attempted integration and balancing of power and mutuality, of self-assertion and love. The grace of God itself operates under these conditions, for meaningful human existence requires both these elements. Power without love is the equation for tyranny. Love without power is ultimately suicide or non-existence. And tyranny in

any of its larger social forms can be unseated or corrected only through the exercise of that sort of mutuality which can organize the power to check it.

Adams ascribes goodness and power to God in apparently equal measure. Wanting to regulate what ecclesiastical authorities commonly claim as their rightful authority (derived from the author of the universe), liberals as children of the Enlightenment have tended to give primacy to divine goodness, God's beneficence, justice, love, etc. But do these liberals now presume to regulate God by the standards of their own minds? Or their own cultural values? Or even the ideology of their own dominant economic or racial group? This is what Marx calls *ideological thinking*. Are we here on the slippery slope that first gives us a God with "no bones" and then puts humanity in the place of God? This is the progression Friedrich Nietzsche sees and even celebrates in his announcement of the death of God, saying we ourselves have killed God.

In this light we can understand why, in the face of the crisis of liberal democracy represented by the rise of fascism, a religious liberal like James Luther Adams can undergo a conversion, a radical change of heart that initiates new intellectual pathways. Now *power* (the capacity to effect) is given an ontological priority over any ethical category, such as goodness, and will (the capacity to decide and act) is discerned as central to the classical tradition of theology. "Humanity is fated as well as free," Adams asserts, and goes on to explain,

> As Wilhelm von Humboldt puts it, "humanity always ties on to what lies at hand."... We are fatefully caught in history, both as individuals and as members of a group, and we are also able to be creative in history. Through the use of this creative freedom, humanity expresses the highest form of vitality that existence permits. Indeed, since this creativity is a manifestation of a divinely given and divinely renewing power, we may say that humanity is created in the image of God, that is, we participate in the divine creativity.

So Adams bids us to revise our perception of the heart and soul of the liberal tradition.

Tragic History

The conflicts among wills in history and in the inner conflicts of the human psyche are expressions of the tragic dimension of existence. This dimension cannot be evaded without trivializing our humanity. The glory of our creative freedom is also the source of an almost compulsive destructiveness, for the greatest achievements of human genius are routinely and ingeniously turned to evil purposes, and utopian aims are regularly turned into justifications for tyranny.

World War I was called, with supreme optimism, "the war to end all wars," an optimism we now hear as deeply ironic. Within a generation, with World War II at its height, Adams reflects upon the tragic aspect of this age, a tragedy invited by human self-deception:

> War is a relentless revealer. It presents humanity as it were in Brobdingnagian proportions, bringing into clearer view our powers and aspirations, our perversities and self-deceptions. The humanity it reveals is essentially the same as humanity in peacetime, but the humanity that is almost hidden in time of "peace," the *homo absconditus*, comes now into full view. This may sound like hyperbole when one thinks of the terrible, the colossal destruction, brought about by this war. If so it is the sort of hyperbole that lies without deceiving.

The shift from intellectualism to voluntarism has profound implications for social-ethical concerns. The issue is not between theism and atheism as concepts of ultimate reality but between authentic and perverted faith or, in traditional terms, between true and idolatrous faith. *Faith* now signifies not primarily a belief but a "believing in," an active devotion. This is a key element in the dividing line between modernity and post-modernity or between liberal theology and liberation theology. It is for the idols of nation and race (crowned by nationalistic and racist religions) that whole societies make war on each other. Acknowledging "the ambiguities of human existence" (Tillich), we may still judge that, in the face of gross injustice, making war can be the lesser of two evils.

Meditations on the exercise of human will in history are likely to become meditations on tragedy, as in Adams's account of the fate of Thomas Cranmer:

> The English martyr Archbishop Cranmer, during his incumbency under "Bloody Mary," six times recanted the views he had previously held under Henry VIII and Mary. On March 21, 1556, he was taken to St. Mary's Church at Oxford and asked to repeat his recantation in the hearing of the people as he had promised. To the surprise of all, he renounced all his previous recantations. "I have written," he said to the hushed congregation before him, "I have written many things untrue; and forasmuch as my hand offended in writing contrary to my heart, my hand therefore shall be the first burnt." He was forthwith hurried to the stake, and when the fire leaped up around him he held his right hand steadily in the flames, that it might be "the first burnt." We must learn somehow to say, along with Thomas Cranmer, "I would fain be to the eternal Goodness what his own hand is to a man."

The image of purification by fire is troubling, for it evokes the thought of intense physical pain; it also places the seal of absolute sincerity on Cranmer's final commitment to serve God. The image of Cranmer's hand is strikingly like the image of Isaiah's lips, purified by a burning coal, taken by an angel from a brazier: "Woe is me, for I am lost," he cries, "for I am a man of unclean lips, and I dwell in the midst of a people of unclean lips"(Isaiah 6:5). It also reminds us of Adams's question, framed during the Second World War: "How much more suffering must be endured before we give up the idolatries of nationalism?" We do not yet have an answer to that question.

Are these reflections theological or anthropological? Adams hardly pauses over the distinction. God's being and human being seem knotted together in ways our minds cannot untangle. God is known, so far as God can be known, in and through the human spirit, expressed through the "divine discontent" that questions all appearances in quest of truth. Michael Novak writes,

> I think those philosophers are correct who stand in the tradition of St. Augustine and St. Bonaventure... who seek God within and through the human spirit. The question, then, is what I take the human spirit to be. In a word, spirit is inquiry, and its manifestation is the question.

What we need is a new heart and a new mind, a newness wrought by an absolute good will—"purity of heart," in the language of the New Testament.

Here Adams reflects on World War II, then in progress, telling the truth of the human condition as he sees it, although it be a report of tragic conflict within the ambiguities of history:

> What the war reveals is that the human condition is a tragic one in which the person of responsibility (as well as of conscience) must choose, not between absolute good and evil, but rather the alternative that promises to preserve or create as much goodness and justice as possible. This is the way in which men and women on earth must use their freedom and power. The axiom, "nature abhors a vacuum," has its spiritual analogue: human nature abhors an empty altar; it is incurably religious. We are always "open to the infinite," whether to the true infinite or to a false infinite. This is our greatness and our misery. Our greatest loyalties have been to false gods, to Mammon and Caesar and the "superior race." War reveals that human nature requires a great deal of suffering before it will abandon false gods.

Conflict is a primary condition of existence, so the very character and meaning of human life is significantly shaped by conflict. We do not readily change; we have our identities, our devotions, our habits of the heart, shaped by our personal experience and our culture. One consequence of conflict is to move us to cling to those identities all the tighter, as when people say, "I'd rather die than change" and mean it literally. Adams notes that it is not only human nature but the nature of nature itself that is felt as fated in ancient Western thought:

> The Greek view from pre-Homeric times was unable to find a principle of transcendence beyond the tragedy of existence. This view finds philosophic expression in the famous fragment of Anaximander: "Things perish into those things from which they have their birth, as it is ordained; for they pay to one another the penalty of their injustice according to the order of time." For Anaximander, Eduard Zeller writes, "the separate existence of things is, so to speak, a wrong, a transgression which they must expiate by their own destruction."

Adams takes the fragment from Anaximander as an expression, in terms of archaic thought, of the "fallen-ness" not only of humanity but of existence itself. The pre-Socratic philosopher is echoed by Paul Tillich, who speaks of the Fall as not only a temporal but also an ontological reality, as something entailed in the transition from being to existence. An "archaic" sensibility has regained currency in our time—particularly in contemporary art. I remember Paul Tillich's comment, in a lecture on pre-Socratic philosophy and art to Harvard undergraduates, that the characteristic smile that we see on the face of Greek statues from the archaic period is the smile that anticipates the breaking forth of a glorious "classical" period. We smile at this extravagant idea—who but a bold and erudite Tillich could get away with such a claim? If we say, "prophetic fore-knowledge can be inherent in a strong sense of destiny," it begins to sound plausible, while focusing our minds on the power of cultural creations. J. S. Bach surely smiled, but did he smile at the thought of W. A. Mozart?

Adams suggests that the art of Alberto Giacometti (1901–1966) is similarly prophetic in our age, redirecting us from the sunny age of Renoir and Monet to the age of anxiety:

> The Swiss sculptor, Giocometti, forcefully depicts the inauthentic, oppressed man found in contemporary mass society. His image of contemporary man is a thin, elongated creature, isolated and alienated from the environing world. The head and feet of this figure are connected by a thin line, an attenuated body. The effect of this thinness is to emphasize the space around the figure which seems to press in upon it. The motionless, vertical figure seems to vibrate in anguished loneliness. Giacometti's friend, Jean-Paul Sartre, says that this man "secretes his own void."

Historical tragedy is more than an idea of the tragic and more than a sense of the ultimacy of death and separation. It is a terror, an immense suffering known in history and sometimes foreseen with painful clarity, as in Adams's report on the prophecy of his friend, Paul Tillich:

> In the summer of 1931, less than two years before the Nazis came to power, Paul and Hannah Tillich spent their vacation at a resort on the island of Sylt in the North Sea. One evening a group of friends, all of them being from Berlin, gathered at a vacation home and talked until dawn about the rapidly moving events in Germany. Around four o'clock as the sun was rising they went out of the house to greet it and to look over the meadows down to the sea. As they stood there together Hannah quoted a poem by Goethe, about a ship at sea. Then there was silence again, each of them being absorbed in his own thoughts. Suddenly Paulus broke the silence, "And all of you," he said, "will live to see the day when sheep will graze in Potsdamer Platz." His words were verily a prologue to the omen coming on. Years later, when Tillich was living in New York City, he was astonished to read a news item from Germany showing that the prediction had come

true. Sheep were grazing the Potsdamer Platz. Not only that, Potsdamer Platz had become a boundary between East and West Berlin.

History continues to be largely the story of warfare—even of increasingly fratricidal and genocidal warfare. Could we but awaken to recognize our brothers and sisters, our fellow humans, in those we fight! Adams several times calls attention to the religious significance of the dramatic recognition scene:

> In Sophocles' *Oedipus Rex* the king has been seeking the one whose crime has brought on a national calamity; he intends to find the criminal and banish him from the realm. But at the moment of recognition he discovers that he himself is the criminal, that he has killed and supplanted his father and married his mother. Greek tragedy was connected with a religious festival, with worship. At its origin and apex it was imbued with an all-pervading presence of a "divine breath of life." On these solemn occasions the high point of religious insight was the recognition scene. According to Aristotle, the scene induced an awesome, cathartic experience impelling the viewer to say, "Oh, I may be like that! I may be just the opposite of what I think I am!"

Without a profound sense of personal tragedy, the motive to change is absent; without a tragic sense of existence, there is no radical change of heart.

Adams speaks of history in terms that are much closer to his great contemporary, Reinhold Niebuhr, than to the theological liberals of his own and preceding generations. Niebuhr's political liberalism is steeled by realism about human failings and human nature. This means accenting human sinfulness and taking seriously a concept anathema to liberals, original sin. In 1949 the American Unitarian Association published a booklet explicitly attacking Niebuhr, *What Is This Neo-Orthodoxy?* Adams commented to me about Niebuhr's bitterness over "the theological ignorance" of this attack, a view that Adams shared. To be sure, Niebuhr himself seems to have obscured his deeper loyalties, or at least Adams thought he had, for Adams suggested that the theological liberalism of Reinhold Niebuhr would be a good topic for an academic dissertation. To my knowledge, it remains to be written. Adams writes,

> When we say that history is tragic, we mean that the perversions and failures in history are associated precisely with the highest creative powers of humanity and thus with our greatest achievements. One might call this the Oedipus motif in the sphere of history: nemesis is often encountered almost simultaneously with the seemingly highest achievement.... The national culture, for example, is the soil from which issue cherished treasures of a people, their language, their poetry, their music, their common social heritage. Yet nationalism is also one of the most destructive forces in the whole of human history.

If tragedy is often laced with irony, a sign that a radical evil has been perpetrated in the name of doing good, then tragedy is tinged with evil. Yet even evil may bring a smile for the very irony of it—for instance, Adams's saying "The dictatorship of the proletariat turns out to be the dictatorship of the bureaucrats."

Adams holds that the optimism of inherited liberal culture—especially its rationalistic ideas of human knowledge and its laissez-faire economics—contributes to the vast historical tragedies of the twentieth century. He was a student, an admirer, and a sometime critic of the sociologist Max Weber. While honoring Weber's famous thesis linking the Protestant ethic and the rise of capitalism, he calls attention to another, less ambiguous outcome of this movement—popular democracy. Adams suggests that Weber reflects in his personal intellectual life the social unhappiness that he laments. He sees Weber joining the ideals of rational, scientific sociological analysis to the sensibilities of a prophet, with a profoundly tragic and prophetic sense of history; still, he calls himself "religiously unmusical." Adams calls attention to the way his words occasionally betray an awareness of the tension between social scientist and social prophet—wanting to speak with passion of moral commitments but feeling constrained by the objective distance required by academic culture:

> The positive aspects of rationality, along with individual freedom and responsibility, are delineated by Max Weber as indispensable elements in civilization, and are of course cherished by him. The negative aspects, on the other hand, illustrate the axiom: *the corruption of the best is the worst*. It is no accident that the account given of the corruption of freedom and reason by Weber, a scholar learned in theological lore, should remind one of the Christian theologian's account of the corruption of the *imago dei* ["image of God," Genesis 1:27]. In this respect one must say that Weber reveals a tragic view of history—in the Hebraic sense. Human freedom and reason are the pivot at once of meaning and of the possibility of the fall into un-freedom, irrationality, and meaninglessness.

Adams goes on to cite Weber's penultimate sentences from *The Protestant Ethic and the Spirit of Capitalism*—we could call it his "concluding unscientific postscript":

> The Puritan wanted to work in a calling; we are forced to do so. For when asceticism was carried out of monastic cells into everyday life, and began to dominate worldly morality, it did its part in building the tremendous cosmos of the modern economic order. This order is now bound to the technical and economic conditions of machine production which today determine the lives of all the individuals who are born into this mechanism...with irresistible force. Perhaps it will so determine them until the last ton of coal is burnt. In [the Puritan Richard] Baxter's view, the care for external goods should lie on the shoulders of "the saint like a

light cloak, which can be thrown aside at any moment." But fate decreed that the cloak should become an iron cage. . . .

There is more. Weber the social scientist turns momentarily into Weber the prophet, after which, as Adams notes, he draws back in embarrassment: "But all this brings us," he says, "to the world of judgments of value and of faith, with which this purely historical discussion need not be burdened." Nevertheless, professor, it's the judgments we remember. Indeed, repealing reticence (as Adams likes to say), Weber continues his oracular denunciation:

> No one knows who will live in this cage in the future, or whether at the end of this tremendous development entirely new prophets will arise, or there will be a great rebirth of old ideas and ideals, or, if neither, a mechanized petrifaction, embellished with a sort of convulsive self-importance. For of the last stage of this cultural development, it might well be truly said, "Specialists without spirit, sensualists without heart, and this nullity imagines that it has attained a level of civilization never before achieved."

Weber describes a cultural failure in the formation of personal identity and human vocation, a humanity whose loss of creative spirit goes unrecognized even by itself.

Metanoia

We are both perpetrators and victims of tragedy. To rise above tragic circumstances we need to undergo a change of heart, mind, and will. Willing the same deep change in others, in good will, we need also to forgive. The New Testament word for this spiritual event is *metanoia*. It is usually translated "repent," as in Revelation 2:5 (King James Version): "I have somewhat against thee, because thou hast left thy first love. Remember therefore from whence thou are fallen, and repent, and do the first works. . . . " James Baldwin once recalled that in his father's church they spoke of "doing your first works over," a phrase that wonderfully conveys the sense of *metanoia* as returning to something precious that one has lost, "thy first love."

Metanoia is a form of religious awareness that underlies the best of the Christian tradition, in Adams's view:

> Theology is, in the language of Bonaventura, "an affective science," the science of the love of God.... Thus our rationalism and our moralism... give us a "poise" that freezes the knees and keeps us erect and "harmonious" in face of the divine demand for repentance, for change of heart and mind.... the creative and redemptive power is not subject to domestication by these techniques. It breaks into a human situation transforming old forms and creating new ones, manifesting the... power of a new affection—*the amor dei*. It is not reason alone, but reason inspired by "raised affections" that is necessary for salvation.

From time to time Adams cites an evocative phrase from Jonathan Edwards: "visible upsets and thunderclaps of grace." He is drawn to the vivid rhetoric of conversion as a dramatic happening, even though he sometimes also speaks disapprovingly of the idea that conversion is once-and-for-all. Here again the answer we reach is not unambiguous but dialectical, a movement between two poles—conversion as a one-time life-changing event versus conversion as a continuous process—that renders a nuanced understanding of the phenomenon. We may think of conversion (today many people are more comfortable with the term *transformation*) as a radical change—a break with the past, a reorientation of one's life, etc.—the positive effect of which can be realized only through an ongoing process—an openness to new learnings, new life habits, new commitments, etc.

Theologian Bernard Lonergan describes conversion on the intellectual, moral, and religious levels, which are both interrelated and build on one another. These conversions may focus on a single, deeply memorable event, such as the experience reported by

Adams of singing in the chorus for J. S. Bach's choral masterwork, Mass in B Minor. But he also emphasizes that "this experience as such was not a new one: it was simply a more decisive one." We may say it is an emblematic event within an ongoing process. What makes it decisive is probably the emotional impact of a sense of guilt—the sense that he is doing little to contribute to the "costly spiritual heritage" that includes Bach's Mass, while being personally exalted by it at the same time. In the classic form of the religious experience, he feels himself both cast down and lifted up at once.

We should not overstate the case for singular, life-changing events. While there may be particular events marking a changed consciousness in a person's life, perhaps at several levels, they probably do not stand in isolation from a host of related experiences and reflections, preceding and following, that reinforce the awareness of a decisive change. This understanding of conversion as once and for all, in one sense, and as a continuous process, in another sense, is consistent with Lonergan's description of conversion as a multi-leveled and therefore continuing and personally deepening process.

Jonathan Edwards also wrote a learned treatise, related to the conversion experience, on "the religious affections." Adams never tired of warning his students against focus on inward feelings to the exclusion of ethical commitments, but it is interesting to see how he links feeling with will. Because we tend to think of will as something hard or even harsh, it comes as a surprise to find it linked to affection and love. He says,

> We become what we love. Not that information and technique are dispensable. Even a St. Francis with commitment to the highest would be impotent when confronted with a case of appendicitis if he did not recognize the malady and did not know what to do.... But something of the spirit of St. Francis is indispensable if the benefits of science and of society are to be in widest commonalty spread, and, for that matter, if even the intellectual problems are to be dealt with adequately. The

desire to diagnose injustice as an intellectual problem as well as the power of action to achieve new forms of justice requires "raised affections," a vitality that can break through old forms of behavior and create new patterns of community. But the raising of affections is a much harder thing to accomplish than even the education of the mind; it is especially difficult among those who think they have found security.

Lonergan speaks of theology as "the science of the love of God." For Adams, we may say theology is the science—the reasoned and empirical study—of human relatedness in its intimate and ultimate dimensions. The original sin in such a theology is willful separation, twisted and broken relationships, segregation in all its forms.

Adams recalls that when he was five, his father carried him "down the sawdust trail" and lifted him up to reach the hand of Billy Sunday on the high platform. Did revivalist preaching gain his secret admiration? He tells this story:

> Winding up his sermon, the preacher warned unrepentant sinners of the coming day of wrath—"And there'll be weeping and wailing and gnashing of teeth!" The oldster in the front row piped up, "But preacher, I ain't got no teeth." The preacher roared back, "Teeth will be provided!"

There are mysterious intersections in human existence, between personality formation and theological conviction, between identity and conversion, between the long processes of growth and the original decisions that re-form our lives thereafter. Parables are tales that tell what life is like, yet without telling us what we must do—for that we must decide for ourselves. Just so, parables beg for elucidation, commentary, and discussion. They are obscure, sometimes deliberately obscure—dark sayings, oracles, allegories, or riddles. We tell them because life itself is obscure, or scary, and sometimes fun or just funny.

"The unraveling of a riddle is the purest and most basic act of the human mind," writes Valdimir Nabokov, in a "review" of his own memoir, *Speak, Memory*, a book that he says offers "conclusive evidence that the world is not as bad as it seems." Adams is dubbed "the smiling prophet" not only because he affirms an ultimate optimism but also because his stories often help us to "lighten up." The following example, told about his own youth, might be called "Repentance Repented Of," but other interpretations would probably yield other titles:

> My father tried his best to "save" me. But I wouldn't respond. And then an itinerant evangelist came to the country church and I was "converted." I walked down the path. I gave my life to Jesus. But I was sorry for it within twelve hours. The next morning—it was a Saturday morning and I wasn't in school—I overheard my father and this itinerant evangelist arguing over Scripture. My father pushed him into the corner. I was proud of him; my father knew the Scripture better than that fellow! But the evangelist finally said, "Carey, you may know the Scripture better than I do, but you weren't able to save your own son—and I did!" I was so sorry, I wished I could have lived over the night before and stuck to my chair and not given my life to Jesus under his auspices.

The boy's sense of personal commitment is intimately connected with his emerging identity and his wish to link his identity to his father. Not an easy task for the young Luther Adams, with such a righteous "man of principle" for a father. Søren Kierkegaard says that we understand our lives backward while living them forward—a formula for self-doubt if ever there was one. Adams remembers this poignant moment as one step in the ongoing process of his spiritual formation. The inward transformation he seeks is an attitude or an inclination of the heart, the mind, and the will—the whole person—toward doing justice and loving mercy. Prayer entails a commitment, Adams says, to maintain this openness to being changed:

> *Metanoia* should be a continuing process. The function of a vital church would be *metanoia* as a continuing process.

There should be an increasing awareness, a raising of consciousness with regard to the evils around us. There should be a specification of evils, including the evils that cause people in our society to become drug-addicted. So there should be moments of commitment, for example, in prayer as a prophetic form of spirituality.

One of my teachers at Marburg University, Friedrich Heiler, drew a distinction between mystical prayer—a sense of communion—and prophetic prayer. Prayer that is prophetic is prayer that aims to share, in a congregation, the sense of responsibility. Prayer, then, is a discipline whereby one offers oneself and the community to the Ultimate for the sake of, for the nourishment of, for the establishment of, authentic community.

Adams's rhetoric, even in the lecture hall, is that of a teaching preacher. Underlying the distinction of mystical and prophetic prayer is the distinction of private and public prayer. Prophetic prayer serves the formation of social-ethical consciousness within the public realm.

Judgment and grace may seem rationally incommensurable, but in the perspective of voluntarism—that is, in our experience as loving and willing beings—they fall together. The judgment that casts us down may turn out to be the grace that lifts us up. Opposites coincide. Adams's prophetic rhetoric likewise invokes both judgment and grace:

In our megapolitan, technological society, with its nuclear power, mass media of communication, military-industrial complex, powerful special interest economic and political pressure groups, widespread poverty and dehumanization, both individual and corporate responsibilities must be reconceived—if religion is to fulfill its vocation: to promote the kind of participation that possesses the wisdom, the audacity, and the power to risk new social decision. Both present and future are at stake. Indeed, we are already living in the future in the sense that what we do or fail to do will affect the future. Authentic religion, relevant concern for meaning, demands eschatological orientation. But hope, alas, can become a form of cheap grace, unless we recognize that we live in the valley of decision that extracts the high price of sacrificial participation. To be sure, the final ends of humanity are hidden. Yet, the kingdom of God is always "at hand." In the translation of Joel Cadbury, it is always "available."

The reference is to Mark 1:15: "The time is fulfilled, the kingdom of God is at hand, repent, and believe in the good news." The verse has been called a summation of Mark's entire gospel. In Adams's interpretation *repentance* is a turning not toward one's own personal salvation but an activation of the self. It points to a "new social decision" with respect to a society seemingly impenetrable to spiritual concern. The eschatological orientation invoked is both present decision and future intention. Jesus' word that "the kingdom is at hand" is not a prediction of an imminent, cataclysmic divine intervention—as commonly understood and promptly dismissed as a "mistake" by rationalist interpeters. Rather, this kingdom is "at hand" in the sense of being available to us, within our grasp, precisely as we are activated by its prospect and grasp its presence.

Theology for Adams is not an academic exercise. As an active participant in local congregations in Chicago and later in Boston, he sees theological reflection at work in people's lives:

In the First Unitarian Church of Chicago we started a program some of us called "aggressive love" to try to desegregate that Gothic cathedral. We had two members of the Board objecting. Unitarianism has no creed, they said, and we were making desegregation into a creed. It was a gentle but firm disagreement and a couple of us kept pressing. "Well, what do you say is the purpose of this church?" we asked, and we kept it up until about 1:30 in the morning. We were all worn out, when finally this man made one of the great statements,

for my money, in the history of religion. "O.K., Jim. The purpose of this church...well, the purpose of this church is to
get hold of people like me and change them."

This is what Adams means by eschatological orientation—the
pressure that the future exerts upon the present.

The purpose of the church is also to expose us to perspectives
that fall outside our commonly circumscribed, self-protected existences, in order that we shall have the opportunity to read the signs
of the times and to change. Adams also recalls consciousness-
changing events in denominational life:

> A national conference of Unitarian Universalists, held in New
> York City in 1967 to consider "The Black Rebellion," turned
> out to be a bifurcated assembly, with most of the black repre-
> sentatives meeting separately. On the final day of the meeting
> the Black Caucus emerged at the assembly, presented a list of
> demands regarding denominational policy with respect to
> blacks, and insisted that its resolutions be approved immedi-
> ately and without discussion. This was shock treatment. A
> stormy session ensued. The white and black liberals wanted
> to discuss the resolutions. In the midst of near chaos, a mem-
> ber of the Black Caucus, a woman, was aroused to such a
> peak of indignation at liberals who want "to go on talking for
> another century" that she left her seat and swayed in rhythm
> up and down the aisle, shouting hot words. A member of the
> audience put her hand on the woman's arm, holding her
> back. With fire flashing from her eyes she shouted, "Don't you
> understand? I don't speak liberalese. Don't you understand? I
> don't speak Unitarianese." Such events bespeak a shock of
> recognition, a rapid change in the perception of certain
> blacks and whites regarding themselves and each other.

I witnessed these events at first hand and remember the sense of
shock I felt. For me it was the beginning of a new recognition of
the radical differences in perception that arise and persist among

long-separated groups, especially racial groups. I began, then, to have my righteous liberal veneer stripped away and when the emotional confusion of the event had dissipated, I began a process of moral conversion, a basic change of heart. The Gospels tell a similar story. The smugly self-satisfied see no need for change, least of all to be changed within, at heart. They do not honor the principle of humility, as expressed by Oliver Cromwell: "By the bowels of Christ, remember that you may be mistaken!"

The idea of a humble Oliver Cromwell seems astonishing and makes the principle of humility he enunciated (if the story is not apocryphal) all the more unforgettable. Similarly unforgettable is the translation Adams reports from New Testament scholar Henry Joel Cadbury. The Hebrew term *messiah*, which literally means "the anointed one," Cadbury renders as "the smeared one." We may say that whoever undertakes transforming spiritual leadership risks becoming another smeared one. Adams says,

> A sense of commitment requires a change of priorities, and a shared commitment involves a change of shared priorities. The concept of *metanoia*, which is falsely translated "repent ye," is properly translated "change of heart, mind, soul." But as Unitarians we tend to assume we are liberated already. It is even said, "You can be a Unitarian without knowing it."

A successful advertising program—successful in terms of numbers of responses—a generation ago asked, "Are you a Unitarian without knowing it?" The question became famous, and a whole generation of Unitarians said they had been Unitarians without knowing it, seemingly unaware it implied that joining a Unitarian church did not entail any particular change of heart or mind, certainly not the articulation of "explicit faith," which Adams identifies as a hallmark of Unitarian ancestry in the Radical Reformation. Was the campaign dropped due to embarrassment at the suggestion that Unitarianism is a religion in which historical roots, institutional commitments, and articulated beliefs are superfluous? Perhaps, but the way of thinking it reflected hardly went out of vogue. For Adams religious liberalism means commitment within a dedicated community to a liberating theological vision, not a negative freedom from something but a positive spiritual freedom, issuing in a capacity for self-criticism and self-renewal. These things are more fully understood when a community is fed by its history. As Adams puts it, "By their roots you shall know them." Here he goes to the heart of the matter:

> The element of commitment, of change of heart, of decision, so much emphasized in the Gospels, has been neglected by religious liberalism, and that is the prime source of its enfeeblement. We liberals are largely an uncommitted and therefore a self-frustrating people. Our first task, then, is to restore to liberalism its own dynamic and its own prophetic genius. We need conversion within ourselves. Only by some such revolution can we be seized by a prophetic power that will enable us to proclaim both the judgment and the love of God. Only by some such conversion can we be possessed by a love that will not let us go. And when that has taken place, we shall know that it is not our wills alone that have acted; we shall know that the ever-living Creator and Re-creator has again been brooding over the face of the deep and out of the depths bringing forth new life.

This indictment and call to renewed faith, redolent with Biblical language, rings no less true today than when it was first uttered more than half a century ago. If so, a movement that professes to welcome change would appear to be remarkably unchanging. It suggests that the function of liberal religion in contemporary society is not entirely to generate commitment, but on the contrary, to serve as a kind of religious decompression chamber for successive generations of "come-outers." The assessment is harsh, but a self-critical religion would welcome the critique from within of one like Adams, himself a self-identified "come-outer."

Identity Formation

At the personal level, power is an expression of a fully developed personality. Adams refers to his belief that "the insistence on discipline enables one to achieve self-identity," in context of describing his own attempt to master the art of playing the violin in adulthood—a humorously failed attempt, as he tells the story. Adams believes that it is important for individuals to form a sense of distinctive identity within a broader sense of human vocation. He develops the concept of vocation in various contexts within his wide-ranging thought on social ethics. While *vocation* originally meant a calling from God to a particular religious career within the church, the Protestant Reformation declared that all socially useful occupations were callings, vocations of equal dignity in the sight of God. In time, however, with progressive secularization, *vocation* has come to mean simply a career—something more than "a job," leaving behind only the vaguest sense of social or moral, let alone religious, significance.

Adams is concerned with professional ethics, particularly standards of education and ethical responsibility. And he universalizes the concept of vocation, as his namesake Martin Luther did in an earlier age, to assert that all persons have, by nature and by education (which is, of course, a moral imperative for every human being), a "human vocation," a nature that they are called to fulfill. In brief, we may say, To fulfill our human vocation, our identities need to be formed and our wills need to be engaged in the life tasks of personal development and the ends of serving the common good and seeking transcendence. Responding to the words of Alfred North Whitehead, "I hazard the prophecy that the religion will conquer which can render clear to popular understanding some eternal greatness incarnate in the passage of temporal fact," Adams says, "This is a demand for the true infinite, a call for the prodigal to 'come to himself' and reclaim his birthright. But the road back is a long and hard way." Here Whitehead is almost aphoristic and yet curiously abstract, even though he talks about "temporal fact." Adams turns it into a story about the moment when we,

like the Biblical prodigal son, affirm what is eternal—forgiveness, a
new beginning—in a present moment and life-shaping decision.

The eternal and the temporal are parameters by which we define our humanity, and more particularly, our identity as unique
persons. Adams reflects,

> We think of the date and place of our birth. We recall the day
> we started to school wearing this little velvet suit with the
> brass buttons, or the day when we first had a bicycle of our
> own. We remember the teacher who first communicated en-
> thusiasm to us. We think of the church in which we wor-
> shiped as a child, or of the college to which we still feel our
> old loyalty. All of these times and places are a part of us;
> without them we should not be what we are. They are, as
> Emily Dickinson said, a "single hound" pursuing us, the sin-
> gle hound of our own identity.

He alludes to Dickinson's poem, cited in the first chapter—
"This consciousness that is aware . . . ." It suggests that our sense of
self and world and the swift passage of our experience between
birth and death—are something that in the mysterious dynamic
of human existence we do not control but that pursues us as "the
hound of its identity." The rendezvous is inescapable and we pray
that the "hound" we meet will be our friend. Her "hound" may be
a symbol of God, as it is later for Francis Thompson in his poem
"The Hound of Heaven"—but she will not be pinned down. Often
religious liberals know more clearly what they do *not* believe than
what they *do*; they need to recognize that faith entails a personal
decision—an existential, yes-or-no decision—about what they believe, as a step toward self-definition.

Those who have passed through profound personal crises
have learned that friendship itself saves us. It releases us from ourselves and enables us to repossess ourselves. When the time is ripe,
crisis becomes opportunity, as Adams affirms:

> Jesus was a member of the race possessing a creative mem-
> ory, a race that had not failed to roast that which it had taken

in hunting. St. Paul used the phrase "the fullness of time" to
describe the point in history when the Christ came. The conversion of a people or of an individual can occur only in the
fullness of time. We need to strike root into a definite plot of
soil. We need somehow to find our place in a continuing and
promising tradition with its sacred books, its communion of
saints and its disciplines. This is just what academic life for
most students seems to prevent. We get ourselves into a spectator attitude. We need the church's community of memory
and hope through the sharing of which we may in the fullness of time first sense our need for conversion and growth
in the grace and knowledge of Christ.

Adams dropped out of high school in order to support his
family by various jobs, finally becoming an assistant to the western division of the Union Pacific Railroad. He finished high school
by studying nights and with his boss's support gained a night-shift
job with the railway in St. Paul while attending the University of
Minnesota. "The people I knew on the railroad, some of these officials," he says, "were admirable—men of integrity, conscientiousness, generosity." Then he tells a story about it:

> When I told my boss that I was thinking of going to college
> he let the word pass up the line and the chief man on the
> railway division decided I wasn't going to leave the railway,
> so he came in—he and his huge plush private car—a self-
> made man accustomed to pushing people around: "What the
> hell could this railway do for you, James, more than we have
> already done? How old are you, anyway? Well, there you are,
> nobody I knew ever had such jobs as you've had on this rail-
> way. Why the hell do you want to leave all of that and go to
> college?" "Oh," I said, "I don't know. I just heard the name of
> Shakespeare. I want to find out what that's about." He thun-
> dered, "What the hell is that about?" I must have had some
> kind of pill that kept me at it—for I stuck to it and then I left,
> saying, "No, I am going to leave." That night I went for a walk

in the car shops, somewhat dilapidated and wondering if I'd made a fool of myself. Finally I ran into the boss's assistant, a man I had met before at the headquarters in St. Paul. "Where have you been, Jim? I've been looking all over for you. I want to shake your hand. I never in my whole life saw anybody talk back to the boss the way you did!"

As a small-town boy with what he feared was an inferior education, Adams read voraciously in order to catch up. He wanted, he said, to "de-provincialize" himself. Audacity and importunity, courage and confidence—these virtues of ego strength and identity formation are often implicitly praised in his stories:

> Speaking of John Maynard Keynes, who had been his classmate at Cambridge University, Alfred North Whitehead said that when he was a student Keynes announced that as a scholar he did not intend to remain at the university, where he would be obliged to climb the tortuous ladder of academic and administrative advancement. No, after graduation he would go up to London, earn two or three million pounds, and then return to Cambridge and achieve his goal despite the bureaucracy. I shall not forget the triumphant, climactic tone in Professor Whitehead's voice when he concluded the story, saying, in rising inflection, "And, by George, he did it!" The story illustrates a favorite idea in Whitehead's writings, that significant innovation requires that one break through the grooves of conventional routine. A major concern of Whitehead was to grasp the nature of a world in which novelty occurs.

It is a world in which creative freedom, the capacity of any person, finds exemplary expression in a few—and we all take notice!

Other virtues commended by Adams qualify "the primacy of will," which might otherwise turn into willfulness, for instance, devotional disciplines and maintaining communication with others. Harry Scholfield, the eminent Unitarian Universalist minister, once said he was too busy *not* to set aside time for meditation every day. Like Jerome Hall, the eminent professor of law, Adams might have said he was too busy *not* to write letters, for over the years thousands must have been recipients of his epistles. Naturally, he admires in Hall the virtues he prizes for himself, "aggressive empathy," "critical acumen," and "a love for dialogue":

> By the flow of Jerome Hall's letter writing I am reminded of Maitland's observation that only the people who have many other things to do write letters. Through his published writings as well as through his letters the whole man radiates, revealing a balance between aggressive empathy and stubborn critical acumen, a balance sustained and nerved by an engaging love for dialogue. By continuing dialogue he has avoided the worm's-eye view of the pedant.

Continuing dialogue is the moral of the story. It was continuing dialogue, I am convinced, that kept Adams's mind going strong into his ninety-third year.

Another duality in Adams's life was his stance with one foot in the church and the other firmly planted in academia. Speaking to a gathering at the Divinity School of the University of Chicago, he tells a story within a story:

> Stephen Leacock, the Canadian political scientist and wit, tells of the young man who said, "All I am I owe to my study of the classics." To which the reply was given, "A grave charge, young man, a grave charge!"... My principal teachers include Shailer Mathews, Alfred North Whitehead, Irving Babbitt, Friedrich von Hügel, Ernst Troeltsch, Rudolf Otto, and Paul Tillich. The older I grow, however, the more I recognize that my roots are in the Baptist fundamentalism. A grave charge, but I assume many of you also have followed the path from fundamentalism to liberal Christianity.

We may note that Shailer Mathews, the modernist Baptist who helped Adams discover a way beyond the fundamentalism of his youth, comes first in this list of teachers. When he moved to the University of Chicago, he was delighted to find Mathews his colleague and his neighbor as well. Recalling Mathews, Adams relates another story of ego-strength—and a quick wit:

> It was said that when Shailer Mathews spoke at a certain Baptist convention, fundamentalists carried placards of protest in front of the convention hall. After the dean finished his address, a stalwart fundamentalist stood up and shouted, "I want to ask you a question, and I want a straight answer. I want only a yea or a nay." "What is your question?" asked the dean. "My question is, do you or do you not believe that every single word of Scripture is inspired of God, yes or no?" To which the dean responded, "If the letter is greater than the spirit, no. If the spirit is greater than the letter, yes."

Not a few of Adams's stories concern confrontations, verbal wrestling matches in which one speaker seeks to pin the other to the mat. Here Mathews uses St. Paul's affirmation of the spirit of God as against the letter of the law (II Corinthians 3:6) to refute Biblical literalism: "The letter" in the sense of Biblical or any other literalism must be negated as a misreading of the text, even in its original sense, in order that the spirit of the text—the true meaning—can emerge.

However, the same terms can be read in the opposite way, and this way is the more characteristic of Adams's polemics. Now "the letter" is affirmed as the concrete embodiment of the "the spirit," the text's meaning, which otherwise remains unconnected with actual existence. Only actual beings—"letters"—can develop in time and space, undergoing identity formation (or malformation). Spirit gains power by incarnation.

Ancient wisdom traditions see "letters"—the "characters" of the alphabet—as signs of hidden meanings; just so, a person's "character" is revealed, gradually or suddenly, in his or her words and deeds. In this perspective the act of "naming," inscribing actual letters, is a potent and creative act. Adams notes,

> T. S. Eliot ingeniously stated the objection to a religion of "pure spirituality" in his revision of a familiar verse of Scripture:

"The spirit killeth, the letter giveth life." Without specific acts, without the letter, the spirit dies.

Adams also ascribes to T. S. Eliot another transposition of St. Paul's dictum—"The spirit killeth, the Word giveth life." It seems improbable that the precise Mr. Eliot would say it both ways, but with either version the moral is clear enough: Having your heart in the right place isn't enough, for you must courageously risk your word, spelling it out in the theater of history.

I'm reminded of Adlai Stevenson's *bon mot*: "Use me, Lord, use me! But in an advisory capacity." Some say Stevenson lost the election to likable Ike because people were uncomfortable with the idea of a jesting president. It is hard to picture the dignified Governor Stevenson as a clown, except for the sense of sadness just under the joking surface, as has often been noted in the case of Abraham Lincoln. We need more than tradition; we need people who devise strategies, in Adams's words, for "breaking through the grooves of convention." Adams notes that "the Polish Marxist philosopher Leszek Kolakowski defines the proponent of religion as 'the priest,' the 'guardian of the absolute who upholds the cult of the final and the obvious contained in the tradition.'" He goes on to cite Kolakowski's characterization of a contrasting figure:

> The jester, although an habitué of good society, does not belong to it and makes it the object of his inquisitive impertinence; he who questions what appears to be self-evident...who detects the non-obvious behind the obvious and the non-final behind what appears to be final....The philosophy of the jester is a philosophy which in every epoch announces as doubtful what appears as unshakable; it points out the contradictions in what seems evident and incontestable; it ridicules common sense and reads sense into the absurd.

The reversal of normal expectations is a dimension of parabolic vision, as when the Fool is wiser than the king in Shakespeare's *King Lear*. As a graduate student in comparative literature, Adams en-

countered the renowned Shakespeare scholar George Lyman
Kittredge, who tells this story of reversed expectations:

> Professor Kittredge once set out to study a Latin inscription
> on an ancient church in Rome. Feeling uncertain about his
> command of Italian, he sought out a knowledgeable monk
> who might discuss it with him in Latin. The monk whom he
> found readily agreed to do so—but first, he wanted to know,
> who was this Latin-speaking American? Did he perhaps in-
> tend to enter the cloister? No, Kittredge replied, in fact he
> was not even Catholic. Eyes widening, the monk asked, was
> he then a Protestant? Yes, a Congregationalist in particular,
> Kittredge said, "and I hold to its tenets." Well, the monk said,
> at once curious and agitated, there are after all so many vari-
> eties of Protestants! How had he happened to choose *that*
> one? Kittredge reflected momentarily and then replied that
> he had perhaps not so much chosen it as inherited it. The
> Congregational church in his native town on Cape Cod had
> been his family's church for as long as they had lived there.
> The monk, too, reflected for several moments, then ex-
> claimed, "You know, I think that's why I'm a Catholic!"

Why are any of us what we are? The story is luminous because
it invites us to reflect on at least two sides of the question. It does
not tell what the monk did the next day, but we can hardly imagine him rejecting his faith only because he discovered it was, in
part, an accident of his birth. We imagine him becoming a wiser
Catholic for his encounter with this Congregationalist. We are, in
part, the products of our upbringing; it could not be otherwise,
nor would we want it to be. And yet the tiny qualifier—"in
part"—is absolutely essential to the validity of the observation. We
are never wholly "bound and determined" by our upbringing; we
can have positive appreciation of other faiths, other traditions,
and when we do we will modify our understanding of our own
faith and tradition, just as we imagine the monk in Kittredge's
story doing. But rather than go on and on in this analytic mode, it

is perhaps enough to let the story stand without commentary, as Adams himself does, observing once again the curious power of parabolic vision.

The story that follows has several layers of meaning, but the deepest meaning is crystal clear. It is about a conversion experience. The experience follows a classic pattern, which Von Ogden Vogt describes as the fundamental pattern of worship itself, on the basis of his analysis of Isaiah 6. The pattern runs from being lifted up ("exaltation") to being cast down ("humility"), then from new understanding ("illumination") to a new decision (an act of "dedication"). But the substance of his experience lies beyond analysis or explanation:

> Nathan Söderblom has remarked that Bach's St. Matthew Passion should be called "The Fifth Evangelist." So was Bach for me. One night after singing with the Harvard Glee Club in the Mass in B Minor under Serge Koussevitzky at Symphony Hall in Boston, a renewed conviction came over me that here in the mass, beginning with the *Kyrie* and proceeding through the *Crucifixus* to the *Agnus Dei* and *Dona nobis pacem*, all that was essential in the human and the divine was expressed. My love of the music awakened in me a profound sense of gratitude to Bach for having displayed as through a prism and in a way that was irresistible for me, the essence of Christianity.
>
> I realize now that this was only the culmination of my *praeparatio evangelia*. For suddenly I wondered if I had a right even to enjoy what Bach had given me. I wondered if I was not a spiritual parasite, one who was willing to trade on the costly spiritual heritage of Christianity, but who was perhaps doing very little to keep that heritage alive. In the language of Kierkegaard, I was forced out of the spectator into the existential attitude. This experience as such was, to be sure, not a new one. It was simply a more decisive one. I could now see what Nietzsche meant when, in speaking of

Bach's Passion music, he said, "Whoever has wholly forgotten Christianity will hear it here again.

My own upbringing in the humanistic Unitarianism of the 1950s was radically different from Adams's. Nevertheless, among the many passages of his that have brought with them a new way of thinking and feeling, this one cut closest to my heart. It has led me to say what Adams says near the conclusion of the essay, "Christianity is no longer an optional luxury for me." I would call the passage a parable of the original decision of faith. But while such a categorization may clarify one aspect of its meaning, the story itself remains multifaceted and brilliant, a gem.

Thou ancient of days, we are grateful that thou hast gathered us into a fellowship of faith, calling us to search and to proclaim knowledge of thy truth and to enter into a covenant with thee and with each other of faithfulness to that truth and in responsibilities both individual and collective. We are grateful for that covenant which has been entered into by men and women of diverse times, places, and traditions. From the covenant opened up for us by Jesus we acknowledge the calling that thou hast given us in the priesthood and the prophethood of all believers. We acknowledge the indispensable place of scholarship in this calling. Remembering the command that we love thee with heart and soul and mind and strength, we in this time of dedication acknowledge that the mind cannot work alone, that to become love of thee it requires also heart and soul and strength. Amen.

—JLA

Confronting the Demonic:
Blessed Are the Powerful

IN THE HEYDAY of the feminist movement, I heard theologian Mary Daly speak to a hall packed with liberal-minded religious folk, concluding with an invitation for questions from, she said, "the women in the audience." A murmur ran through the hall. A woman forthrightly raised her hand and demurred, voicing an objection doubtless widely felt. Many men present, she said, entirely support feminist concerns and they should be heard from as much as anyone! Professor Daly coolly scanned the audience for another hand and said, "Now that we've heard a man's point of view, I'll take a question from a woman." After the nervous laughter subsided, we submitted without further dissent to Daly's Rule. Her symbolic action—years later, I remember it vividly—delivered her message with precision and power. Women must speak for themselves, and men must listen.

Such are the uses of power—the power to determine what voices will be heard and what voices will be silenced—in the struggle to effect social change. Radical change starts with a changed consciousness, and its agents, like Mary Daly, resort to offensive tactics. By scorning liberal attitudes and demanding liberating actions, radicals have often outflanked liberals. Still, the silencing of some voices in favor of others is ethically troubling. It is an old problem: How, if we are to confront evil, can we keep from taking on "the face of the enemy"? Those like Adams who choose the path of confronting demonic forces—destructive, possessive forces—need a keen sense of irony and a distinct tolerance for moral ambiguity. They need to know that their own motives are impure, and to know that, as surely as coercive violence tempts anyone, it also beckons to them.

Adams speaks boldly and risks misunderstanding when he ventures a new beatitude—"blessed are the powerful." To exercise power is among the most common of human ambitions and the most dangerous, perhaps, to both others and one's self. Accordingly, his beatitude provokes the question, What is the power that does not curse but is a blessing? People of faith must speak boldly and risk misunderstanding—if the world is to listen.

As we see in this chapter, Adams is centrally concerned with the uses and the abuses of power in interpersonal and societal life. He understands power not only as the capacity to exercise influence—a sociological concept—but also as a mark of being as such—an ontological concept. As such, power is a fundamental and unavoidable aspect of human existence. Similarly, Adams understands evil not only morally, as deliberate wrong-doing, but also theologically, as a perversion of the original goodness of "the creation."

With its optimistic assumptions about human nature and historical progress, liberalism has had difficulty dealing with problems that cannot be "solved"—the aftermath of evils, such as destructive and cruel acts, and conscious or unconscious abuses of power. In Adams's view this is a spiritual as well as a moral problem. Often it is rooted in idolatry, that is, false devotion to nation, to race, to wealth, or to another object that is less than ultimate. The ineffectuality of much religion in the face of evil he attributes to its "pious" other-worldliness—its focus on individual rather than social salvation and its avoidance of conflict.

Adams says that the good is to be won "not without dust and heat." To have the courage to confront evil, liberalism needs to affirm both personal and social power, and to recognize the affinity between the responsible exercise of power and authentic faith.

Power, the Mark of the Real

Adams tells several stories of "interrupting the meeting"— importunate words and impolite utterances that change the course of events in small or large ways. Those who figure in such stories are a radically diverse lot: his father James Carey Adams; the humanist minister and social activist David Rhys Williams; the neo-Reformation theologian Karl Barth; and Adams himself. Such events display "an aspect of power," in Adams's phrase as the following story reflects:

In 1936 I attended in Switzerland an international conference of students and faculties of Protestant theology, a conference at which the Swiss theologian Karl Barth was a participant.... The first paper, presented by a theologian from the University of Geneva, dealt with the concept of religious experience, and it employed the language of psychology as well as of Christian theology. Before the speaker was well under way, however, Barth suddenly arose in the audience, interrupted the speaker, and addressed the chairman. "I cannot wait any longer. I want to ask the speaker a question now," he said, thereby of course throwing the meeting into a uproar of consent and dissent. The chairman replied that it is customary for questions to be withheld until a paper is finished, but that he would leave the decision to the speaker. With questionable judgment the theologian reading the paper agreed to accept the question immediately. Barth thereupon made a frontal attack. "Is the speaker reading to us a paper on Christian theology or on the psychology of religious experience? If the paper is on the psychology of religion, why should we here listen to it? This is a conference of Christian theologians; only the Word of God, not talk about psychology and religious experience, is appropriate here." Immediately the assembly plunged into heated argument, a debate on the place, or lack of place, of secular science and even of apologetics in a Christian discourse. The heat of the controversy pervaded the remaining sessions of the conference.

Is there not something demonic in Barth's disruptive action? Perhaps, but Adams evaluates neither the tactic nor the substance of his claim, namely, that the word of God is independent of the human sciences. As a religious liberal and indeed a founder of the Society for the Scientific Study of Religion, he is not sympathetic with the Barthian theological program. He sharply criticizes the "proclamationism" that stems from Barth's attempt to "proclaim the Gospel"—the Christian *kerygma*—independent of a universally available "natural theology" or any other philosophical foundation. But here, characteristically, he only notes with wondering smile Barth's brassy skill at "interrupting the meeting."

Adams tells the story as an emblematic moment in the history of theology in the twentieth century; indeed, Christian theology has unalterably changed in the decades since the reported incident. Barth's attack is directed against movement of liberal Christianity through the previous century, seen as a defensive stance against "the acids of modernity," a general secularity. Adams holds that liberalism in all its forms—social, political, religious—that does not reckon with the dynamics of power is, if not already dead, moribund. His thought has a bent that runs counter to what is typical of liberalism. As social ethicist, social scientist, and theologian, he gives description ("the indicative mood") priority over prescription ("the imperative mood"). So too he gives power precedence over goodness. Most strikingly, he gives *will*, the deciding faculty, precedence over *intellect*, the reasoning faculty. Accordingly, Adams observes the operations of power in human affairs first and moralizes, if at all, only afterward:

> Nietzsche pointed out...that in the ancient Greek tradition we find two typical estimates of human nature and the human situation. One view is associated with the classical

philosophers, and is usually called the intellectualistic or rationalistic view, the Apollonian view. According to this view, reason is the masterful principle of creation, and the cosmos is a moving shadow of a world of eternal ideas, essences, or forms.... The other view of human nature in the Hellenic tradition to which Nietzsche drew our attention—the Dionysian view—interprets existence more in terms of vitality than of form, a vitality that is both creative and destructive, that embues every form but also eludes and bursts the bounds of every structure.... We are believed to be confronted by divine and demonic forces that either support and inspire us, or else thwart and pervert us, in our attempt to fulfill our destiny.

Adams proceeds to describe a third view, the Jewish and Christian view, as a synthesis of the Dionysian and the Apollonian views. However, insofar as Biblical faith sees human existence as a struggle between divine and demonic forces—for instance, in the *agon* of the Passion Story—he suggests that it lies far closer to the Dionysian view. The life of faith is no serene confidence or balanced sense of inner peace; rather, it is a way of wrestling with "the forces that sustain and the forces that disrupt" meaningful human existence. Adams sees theology as the delineation of these contending forces in human existence.

In spite of his characteristically genial spirit and analytic calm—a fundamentally Apollonian sensibility--a Dionysian streak runs through Adams's thought. The tension, never neatly resolved in his life and thought, is reflected in the epithet accorded him by friends and happily accepted by himself, the Smiling Prophet. If we give primacy to the will over the intellect—or as Tillich would say, giving primacy to "the form-creating power" over the self-subsisting or eternal form—we find that power rather than goodness becomes the primary characteristic ascribed to God. But it may be surprising that, in an avowed religious liberal, power becomes the primary stuff in terms of which faith is defined. According to Adams,

The first tenet of the free person's faith is that our ultimate dependence for being and freedom is upon a creative power and upon processes not of our own making.... The second tenet of the free person's faith is that the commanding, sustaining, transforming reality finds its richest focus in meaningful human history, in free cooperative effort for the common good.... The third tenet of the free person's faith is that the achievement of freedom in community requires the power of organization and the organization of power.

While the idea of power figures in each of these three tenets, Adams recognizes the moral ambiguity of power. In fact many of his ethical reflections largely consist in descriptions of the corruptions of power. Power may be used destructively and for evil ends but, as such, power is not corrupt or evil, as a dualistic view of human existence suggests. Adams notes that the extended version of the Lord's Prayer, concluding, "Thine is the kingdom, the power and the glory," is hardly a glorification of powerlessness.

It remains true that whoever acknowledges the reality of evil opts for a limited dualism. New Age spirituality, typically insisting on monism, is by these lights an ideology of conflict avoidance. For Biblical faith the dualism is not ultimate, however; faith signifies precisely the belief that, with powerful good will and God's grace, we shall overcome. In "Our God Is Able," a sermon reflecting a sense of faith as empowering, Martin Luther King Jr. affirms that "though the arc of the universe is long, it bends toward justice."

A faith for the free, Adams says, is rooted not in right thinking and believing but in right willing and acting. From time to time he criticizes the Buddhist focus on individual spirituality and its tendency to withdraw from the world. But there is something remarkably Buddhist about the accent on right action and the disdain of metaphysics, with its disputes "that do not tend to edify." It's also interesting to note that Adams first encountered both the serious study of Buddhism and the idea of the primacy of the will in the work of the "literary humanist" Irving Babbitt.

Freedom is not a formal right, the right to act as one pleases. Rather, freedom is the capacity for self-determination exercised within the limits of the human condition. Hence, it is an aspect of power. To exercise power is to exercise free will, and when this capacity is exercised in concert with others, we call it social action. "The decisive element in social action is the exercise of power," Adams comments. By reaching for a theological and ontological understanding of power, he goes beyond morally neutral or ambiguous conceptions of power—for instance, the sociological definition of power as simply the capacity to influence:

> In some circles power has a very bad reputation. Everyone is familiar with Lord Acton's maxim, "Power tends to corrupt, and absolute power corrupts absolutely." Henry Adams is more blunt when he says, "Power is poison." Jacob Burckhardt, the eminent Swiss historian, formulated a basic axiom of his philosophy of history in these words: "Power is not a stability but a lust, and *ipso facto* insatiable; therefore, unhappy in itself and doomed to make others unhappy." Looking back at the period of the Reformation and the Protestant-Catholic struggle, Burckhardt concludes that the confession that became dominant in any region of Europe was the one that possessed the strongest battalions.

Power tends to corrupt because in our self-centeredness we forget that we are one among multiple centers of power, each of us with our own created dignity. It is not only because we forget but also because we feel insecure that our wills are corrupted, for instance, in aggressive or subservient behavior. It is a problem of will and a problem of good will.

Acton's famous maxim is often cited without the qualifier *tends*, making it an assertion that power inevitably corrupts. A commonplace manifestation of this attitude is the cynicism, rife today, toward politicians—who are believed to seek and to hold onto political power for their own glorification or enrichment. This *tends* to happen to be sure, but a blanket judgment contributes to alienation from the political process and leads to withdrawal from even the most rudimentary form of participation, voting. Adams often laments the almost continuous decline in Americans' exercise of the franchise. The question of power, he argues, is at root theological:

> Power can be understood to corrupt absolutely only when the socio-political power is sundered from its theological ground, God's law and love.... When accepted so superficially, such dicta give plausibility to Candide's admonition that in a world of corruption we should simply cultivate our own garden. This interpretation has given both religious and irreligious people a spurious rationalization for a retreat from social action.... But... Candide could not even cultivate his garden without exercising freedom, human power.

There is no retreat from exercising freedom and power. One's garden is protected by the civic society or it could not exist; so even gardening falls within the socio-political realm. And the socio-political realm falls within the theological realm—the realm of necessary and contingent being. The civic society is limited by the freedom and dignity of the person, for the person's relationship to God is prior to (not dependent on) his or her relationship to society. Adams reduces these complex relationships to their underlying elements:

> Power has always a double character: first, as the expression of God's law and love; second, as the exercise of human freedom. To understand power as God's law and love is to understand it as Being; to understand it as human freedom is to understand it as the person's response to the possibilities of being, a response which is both individual and institutional.

When we exercise freedom within the context of God's law and love, we exercise it within limits. This theological matrix of freedom allows a moral domestication of power, that is, a limited right and a limited capacity to work one's will. Much is permitted, but not everything. Neglecting its theological matrix, liberals have tended to turn freedom into the exercise of individual preference. It has been observed that, historically, Unitarianism grew from the soil of Calvinism; not surprisingly, it remained closely akin to the parent it rejected, the parent it believed it had left utterly behind. Calvin's strong doctrine of predestination attenuated the doctrine of Christ's atonement; Unitarians, then, could discount both doctrines the more easily in favor of human freedom and righteous endeavor, with Jesus as teacher and exemplar. The strong kinship with Calvinism that remained is seen in the rejection of sensory representations of the divine as idolatry, and in the reformist drive to create a "holy commonwealth"—in modern terms, the welfare state. Unitarians, we may say, are Calvinists gone to seed.

The contemporary Unitarian Universalist minister and theologian Joseph Bassett comments on John Calvin's understanding of the church in terms that are both theologically enriching and congruent with Adams:

> In his commentary on Psalm 135, Calvin maintained: "All the world is a theater for the display of the divine goodness, wisdom, justice and power, but the church is the orchestra, as it were." The Geneva preacher and teacher had in mind a Greek amphitheater where the chorus occupies the orchestra in the very front part of the theater... [and] comments upon the action. Calvin's figure suggests that the church is that place in the world where the people of God play the chorus and comment on the display of God's goodness, wisdom, justice and power in the world.

Here, as in Adams's thought, neither the *soul* nor the *church* but rather, the *world* is the theater of God's action. The function of the church is to interpret God's "mighty acts" and its theology is fundamentally rhetorical, a dramatization of those acts.

The missing link in this theological discussion, which Adams sees and responds to with his emphasis on institutions, is a doctrine of the church, the community of God that takes our freedom to do good or ill seriously. He cites Emerson and Plato on power as an ontological concept, a primary quality of being that immensely deepens our understanding of power as a psychological and a social reality:

> "All power is of one kind," says Emerson, "a sharing in the nature of the world." One is reminded here of Plato's laconic remark, "And I hold that the definition of being is simply power.".. . in the typical modern generic definition, [power is understood as] simply the capacity to exercise influence. The modern definition is true so far as it goes. But it is true only with respect to the power of freedom, the power to influence others.... Plato observes in the *Sophist* that power is present equally in the capacity *to be influenced.*

This is fundamental. Power is the capacity to influence or to be influenced. For instance, it is not only the capacity to teach but also the capacity to learn. (Some are tragically disabled from learning due to psychic or societal factors in their lives, and some are what we call invincibly ignorant; both are disempowered.) Again, power is the capacity to act and move others, but it is equally the capacity to be acted upon, to be moved and to suffer. Eminently, love is such a power.

Plato's "laconic remark" is also an obscure remark. The translation cited by Adams is Benjamin Jowett's. Francis M. Cornford renders the passage: "I am proposing as a mark to distinguish real things, that they are nothing but power." Cornford comments, "The implication seems to be that the simple and unanalyzable nature can only be manifested and known by the effects it produces or suffers." Adams notes that the idea here expressed is akin to C. S. Peirce's "pragmatic theory of meaning" and to Jesus' principle of discernment, "By their fruits you shall know them." For the seminal Plato, as for the aphoristic Emerson, as for the prolix Paul Tillich, power is that which causes a being to come into existence or causes an existent being to pass out of existence. For

Hamlet the issue is not hypothetical but existential: "To be or not to be, that is the question."

We are most drawn to the dramas in which power is given or taken away, dramas in which power is surrendered or held fast, and dramas in which we are enabled and empowered or else disabled and marginalized. Adams comments, "I heard a definition recently at a church conference on black power: 'Power is not something to be shared. It is something you have to take away from others.'" In spite of its moral ambiguity, the statement is a realistic commentary on "the way things are." It reminds us of the human desire to hold onto power over others at all costs (an instance of the Calvinist recognition of idolatry) and suggests that one may rightly use force, even violent force, to wrest power from others (an instance of the Calvinist legitimation of legal coercion in the interest of social justice).

Still, the assertion that power is never freely and willingly shared, especially when it is asserted at a church conference, seems shocking. Certainly it lacks any sense of power as "the capacity to be influenced." Probably the assertion is intended to shock and to alter consciousness. It resonates with an idea religious liberals have neglected, the idea of a fallen world, a world yet to be liberated from the power of original sin. But such ideas need not be treated as foreign. The liberal-minded William Ellery Channing articulates a theory of original sin without ever using the term: The most pervasive and destructive human sin, he asserts, is the drive to dominate others, leading to the loss of democratic freedoms and even slavery. Channing could hardly be more emphatic:

> Christianity has joined with all history in inspiring me with a peculiar dread and abhorrence of the passion for power, for domination over men. There is nothing in the view of our divine teacher so hostile to his divine spirit, as the lust of domination. This we are accustomed to regard as eminently as the sin of the arch-fiend. "By this sin fell the angels." It is the most satanic of human passions, and it has inflicted more terrible evils on the human family than all others.

The drive to dominate is a drive for power *over* rather than power *with*. The difference, Adams indicates, is a difference in social relationships:

> In the face of the alienated, of the marginal men and women and children, power must be newly defined: as a creative, innovative relationship between those who have the freedom to participate in making social decisions and those who do not have that freedom. There is a good deal of evidence to show that the deeper the sense of alienation the greater the sense of hopelessness and the more likely the resort to violence. In this context, the people with power engender the violence. One theological tradition has called this process the wrath of God, the strange work of God's love. The Old Testament calls it hardening of the heart.

There is also a renewal of the heart, felt as God's grace. If Jesus' word that the "kingdom of God is at hand" means—as Adams, following Henry Joel Cadbury's translation, suggests—that the kingdom of God is available, hence within your grasp, then the act of grasping it is itself a powerful act. Richard R. Niebuhr proposes another translation for the term *kingdom of God*, namely, *God-ruling*. The term is linguistically awkward, but it underscores the dynamism and active character of *basiliea thou theou* (the New Testament Greek term that is usually translated "kingdom of God"). Niebuhr's language suggests that the kingdom (or reign or rule) of God is not a place, either worldly or otherworldly, but an active presence and a manifestation of divine power.

We are empowered by exercising our power and liberated by exercising our liberty, even in spite of ourselves. Sometimes, Adams notes, the problem is not the power we exercise but our powerlessness. Sometimes the problem is not controversy but the suppression of controversy and, in consequence, the destructive or violent turn that controversy takes:

> Impotence tends to corrupt. Absolute impotence corrupts absolutely. Power is the capacity to participate in creative

controversy. Power is the ability to make one's self heard, the capacity to cause others to take one's concern seriously. It is the capacity to make one's concerns felt as a impact in the communal decision-making process. It is also the capacity to listen. It is the capacity to respond creatively to others, to the needs of others. In all these dimensions, power engenders conflict.

These are aspects of the power that we hold and express as individuals and communities. We do so with consent to "God's law and love"—the primary forms in which "the power of being" is expressed. But our consent cannot be coerced or it is not consent. Therefore, freedom is a necessary part of the equation, as Adams notes:

> Kierkegaard would say that the perfection of God's power is to be seen in his giving to the human being the power to turn against him; for communion with God is not possible if no alternative exists. Here we approach the paradox contained in the dialectic between divine and human power. Human freedom is a gift from God. From a religious perspective, both God and the human being would be impotent but for this grace of freedom.

This double awareness may also be stated this way: God empowers humanity by giving us a Godlike freedom. However, it is a freedom that must function within the limits of human finitude— we are frail, faulty, and mortal— and a moral covenant. These limits are difficult to discern and define. They are difficult to gain consensus on without political coercion, violating human freedom and dignity. In consequence we are constantly tempted to violate the limits, whether for the sake of self-aggrandizement or from pure malice. Hence, evil reasserts itself.

Evil remains an enigma in spite of the many attempts to explain it, for it is irrational and our attempts to explain it seem only to "explain it away." We can at best observe and elucidate its spiritual forms, the demonic and the idolatrous.

The Demonic

Evil distorts the good, with tragic consequences. It twists what is intended for creative ends to destructive ends. It stands against the original created goodness of being—a goodness that is latent within and a potentiality of all actual beings. Evil often has a demonic, that is, a possessive and compulsive, character. Demonic evil is more than a bad deed or a singular sin. It is self-justifying, self-sustaining, and self-replicating. It is a perversity with a life of its own.

Discussions of evil readily provoke concern that a philosophical dualism is implied. We want to take evil seriously, but we are afraid that if we take it too seriously, we will fall into seeing life as a struggle between the children of light and the children of darkness. Curiously, *angelism* seems to lead to dualism as surely as *satanism* does; the one tries to ignore evil, while the other is fascinated by it. Both orientations are unstable and, in time, prove themselves untenable and unsustainable.

The texture of Adams's thought is especially interesting at this point, for he understands whatever persists in time as having some sustaining power; it participates in the creative power of God. Since demonic realities sustain themselves in time, they cannot be seen as purely evil. Rather, they are tragic distortions of the good and in some degree participate in the good. Adams notes an old distinction between the *satanic* and the *demonic*:

> There are elements in reality that sustain mutuality. An element of mutuality runs through all of nature, despite the struggle for existence. Anything completely lacking the capacity for mutuality with other beings is on the way out of existence. Now the sustaining power—the capacity for mutuality—is a quality built into reality; we didn't make it that way—it is indispensable. If it is completely lost, one reaches nonexistence. The distinction has been made since the seventeenth century between *the demonic* and *the satanic*. The satanic is that which is nonexistent because it has

no relationship to the structures of being. The demonic is therefore defined as the perversion of these qualities, but perversions are able to maintain themselves for a time. So there is a sustaining quality present in whatever is.

The distinction helps us recognize that, while we need to take evil seriously, we cannot give it ultimate ontological status. Evil is always derivative or contingent in relation to the good. It is quite possible and not at all uncommon to take evil idolatrously, that is, to be religiously devoted to it. Satanism, White Supremacy, and Nazism are examples. W. H. Auden defines *idolatry* as "taking what is frivolous seriously." Just so, we recognize that satanism is a myth, a story that, taken literally, can lead to radical distortions of the truth, often with tragic consequences.

The moral of the story is that we must recognize the ambiguity of the human condition, and especially our personal existence. By faith we are freed from the myth of the Evil One who supplants God and may even command human devotion. Faith enables us to be critical realists, persons who recognize that we shall go on living with our demons and others' demons until the end of time, and yet we may still, by faith in the goodness of God, live blessed lives. Describing his faith, Adlai Stevenson recalls the Psalmist's words, "I had fainted, unless I had believed to see the goodness of the Lord in the land of the living" (Psalm 27:13).

The awareness of demonic evil is deeply rooted in the New Testament. For a sermon on the demonic powers of the present world age, Adams takes the striking text traditionally attributed to the apostle Paul: "We wrestle not against flesh and blood, but against the principalities, against the powers, against the world rulers of this present darkness, against the spiritual hosts of wickedness in heavenly places" (Ephesians 6:12).

Tender-hearted interpreters often have difficulty with strong language like Paul's. Once I heard a minister use Albrecht Dürer's famous image of St. Paul to illustrate the "shadow" side of the human psyche. This neo-gnostic turn of thought confuses power with evil. The figure of Paul in the oil painting is standing, looking at the viewer from an oblique angle, together with the apostle John, who gazes downward, a pensive image. Dürer juxtaposes two human types; John's image is tender and modest, whereas Paul is shown as a singularly powerful figure, a man with penetrating, forceful vision. As one to whom Martin Luther is a spiritual hero, we must suppose that Albrecht Dürer holds Paul, Luther's spiritual hero, to be a true saint. That Paul does not look angelic, as compared to the figure of John, does not make him a Jungian "shadow" figure. Rather, he looks exactly like one ready to take on the principalities and powers of the world. The distinguished art historian Erwin Panovsky comments at length on Dürer's masterwork, "The Four Apostles," among whom Paul represents the melancholic temperament: "St. Paul was the hero of a new creed, just as melancholy was the signature of a new human type which we call genius."

Jesus' utterances are suffused with the awareness of demonic possession. Indeed, there is a close connection between his speaking in obscure parables about the "mystery of the kingdom of God" and the belief in his time in the prevalence of demonic powers. The kingdom must be kept secret precisely because the demons must be eluded; only then can they can be defeated. Small wonder that Jesus was himself accused of being possessed by Beelzebub (see Matthew 12:24). According to Adams,

> Jesus viewed the kingdom of God as carrying on a struggle against an enemy, against invisible powers of darkness. "If I by the Spirit cast out demons, then is the kingdom of God come upon you. Or how can one enter into the house of a strong man and spoil his goods, except he first bind the strong man? And then he will spoil his house" (Mark 3:27). In this fashion the power, the *exousia*, which Jesus represents comes to mortal grip with the power, the *exousia*, of the demonic world. Jesus apparently viewed himself as the herald of the power of God that can overcome the principalities and powers, "the rulers of this present darkness."

Taking the demonic seriously does not mean that we are being asked to believe in the objective existence of mythic supernatural beings. Adams notes that the myths, in the proper sense, are stories of the conflicts of the gods. The ancient myth of a struggle between demonic and angelic powers is a way of grasping, if not explaining, the struggle between evil and good forces in the world. Moralizing about such things is plainly inadequate. Moral exhortation cannot address what Tillich calls the ambiguities of history and historical action. The evils we wrestle with, always with uncertain outcome, are not simply the conscious decisions of moral agents—people making wrong choices, whether from ignorance or malice or some combination of the two. They are irrational, destructive, and often self-destructive forces. Evil has been described as a moral virus that invades its host; unopposed, it tends to become radical. Radical evil is evil that justifies itself, and even exalts itself, as do fascism, extreme nationalism, or religious fundamentalism. It becomes a possessive power with an insatiable, and finally a self-destructive, appetite. So Shakespeare's Ulysses says, calling unbounded appetite the "universal wolf" that is so voracious, it must finally "eat up himself."

Coming to terms with the reality of evil is another instance of the primacy of the will over the intellect. The principle reminds us that we cannot rationalize evil; we can only suffer and endure it or else exorcise it. To cast it out requires a still greater *exousia*, "from being" in Greek, a word we translate as "power." Modern rationalism, having swept the demons out the front door, is beset by a dozen new ones entering through the back door—in the imagery of the parable teller Jesus (see Matthew 12:43ff.). Adams says,

> Nazism was the expression of a major driving force of modern history, so pervasive a force that nationalism has been called "humanity's other religion." Paul Tillich is the major theologian who has given currency to the term, "the demonic." But the term is applicable not only to the totalitarian state.

Adams names two other possessive powers prominent in our time as worthy of the label. One is an economic system that compulsively depends on the production and consumption of ever more things. "One is reminded of William Hazlitt's word that the image of America [he took home to England] was that of one long bargain counter." Another, he says, is racism:

> A few years ago I delivered an address in Tokyo to representatives of various religions, endeavoring to indicate the bases for bringing about a better understanding and a closer cooperation between the religions. Immediately after my address, a Buddhist monk stood up to pose a question, and he spoke for fifteen minutes, centering his attention on the destruction of Hiroshima and Nagasaki by atomic bombs. He concluded his remarks by asking if the Americans would have destroyed these two cities if they did not assume that the Japanese people were a subhuman species. Race, he said, is the religion of the West.

Demonic possession is itself a spiritual phenomenon. A demon is an alien and possessive power—something that displaces reason and will, something that puts individuals and perhaps whole institutions in the service of something they consider greater, often a political system or cause. It spreads through the manipulative use of a "big lie," often a slander of a person or a group and often linked to a conspiracy theory. It develops engines of propaganda. It is an ancient as well as a modern phenomenon, variously rooted in the drive of rulers to subject peoples to their rule or of discontented, dispossessed groups to subvert institutional leaders. Patriotism (the religion of nation) and religious orthodoxy (nondeviation from traditional ideas and norms) are often invoked to aid the cause or to cover its true motives.

Such recognitions are likely to prove controversial, as Adams once found:

> When I visited the Byzantine monastery at Daphni outside Athens, I with binoculars lay on my back on the floor in

order to scrutinize the mosaic high on the dome. Especially impressive is the grim Pantocrator, Christ the Judge and Redeemer [ca. 1100 C.E.]. Years later at the home of a professor of art history, in the company also of an eminent scholar of ancient Greek culture, I raised the question: What is the most numinous work of art you have ever seen? Within a short time we agreed that the Pantocrator mosaic at Daphni is the most impressive. Whereupon I told of my experience at Daphni and also of my feeling that this grim Christ, ruler of the cosmos, provided religious sanction for the autocratic rule of the Byzantine Emperor. I added that in the liturgical procession in the Byzantine church the Emperor led the way with the representatives of Christ later in the line. Immediately we were engulfed in a vigorous argument. The art historian hinted that my remarks were sacrilegious. To my frustration the Greek scholar would not take sides in the discussion, nodding with seeming approval after each of us had stated our opinions. When I went home that evening I was oozing with guilt, for I thought I had spoiled the evening with my comments. But then, two months later, I encountered the art historian at the Harvard Faculty Club. He said that he owed me an apology, that he and his wife since that evening had spent much time discussing the mosaic. But, he said, we have finally come to agree that the Pantocrator is a divine sanction for the autocratic monarch!

In this tale a Christological question lies just under the surface. The Christ wholly exalted as "Pantocrator," that is, the divine agency of all creation, loses the sense of the Christ made present by Jesus of Nazareth, the historical person who subjects himself to the powers of evil and overcomes them through compassion and forgiveness. A kind of double vision is needed to see Jesus as revealer of the divine and yet as entirely human—indeed, to see that only a fully human Jesus could authentically mediate God's goodness and power.

The contrast drawn by Adams between images of Jesus is similar to the contrast drawn by the novelist and art critic John

Updike in a review of a major exhibit of works by El Greco, the Greek painter who flourished in Counter-reformation Spain. Updike acknowledges the spiritual power of El Greco: "An acquaintance, a distinguished painter and caricaturist, told me that he, although an atheist, now found himself, after the show, willing to be converted." Updike's own viewpoint—possibly due, he says, to his "stubborn, hard-shelled Protestantism"—leads him to contrast El Greco with other old masters:

> [An] ecstatic androgyny…permeates El Greco's images of Christ, with their long-fingered hands, airy gestures, and fine-grained pallor. What I miss in them is a sense of God's Incarnate, a walking-around Jesus, a man among others, as we see in Giotto and Titian and Rembrandt's etchings and Dürer's woodcuts. El Greco's divine personages, once he has reached maturity, are like movie stars, perfect and untouchable.

The Roman Catholic Counter-reformation exemplifies the way in which an otherworldly spirituality often unites with a quest for worldly domination.

A religion that becomes a worldly power is not unlike a political movement that becomes a religion, as Adams himself witnessed:

> "Believe, follow, act," said Mussolini, "Fascism before being a party is a religion." Human history is not the struggle between religion and irreligion, but between authentic and idolatrous religion. It is veritably a battle of faiths, a battle of the gods who claim human allegiance. Once I heard a German exile tell a story of Nazi horror. As he reached the end of his story he became mute with revulsion and indignation. How could he speak with sufficient contempt of what the Gestapo had done to his friend? "Are these men completely without awe, are they completely without faith?" Immediately he answered his own question: "There is no such thing as a man completely without faith. What a demonic faith is the faith of the Nazis!"

Adams tells various stories of the way in which twentieth-century liberalism is unprepared for the challenge of nationalistic fascism, including this one:

> I recall especially a conversation with one of the Nazi student leaders [in Germany in the 1930s]. I had met him in a restaurant. Eventually the discussion came round, as it always does, to the subject of politics. "Oh," he laughed, "you are one of those American who believe in talk, or as you call it, democracy! Listen here, my friend, democracy is finished. Government by talk! Government by opinion! You have no government, you have no authority, you have no leadership. Germany," he said—he meant National Socialism—"has found out democracy for the vile disease it is. It is a form of paralysis. Well, Germany is not paralyzed. She has a leader who believes in action and who acts."

The shift to post-modern thought comes when we recognize that the question of faith is not one of theism versus atheism, but rather one of authentic versus idolatrous faith. For believing in something that gives meaning to one's life, as Adams often says, is humanly inevitable. If so, an inauthentic or idolatrous faith can be true in a paradoxical sense; it stands in judgment against a formally authentic but practically impotent faith. Thus a democracy that is paralyzed—because it is irreconcilably divided, a "house divided against itself"—is in a state of absolute crisis. Some will think it perverse to recognize the truth, however paradoxical, in the words of a Nazi, but the same problem arises today when we seek to understand the motives of terrorists or other perpetrators of manifestly evil deeds without justifying them. It is not easy, but it is morally imperative.

In the rise of National Socialism in Germany, Adams sees the crisis of liberal democracy in the twentieth century. Fascism—still evident today in extremist nationalistic states and in the alienated sub-cultures of every state—did not come from without, but from within Western culture. So all religious bodies, upholders of transcendent values and faith, share some responsibility for the world-historical failure that the rise of fascism represents. One event more than any other brings the very foundation of faith communities into question: the Holocaust. Nevertheless, what is most lacking in discussions of its meaning, Adams says, is a theological dimension:

> In the face of the incomprehensible and fearful mystery, the incredibly bestial mass murder attaching to the Holocaust, we recognize the moral necessity of remembering the Holocaust and our responsibility for preventing its recurrence. The word "Holocaust" still falls too easily from our lips. We are reminded that we require a more adequate conception of human nature than was characteristic of the sweet gloss of old-fashioned liberal religion. The lack in the West of heed to the Holocaust for over a decade may be in part due to nicely reasoned interpretations that confine themselves to the anthropological, the human dimension, interpretations that do not venture to give a theological interpretation.

The notion of a problem that we cannot solve by doing something to fix it, an evil that we cannot resolve by finding out who to blame and punish, and a theological enigma that we cannot get rid of by moralizing—these tough cases profoundly disturb us. Some deny that such cases exist. The Holocaust of the Jews and the other victims of genocide, and more recent atrocities of murder, violent oppression, occupation, and territorial expulsion outstrip moral interpretation. People do not simply do evil things; they do evil things that they could not do without believing them to be good and necessary. They dress their actions in moral justifications.

Thus garden variety evil deeds become demonic evil, a force with a life of its own. Adams wrestles with the paradoxes of demonic evil:

> In *Crime and Punishment* Dostoyevski, a relentless theologian, views freedom as a burden and the tragedy of human existence, yet also as a divine gift accompanied by the occa-

sion for responsibility. For the human being, individually or collectively, no limits to the abuse of freedom are imposed, for if any limit is imposed, it simply is not freedom. Everything is allowed, whether it be Raskolnikov's murdering of the old usurer, or the sufferings of Job, or the destruction of Hiroshima and Nagasaki, or the Nazi Holocaust. Guernica must be possible. Dostoyevski at great length studied the demonic, Raskolnikov writ large. Every abuse of freedom issues from freedom's deteriorating into self-will, into defiant self-affirmation. Raskolnikov commits the crime of murder for the sake of a "higher idea"—he plays the role of superman, as does the Grand Inquisitor. He therefore resorts to coercion. Wasn't the usurer anyway a greedy, inferior, and worthless creature? But enforced goodness is itself evil, as is every authoritarianism. Compulsion is the Anti-Christ, for Christ gives liberty of conscience, "the glorious liberty of the children of God" (Romans 8:21). A person obsessed is no longer free. In this view the abuse of freedom is the tragic destiny of humankind—and of God.

Adams goes on to cite a parable of the nexus of human freedom and evil from the thought of Hans Jonas, a Jewish refugee from Nazi Germany and a scholar of ancient Gnosticism and modern existentialism:

Hans Jonas has suggested that in making unlimited freedom possible for the human being, God has taken a great risk, has made a wager. Therefore, it is up to us to accept the challenge of attempting to vindicate God's wager. In a sense God is betting on us. This is the ontological, theological meaning of divine given freedom and responsibility. In the face of Hiroshima and the Holocaust and of humanity's multiform inhumanity among the brothers and sisters of Job, God the Great Wagerer is not powerless, for God offers us the mystery of grace—sustaining, renewing, and transforming. Grace is the ground of hope. What was the alternative for

God? Either to intervene to limit human freedom, or to "condition" freedom in the manner of *A Clockwork Orange.*

We might say that in a burst of optimism God wagered that we humans would use our freedom with a Godlike creativity, or at the very least, that we would use our freedom humanely. If that is what God had in mind, then God has lost the bet and lost it badly. If our theology does not take evil seriously, recognizing that evil is a universal element in human life, including our own lives and even the lives of our beloved communities, then our theology speaks neither from the heart of this age nor to it.

Contemporary Idolatry

When Adams says that faith requires an "eschatological orientation," he refers not to prediction of the future but to the pressure of the future on present decisions, or actions oriented to ultimate ends, "last things." W. H. Auden similarly draws upon the eschatological consciousness reflected in certain words of Jesus in order to define an ethical stance toward history: "The past is not to be taken seriously (*Let the dead bury their dead*) nor the future (*Take no thought for the morrow*), but only the present instant and that, not for its aesthetic emotional content but for its historic decisiveness. (*Now is the appointed time.*)" Idolatry is misplaced or truncated devotion, or in Auden's terms, "taking what is frivolous seriously." It is devotion to gods who are impotent and dying. It is devotion to that which we make or can manipulate rather than that which makes us and on which we ultimately depend. Adams observes,

> Human history seems to be a history of the recurrent fall of old tribal gods and the rise of new ones. Half-gods are Protean creatures. They disappear only to reappear in new forms. Observing this recurrent tendency in the history of the race, the philosopher David Hume once suggested that the "natural" religion of humanity is polytheism.

In England I saw a billboard showing young men standing in a stadium and yelling; the caption was "Football Is Our Religion." A small logo indicated that the advertisement was placed by a major television network. To an American such blatant secularism was astonishing, but my English friends shrugged it off. The realms of sports and entertainment celebrities overlap and are among the several forms of "religious" devotion that coexist in our polytheistic souls. We may feel that they are entirely harmless, relative to serious faith. On further reflection we may not be so certain what "serious" faith would be, especially in a day when religion, too, is so deeply drawn into the realms of entertainment and celebrity. Nations that have lost a sense of historical purpose in the political realm often seem to have lost it also in the spiritual realm. What, we must wonder, will arise in the future to fill the void so lightly occupied for so many millions by the icons of popular culture?

In spite of our secularity, Adams reminds us that in the face of manifestly just historical struggles, Biblical imagery and its underlying convictions gain fresh meaning.

> The basic image of the Old Testament is that of a people being led by God into every new situation, journeying through the wilderness into a Promised Land. The exodus from Egypt was viewed as a divinely given liberation from bondage and as a thrust toward fulfillment, under the covenant with the Lord of history. As John Donne would say, this people of God was on pilgrimage; it had a future engagement with its higher self.

The story gains renewed significance where people are awakening to a sense of being a "people of faith" engaged in events that dramatize historical meaning. The prophetic tradition of ancient Israel is reflected, for instance, in Richard Niebuhr's comment that history is "the story of the global struggle for justice" or equally in the worldly voice of Voltaire: "History is the sound of silk slippers coming down the stairs, wooden shoes going up the stairs."

The Bible is not only the story of authentic religion, it is also the story of idolatrous religion, hence the recognition that religion per se is not good. Adams notes both sides:

> In the Book of Exodus we find not only the image of a faithful people, but also a counter-image, that of the disobedient, the stiff-necked people. The children of Israel in the wilderness murmur against God and fall into temptation. Trying vainly to manipulate the Determiner of Destiny, they make a Golden Calf. In this yielding to temptation they give themselves to something unreliable; they adopt self-worship.

Arnold Schönberg's opera *Moses and Aaron* raises the question: Who is to say that a Golden Calf is not as good an object of devotion as Yahweh, the god of whom no image can be made, and possibly better? Contemporary consciousness is open-minded on this issue and can barely understand what it would mean to be "a people of God on pilgrimage"—trekking through a spiritual desert.

One of Adams's most interesting—and due to contemporary ecological consciousness, most controversial—polarities is the temporal and the spatial. He draws a sharp distinction:

> Idolatry is a form of spatialization, a belief that you can identify particular spaces as ultimate—"my church, my national tradition." "This Bible which I can carry right in my pocket will protect me if a bullet comes...I can also pull it out and I can answer any question you like." All of these exaggerated claims represent forms of idolatry, a spatialization of the divine. Frank Cross [colleague at Harvard Divinity School] has reminded us that Yahweh resided in a tent, not to be confined to a particular space.

Cross drew on the many interpretations of the Book of Job that seek to soften its uncompromising outcry against God's apparent injustice. He titled a convocation sermon at Harvard Divinity School "Will Ye Speak Falsely for God?" The temptation "to speak falsely for God" is precisely the temptation to set up a God we can control, an idol. Space and time form a polarity in Adams's thought. Adams sees in Nazism an idolatrous attempt to "spatialize" the divine:

> A good illustration of demonic loyalty to spaces and the denial of a universal loyalty is seen in the Nazi slogan, *Blut und Boden*, our blood and our soil.... The temporal element brings all spaces under judgment. At the same time, all spaces are supported by the divine, so there is... a recognition of divine creativity with respect to space. But in the last analysis time informs and overcomes space.

In the prophetic tradition of the Hebrew scriptures Adams finds a God who is deeply involved in time and history, a God who had acted in the past and will act in the future. This is the language through which a prophetic faith is defined, delineating that which is ultimately reliable and worthy of our devotion. These highly abstract ideas are the means by which the theologian provides basic orientation to human existence and asserts the ways in which we see God as impinging on our lives. Adams's sharp contrast between time and space, and between history and nature, is characteristic of his generation. The contemporary revaluation of nature and space, driven by awareness of life-threatening environmental degradation, suggests re-evaluation of these dichotomies. Nevertheless, it does not obviate Adams's basic point, because the *natural* world itself is a central *historical* concern; human "dominion" over the natural world is (in a qualified sense) an historical fact and therefore poses great social-ethical issues and responsibilities.

Is time more fundamental than space, as Adams seems to assert, or are they two aspects of the same reality, the Einsteinian space-time? The latter seems to be the case, but the attempt even to speak of space-time catches us up in yet more abstractions—ideas that are far removed from personal experience. Such unimaginable ideas have sometimes been given imaginative or symbolic representations in order to illumine mysterious processes such as creation. Thus the prophet Isaiah speaks of Yahweh as "he who sits above the circle of the earth, who stretches out the heavens like a curtain, and spreads them out like a tent to dwell in..." (Isaiah 40:22). The imagery suggests that *time* is like raising the poles of a great tent and that *space*, like our circus tent world, would collapse without them. Perhaps space-time is the very breath of God, perpetually blown into the tent of cosmos, keeping it inflated. The atomic structure is itself a kind of tent, with forces that keep it from collapse; further, this structure may be seen as a microcosm of the physical reality writ large. The story also suggests that creation is a continuous, present process, not an event at some past date. These are not, of course, literal descriptions but forms of parabolic vision that enable our minds to grasp astonishing things that would otherwise remain abstract and lifeless.

Devotion to place, to the very soil, Adams argues, is one of "the major religions of humanity." We are today less inclined to take that as a bad thing, however. He does not consider, as for instance Wendell Berry does, that when we lose all love of particular plots of earth, we exploit and despoil nature, treating it as an infinite economic commodity. A provocative bumper sticker reads, "Farmland lost is farmland lost forever." The religion of place and soil is reflected in a story from Hebrew scripture (II Kings 5) related by Adams:

> Naaman was a commander of the army of Syria, and a mighty man of valor; but he was also a leper. In search of a cure, he made a pilgrimage to Samaria to appeal to [the prophet] Elisha. In response to his plea Elisha told him to dip himself seven times in the River Jordan. Naaman obeyed the instruction. "He went down and dipped himself seven times in the Jordan; and his flesh was restored like the flesh of a little child, and he was clean." Out of gratitude Naaman now returned to Elisha and offered him a present. But Elisha would accept no gift. Then Naaman made a strange request. He asked that he be given two mules' burden of earth, saying

that henceforth he would not offer burnt offering or sacrifice to any god but the Lord of Israel.

Why did Naaman wish to take with him two mules' burden of soil from Samaria? The answer is that he, like his contemporaries..., believed that in order to worship the god of any country it was necessary to stand on earth taken from that god's territory. The gods of the time were territorial gods.

Territorial religion is a highly symbolic term for Adams. It signifies the spatialization of human consciousness—being attentive to objects rather than to acts or devoted to what is given by a higher authority or embodied in a mass culture rather than to personal and communal goods that must be created and shared in time. Adams comments,

> Viewing the mass media as a whole, we must see in them an illustration of the old principle, the religion of the prince is the religion of the territory. Our princes of the mass media are the principal purveyors of our increasingly uniform territorial religion. These purveyors, to be sure, claim to give the public what it wants, but the claim cannot conceal the compulsive desire of the purveyors to define what the public wants.

Prophetic preaching readily takes on oracular forms of expression, such as ecstatic denunciations and visions. Like parables, oracles uncover what lies hidden and will in due time be revealed, as the latter-day prophet Jesus of Nazareth says. Ezekiel's famous images, "the wheel within the wheel" and "the valley of dry bones," are highly developed parabolic visions. Adams alludes to Jeremiah's prophetic denunciation: "They have forsaken me, the fountain of living waters, and hewed them out cisterns, broken cisterns, that can hold no water" (Jeremiah 2:13). Adams comments,

> We recognize that overcoming poverty is not equivalent to the advent of the kingdom of heaven. A rise in the standard

of living is no guarantee of improved standards of life. But this truth does not conceal the price exacted by the territorial religion that preaches comfort to the comfortable and that cultivates blindness to the broken-ness of our cisterns. Nor does it cancel the stupendous difference between the size of the military budget and that of the anti-poverty program. Karl Marx has astutely observed that whenever the economic system is under attack, one protects it by wrapping the flag around it.

Specialization is also a form of spatialization, tending to isolate highly educated persons from one another more and more as they advance in their fields, with ironically dehumanizing effect, according to Adams:

> Dean Willard Sperry, of Harvard Divinity School, used to tell the story about his first evening as a graduate student at Yale. In the refectory he spoke to the student sitting next to him, announcing that his specialty was New Testament Greek; the other student said that his field was mathematics, whereupon the conversation ended!

Education and specialization need not incapacitate our humanity, but conscious effort must be made toward broadening and interconnecting. Adams writes about "the purposes of a liberal arts education," which he sees as essential to education for citizenship. He also advocates interdisciplinary study and interchange between professional and religious groups, to work against the isolation of specialists. His doctoral student Max Stackhouse recalls:

> In a small seminar, really one of his famous "evening sessions" in his home, with several of us who were nearing the end of our studies, Professor Adams injected a plea that each of us should not only read and study the materials proper to our particular teaching or research tasks, but that we select some of the great classics of literature, the arts, history, phi-

losophy or religion, and study them a little bit each day. It prevents constriction of perspective. The suggestion was one which he exemplified in his own habits.

Adams also holds that "bringing together people from differing life experiences and perspectives" is a major function of an *authentic* voluntary association. Indeed, it is precisely the vocation of the church to bring together "all sorts and conditions" of humanity in an inclusive covenant. Adams tells the following story, showing that it is difficult to overcome the separations of class and education, even with the best of intentions, perhaps especially in the church:

> I saw a lot of a CIO organizer and his wife because a good deal of our political activities in Chicago and Downstate involved collaboration between the IVI—the Independent Voters of Illinois—and the CIO. This man was very articulate, what you call a rough diamond. Eventually the question came around, "Say, Dr. Adams, what is that Unitarianism?" I told him about it. His wife said, "I didn't know there was any such thing." I said, "Come on down." So they came around to our Gothic cathedral, attended two or three times, and then we didn't see them any more. The next time Margaret and I encountered them, we did not ask any questions. They said, "Well, you notice we haven't been back?" "Yes, what was the trouble?" "Well, I liked what the preacher said," he said. "That was good. But those hymns—my wife said they were all strange hymns. She was brought up on gospel hymns, and there wasn't a single gospel hymn there. Well, it was worse than that. You know, I could just see it as you and Margaret introduced us to people. You know what they did? They looked at my necktie! My wife and I, we talked about it. I took hold of my necktie like this and I started to yell, "What the hell's the matter with my necktie?" My wife and I, we're just people with bad taste.

Churches notoriously reflect the class divisions in society, a darkly ironic fact when set beside their devout professions to a universal and undivided community. What we learn, ever so reluctantly, is that a faith that has lost its critical, self-critical, and socially prophetic edges fails to draw people into significant, outwardly directed purposes. Their place is readily taken by the spiritual sandbox, churches where small egos contend for attention, grab toys, and throw sand. Joseph Barth comments on the growing tendency to substitute talk of "community" or even "the beloved community" (Josiah Royce's idealistic term) for concepts of real transcendence, an Other standing over against you and your group. A sentimentally formed God is likely to betray you, because such a God is not sufficiently separated from human interests to provide a critical distance, as Adams emphasizes:

> One of the greatest mistakes we can make is to suppose that all religion is good, or that religion is something sacrosanct, something that should be exempt from criticism, something that can escape the wrath of God. The prophets of Israel and the prophet of Nazareth knew better. They knew that the Devil is a gentleman, that evil in order to make headway in the world needs the cloak of religion. I once heard the Nazi Archbishop of Germany say that Hitler had been sent by God to fulfill German destiny. I ventured to remind him that the God of the ancient Hebrew prophets had a controversy with the people of Israel. For they thought God had a special destiny for them because of their blood and soil and regardless of their disobedience to the commandment of justice. The archbishop jumped up from his chair and shouted, "How could God be against us? God is in us!"

Karl Barth's naysaying to religious liberalism is aimed in part at its tendency to idealize and accommodate the contemporary world, thus becoming "a culture religion"—a religion that accommodates to current cultural ideas and social practices, "gaining the whole world and losing its soul." Adams absorbs this critique and

makes it a double-edged sword of his own, against both a sentimental Christianity and an arrogant scientific or secular humanism. He makes Barth's term, "no-God"—the popular god-in-us,
the god who stands at no critical distance from us—his own:

> One of its [prophetic theology's] decisive features is its in-
> tention to expose the human assistance, and particularly the
> religious person's assistance, "at the birth of 'no-God,' at the
> making of idols." Like the Old Testament prophets, it em-
> phasizes the Commandment, "Thou shalt have no other
> gods before me." Neither Christianity as a historical phe-
> nomenon, nor the Bible as a cultural creation, nor culture
> with all its "riches," nor anything that is of the order of crea-
> tures can be the proper "object" of faith. False faith places its
> trust in such idols. As Augustine observed, it gives to the
> creature that which belongs alone to the Creator. Thus it be-
> comes a form of self-salvation, denying the need for grace
> from the invisible Origin. Prophetic theology, therefore, re-
> jects the notion that Christian faith can provide sanction for
> a culture-religion.

In recent years the idea of grace has become popular among
religious liberals; many sing "Amazing Grace" with gusto and
some even sport the bumper sticker "Grace Happens." But the theological basis of the idea of grace, divine transcendence, is often
attenuated, becoming a vague spiritual feeling, or totally collapsed
in favor of Humanism. Sometimes, turning Augustine's assertion
on its head, it is even said that liberal religion honors "the creature" rather than "the Creator," but such an oppositional interpretation is unfortunate. In a time when protection of the ecosystem
is imperative, honoring "the creature" can be an important way of
honoring "the Creator," for instance, by seeing sacramental qualities in nature and in human creations. But the distinction Adams
draws within prophetic theology remains important: We do not
(for instance) worship light itself, but we honor light as a gift that

enables us to see and as a symbol of transcendence, of "that by which we see."

Adams calls attention to the ways in which moral righteousness is insufficient to challenge "the principalities and powers" of this world. Demonic powers can be challenged and overthrown only by a greater spiritual power, as mythologies have always told. We should not mistake this as an otherworldly outlook, for it arises precisely from ethical and political engagement in worldly concerns. This line of thought about demonic social evils led the radical Lutheran pastor Christoph Blumhardt to abandon parish ministry for electoral politics. Karl Barth calls him "the theologian of hope." Blumhardt speaks of the necessity of God's being not an abstraction but a living, speaking, laboring, and suffering God, if there is any real work of justice-making to be done in this world. Adams interprets the largely forgotten Blumhardt in contrast to the modern tendency to spiritualize and thus to domesticate faith:

> The kingdom of God comes bringing unrest as well as hope. To the spiritualizers Blumhardt said, "You set up a God without hands, without a mouth, without any feet, so that we can do simply as we like. No thanks, I cannot believe in such a God."

Blumhardt's words echo the Psalms:

> Their idols are silver and gold, the work of men's hands. They have mouths, but they speak not: eyes have they, but they see not: They have ears, but they hear not: noses have they, but they smell not: They have hands, but they handle not: feet have they, but they walk not: neither speak they through their throat. They that make them are like unto them; so is every one that trusteth in them. (Psalm 115:4-8)

The psalm teaches precisely what idolatry is: the worship of objects, ideas, or anything we have ourselves made—things literally deaf and dumb. Being lifeless, idols are incapable of either responding or acting; they are powerless, and the worship of such things renders the devotee spiritually deaf and dumb. The English philosopher Owen Barfield interprets the attack upon idolatry in the Hebrew scriptures—directly expressed in Psalms 115 and 135—as expressions of the historical evolution of human consciousness itself. He relates the "numbing" effect of idolatry to the inability to comprehend parabolic or symbolic forms of expression, reflected also in the New Testament when Jesus speaks about comprehension and incomprehension of parables (see Mark, chapter 4). Barfield's seminal work relates "idolatry" to the modern idea that *all* knowledge or *real* knowledge is scientifically objective and verifiable.

Adams seeks in a similar way to transform modern, liberal consciousness by breaking open naïve, "idolatrous" forms of religious thought, often deploying imaginative rhetorical forms. He undertakes the effort not for the sake of rescuing tradition but for the sake of an enlarged humanism. This is the central point in what the Jewish theologian Martin Buber calls Biblical humanism, that is, Biblical faith as the substance and support of an authentic humanism, as distinct from an anti-theological or secular humanism.

Impersonal, abstract, or static images of God are defective because they suggest definition and delimitation of what is necessarily indefinable and illimitable. Rationalists read personal, concrete, and dynamic images of God as hopelessly mythological rather than as a recognition that God is known, so far as God is known at all, by His/Her effects. Ideas that continue to inform our religious imagination and our moral sensibility follow from this Biblical form of theological reflection. Prime examples are the idea of prophetic calling as a moral directive to act in history and the idea of divine incarnation as the embodiment of God in living beings—ideas that Adams gives renewed currency:

> "They have forsaken me, the fountain of living waters, and hewed out cisterns for themselves, broken cisterns that can hold no water" (Jeremiah 2:13).... In the view of the

prophet Jeremiah, territorial religion—the worship of
Baal—puts its confidence in broken cisterns that can hold
no water....It tries to live from a narrow self-enclosure that
cuts it off from the judging, transforming power of God.
Jesus likewise took up the struggle against territorial reli-
gion. In the face of the pagan city-state the early Christians
appealed to Jesus' words, "Render unto Caesar that which is
Caesar's, and unto God that which is God's" [Mark 12:17].
They asserted that there is an authority higher than that of
Caesar and the territory.

Theirs is not the no-God of the Roman Empire, with its idolatrous apotheosis of Caesar Augustus and the emperors who followed him, nor what Pascal calls "the god of the philosophers," but
rather "the God of Abraham, Isaac, and Jacob."

Worldliness and Otherworldliness

Satan—the representation of moral self-centeredness and spiritual pride—is the symbolic agent of temptation. When we sell our
souls, that is, our devotion and loyalty, to false gods, such as class
supremacy or racial superiority, "there's hell to pay." Adams describes the way Thomas Mann uses the Faust legend to show how
Germany fell under the spell of Adolf Hitler:

We find a telling parable in Thomas Mann's *Doctor Faustus*.
Adrien Leverkuhn, Thomas Mann's Faustus, made a compact with the devil, agreeing that in return for fame as a
composer he would sever the bonds of normal affection and
social responsibility. The outcome was disaster for Adrien
and for his nation: his disease became endemic.

Moralists are good at seeing the motes in others' eyes, less
good at seeing the beams in their own. Adams knows that before
it becomes a moral issue, evil is a spiritual issue. Thus he cannot
simply denounce the evils of another nation, for instance the
German Nazism to which Thomas Mann's rendition of the Faust

legend points. Rather, he must use the German tragedy as occasion to pose to himself the question of selling one's soul. Implicitly he says that we must "go and do likewise"—not point the finger at others without first pointing it at ourselves:

> Let me put it autobiographically and say that in Nazi Germany I soon came to the question, "What is it in my preaching and my political action that would stop this?" Maybe it was an extreme judgment of myself, but I said, "If you have to describe me, you'd say I'm not really involved, for example, in combating anti-Semitism as it is in the United States." It is a liberal *attitude* to say that we keep ourselves informed and read the best papers on these matters, and perhaps join a voluntary association now and then. But to be involved with other people so that it costs and so that one exposes the evils of society—in Boston we're right across the tracks from poverty—requires something like conversion, something more than an attitude. It requires a sense that there's something wrong and I must be different from the way I have been.

A lack of critical distance, an abandonment of intellectual and moral judgment, can be an invitation to the demonic. The principle is similar to the concept of self-differentiation in family systems theory: A healthy social system depends on the leader's ability to stay emotionally in touch with the group but also to be self-defined. The psychologist and rabbi Edwin Friedman applies these ideas to churches and synagogues as "family systems." He emphasizes that because effective leadership is constantly under attack by the insecure and immature members of the group, who seek "fusion" between themselves and the leaders, self-differentiation requires constant, conscious effort. Psychic fusion can be seen as precisely the goal of supposedly "mystical" religions, or religions primarily focused on feelings of well-being. Adams recalls,

> After my three long stretches in Germany, the last two being under Nazism, I was more than uncomfortable when I came

home and went to the summer church conference at Lake
Geneva, in Wisconsin. What do you suppose the worship
service was? After dark we went down into this little cove by
the lake. Somebody had built a log fire. Ideally, the stars were
out. We had a nature service. So darned similar to what was
going on in those "German faith" movements! Friedrich
Schelling said that the great advantage of naturistic categories and certain types of mysticism is that they promote a
sense of unity. Merging with nature, you all feel the same vitality together, and so on. But the built-in defect of this type
of mysticism is that the concept of guilt does not appear. I
think that this is a profound observation. The emphasis on
nature—"We are all one in nature, we have the same blood
and soil"—means that there is no transcendent dimension
to bring judgment.

A liberal church magazine once depicted on its cover a small
white clapboard church with the signboard in front saying, "We
don't do guilt." The slogan is a contemporary version of the
Pharisee's prayer: "Thank God our church is not like other
churches but guilt-free!" The thought is characteristic of the negative identity formation of adolescence. Mature individuals tend
to withdraw from such groups because they are deficiently self-
critical, failing, for instance, to differentiate between real guilt, a
fact of life wherever moral responsibility is taken seriously, and
neurotic guilt feelings.

Evils are tolerated and sustained by the manipulation of symbols of the good and by the human capacity for self-deception;
they can be met and overcome only by authentic power.

The two impolite topics for the dinner table are religion and
politics, for both concern loyalties that are part of a deeply felt
sense of identity. Consequently, both readily inflame feelings
when strong views are expressed, and this is not good for digestion
and *Gemütlichkeit* at the dinner table. But the great prophets, ancient and contemporary—Mohandas Gandhi and Martin Luther

King Jr. are examples—could not have been what they were without combining religion and politics. Christoph Blumhardt is another, as Adams notes:

> The Lutheran pastor Christoph Blumhardt (1842–1919) was the first pastor to join the party of Social Democracy in Germany, and became its representative for six years in the Würtemberg Parliament. As a consequence his ecclesiastical superiors demanded that he renounce all rights and privileges of his vocation. He complied immediately, but not without great pain. Yet he did feel that the church had little contact with social realities and little concern for social justice. "Our Christian concern," he said, "has been spiritualized so much that people have drowned in the spirit." He refused to divide the world into a spiritual and a physical sphere. Moreover, he saw that corruption of spirit could infect and distort all realms of life. This infection and distortion he interpreted to be a demonic "possession." Observing demonic possession in the psychosomatic sphere (in the healing miracles of the Gospels and in contemporary psychopathology) he discerned a kind of demonic possession in society at large, in the family and in economic and political institutions. Even the church in its rigidity and its class orientation he interpreted as possessed by demonic powers; and to the surprise and shock of his fellow-churchmen he saw in atheistic socialism elements closer to the advance of the kingdom of God than were evident in the churches.

Atheism is not, of course, a free ticket to prophetic truth; as a counterculture ideology, it does not distinguish between "culture religion" and authentic faith, faith that maintains a critical distance from the culture. When atheistic doctrine becomes official "truth," promulgated by the state—when it loses all critical distance—it is readily twisted into a tool of oppression rather than of liberation. Adams cites the words of the great Russian composer Aram Khachaturian, who confesses his "crimes" in an issue of the *Information Bulletin of the U.S.S.R.* in the late 1940s:

> Aram Khachaturian wrote: "The roads to error are many. The one which I took...endeavored by artificial means to unite simultaneously the eleven-voiced sound of the wind instruments with the voice of an instrument such as the organ. I went to an extreme, and the result was an unnecessary conglomeration of sounds. Instead of upholding the tradition of Russian music, I followed a formalistic path alien to the Soviet artist." As a consequence of this deviation, Kachaturian says, he was properly censured by "the Soviet people." He concludes his confession with the bending of the knee: "I hope that my future work will give evidence that I have rightly understood the beneficial criticism of my great people." The super-patriots have cracked the whip, and the composer pipes to their tune.

Neither are super-patriots always modern-day nationalists. In connection with the sad story of Khachaturian, Adams cites the story of the prophet Jeremiah, who is accused of "deserting to the Chaldeans" and in consequence suffers abuse, imprisonment, and the destruction of his writings at the hand of Zedekiah the king (Jeremiah 37:13-17). (Perhaps such a prophet to "King Sharon"— as his supporters call him—may yet arise among the Israelis today.) Adams also recalls the attacks on leaders of the dissenting churches in England during the hysteria over the French Revolution, including the Unitarian divines Joseph Priestley and Richard Price:

> Already in 1790 in his attack on the Unitarian Richard Price, Edmund Burke had criticized those churches that permitted the minister even to discuss political and social-ethical issues. He urged that what he called "political theologians" should be discouraged from proclaiming their views from the pulpit. Here are his words, from *Reflections on the Revolution in France*: "Politics and the pulpit are terms that have little

agreement. No sound ought to be heard in the church but the healing voice of Christian charity. The cause of civil liberty and civil government gains as little as that of religion by this confusion of duties. . . . Surely the church is a place where one day's truce ought to be allowed to the dissensions and animosities of mankind." On these principles Burke would prevent the churches from "meddling" with the discussion of human rights.

Far from viewing Burke as a historical villain, Adams elsewhere cites with admiration his words on society as formed by a social contract, the unwritten compact that elicits the loyalty and participation of the people of a civil society by voluntary consent. But no one, not even the esteemed Edmund Burke, lives always on a pedestal, exempt from criticism. The idea that nothing is exempt from criticism is where the prophetic principle and the liberal principle come together in "the gospel according to Adams":

> In our concern for our day-to-day interests and obligations, we find ways to ignore the plight of those who are deprived of full participation in the common life, the plight of those who live in poverty of body or of spirit. This fragmentation of the common life is the fate of living in a segregated society. We live in neighborhoods segregated from other neighborhoods in terms of education, occupation, and income, also separated by class and pigmentation, that is, race. The segregations of sexism cut across all of these boundaries. In a great measure the churches are a function and, indeed, a protection of these segregations. In this situation the middle classes are tempted, indeed almost fated, to adopt the religion of the successful. This religion of the successful amounts to a systematic concealment of, and separation from, reality—a hiding of the plight of those who in one sense or another live across the tracks. In the end this concealment comes from a failure to identify and to enter into combat with what St. Paul called the principalities and the

powers of evil. The religion of the successful turns out, then, to be a sham spirituality, a cultivated blindness, for it tends to reduce itself to personal kindliness and philanthropy costing little. Thus it betrays the world with a kiss. One of his paintings Pieter Brueghel the Elder called *The Blind Leading the Blind* is perhaps a satire on the churches. As has been said, "he penetrated into the vanity of human pretensions." For Brueghel "the religion of the successful" was a symbol of a lost humankind.

If we think this is harsh, consider what Jesus advised "the rich young man"—give it all away!—and what he said after this fortunate fellow "went away sad" (today we would probably say "deeply conflicted"). Jesus comments, "It is easier for a camel to go through the eye of a needle than for a rich man to enter the kingdom of God" (Matthew 19:21-24). Adams's oracle against "the religion of the successful" also calls to mind his summary of a story by Nathaniel Hawthorne—a bluntly pointed parable:

> In his story *Lady Eleanor's Mantle*, Hawthorne deftly set before us the alternatives of responsibility or irresponsibility. An aristocratic lady from the old world disliked to be seen on occasions where the commoners congregated. Lady Eleanor wore a beautiful scarf, a sign of her aristocratic breeding. With his characteristically pungent symbolism Hawthorne presents a commoner who approaches Lady Eleanor and begs that she will drink from a communal chalice in recognition of her identification with the common lot. The Lady declines the offer. A few days after she had refused to drink from the proffered common chalice, an infectious disease broke out in the colony. In the end it was discovered that the initial germ of the disease had been carried by Lady Eleanor's scarf. Willy-nilly she was a part of the total community.

Lady Eleanor, we may say, is insufficiently self-reflective and excessively self-protective, not to mention vain. Where Socrates says, "An unexamined life is not worth living," Adams says, "An unexamined faith is not worth having." There is undoubtedly a tension between the positive resonance we feel in expressions of religious feeling and the emotional distance we feel in expressions of intellectual and ethical critique. Adams indicates a way beyond this impasse. He suggests that the latter, a rigorously examined faith, protects the integrity of the former.

When he was young the family called Adams "Luther" and his father, "Carey." His relationship with his father and namesake, James Carey Adams, was intense and difficult. His father's strict piety demanded separation from worldly influences so resolutely (and not unlike Jesus, we might note) that it produced what to the outsider could seem an insufferable self-righteousness. Still, Adams clearly admires his father for living by his convictions:

> My father was as otherworldly as the head of a family could possibly be. Very often he would tell us after family prayers before retiring at night that we might not see each other again on this earth. Christ might come before morning and we should all meet him in the air. After he joined the Plymouth Brethren he refused on religious principle to vote. He gave up his life insurance policy because he felt it betrayed a lack of faith in God. When he was employed by the American Railway Express Company he refused to join the union on the ground that it was a worldly organization with worldly aims. Indeed he had taken up railway work because of his decision to follow St. Paul's example and refuse to accept wages for preaching the Gospel. In short, my father was a man of principle.

After joining the Plymouth Brethren, Adams's father earned a living from farming, but later, when he became disabled, Adams was forced to drop out of high school to help support the family. In personal terms the story is shocking, for this was the man who tyrannized the family with his ever-narrowing fundamentalism, and yet the son never uttered a word of resentment. Was forgiving his second nature? Shocking also is the father's "principled" rejection of every form of social responsibility that Adams puts at the center of *his* gospel. The irony of a strictly principled sense of responsibility is that, by striving to keep itself free of the stain of this world, it produces a puritanical ethic, a ethic that cares more for its own purity of conscience than for the consequences of its engagement or nonengagement. These issues afflict secular and especially political pursuits as much as religious pursuits. Adams quotes the political scientist T. V. Smith:

> There's nothing quite so dangerous in Congress as a man of principle. You can't talk to him. You can't get some kind of compromise.

Which is to say, he does not exercise power responsibly, with due regard for consequences, nor does he recognize the ideological bias that adheres to his "principles." He is otherworldly.

The Courage to Confront Evil

The central social-ethical issue is the use and the abuse of power. Adams returns frequently to the question of the authentic or creative uses of power. To have the courage to confront evil, he believes, we must be able to affirm and to use responsibly the power that is ours. Authentic power unites good ends and good means:

> The authenticity of power is determined by the ends it serves and the means it uses. The truly powerful are those who serve large purposes and can accomplish them. This kind of fulfillment requires "power with," not "power over"; it requires love.

It also requires social change, or a redistribution of power in society:

> Progress in the authentic use of power has been marked by the inclusion of the marginal people in the systems of power. Just as language is constantly enriched and enlivened from below, so society can be constantly enriched and enlivened by the marginal people with their highly creative potential.

Let us hearken to the Exodus theme as expressed in the black spiritual "Way down in Egypt land,...let my people go!"

Social conflicts and power struggles are not necessarily evil. They can, Adams says, "provide the occasion for the renewing, community-forming power of God to work." So Adams conceives God to be at work even through the tragic conflicts of history:

> Authentic power is a gift to the human being, issuing from response to the divine power. To them who have the power to hear, the saving Word of reconciliation will be given. From them who have not this power, even what they have will be taken away.

He alludes to the words ascribed to Jesus (words that the Gospels associate with the parable of the sower): "For to him who has will more be given, and he will have abundance; and from him who has not, even what he has will be taken away" (Matthew 13:12). The words are nonsensical unless they are understood as a parable of the hidden workings of divine power. So Adams understands the parabolic saying to mean that to some, capable of receiving this power, it is empowering, a blessing; to others, incapable of receiving it, it is disempowering, a curse. In the imagery of another parable, Jesus suggests that some people are incapacitated by the "leaven"—the worldly or self-seeking spirit—that they carry within themselves.

These reflections set the stage for one of Adams's boldest parables, an assertion comprehensible only in the context of a theological sense of history:

> Authentic power is neither poison nor insatiable lust, neither coercion nor corruption born of pride. It is the power that can exhibit the imagination of bold invention, the power that can respond to the ultimate power that shapes new communion with God and new community among men and women. It is in this sense that we venture to make a beatitude: *Blessed are the powerful.* Blessed are the powerful who ac-

knowledge that their power is a gift that imposes ever new responsibilities and offers ever new gifts through costing joys. Blessed are the powerful who acknowledge that authentic power is the capacity to respond to the covenant, the capacity to secure the performance of binding obligations.

"Speaking truth to power" is an exercise of power; truth-telling that effects authentic change takes the forms of courage, commitment, dissent, and self-sacrifice. Being a person of courage is not the same as being a person of principle. Courage requires us to act in accord with one's best understanding of what makes a community just. It means dealing with power as well as with kindness. Although Adams wrote the words that follow for an occasion honoring Professor Alvin Pitcher at the University of Chicago in 1977, his presence was precluded by his wife Margaret's illness at home in Cambridge, so the address was read for him. He writes,

> Al Pitcher has been a creative and dedicated leader in race relations projects in Chicago. Paradoxically, the human relations approach had to be combined with a law and order approach in his work. Speaking of the situation in Hyde Park, an old-timer once said, "It was a schizophrenic experience to live here. There was Jesus Christ walking down one side of the street and Julius Caesar marching along the other." Al Pitcher as a leader walked with faith and fortitude on both sides.

"Speaking truth to power" is a noble ideal but not necessarily a prudent one, and yet friendship and gratitude and courage may rescue us. These meanings are contained in an autobiographical story Adams tells several times, with different accents but always with the same punchline:

> In 1927 in the city of Nuremberg, six years before the National Socialists came to power, I was watching a Sunday parade on the occasion of the annual mass rally of the Nazis. Thousands of youth, as a sign of their vigor and patriotism,

had walked from various parts of Germany to attend the mass meeting of the party. As I watched the parade, which lasted for four hours and which was punctuated by trumpet and drum corps made up of hundreds of Nazis, I asked some people on the sidelines to explain to me the meaning of the swastika, which decorated many of the banners. Before very long I found myself engaged in a heated argument. Suddenly someone seized me from behind and pulled me by the elbows out of the group with which I was arguing. In the firm grip of someone whom I could barely see I was forced through the crowd and propelled down a side street and up into a dead-end alley. As this happened I assure you my palpitation rose quite perceptibly. I was beginning to feel Nazism existentially. At the end of the alley my uninvited host swung me around quickly, and he shouted at me in German, "You fool! Don't you know? In Germany today when you are watching a parade, you either keep your mouth shut, or you get your head bashed in."

I thought he was going to bash it in right there. But then his face changed into a friendly smile and he said, "If you had continued that argument for five minutes longer, those fellows would have beaten you up." "Why did you decide to help me?" I asked. He replied, "I am an anti-Nazi. As I saw you there, getting into trouble, I thought of the times when in New York City as a sailor of the German merchant marine I received wonderful hospitality. And I said to myself, 'Here is your chance to repay that hospitality.' So I grabbed you, and here we are. I am inviting you home for Sunday dinner." This man turned out to be an unemployed worker. His home was a tenement apartment in the slums. To reach it, we climbed three flights up a staircase that was falling apart, and he ushered me into a barren room where his wife and three small children greeted their unexpected American guest in astonishment.

It is also a story of the demonic power of fascism to exact conformity, and a story of foolish courage and courageous comradeship. So a bad situation may be redeemed by acts of courage and friendship, acts having a saving power of their own. Adams enjoyed returning to the punch line, a comment of the costliness of dissent when people are being called to march in lockstep: "In Germany today you keep your mouth shut or you get your head bashed in."

The following story, as extemporized by Adams—I call it "You don't have to bring in your spies!"—touches some of the same themes:

> The man that I knew best in Germany, Peter Brunner, got his degree from Harvard Divinity School the same year that I did, and I had lived with his family there for a while in 1927. I didn't receive any response when I told him that I was coming to Germany again, and I couldn't understand that. He had been teaching theology at the university at Giessen, north of Frankfurt. So when I arrived there I learned he was in Dachau concentration camp. His wife was ill and in the hospital, so I went to that hospital, and there she was. She was somewhat disturbed that I should be there. She said, "Bring your chair close to the bed. We've got to make this very short. You are an American and my husband is accused of being a traitor. This place is full of Nazis, and the nurses get credit if they can tattle or say something. I have to tell you that my husband— *mein Mann*—was sent to the concentration camp because he preached against the Nazis." Now she had to do all this in three and a half minutes. "My husband has connections with the outside and we hear from the grapevine that he will be released from the camp a week from Wednesday." Imagine, the anti-Nazi underground had that good a spy system! "What is the name of your hotel?" "Schmidt," I said. She said, "All right, be back there a week from Wednesday and stay there at ten o'clock every night for three or four nights. If he gets out, he will call you. You are not to talk about anything substantial— just chit chat, the weather. That will be a sign to you that he

will meet you on the edge of the city at eleven o'clock the same night, no matter what the weather." She drew a little map of the place, with the names of all the streets. And she told me what he said to the Nazis when they warned him against speaking out: "You don't have to be uncertain about me. I will be loyal to my ordination vows. And so far as my vows demand, I shall be opposed to totalitarian Nazism. I can tell you right now that I will be preaching that way. So you don't have to send in your spies!"

Adams also tells that Pastor Brunner had been appointed by the Confessing Church to teach at an underground theological seminary in Westphalia and that after their clandestine meeting in Giessen, he agreed that he would see him again there:

> Peter Brunner told me where to find the boarding house for the theological students. It was early spring and I remember wearing a light topcoat. They were expecting me. I hadn't taken off my coat, and was standing in the front hall when one of the students said, "Look! Look! Police are coming!" They were coming up the front walk. A couple of fellows went to a cupboard and grabbed pamphlets. They filled my pockets. I didn't know what was going on, but they filled my coat pockets, my hip pockets, everything, with as many of those pamphlets as they could get in. Before they answered the door they took me off to the kitchen. I said, "What's going on here?" "Well," they said, "these are pamphlets that two young ministers have written against the Nazi persecution of the churches. We think they're coming looking for the pamphlets." We were all palpitating, but one of the students went to the door. They asked about one of the young ministers, and were told he isn't here. "This isn't a very good time to be visiting," they said. "A new visitor here from the United States has just arrived and it won't make a very good impression for his first moment here for us to be visited by the police. He is out in the kitchen—see, there is his suit-

case." Whereupon the police said, "Oh, say nothing about it." The police saluted, "Heil, Hitler," and they were out of the house within a minute.

The source of the courage reflected in these stories can be surmised, but finally it is hidden from view; we must call it a mystery, or perhaps a miracle, insofar as it outstrips normal expectations. How is it possible that a person dispenses with giving first consideration to safety or success and acts instead upon what one affirms as true, right, just? We cannot know with certainty. Adams answers in terms of faith, as a principle that is both critical (because it denies false securities) and creative (because it releases the person from fear).

Here Adams follows Paul Tillich's re-interpretation of Martin Luther's central theological principle, justification by faith, a principle that also gives him the courage to act upon his convictions in a way that has revolutionary consequences:

> Tillich restates Luther's doctrine of "justification by faith alone" in terms of the existentialist concept of the "boundary-situation." He uses this concept to expose the spurious search of the individual for security in terms of his own resources; he applies it also to the church's claim to have something securely in its possession. The individual and the church (and also the culture) must be driven to the "boundary-situation" where every human possibility reaches its limit and where "every secular and religious domain is put in question." According to Tillich the experience of the boundary-situation was for Luther a liberation from false gods, from false securities. Tillich sees here an anticipation of Marx's concept of ideology, that is, ideas or cultural creations which through false consciousness serve to conceal rather than to reveal the social realities (especially class conflict) and which in doing so support the special, hidden "interests" of the adherent. But prophetic criticism (or the experience of the boundary-situation) does not bring merely

a forbidding *No!* It presents a releasing, promising *Yes!* Luther in the experience of justification discovered not only a critical but also a creative power. This is the paradox of justification.

The radical spirit that underlies such reflections has appeared repeatedly in Western history. In the thirteenth century Joachim of Fiore foresaw and called for the "Third Age," an age identified with the Holy Spirit, a new dispensation bringing justice to the poor. In the early sixteenth century Thomas Münzer appeared in Germany during the Peasants' Revolt, a mass movement that was denounced by Martin Luther—ironic as it seems for the radical to turn reactionary—and was violently suppressed by the German princes. Adams comments,

> A revolutionary spirit is contained in the proclamation of a coming, new era, when there will be a new social structure and even a new church and a new art. Of special interest to the Marxist is Thomas Münzer, the most violent of the revolutionaries with his demand that economic transformation must be accomplished by force, indeed that this economic revolution must be achieved first if the religious reformation is to have validity. Here a special place assigned to suffering (depicted in the paintings of Mathias Grünewald) is peculiarly significant.

Adams characterizes Münzer's outlook in a lecture:

> When one suffers, then the Holy Spirit comes in. Revelation appears to us at the point where we realize our limitations, where human nature finds its limits, where God is acting in history. For Münzer grace overcomes nature; the human spirit must be denuded, the Gospel is for "the poor in spirit." Genuine faith is courage for the impossible. It springs from the abyss in one's own heart.

Adams both evokes this revolutionary spirit and explicitly disavows its embrace of violent means. Power that depends on the use or the threat of violence is not "blessed." Still, passive acceptance of—consent to—injustice is also a form of violence, and dissent from social injustice, while producing social conflict, is an authentic and nonviolent exercise of power. Adams affirms in his own words the prophetic thrust of the Radical Reformation: "The tide of the Spirit finds utterance again and again through a minority."

Blessed are the powerful? Those who resort to violent means in response to societal or "official" violence are not themselves "accursed," any more than those who fight in just wars are. The historical struggles of peoples for self-determination and social justice, no less than the concept of just war, are replete with moral ambiguities. To choose and to act for the good, with full awareness of the moral ambiguities of every social-historical situation, is the price of moral responsibility.

Adams reports that Paul Tillich once called Matthias Grünewald's monumental "Crucifixion," in the museum at Colmar, France, with its depiction of Christ's horrible wounds, as "the most religious of all paintings." Its expressionistic depiction of Christ's suffering and intense grief among the onlookers to the Crucifixion confronts the viewer with something horrible; it is not the kind of cross that one could, in Adams's phrase, "smother with lilies." Adams comments,

> Grünewald's Isenheim altarpiece, with its central panel of the Crucifixion, is not a study in naturalistic realism. It is a burning symbolic representation of intense emotional power. In Grünewald's mind it probably was in part a bitter comment on a time that was out of joint. He was apparently close to the peasants' revolts of the region. Perhaps for this reason he was dismissed as a court painter. His compatriot, the sculptor Tilman Riemenschneider, was tortured on the rack for this participation in the rebellion. The Issenheim Altar was completed only shortly before the revolt was condemned by Luther. Tillich spoke of Thomas Münzer, a leader in the revolt, as a "depth sociologist." The suggestion has

been made that the open sores of the Issenheim figure represented, in Grünewald's mystical view, the injustices inflicted by the tyrannical forces of his time. "As you did it to one of the least of these my brethren...."

The concluding allusion is to the New Testament parable of the last judgment (Matthew 25). The prophetic word is simply the word of truth. Truth-telling turns out to be the central act and commitment of prophetic faith. And this penetrates the veil of lies that conceals the truth. In situations in which evil has taken control or no uncompromised voice remains, perhaps no truth at all can be spoken. Then "a time to speak" becomes the opposite, "a time to keep silence" (Ecclesiastes 3:7). At the end of a long evening's colloquy, Adams said,

So I have spoken about "intimacy and ultimacy" and have tried to show that intimacy is to be understood in the social and not merely individual context, to be authentically personal.

Before we came together this evening I recalled a story that joins these two dimensions of existence. In Germany there was a vigorous anti-Nazi, a professor of the Old Testament at Marburg, Professor Balla. He had acquired national notoriety among the Nazis when he translated a passage from Jeremiah, "My people say, 'Heil, Heil,' and they know not what they mean." [See Jeremiah 8:11].

One evening shortly before I went back home some of the faculty at Marburg arranged a farewell party for me. There Professor Balla had a newspaper clipping from London in his hand which he read to me—a report on what the Dean of St. Paul's had told about his experience in Nazi Germany. Among other things he said the British were astonished to hear the people speak of the Fuhrer as "our redeemer." He said there couldn't be anything more blasphemous than that. And Balla, ashamed of what the Nazis were doing, sarcastically complained about it. He held out the clipping and said, "He accepted our hospitality over here, and then he goes home to London, and look what he says about us! Aaah!" A silence fell over the room.

"Well," I said, "I really am stuck. Here's a farewell party for me, and I'm going back now, and the word will come back to you about what I say about Germany. I have accepted hospitality, right here and in plenty of other places. If I go home and—recognizing that I'm indebted to you for your hospitality—say, 'The trains are running on time, things seem to be going very well,' you'll look at each other and say, 'I didn't know he was half as stupid as that!' But on the other hand, if I tell what I have seen, then you'll say I have violated my hospitality! So I have to ask you, what should I say?"

Balla was so excited—he had a wineglass in one hand and the newspaper clipping in the other—and he came across the living room to me with his hand shaking. I said again, "I ask you, What should I say? What should I say, then? I've accepted hospitality here." He shouted back at me, "Say *Nichts! Nichts!*" Belatedly, I recognize that now is the time for me to say *Nichts!* ["Nothing!"]

I have wondered what this flawlessly extemporized story can mean. Adams was in his eighty-seventh year and we the audience could ourselves only "keep silence" when he finished. He did not explain the story, but simply let it serve as a closing to a long evening's conversation among colleagues and friends. I heard it as a story of intimate pain in the face of ultimate horror, of personal agony in the face of the vast, descending night of historical tragedy. I heard it also as a parable of a solitary person's facing into the mystery of existence—as we can only do, and yet are enabled to do—among friends. This is the grace of friendship. Friends are those who, even if they cannot tell each other whole truth, are still bound not to lie. They know that if no true word can be spoken, then nothing at all should be spoken. *Nichts*. At the end of his *Tractatus Logico-Philosophicus* (1922), Ludwig Wittgenstein says, "Whereof one cannot speak, thereon one must remain silent." The statement reflects his "logical mysticism," a recognition that language is always caught up in self-referential "games," with the result that "literal truth" can never be directly spoken, and yet language manifestly produces meaning. In Adams's story of his exchange with Hans Balla, the truth about the political situation in Nazi Germany cannot openly be spoken, and yet in the ironic play of language a moral commitment and a friendship are told.

> *O God, we offer thee our earnest and humble thanks for the gifts of nature and of grace, for the support of every moment and for the joys and strivings of our common life. In thy presence our disguises and pretenses do not avail, and under the light of thy holiness we know ourselves for what we are, stumbling and struggling creatures of vision and of blindness and of perverted vision, of love and of strife. We confess the distressed confusion of our common life, our common guilt, and our common responsibility. Amen.*

—JLA

Confronting Injustice:
By Their Groups Shall You Know Them

"Perpetrate a lie, and then qualify it." According to Adams this is the formula for effective teaching espoused by eminent Shakespearean scholar George Lyman Kittredge. Memorable "lies" of simplification, followed by qualifications and elaborations, are commonplace in Adams's pedagogy. His thought is both astonishingly simple, blunt, uncompromising, and at the same time subtle, qualified, elaborated. He taught as he did because he wanted not only to inform but also to affect. No doubt some of his students were indifferent or took offense, as every powerful teacher finds, but many of his students have attested to the deep effect Adams had on them.

Adams tells the story of a Harvard geologist of an earlier generation, Nathaniel Shaler, who "to the great annoyance of his colleagues on the faculty, persists in objecting to the award of a top scholarship to a certain student" despite his straight-A record:

> Barrett Wendell put the question squarely to Shaler: "Why are you set against this man who has such a superb record?" In reply the tall, red-bearded Scotsman stood up and said, "I am voting against this student because of his cantankerous whatlessness." A liberal arts education is a failure if it develops the ability to think, but still issues in whatlessness, a Laodicean lack of commitment.

Adams is not dispassionate, not detached, and certainly not Laodicean. He is probably best known in academic circles for two seemingly disparate scholarly interests, the interpretation of the thought of Paul Tillich and the study of the nature and role of voluntary associations in contemporary society. But the subjects are connected. Adams is drawn to Tillich not only on account of the theologian's vast erudition and boldly constructive thought but also because he finds in Tillich a thinker who "takes time seriously." That is, Tillich sees that serious philosophical and theological thought must both respond to contemporary history and speak prophetically to its central spiritual issues. Adams's social-ethical thought is likewise a call to responsible action in history, especially through the agency of voluntary associations—groups motivated by a vision of the good society and working to build effective agencies of social action.

Paul Tillich offers a radical reinterpretation of Christian faith. His method of "correlation" interprets affirmations of faith as answers to the central questions of human existence. In this way he has helped many students, such as myself, to rediscover their theological roots and to deepen their sources of spiritual nourishment. A significant reappropriation of faith is not, Adams insists, "for old times' sake." It is for the sake of our ability both to learn to be more fully human and to confront the injustices of our age—both/and! This quest is complex, for it must take into account questions of decision and action at both the personal and the societal levels. In brief, the groups we identify with—the groups we shape even as they shape us—must be taken into account.

A liberal arts education, in Adams's aspiration, would attend to the formation of character, especially in relation to its social dimensions, for instance, vocation and citizenship:

> Dorothy Canfield Fisher used to say that the college degree should perhaps be granted only ten years after the customary graduation day, on the basis of the graduate's perform-

ance as a citizen, as a professional person, and as a parent. This would constitute a severe test for most of us. The suggestion does, however, accentuate the view that the liberal arts education aims to develop the rational powers of men and women, so that they may become responsible in the criticism and the service of worthy and viable ends shared by a community of free men and women. Hence the pertinence of our two tests: *By their roots you shall know them;* and *By their groups you shall know them.*

Adams refers here to Jesus' principle for discerning authentic faith: We cannot judge the faith of another externally or by any formal criteria; rather, "by their fruits you shall know them" (see Matthew 7:20). The principle is also the charter of an ethics of *consequences* as distinct from an ethics of *conscience*, an ethics concerned not only with right *means* but with good *ends* and not only with *motives* but with *outcomes.*

In this chapter, Adams develops his social ethics in terms of the moral imperative to confront injustice, a conception that he identifies with the prophetic traditions of the Bible. To be human, he argues, is to live in relationship, and to be a moral being is to uphold just relationships with others. The prophets of ancient Israel establish a tradition that names a constellation of covenant-sustaining values; this tradition, with its central values of justice, compassion, truth-telling, and peace, continues today in prophetic faith.

Adams argues that the free church tradition, in which the church is a voluntary association independent of state support or control, is the bearer of the prophetic tradition. The rise of voluntary associations in civil society in the modern era, following the free church model, is central to the historical rise and the present-day defense of liberal democracy. When Adams speaks of our "human vocation," he means not only our work or profession but, more fundamentally, the imperative to sustain justice in both the personal and the public spheres of life.

The Moral Imperative

We live under the moral imperative to confront injustice. We must do so not only conscientiously but also effectively, as far as we are able, in the face of the ambiguities of history. Adams notes,

> A century and a half ago William Ellery Channing, on hearing an advocate of the use of the lash in the army, the navy and the prisons, broke forth with, "What? Strike a man?" A long period of time was required to bring this practice more generally into disrepute. An equally long period of time has been required for America to awaken to poverty (and unemployment and racism) as a social problem and as a common responsibility. The late Bishop Francis J. McConnell used to say, "The trouble is not that we don't get mad. It's that we don't stay mad!"

The prophetic voice is a voice of protest. It gives voice to the stung conscience and seeks to sting the conscience of everyone within earshot. Ethical protest is not autonomous but speaks in the name of something held sacred. For Channing the idea that the human being is made in "the image of God" (Genesis 1:27) is the basis of his commitment to the dignity and liberty of every person. Channing declares,

> I have lost no occasion for expressing my deep attachment to liberty in all its forms, civil, political, religious, to liberty of thought, speech and the press, and of giving utterance to my abhorrence of all the forms of oppression.... Christianity has taught me to respect my race, and to reprobate its oppressors. It is because I have learned to regard man under the light of this religion, that I cannot bear to see him treated as a brute, insulted, wronged, enslaved, made to wear a yoke, to tremble before his brother, to serve him as a tool, to hold property and life at his will, to surrender intellect and conscience to the priest, or to seal his lips or belie his thoughts through dread of the civil power.

Adams often calls attention to the way theological ideas shape and motivate ethical commitments; in fact, he understands ethics as an extension of theology. *Theology* he defines in accord with the ancient formula—faith seeking understanding—and *ethics*, he says, "is faith seeking understanding in the realm of moral action." The "two tablets" of the Decalogue—Commandments 1 to 5 in one, Commandments 6 to 10 in the other (Exodus 20:2-17)—have been seen as enumerations of religious and moral commands, respectively; however, the Bible never distinguishes between theology and ethics but treats them as two sides of one coin. The uncertainty about whether to call Adams a religious ethicist or a theologian is rooted in his conflation of these fields, which are probably only sharply distinguished in academia. Adams is not a narrowly focused "academic's academic," but ventures broad-brush and insightful judgments in both realms.

In his discussion of the prophets of ancient Israel, Paul Ricouer speaks of the prophetic sensibility as "hyper-ethical," that is, as seeing ethical violations not merely as the violation of an accepted moral code, and still less as violations of individual conscience, but as attacks on the foundations of a divinely established moral and spiritual order. For example, the prophet Ezekiel speaks of "the covenant of peace" (Ezekiel 34:25); peace is one of the fundamental conditions that constitute Yahweh's sacred covenant with His people. Truth-telling is another. Announcing peace in order to mask or to justify an injustice is not just "unethical," it is "hyper-unethical" in Ricouer's sense. It violates the divine covenant—as Ezekiel and Jeremiah announce, speaking of ancient Jerusalem (Ezekiel 13:10, Jeremiah 6:14), and as professor Hans Balla announces, speaking of Hitler's Berlin. Adams says,

> The Hebrew word for peace, *shalom*, means more than the absence of war. It is a profoundly religious term, used to describe material and spiritual well-being, cognate with heal, healthy, hale, whole. Sometimes God is spoken of as *Shalom*. In Yiddish the word is pronounced *sholem*, and in popular usage means both "hello" and "goodbye." Asked how the

same word may be used for both "hello" and "goodbye," the Israelis have said, "It is because we have so many problems we don't know whether we are going or coming." In the form *shalom aleichem* the term means "peace be with you...."

Shalom, then, possesses a striking breadth and depth of meaning. It signifies the wholeness of authentic human life, God's intention for human being and community. *Shalom* is holistic. Nothing is secular and beyond scrutiny. All is sacred. Just this is contained in the words from Jeremiah, "You have healed the wound of my people lightly, saying, 'Peace, peace,' when there is no peace." The full force of the word *shalom* became electrically alive in the Nazi period in Germany when the common greeting imposed upon the nation was "Heil Hitler." Hans Balla, a Christian professor of Old Testament at Marburg University, paraphrased Jeremiah, "My people say, 'Heil, heil,' and they know not what they mean." The memory of the Jew Jeremiah was still alive, although the Old Testament was no longer read in pro-Nazi churches and photographs of Hitler the Jew-hater were placed on the altars of some churches.

Moral protest begins with holy indignation, a gut-level reaction to a felt violation of what is sacred and good. While ethical reflection regularly begins with a sense of violated conscience, Adams moves insistently from an ethics of conscience to an ethics of consequences. An ethics of conscience readily serves as the basis for a rule-oriented (deontological) ethic, finding justification in right conduct. An ethics of consequences is goal-oriented (teleological), finding justification in good purposes, efficacious action, outcomes.

A third form of ethical thought focuses on character and virtues, a form reflected in Adams's discussions of "identity formation" and vocation. It is also implicit in his reflections on "covenant" and the ethical qualities that uphold moral and spiritual covenants. Covenants join deontological and teleological forms of ethics by fitting moral stipulations to ideal ends; also, individuals enter into covenants as autonomous agents, but not for individualistic or purely self-serving ends. Without denigrating conscience, clearly Adams sees it as susceptible to individualistic and idealistic understandings, inadequate to social-ethical concerns. The American transcendentalist movement, with its emphasis on intuition and inner authority and its denigration of tradition or any outward authority, exemplifies the limitations of this way of thought. Actual human consciences are always socialized, historically located, and educated (or else miseducated).

Neither does Adams believe that all ethics can be rooted in a single rule, such as Kant's categorical imperative—"Act only on that maxim through which you can at the same time will that it should become a universal law"—or its twin, "the golden rule." He can wax indignant at union-busting business executives who liked to say that their whole religion comes down to Jesus' word, "Do unto others as you would have others do unto you" (Matthew 7:12).

Adams's thought is sociological and dialectical. With him, Marxism has made its mark. He is attuned to the inner contradictions of history and of the human heart. History moves forward dialectically, through stages of conflict and resolution. His thought is also metaphorical and parabolic, for it is through analogies and stories that the conflicts of life and their resolutions are given comprehensible form; in the act of dramatizing them, the storyteller becomes an actor, perhaps even a prophet. Stories convey moral import by showing consequences that are implicit human motives and actions; "ultimate ends" are symbolically teleological, for they are implicit in present decision and action, as the oak is implicit in the acorn. According to Adams,

> In order fully to understand any religious movement—and indeed, any secular ideological movement—one must include the answer to the question: What consequences do the ideas held by the group have in the sphere of action? A belief is effective when people are prepared to act in accordance with it. "By their fruits you shall know them."

Adams tells of standing on a speaking platform with Billy Graham and challenging Graham to answer the question: How, after having "given one's life to Jesus," would a person's attitude or actions be changed with respect to, say, the labor movement, or racism, or war? Not surprisingly, no reply is forthcoming. This does not mean that Adams is simplistic in his approach to such complex social issues; it means that he presses, as the criterion of authenticity for any professed religious belief, the moral qualities or commitments that follow from it.

The principle is also a principle of religious tolerance, for it says that there is no way to judge the faith of another person in abstraction from its ethical import. Rather, "you shall know them"—the truly faithful—"by their fruits"—by the righteous, courageous, caring deeds that flow from their lives, their personal and shared commitments, their *faith*. The assertion is validated not by appeal to authority or tradition but by common sense and observation. Without appeal to authority or tradition, but in his characteristically rhetorical mode, Jesus asks an absurd rhetorical question, "Do men gather grapes from thorns, or figs of thistles?" (Matthew 7:16) and draws out its parabolic implication: obviously not.

"By their fruits you shall know them" is a miniature parable, a comparison and an image that shapes what we see and value. It is a principle of discernment, a guideline for decision and action. Substantively, it is also a norm inherent in an ethics of consequences. Adams finds in C. S. Peirce's "pragmatic theory of meaning" another expression of what is, at root, the same idea. To this principle he adds a corollary: "By their *groups* you shall know them." The just can be recognized by their participation in groups—organizations, communities, voluntary associations, churches—that are deliberately engaged in sustaining or perhaps kindling the fires of social justice. Adams likes to say that there is no such thing as a good person, as such; there are only good teachers, good parents, good artists, and so on. The human good, insofar as it is deliberately chosen, is always embodied in a relationship or a social role such as a vocation, a public office, or a familial or employment or community responsibility.

Adams goes on to offer a second and equally memorable corollary to Jesus' principle of discernment:

We know the axiom from the New Testament, "By their fruits shall you know them." Of the believer and of the congregation we may also say, "By their roots shall you know them." They are hidden roots to be sure, but roots that ever give life and newness of life to the faithful, to the transformed and transforming community of faith, which can hear the call of human need. This need is for the community seeking for mercy and justice.

Adams's use of the metaphor "roots" signifies his belief that we should know and draw upon our historical roots as significant contributors to our present identity; however, it seems to mean more than this when he speaks of "hidden roots" as that which feeds the human need that is met in authentic community.

Adams is keen to remind religious liberals—often people who have been uprooted from traditional faiths—of their history and heritage. He traces three great "ages of liberalism": the Radical Reformation of the sixteenth and seventeenth centuries, the Enlightenment era of the eighteenth and nineteenth centuries, and the present postmodern age, an age marked by the twentieth-century failure of the modernist myth of scientific and moral progress. (Those who find this judgment excessively negative must reckon with the fact that the twentieth century is indisputably the most violently deadly and destructive in human history.) To deepen our understanding of religious liberalism, one needs to understand its sources in each of these ages or epochs and the historical progression within religious liberalism that they represent. We need, he says, "epochal thinking," that is, an understanding of history in terms of major stages of development.

The term *roots* has not only historical but also theological reference in the thought of Adams. Roots are the means by which we tap into sources of meaning and strength that are hidden, even from our own rational understanding—hidden, as Paul Tillich might say, in "the ground of being." (Sometimes Tillich turns the metaphor in the opposite direction and speaks of "the God above

God.") This exemplifies the parabolic principle that, aided by an artful story or a wide-reaching metaphor, we may tap into hidden and even sacred meanings.

Whence comes Adams's notion of a God-given moral directive toward a community characterized by mercy and justice? The source of these fundamental commitments—they are at once theological and ethical—is the prophetic tradition of ancient Israel:

> Some of you will remember the story I've told about Erich Fromm. One night I was talking to him until three o'clock in the morning, and I finally said, "I don't know how I'd answer this question...." "Go ahead," he said. So I asked, "Erich, what makes you tick?" "Well," he said, "I think I know what makes me tick. I learned from the Old Testament prophets that the meaning of human existence is the struggle for justice." That's a very interesting notion—the idea that we get a basic drive toward meaning from the prophets' demand for justice.

Martin Luther speaks of the priesthood of all believers. To this radically egalitarian principle Adams adds a correlative principle of his own devising, *the prophethood of all believers.* For this term and insight, I believe James Luther Adams wins a place in religious history, although the concept is not novel. Just as all believers are priests, with a ministry of blessing and healing, they are also prophets, with a ministry of truth-telling and moral commitment, as a story from the book of Numbers perfectly reflects:

> And a young man ran and told Moses, "Eldad and Medad are prophesying in the camp." And Joshua the son of Nun, the minister of Moses, one of his chosen men, said, "My lord Moses, forbid them." But Moses said to him, "Are you jealous for my sake? Would that all the Yahweh's people were prophets, that the Yahweh would put his spirit upon them!" (Numbers 11:27-29)

The story reflects an ancient period of Israelite history, but Adams gives the concept—he names it "radical laicism"—an entirely contemporary meaning:

> A church that does not concern itself with the struggle in history for human decency and justice, a church that does not show concern for the shape of things to come, a church that does not attempt to interpret the signs of the times, is not a prophetic church. We have long held to the idea of the priesthood of all believers, the idea that all believers have direct access to the ultimate resources of the religious life and that every believer has the responsibility of achieving an explicit faith for free persons. As an element of this radical laicism we need also to affirm belief in the prophethood of all believers. The prophetic liberal church is not a church in which the prophetic function is assigned merely to the few. The prophetic liberal church is the church in which persons think and work together to interpret the signs of the times in the light of their faith, to make explicit through discussion the epochal thinking that the times demand. The prophetic liberal church is the church in which all members share in the common responsibility to attempt to foresee the consequences of human behavior (both individual and institutional) with the intention of making history in place of merely being pushed around by it. Only through the prophetism of all believers can we together foresee doom and mend our common ways.

This Adamsean version of the Gospel seems immensely demanding, but certainly not more so than Jesus' own version.

The prophets are certainly not moralists in our sense of the word. Paul Ricouer calls them "hyper-ethical," for they speak not simply of wrongs but of "the people of God" being in conflict with or perhaps indifferent to God's historical-ethical directive. Moralists ask us to see and affirm what is right and then simply to

do it. Prophets see a more radical evil. They see that we are burdened by the weight of past injustices we have both suffered and
inflicted on others. They understand hatred, revenge, deception,
and self-deception. They decry the weight of cultural commitments and social structures that perpetuate terrible injustices.
Adams comments,

> In some quarters in Germany the memory of the Nazi period
> has elicited only rationalizations that aim to explain away the
> evils of Nazism and responsibility for them. In attacking and
> revealing these evasions of responsibility the more healthy-
> minded Germans have asserted that the rationalizations are
> bound to leave Germany corrupt, indeed to make it more
> corrupt. These healthy-minded Germans insist on reminding
> Germany of what they call its "unconquered past," *eine unbe-
> wältigte Vergangenheit.* We Americans, too, have an uncon-
> quered past. But nothing is improved if we only let the walls
> drip with guilt. What we must seek is a new and common
> self-identity that is inclusive and that can be shared, an iden-
> tity that is determined not to leave the past unconquered.
> That unfinished business of American democracy obviously
> calls for the recognition of guilt, but more than that it calls
> for new works that are meet for repentance—in short, for
> new beginnings.
>
>   An oracle of Isaiah is a poem about two peoples, Judah
> and Moab, who had been at strife with each other. Yet in the
> face of catastrophe for Moab, the prophet Isaiah in the name
> of the Lord of history asks Judah to take counsel and grant
> justice. And he points to the promise of the future:

> When the oppressor is no more
> and destruction has ceased—
> and he who tramples under foot
> has vanished from the land,
> then a throne will be established in steadfast love,
> and on it will sit in faithfulness one who judges
> and seeks justice and is swift to do righteousness.

The Prophetic Tradition

The sense of standing under a divinely given moral imperative is rooted in the prophets of ancient Israel and in the prophetic tradition generated by those who honor and preserve their words. What is the ethical content of this imperative? Consider the preceding citation, Isaiah 16:4. Four fundamental values—I call them "covenantal virtues," since they are the commitments that sustain the founding charter and covenantal bond of a human community—are named in this one brief passage: justice, steadfast love, faithfulness, and righteousness. There is no precise enumeration of the covenantal virtues, for the Israelite prophets are anything but systematic. But these four, together with two other frequently named virtues (qualities of moral relationship), truthfulness and peace, are announced repeatedly in the books of the prophets, especially Isaiah, Jeremiah, Ezekiel, Amos, Hosea, Micah, and Joel.

Among Biblical prophets, Elijah, Moses, and Jesus are special cases, as early Christian tradition recognizes in the story of the Transfiguration of Jesus (Matthew 17:3). Elijah, the chief precursor of the "literary prophets," is the prototypical prophet—one who denounces the confluence of cultic devotion and self-aggrandizing royal power. Apparently, Moses, notoriously obscure as a historical figure, was cast in the prophetic mold by later generations. He brings from Mount Sinai "the Ten Words" (Commandments), the text of the original covenant of Israel with Yahweh. Jesus of Nazareth is perhaps best understood as a latter-day prophet, understood by early Christians as a successor to Moses, proclaiming in his Sermon on the Mount a new covenant, and as a successor to Elijah, the prophet who is taken up into heaven in "a chariot of fire" (II Kings 2:11) and who is to return to announce the arrival of the Messianic age. Jesus' eschatological consciousness—a matter of continuous controversy among scholars—radicalizes the prophetic critique of religious tradition; his "new wine" cannot, as his parable says, be put into "old wineskins" (Luke 5:37).

Justice, steadfast love (also called kindness or mercy), faithfulness, truthfulness, righteousness, and peace form a constellation
of prophetic virtues, the moral commitments that create and sustain the covenant, the charter of a good community. They are validated by the quality of social and personal life that flows from
them; in other words they are teleological virtues. They also renew
the covenant when it is broken; indeed, all historical covenants are
in some respects broken covenants. All persons and all communities need "repair" by recommitment to these virtues. They may
imply rules or they may be developed into a legal code, but in
themselves they are not rules or laws imposed by external or
higher authority. Rather, they are constitutive elements of the
covenant as a social and a sacral bond. We may even say that the
covenant could not exist without them.

Charles Hartshorne develops the distinction between "internal" relationships, which are intrinsic, organic, or constitutive (for
instance, the relationship between a body and its members or the
bond between parent and child) and "external" relationships,
which are extrinsic, deliberately chosen, or superimposed.
Internal relations in Hartshorne's sense of the term help us understand the sacred dimension of some (not all) covenants—the
sense that we are changed in fundamental ways by our committed
relationships.

Thus *covenant* is a principle with various historical embodiments, of which Yahweh's covenant with the Jews is, at the historical level, one instance. At the theological level, the covenant with
Yahweh is a definitive parable of the sociological process of
covenanting as experienced in every human community. These
qualities of personal and social life are morally imperative because
covenants cannot be sustained without them. A covenant is at
once societal and sacred. It is a covenant among persons in community, and because the commitment is sacred, it is also a
covenant with God, the third party to our solemn commitments.
Sacredness is an internal relation: That which I cannot violate

without doing violence to my own being, as well as the being of the other, is sacred.

Adams recalls,

> We had an oral tradition at Harvard Divinity School in my youth. You were likely to get one question almost for sure on the final exam—an oral exam. (I sat before thirteen professors for three hours and they all took turns at me, a little peewee sitting down at one end of that long table.) You would surely be asked to define a prophet. According to the oral tradition you could get away with it if you said, "A prophet is one who proclaims doom."

The definition is one of those pedagogical "lies" that needs qualification: The prophetic voice is almost invariably driven by a sense of eschatological crisis, the sense that something is coming to an end and something else is being born. The human task is to discern and descry those transitions, the action of God in history, whether they portend doom or triumph.

George Foote Moore, a professor of the Old Testament during Adams's studies at Harvard Divinity School, accented the overwhelming pessimism of the prophets. We read them so sparingly because they bewilder and depress us. Still, the doom they prophesy is conditional upon repentance, reform, mending our ways, so there are glimmers of hope in their words. In fact, in the eyes of a Biblical faith, no situation is wholly desperate or doomed but, given a change of heart among the people, may find miraculous rescue. Miracles, commonly thought of as events contradicting laws of nature, are comprehensible as parabolic signs of inexplicable benign powers, such as creative freedom, *agape*, forgiveness, grace, and wonder. Walt Whitman finds a myriad of miracles in "a single blade of grass."

Adams is himself popularly dubbed the Smiling Prophet, for he is never abject, moralistically judgmental, or without a sense of humor. If the future can be predicted, even with a margin of error due to our fallibility and life's changeability, then the future is not fated and we have grounds for hope. We and others, even our enemies, can mend our ways. Foreseeing the future (in the qualified sense of seeing the consequences of human actions) remains a central prophetic task. Adams takes up economics and the other social sciences as the handmaidens of religious social ethics in our time. In this vein he cites the social scientist Edward Alsworth Ross: "From the days of Comte our slogan has been *Voir pour prevoir*, See in order to foresee."

The popular idea that a prophet is a clairvoyant or able to foresee the future by divine inspiration is true only in a highly qualified sense. The Biblical prophets have many visions of coming catastrophe and a few visions of a peaceable kingdom of God. Baalam's prognostications are almost clairvoyant curses (Numbers 22-24). Because he is a gentile who prophesies for a fee, Baalam is held deeply suspect in Biblical history. He succumbs to the temptation to manipulate the divine powers for his client, King Balak. Even in his repeated failures to do so—he blesses Israel in spite of himself—he fails morally. To prophesy, even truthfully, for hire and not for heart, or for advantage or anger or revenge and not for authentic love, is perverse. This is why T. S. Eliot's character, Thomas Becket, says, "The last temptation is the greatest treason— / To do the right deed for the wrong reason." He is tempted to court his own martyrdom because he knows that his death will make him famous, and perhaps even a saint. The story of Baalam serves to refine awareness of the difference between sacred and evil prophecy, or as Adams would say, between authentic and spurious prophecy.

The authentic prophet foresees and announces the consequences of the people's evil or faithless doings. Dire consequences are not fated but may be radically altered by a change of heart, whether in the community or in an individual person. In some Biblical stories even God "repents" of his former intention. Thus God's grace and our spiritual freedom enter the picture as theological supposition and moral imperative, respectively. Adams has a way of making difficult propositions such as these plain; he speaks of the priest's ministry of healing and the prophet's liberty of prophesying:

> I call that church free which in covenant with the divine community-forming power brings the individual, even the unacceptable, in a caring, trusting fellowship that protects and nourishes his or her integrity and spiritual freedom. Its goal is the prophethood and the priesthood of all believers, the one for the liberty of prophesying, the other for the ministry of healing. It therefore protests against the infringement of autonomy or participation, whether it be in the church, the state, the family, the daily work (or the lack of it), or in other social spheres.

"The divine community forming power" is Adams's simplest definition of God and his most profound. It locates God's creativity in the formation and the healing of communal relationships and God's judgment in the exclusivity and betrayal of communities.

Because we make promises and, as Auden says, we "cannot keep our promises for long," our covenants are repeatedly (yet not utterly) broken, repeatedly in need of healing and renewal. The contrast of creation/healing and judgment/breaking is further reflected in the typology of priest and prophet—or the priesthood and prophethood "of all believers." Adams dramatizes the contrast by reference to the prophets Amos and Hosea—not, to be sure, by way of close exegesis of their words but by making them into contrasting types in a theological parable.

> Amos is the prophet who says, "You've got to do justice or you're gonna get it in the neck." Amos voices a salutary doctrine, putting the fear of God into some people. But Hosea says, "Look, if that's the whole story, we're all doomed because we've all been involved in injustice." Hosea really rejects the Greek idea of *nemesis*, an idea that is similar to Amos's at this point: "Once violation of the covenant has taken place, then from generation to generation the curse is

on you." Hosea says, "Well, we're all lost then." The creative principle is heard in Hosea. Hosea is asserting that you have to understand the covenant as providing the occasion for new beginnings. If you have only a doctrine of retributive justice, or nemesis, there cannot be new beginnings. There is just constant suffering from violations of the past. Forgiveness means: What has happened in the past—I won't say whatever, for judgment is not ruled out—shall not completely determine the future. You can make a new covenant; you can renew the commitment and you can start again.

In one of his great leaps across intellectual history, Adams comments,

> Hosea is a great anticipator of Henri Bergson and Alfred North Whitehead, and others who have emphasized the idea of novelty in history, the possibility of a new event. In human terms this means that we are not caught in the vise of cause and effect, the past determining the present. It is possible to introduce something new: that is the meaning of forgiveness.

Morally, to be forgiven means to be released from moral obligation or from punishment, that is, to have the negative consequences of one's actions removed. But Adams accents the metaphysical dimension of forgiveness, seeing it as an expression of absolute "novelty," something undetermined by prior causes, a form of creativity.

While commending the idea of forgiveness, Adams also reminds us that this too cannot be made into an invariable rule, a trump card that takes all tricks. Forgiveness must serve the ends of justice:

> I used to say to my classes at Harvard, "I will immediately with great delight give ten dollars to anybody who can come in on a Monday and say "The Lutheran Hour" did not solve all the problems yesterday by saying, 'forgiveness.'" I never

had to spend that ten dollars. The idea of forgiveness, taken alone, is another form of idolatry. Forgiveness has to be related, somehow, to the creative maintenance of justice.

Judgment and forgiveness, like the prophet and the priest, must finally be brought into dynamic relationship with each other. Thus Paul Tillich speaks of "creative justice" as justice that does not seek revenge or retribution but seeks, rather, the healing of the broken bonds of trust in the community. However stated, it is not an either/or but a both/and proposition. Both justice and love must be fulfilled together. According to Adams, prophetic awareness resists premature closure and insists that the tension between justice and love, or justice and peace, must remain so long as injustice remains; it sees, then, a directive in history:

> The prophets in the very name of the divinely given creative and fulfilling powers oppose every bondage that cramps the human spirit. They understand human fellowship to be inextricably bound up with obedience to and inward fellowship with the divine power that is sovereign over all of life. They believe that history is going somewhere and on the way they see persons as responsible under God for the character and direction of their social existence. For the sake of these convictions the prophets devise dramatic means of communication and agitation that anticipate the modern free press and other modern implementations of public opinion. In the Old Testament prophetism our relation to the final resource—to the Lord of history—is intimate and ultimate; and its active thrust is toward corporate life, for salvation is for time and history.

According to T. S. Eliot, "Only through time time is conquered."

Adams bears an interesting—perhaps an ambivalent—relationship to his own religious upbringing. Or perhaps a dialectical relationship: If childhood is the thesis and adolescence is the antithesis, then maturity is the original genius we carry over from childhood, after it has passed through the fire of disillusionment, rejection, and reappropriation. Adams is keenly aware of what he carries from his own past, as well as what he has rejected:

> One of the more vivid recollections of my youth in a funda-
> mentalist group is the memory of their eager interest in the
> prophecies of the Bible. These prophecies were believed to
> encompass almost the entire range of human history. One
> all-embracing "prophetic" image that looms in my mind is
> that of an immense chart that adorned the wall of the church
> auditorium. It depicted the pivotal events of creation and re-
> demption, beginning with the original chaos and proceeding
> through the six days of creation, the first day of rest, the fall,
> the various dispensations of Old Testament history on down
> to the annunciation, the incarnation, the crucifixion, and the
> resurrection and thence on to the Second Coming of Christ,
> the Battle of Armageddon, the seven years of tribulation, the
> thousand-year reign of Christ, the chaining of Satan in hell,
> the last judgment before the great white throne, and the eter-
> nal peace and unquiet of the respective final destinations of
> all human souls. In short, the epochs of "salvation history"
> were set forth as "by prophet bards foretold."

Modern secularism sets aside any such scheme of "salvation history" as naïve and replaces it with either the myth of material and scientific progress or with nothing. But clearly the idea made a lasting impression on Adams and underlies his passion for social justice.

The elaborate scheme informs the child Adams that history is a vast parable; a sacred history is woven through it, without which the course of human events is truly meaningless. He learns that the cosmic sweep of time has a meaning and he has a place in it. He learns what we must do to be saved from oblivion, the fire and ice of Love's negation. As he matures, he learns that the meaning of history is found in terms of its ages or epochs. He comes to see that there is a pattern among these epochs, on the basis of which prophetic foresight—social ethical vision—is exercised. To be sure, he rejects the idea of reading Biblical "prophecies" as keys to unlock the esoteric mysteries of present and future. He keeps the idea that all persons of authentic faith share in the prophetic vocation of speaking out against injustice and calling for renewed commitment to justice—a universal justice that will be tested in concrete, historical terms. Adams cites Martin Luther King Jr.: "Nonviolence, the answer to the Negroes' need, may become the answer to the most desperate need of humanity," and comments,

> For us in the United States the question is whether or not the coming years will bring a rebirth of American society—the Second American Revolution. The litmus test will be what happens in the relations between whites and blacks, and between "the haves" and "the have-nots."

Once I suggested to a professional religious educator that our children should know something about the great Biblical prophets. Not a great deal, just something. She said brightly that she thought it more important for them to know about contemporary prophets like Martin Luther King Jr. Exasperated, I said, "Well, the name of Mount Nebo—where Moses espied the Promised Land in the distance—may mean nothing to them. But if they have never even heard the story of Moses, what on earth will they make of King's 'I have a dream' speech, where he says, 'I've been to the mountaintop'? He is saying that he, too, from his own Mount Nebo, has seen the promised land, and that he, like Moses, will not live to cross over to it. But all this will be lost on them in their Biblical illiteracy!" Her blank response suggested I was speaking of something arcane and irrelevant, not (as I viewed it) of the very heart of our sacred tradition.

Martin Luther King Jr.'s persuasive power lay, in large part, in his ability to speak our culture's language of sacred history and be profoundly understood; but it is not clear that young people today would understand and be moved. Douglass Coupland, who names his generational cohort Generation X, comments incisively, "Ours is the first generation raised without religion." This, too, is a "lie" that must be qualified, but the truth it contains is immense. Coupland does not mean that his generation grew up without spiritual feelings and ideas, for these spring up as spontaneously as weeds. It means, rather, that they have been raised without the religious roots that provide a vocabulary and a sense of being part of a sacred tradition, something that alone provides nourishment and depth in times of spiritual drought.

Moses is the archetypal prophet; his brother, Aaron, is the archetypal priest. Adams elaborates this ancient typology. The prophet decries the divine absence, in a world that is broken and defiled; the priest celebrates the divine presence, in the sacramental elements of the liturgy, the healing "work of the people." But these simple oppositions are dialectically related in Adams's view:

> The prophet appeals to a covenant which is above both the sacramental and the prophetic. The authentically sacramental element, then, contains a prophetic demand. Consequently, the inauthentic attitude appears when one hears some say gushingly, "I just love the liturgy."

Adams recalls the following story:

> A few years ago I discovered a letter from Karl Marx to one of his friends complaining about his wife and daughter putting on their Sunday-go-to-meeting clothes to go off to a Methodist chapel. He said, "I've tried to be tolerant with them, but I really had an outburst last Sunday. I thundered, 'If you are so damned much interested in religion, why don't you stay home and read the Old Testament prophets? Then you'll see what it's all about!'"

Karl Marx is keenly interested in the future and believes that it will unfold dialectically through the class conflicts engendered in ages past. That he allows no place for a transcendent dimension in his thought is a serious defect—considering the emergence of Marxism as a key historical force in the twentieth century—with vast and tragic consequences for world history. Marx as "scientific socialist" is a creature of his age and fails to rise above it. Still, he is an authentic prophet in that he decries the reactionary effects of religion—"the opiate of the masses"—and of a capitalism and an imperialism that oppress and exploit the masses. He is Biblical in spite of himself, Adams suggests, in a way that the hyper-Christian Søren Kierkegaard is not:

> One does have to make qualifications, but it seems to me that, in the main, the name of Søren Kierkegaard in the last fifty years in Protestantism actually has come to symbolize the loss of orientation to the God of the Bible, the God who is the Lord of history and who holds Christians responsible for the character of their society. Kierkegaard's exclusive emphasis on the individual directly before God, without reference to the political symbolism of the Bible, has made it possible to reduce the majesty of God, and the demands of God upon us, and to reduce our conception of responsibility.

In another context Adams pairs Kierkegaard and Marx as "the yogi and the commissar," respectively, each "lopsided" and, while brilliant and vastly influential, not in themselves wholly reliable spiritual or intellectual guides.

Adams distinguishes an authentic from a false prophet by several criteria, articulated in various contexts. An authentic prophet, he says, is not so much concerned with comforting people as with calling them "to make some new sacrifices"; an authentic prophet is not on the payroll of the king or other powers that be; an authentic prophet is not self-proclaimed but is recognized and celebrated by the people; and an authentic prophet is likely to be in trouble with the authorities. I recall Adams telling a story to illustrate the last of these criteria. He said that a brief news item that appeared in a London newspaper during the period of the English colonial domination of India: "A new mahatma has appeared in the Ganges Valley. The police are after him."

Our typical image of a prophet or a *mahatma* is of a solitary individual. And yet the concept is a social construct, developed within a culture over a long period of time and rendering the individual visible and powerful—"by their roots shall you know them." Adams says,

> A kind of institutionalization of the concept [of a prophet] had to take place. You have Amos declaring, "I am not a prophet or a son of a prophet, but....." You see, something is getting defined there.
>
> An analogous thing can be said regarding the concept of a mahatma. Isn't that a striking idea! There comes a time in history when a special figure appears, and then somebody says, "Ah, a mahatma!" The person fits a form that has been culturally created over centuries.

An authentic prophet is independent of established authorities and at the same time committed and responsive to the fundamental and sacred charter of the community. Adams refers to this as a nascent form of the idea of the separation of powers, or of the separation of church and state. Authentic prophets are not court prophets, soothsayers attached to the king, but precisely those who call the king to account in the name of the covenant both as a voluntary social contract and as a sacred testament given in love by God:

> The prophets of Babylon were on expense accounts, but the prophets of Israel were not. They had "no place to lay their head." I saw in the Old Testament prophets the voluntary principle working in a twofold way. On the one side, they appealed to the broader covenant of Israel; on the other side, they developed the capacity to organize schools of the prophets, and the concept of the role of the prophet.

On account of Adams's political activities in Chicago in the 1930s and 1940s, the right-wing *Chicago Tribune* sought to smear him as a fellow traveler of the Communists. He tells with considerable relish of a certain *Tribune* reporter who was assigned to cover his public speeches:

The reporter would come to talk to me after I made a speech and say complimentary things. But the next day in the paper I was presented as an ass, a bumbler in politics. So one evening I asked him, "Why are you doing this to me? You tell me my speeches are pretty good and then I pick up the paper and you present me as a first-class fool. How come?" "That's my job," he said. "I'm just doing my assignment. I'm to follow you around and write you up in this way." So I said to him, "I'd just like to know, what's the difference between you and a whore?" "Well," he said, "we have a good vacation policy and fringe benefits and insurance." He listed that sort of thing. "Oh, I see," I said, "you're not a whore. You're just a very well-paid prostitute!"

In another context Adams comments,

The Hebrew prophets condemned as false prophets those who simply served the king. The singularity of the Hebrew conception of the liberty of prophesying—a separation of powers—must be understood in terms of the historical context of the time.

The king represents the powers that be, the powers in any age, nation, or institution that go unquestioned because they hold supreme power. The prophet represents and speaks for a transcendent principle to which even kings and college presidents are accountable, a principle that Adams names "the liberty of prophesying." He writes,

David Rhys Williams, who graduated from Harvard Divinity School in 1914, felt that much that went on in the school was irrelevant to the tasks of the minister and the needs of the churches. No doubt mindful of his father's experience in the mill town controversy in Huntsburg, Ohio, and of his mother's even greater concern for social justice, he as a socialist had gone to Lowell, Massachusetts, to observe the strike of the textile workers. There he had seen a mounted policeman who, with murderous intent, had caused his horse to trample on one of the striking women, and he had seen her lie in the street in blood. Being shocked by what he witnessed, he was determined to exercise the liberty of prophesying during the graduation ceremony. Never timid, Williams after the speeches were concluded arose and approached the podium. The faculty member in charge gestured for him to return to his seat, but instead of acquiescing he beckoned for the faculty member to take *his* seat. The president of the university, Charles William Eliot, was on the platform, and it is said that he gave a welcoming gesture. With the eloquence for which he was later to become noted, Williams asserted that theological education at Harvard fell short if it did not show concern for social justice. If the study of the Old and the New Testaments did not induce the faculty and the students to do something in the face of the cruelty to the workers in Lowell, then they had not understood Amos and the prophets and Jesus.

Adams, who delights in this scene, sees Jesus as one "who has no place to lay his head," one harried like the destitute poor with whom he lives and for whom he speaks. Of him John the Baptist declares, as it were, "Ah, a messiah!" With him, disciples form a "school," preserving his words and carrying forward his mission. The number of disciples, twelve, is an idealization of a group that some scholars now believe included a band of men, women, and children, impossible to number. Adams says that the early Christian church is one of the great historical examples of a voluntary association.

Jesus may seem to us an apolitical figure, until we reflect that in his name Caesar is challenged and his empire transformed. "Render unto Caesar the things that are Caesar's; and unto God the things that are God's" (Matthew 22:21) is not an accommodative but a subversive formula, for it denies the worship that the Roman emperors, beginning with Augustus, demanded. Jesus introduces by parable and example the principle that underlies the continuing transformation of the social order, the principle that the apostle Paul and William Ellery Channing call "spiritual freedom."

Adams traces the democratic conception of the separation of powers and the separation of church and state to early Christianity:

> In this separation of powers the early Christians broke not only with Rome but also with the theocratic conception of the Jewish state. More than that, they broke the connection between religion and ethnic heritage; they also broke the bond between religion and family, in the sense that the individual might join the church independent of the family. Yet no one of these institutions of the world was in their view consigned to "outer darkness." In accord with their eschatological orientation, they held that with the fulfillment of the kingdom of God, when God will be "all in all," social institutions as well as individuals (and even nature) will be redeemed. Hence the message of the prophets was confirmed. According to Father George Tyrrell, the Christian eschatology moved from immediate pessimism to ultimate optimism. The divisions of power were to be overcome through the power of God. Hope became an evangelical virtue. . . .
>
> Alfred North Whitehead, commenting on the admonition of Jesus about rendering unto Caesar that which is Caesar's and to God that which is God's, was wont to say that "however limited may be the original intention of the saying, very quickly God was conceived as a principle of organization in complete disjunction from Caesar." This principle of organization had shocking consequences, because it meant that not everything belonged to Caesar. Here we observe a claim analogous to that of the prophets: the early Christian church assumed the status of an intermediary between the transcendent and the individual.

Just this is also the basis of a doctrine of the church—the church as a mediating, connecting, symbol-forming institution, between the

ultimate and the intimate, between the transcendent and the individual. The "free church" tradition sorely needs a doctrine of the
church going beyond the notion of "an aggregate of like-minded individuals." It needs a functional and theological conception in which
the religious congregation is recognized as a provisional structure,
not an end in itself—a structure that serves ends beyond itself and is
a constituent member of the community of faith of all peoples in all
ages, sometimes called the church universal. Adams declares,

> I call that church free which is not imprisoned in itself or in a
> sect. In loyalty to its own historic character and norms, it is
> open to insight and conscience from every source. The church
> that would be free yearns to belong to the church universal,
> catholic and invisible.

Liberals may feel difficulty with Adams's affirmation of the church
as "catholic," even if they understand that by "invisible," he means a
community that is not embodied in any particular historical institution. However, neglect of the idea of "the church universal" has
had the unfortunate effect of giving the impression that particular
churches and denominations are not spiritually united to others in
something much larger than any one group. Since the common
translation of *catholic* as "universal" may seem to retain an imperi-
alistic connotation, an alternative translation may help, namely
"comprehensive." Taken etymologically, *catholic* joins *cat-*, meaning
"by or in accordance with," and *-holic*, meaning "the whole." We
might say, then, "I believe in the church comprehensive, the church
of the whole, by the whole, for the whole."

The Institutionalization of Prophetic Faith

As against individualism, whether of libertarian or anarchistic
stripe, Adams preaches a gospel of social institutions:

> Miguel de Unamuno, the Spanish philosopher, poet, and
> novelist, tells of a conversation he had with a young philo-
> sophical anarchist, not the kind carrying bombs but one be-

lieving in radical individualism, in going his own way, or as we say today, "doing his own thing." The young man said, "I am an individualist. I never ride in a car if I can help it. I ride on a bicycle so that I may go my own way." Unamuno responded, "I suppose, then, that you do not ride your bicycle on the road. You pedal across field and hill avoiding every path where anyone else has ever been. And, by the way, who made your bicycle? Did you make it? And if so, where did you get the parts?" In this fashion Unamuno dissolved this fellow's claim to be a radical individualist.

The prophetic tradition finds continuing institutional expression in the traditions of the free church and liberal democracy. The two arose together and will, Adams holds, either fall or be renewed together:

> Social scientists have been studying...how long it takes a group of fowl to form a social organization. As I recall the findings, only eighteen to twenty-four hours elapse before a group of chickens hitherto unacquainted with each other form a tightly structured social organization, a flock.
>
> The social organization turns out to be a rigid hierarchy. At the top is one chief hen who by dint of pecking the other hens has established her prestige: she is able to peck any other hen and none other dares peck back. Immediately beneath her in pecking rank will be three or four hens who are second in command; they have established their power and "right" to peck all the other hens in the yard except Number One. And then gradually the hierarchy broadens out to *hoi polloi*, the common hens, who may be pecked by any of the hens in the higher echelons but may not peck back. Food and other privileges become accessible in accord with these rankings. This hierarchy is called a "pecking order." Liberal Christianity...began in the modern world as a protest against ecclesiastical and political pecking orders. Protest in the economic sphere also soon appeared.

Adams here alludes to criticisms by liberal Christians and Unitarians of the economic pecking order resulting from the *laissez faire* capitalism of early nineteenth-century America. In the essay "God and Economics" he cites examples, including the utopian experiments such as Brook Farm and the words of William Ellery Channing, his nephew William Henry Channing, the music critic John S. Dwight, and the education reformer Horace Mann. Mann writes,

> Wealth, by force of unjust laws and institutions, is filched from the producer and gathered in vast masses, to give power and luxury and aggrandizement to a few. Of production there is no end; of distribution, there is no beginning.

Adams's broad-brush interpretations of intellectual history are undergirded by erudition and insight:

> One of the principal sources of liberal Christianity is...the left wing of the Reformation...a composite movement that in part originated as a protest against the authoritarian organization of the churches that were ruled from the top down. Another source is the Enlightenment, with its demand for individual, rational self-determination. (Subsequently, Romanticism emphasized individualism still more, and uncovered something deeper than reason—intuition and feeling.)

The winds of doctrine do not blow all in the same direction, as Adams makes clear. The fate of liberalism, if it only runs after ever-purer expressions of individualism, is dissolution. The right to freedom of association and the will to form public-regarding voluntary associations are essential to the maintenance of freedom in a society. According to Adams,

> The history of effective freedom in the West is the history of the organization of freedom. Effective freedom requires freedom of association. To be sure, if such freedom is not to issue in anarchism, there must be an overarching loyalty or covenant under the roof of which freedom of association is exercised.

Freedom of association is the hallmark of democracy. For instance, when Communist regimes loosened restrictions on freedom of speech and still restricted unofficial organizations, that was a positive step, Adams says, but it was hardly enough to qualify the system as a full democracy.

All Adams's students can recall him quoting the seventeenth-century political philosopher Thomas Hobbes to the effect that voluntary associations are "worms in the entrails of the sovereign." Then he would add, "And what do you do with worms? Growing up on the farm I learned about these things. You worm them." But the farm boy had also been to college, and in his published version, he recognizes that Hobbes does not refer directly to the sovereign (the king), but to "the natural man," that is, human nature. So he is speaking philosophically, not politically, unless we say that a professed philosophical idea often masks a political ideology. Adams says,

> Hobbes the totalitarian warns against "the great number of corporations which are as it were many lesser commonwealths in the body of the greater, like worms in the entrails of a natural man." The late Senator Joseph McCarthy worked in the spirit of Hobbes when he tried to smother freedom of association.

According to Adams, "James I of England had predicted: 'Today they are attacking the bishops, tomorrow they will be attacking me.' His prediction was correct." The rise in the demand for democratic freedoms followed upon the rising demand for religious liberty. Democracy in turn furthered the principles of the separation of church and state and the rights of dissent, or nonconformity. Adams is interested in the religious roots of this complex of ideas and in the continuing responsibility of religious communities—the free churches above all—to sustain these traditions. He cites the case of the eminent English jurist, Sir Edward Coke, who protested to King James I:

> The King "cannot properly take any cause out of any courts and give judgment upon it himself." On another occasion,

Sir Edward confounded and offended the King by citing Bracton, saying "that the King should not be under man, but under God and the Laws." Sir Edward reports that on this occasion the King "fell into that high indignation as the like was never known in him, looking and speaking fiercely with bended fist, offering to strike him. Which the Lord Coke perceiving fell flat on all four."

Sir Edward continued to defy the King and in consequence suffered imprisonment in the Tower of London. Adams concludes the story with words from the book of Numbers, evidence of a dissenting tradition within the Bible itself: " 'Notwithstanding, the sons of Korah did not die.' The Boston Tea Party and the Declaration of Independence were of their doing." Thus several historical moments cohere, in Adams's view. He tells the story:

> In the Old Testament we find an account of one of the first protest marches in history, following upon the freedom march that took the children of Israel out of Egypt and across the Red Sea. But now the protest is not against Pharaoh, it is against Moses and Aaron. Korah and his colleagues, spokesmen of the protest march, say to Moses and Aaron, "You have gone too far! You take too much upon you, seeing all the congregation are holy, every one of them, and the Lord is among them. Why then do you exalt yourselves above the assembly of the Lord?" (Numbers 16)

The story ends badly for Korah and his associates, who together with their families and possessions are swallowed up by a great crack that suddenly opens in the earth. Adams notes that Korah's protest march is a demand for recognition of "the prophethood of all believers."

Once I spoke to a clergy group about Adams's call for recognition of "the prophethood of all believers," and cited the story from Numbers, in which Moses says, "Would that all the Lord's people were prophets." Rabbi Marvin Bash commented, "Yes, but there's also the story of Korah." Which goes to show that, in its main lines, Hebrew scriptural history was also written by the victors—the party of Moses and Aaron, not the party of Korah and his rabble. Nevertheless, remarkably, Korah's protest was not forgotten. Several chapters later a reminder that even a violent act of divine retribution does not settle the matter was preserved in the ancient record, as Adams reminds us: "Nevertheless, the sons of Korah did not die." Dissent often takes the form of truth-telling in the face of the "official account." Adams comments,

> The history of Judaism is the history of a great variety of interpretations. Harry Wolfson at Harvard, probably the most learned Jew on this continent, used to stress the point, saying, "We Jews are always proud that when a decision was made by the rabbis, the dissenting opinion had to be recorded." In the long history of Judaism you find that repeatedly the dissenting opinion of one century becomes the majority opinion of another.

Paradoxically, the very sovereignty of the scripture in Jewish understanding becomes the basis for the free play of thought and commitment. It is recognized that every learned reader, every rabbi, can offer an interpretation of the sacred text. Law and tradition, then, are not the enemies but the friends of freedom. Adams says,

> The demand for a rule of law to bring tyranny into account is what John Milton and other radical Protestants of the seventeenth century called "the Good Old Cause." They said that the cause was "*good* because it hath a tendency to the securing of people's just rights, liberties, properties, privileges and immunities against tyranny, arbitrariness, and oppression, and *old* because anciently and originally all power was in the people" (*The Good Old Cause Explained*, 1659). By this Good Old Cause kings and bishops and super-patriots were brought to book.

On church and state issues Adams is a staunch separationist, in keeping with his membership and sometime leadership in the

American Civil Liberties Union. He adopts the maxim that Robert Frost takes from his neighbor, "Good fences make good neighbors," to reinforce the point that formal separation helps both church and state to maintain their integrity.

A caveat should be entered at this point. Some argue that "the separation of church and state" means that religious bodies should be legally barred from seeking to influence public policy. Nothing could be further from Adams's intent. The maxim, "Good fences make good neighbors," is usually cited as Frost's own, but in the famous poem, "Mending Wall," it is Frost's *neighbor* who voices it as abysmal wisdom passed down from his father. Frost's language in the poem indicates that he considers it a kind of "stone age truth"; the fuller truth, that Adams would also affirm, Frost states in the first line of the poem: "Something there is that does not love a wall."

Adams argues that by seeking an amendment to the U. S. Constitution to allow prayer in public schools, President Ronald Reagan took a long step backward:

> Defending his proposal the President has said that ancient Greece and Rome declined when they began to abandon their gods, and the Supreme Court's ban on organized school prayer for the past two decades has "diminished the importance of religion and morality." He of course did not call for the recovery of belief in the gods of ancient Greece and Rome. But he is calling for the revival of a compulsory feature of the authoritarian government of the Roman Emperor Constantine in the fourth century. In this policy the magistrate with the support of the church had the right and the duty to maintain the faith and to wield the secular arm on behalf of God and country. This practice obtained for almost 1,500 years.

A corollary of religious liberty is voluntary financial support. The idea of the churches having to "make do" without state support shocked Adams's church friends in Germany, since they could not conceive the survival of the church without it. (A compromise system now obtains there, in which the state acts as tax collector for the church or other religious group of your choice, or no group. We should also recall that religious groups in the United States enjoy large benefits under the tax system.) Adams says,

> From the seventeenth century on, the free churches rejected any financial support from the state. I've always said that the collection plate at that time became a sacrament. The passing of the collection plate was viewed as a symbolic statement: "It is our show. We run it. We don't want anybody to pay for it who isn't in it. We pay for it." We should remind our congregations again and again that the collection plate is a symbol of our saying: We do not want to coerce other people to pay taxes for this church. We only want the people who believe in it to pay for it.

But are we willing to pay for it? Sometimes we adopt the rationale toward our churches that Governor George Talmadge of Georgia used to justify low salaries for teachers; he said, "Keep 'em poor, keep 'em honest." In some religious groups the members do not tax themselves heavily in order to keep the group relatively marginal and impotent; power may seem too risky or demanding. Adams recalls,

> A friend of mine said that he had been told that a political scientist was going to give an address at a church conference on the subject, "The Challenge of the Church to the Modern State." In response the political scientist said sarcastically, "I do not think the church could challenge even a rabbit."

The primary sources of the weakening of religion are the privatization of religion, resulting in the elimination of the associational and public dimensions of faith, and the closely related effort by secularists to remove all expressions of religion from public life, sometimes even including "social action" by religious groups. Adams often speaks against these ideas:

> One of the major ways in which the devil works in history is this. If he can only persuade us that the important thing in religion is personal relations. "Well," the sermon goes, "when I was a young man there was a great deal of talk about the social gospel, but the older I grow...." Let me give you the intonation, "*But the older I grow* the more I realize it doesn't make any difference the kind of economic and political institutions you have. I realize that what we need is men of character." The most reactionary people, the people with the tightest hearts down in the pews—oh, how they snuggle up to those sermons!

In consequence the churches suffer a credibility gap. Serious people do not take them seriously. In 1964, during the struggle of the Civil Rights movement, Adams comments on the judgment rendered by a young black man from a deeply religious home who comes to believe he is wasting his time with doctoral studies in theology, when the church itself does not take seriously its Biblically rooted moral commitments:

> Primarily as a consequence of what I have learned from my students, my Negro students, I have to say that I think most of us white people are about a hundred years behind the times. We do not appreciate what the term white even symbolizes for blacks. One of my students, a very gifted doctoral student, has now left Harvard Divinity School. When you ask him why he says, "The Protestant churches simply don't mean it. They have these mealy-mouthed generalizations about love. I would like to have a spoonful of justice. I wish they would stop talking about love and just give me a spoonful of justice." Here is a man who says "I am leaving the church and I don't want a theological degree, and I am going into the study of Africa."

Adams often says, "The road to hell is paved with good attitudes. They require institutional embodiment." In his *Letters and Papers from Prison* Dietrich Bonhoeffer observes that the most common source of our moral failings "is not our wickedness but our weakness." It is our lack of what Bonhoeffer calls "costing commitment"—being unwilling to pay a price for our supposed commitments—that undermines our good intentions. If those committed to democracy are inclined to dismiss lone, dissenting, and abrasive voices, it may be because they have forgotten where they came from. Adams reminds us:

> Modern democracy was born in the seventeenth century in England when the left wing Puritans attacked the centralized power of the monarchy, in conjunction with the state church. It began as an economic and political struggle to disperse power. Thus they formed small churches, emphasizing that every member has the responsibility to participate in the policies of the organization. Another thing that was remarkable—and you see this especially among the Quakers— was the idea that these small groups have a responsibility to protect the minority view. Indeed you'll find words to the effect: "If the Holy Spirit is going to speak to us, probably it will speak *against* the majority. So we are bound by covenant not only to protect but also to listen to the minority."

The Quakers, being sensitive to the minority ("a majority of one," Henry David Thoreau calls it), developed the principle of group action by "the sense of the meeting," or consensus. In practice this means that one person may sometimes stymie action by the whole group. Adams relates that he once asked a group of Quakers how they dealt with obstinate members who had, in effect, veto power over the group. They said that, well, after discussion had run an hour or so and one fellow would not budge, they would suggest that he go out for a cup of coffee. He would oblige, and once he had left the room the group achieved their consensus! So "honoring the minority" or even "the lone" voice is a two-way street: The group needs to hear the minority voice and the minority voice needs to hear the group. Adams says,

> Our liberal forebears were upstarts, rebels against established authority in the name of a new conception of authority. Colonel Rainsborough of the Cromwellian army defended this rebellion saying, "Every English, he hath his own contribution to make." The demand for a democratic constitution, the demand for separation of church and state, the demand for respect of the minority and of a loyal opposition, the demand for the extension of suffrage, the demand for a pluralistic education—all of these innovations were initiated or carried through by "outsiders."

Voluntary Associations

Adams sees society as a community of associations, both nonvoluntary (the family, the state) and voluntary. Together these constitute what he calls "the principal social spaces." He says in an interview,

> In a totalitarian society the spaces of voluntary associations are eliminated. The democratic, pluralistic society is precisely the society in which voluntary associations exist and overlap. Through them the citizen may pursue a great variety of interests. Moreover, the voluntary associations may attempt to exercise influence upon the non-voluntary associations—and vice versa. But none of these associations may be considered ultimate. All of them are expressions of a larger, embracing community—or "space"—and in principle they are accountable to that community. In democratic theory this means, for example, that the state is the creature and not the creator of the community. The community— "we the people," functioning through the political order— delegates certain functions to the state, and these functions are subject to change under law.

Voluntary associations have a special role in the history of liberalism, both religious and political. In particular, they link the ethical convictions of liberal faith and the social commitments of liberal democracy.

In 1927 Adams invited Samuel McChord Crothers, a widely read essayist who for more than thirty years ministered in the First Parish Church of Cambridge, to preach at his ordination in Salem. A simple idea, clearly enunciated, can gain lasting resonance and become a principle:

> One of the reasons I invited Dr. Crothers was because of his idea, which he memorably expressed again in the ordination sermon: "There is no social problem that is not also a personal problem, and no personal problem that is not also a social problem."

The individual and the institution, the person and the community, are always bound together in Adams's thought. The prophets of ancient Israel speak and act as solitary individuals— Jeremiah has his Baruch, but no other example of collaboration comes to mind—yet without devoted followers and friends their words would not be preserved and passed down. Adams is interested not only in prophetic individuals but also in the institutionalization of the prophetic function in the churches and in voluntary associations concerned with public policy:

> I have often told of the experience in Germany when a man— an anti-Nazi—warned me, "In Germany today [1927] you either keep your mouth shut or you get your head bashed in." In the democratic society the nonparticipating citizens bash their own heads in. The living democratic society requires the disciplines of discussion and common action for the determination of policy. The differences between persons are determined by the quality and direction of that participation. In this sense we may understand the New Testament word, "By their fruits shall you know them," but to this word we should add the admonition, "By their groups you shall know them."

Pentecost should be the major holy day in the liturgical calendar of the free church, because it tells the miracle of unity in diversity, even to the point of seeing that the greater the diversity, the greater the (potential) unity. Adams says,

> I call that church free which promotes freedom in fellowship, seeking unity in diversity. This unity is a potential gift, sought through devotion to the transforming power of creative interchange in generous dialogue. But it will remain unity in diversity.

John Buehrens notes that Henry Whitney Bellows's saying, "the Holy Spirit speaks most reliably through a group," is a hedge against fanatics who claim to have a "direct pipeline" to God and are in effect laws unto themselves. It is equally a warning against what Adams calls the "fissiparous individualism" of rationalist or romantic thought. A valid theological concept of revelation depends on a principled safeguard against any idea of divine revelation as inherently solipsistic, that is, self-authenticating and arbitrary; as Bellows's words reflect, a calling to spiritual leadership is necessarily authenticated and sustained by a historical, self-governing community.

Adams would also have us recognize that the "small church within the large"—the purposeful, disciplined group with an agenda for the large group, whether churchly or secular—plays a decisive role in historical change. Among other things, it seeks to protect the rights of a minority, and it may even see the minority, the "outsiders," as having a prophetic authenticity in relation to the majority, the "insiders." So the Holy Spirit is discerning the *character* of those groups it deigns to inspire, favoring the poor, the dissenters, and the reformers. According to Adams,

> The vitality of the church ... depends upon the small groups of the church, often across denominational boundaries. The vitality of the church depends on what Luther called the *ecclesiola in ecclesia*, the small church in the large. In this in-

volvement of the laity we are ideally led not only to the priesthood but also to the prophethood of all believers, recognizing that God moves in mysterious ways, even through secular agencies and figures and, of course, with the assistance of the other professions.

Methodism grew explosively under the leadership of its chief founder, John Wesley. Adams notes that Wesley insisted upon small "class meetings"—

...a dozen members who met regularly for interpersonal discipline, for self-examination, prayer, and guidance in the daily problems of the Christian life.... Within one or two generations these people gained a vigorous capacity to assert their freedom, indeed to exercise power in the sense of participating in social decisions.

Thus "the small church in the large church" becomes the schoolhouse and the model for voluntary association bent on exercising power for social reform.

In 1981 Adams commented on a "Freedom of Conscience Resolution" which, he said, would "abandon the practice of proposing and debating resolutions on matters of public policy at the General Assembly" of the Unitarian Universalist Association. He opposed the move, again choosing the ethics of consequences (consensus formation for the sake of a unified voice and action) over the ethics of conscience (individual freedom to decide and to act, if at all, outside the sphere of the church). Adams did not waste his breath arguing that denominational resolutions sway public policy in themselves; rather, he saw their significance as the educational impact of the deliberative process itself and as the formation of "a clearer and stronger sense of identity" within and among the congregations. They enable the churches to say, in Adams's words, "We are a people who stand for something—for we have hammered it out on the anvil of our times. In fact, this corporate decision-making is what makes us 'a people.'"

In the prophetic tradition the "people of God" is a single body, not an aggregate of individuals, as Adams emphasizes:

> The prophet Joel could say to our churches, "Multitudes, multitudes, in the valley of decision. The day of the Lord is near in the valley of decision." Joel was not in this time addressing an aggregate of individuals but rather a covenanted people, a "corporate personality." In this spirit William Ellery Channing succinctly put the issue when in a sermon of 1820 he declared, "Religion is a social principle, for it is a subject in which men and women have a strong tendency to feel and act together, and thus it is a strong bond of union."

Adams comments that the phenomenon of voluntary associations is noted and promoted by a series of illustrious figures in American history: Cotton Mather, Benjamin Franklin, William Ellery Channing, Alexis deToqueville. Of course, associations are of many sorts. Those that interest him most, because they are the most significant in terms of social-ethical concerns, are groups seeking to influence public policy and professional associations. Taken together, the plethora of independent and sometimes cooperating associations give substance to the recognition that the *state* is not coterminous with the *society* but is the self-limited governing function within the society.

Adams asks, "What are the marks of an authentic voluntary association?" and he answers:

> The major thing is that a voluntary association brings together people of differing perspectives. The sociology of knowledge points to the significance of associations that reflect some kind of common mind, but they also bring together individuals with differing social rootages [perspectives that are rooted in their own social experience]. That was [Karl] Mannheim's insight. There are various types of voluntary associations, but in the authentic voluntary association the *group* must come to a decision....A voluntary association that is significantly functioning is not only one

that achieves some kind of consensus, through an interplay of perspectives. Through compromise, rough experience, and the like, it also finds some way of making a decision. I learned this in the Independent Voters of Illinois, of which I, together with Charlotte Carr of Hull House, was one of the founders. The I.V.I., founded in 1941, is still going strong.

These are not, to be sure, the kind of groups that Max Weber complains of in Germany, "the singing academies, draining off the national energy into 'warbling.'" American society generates as many or more such affinity groups. Rather, he is thinking of social and political action groups, like the I.V.I., a group that brought together Adams, Unitarian and professor, and John Lapp, Roman Catholic and labor arbitrator. Together they ran a weekend seminar for Chicago voluntary associations strategizing on common goals:

> There would be about ten or a dozen of us, and we would spend the whole weekend together, discussing group interrelationships and such questions as, What were we trying to do, anyway? By one o'clock the question would be, Why are we trying to do it? And then someone would ask, "Jim, what does the theologian say?"

Adams recalls Lapp saying, once when they had to cough up $50 per person to pay the rent, "Any organization that doesn't have trouble paying its bills isn't worth its salt."

A meeting must be more than a good bull session. It must be a process that includes building trust, defining issues, developing consensus, and making decisions for common action. Adams tells a story about it:

> Eventually a group has to make a decision. For instance, in the I.V.I. we had to endorse candidates for public office. After we had established a reputation as being not merely a self-interest group, we were ourselves astonished at the influence we had. We simply had to pass out sample ballots....

Our workers would simply stand in front of voting booths and people would come by and ask, "Where's the I.V.I. ballot?" We'd say, "Just take a copy of it here!"

On one occasion we refused to support the handpicked candidate of the mayor of Chicago, a Democrat. Finally [the mayor] called me in and said, "Do you mean to say you're willing to have the Republican isolationist go to Congress?" I said, "We don't care. It's just as good for an isolationist to go as this fellow." But the next day he called me up and said, "I'll give you twenty-four hours. If you can name a candidate that I can accept, I'll throw my fellow out." We did. And he did throw him out. The reason for that was we controlled two hundred precincts. That's an aspect of power.

The associational principle takes many forms. In addition to the political action group there is also the professional association, which maintains standards of professional practice and ethics. Isolation breeds irresponsibility in either realm. Adams recalls encounters with Professor Leo Szilard, one of the team of nuclear physicists who developed the atomic bomb:

> I first met Leo Szilard by reason of my being head of the Independent Voters of Illinois. He came by my office to make a contribution, but otherwise was uninvolved. Later, in 1945, Professor Szilard came to my office immediately after the bombings of Hiroshima and Nagasaki and said that after a century of separation, "It is time for religion and science to work together." He suggested that I communicate with representatives of the major disciplines at the University of Chicago toward the end of issuing a statement of protest and penitence with regard to the destructive use of atomic energy.

Adams worked with Charles Hartshorne and other faculty members of the University of Chicago (not, however, including Szilard himself) to develop a statement that was published in the *New York Times*; it was the first public protest against the use of atomic bombs against Japan and the first warning against an international nuclear arms race. He says,

> Human sinfulness expresses itself in the indifference of the average citizen who is so impotent, so idiotic in the sense of the word's Greek root—that is, privatized, as not to exercise freedom of association for the sake of the general welfare and for the sake of becoming a responsible self.

Adams admires Szilard immensely, but still doesn't let him off the hook for his unwillingness to do what he calls "the hum-drum work of a democracy." He also admires Kierkegaard, whom he excoriates for preening the individual soul and ignoring the institution. And he admires another cultural icon, William James, in particular for his exemplary prose style. But Adams sees James's individualistic and noninstitutional approach to "religious experience" in his most famous work, *The Varieties of Religious Experience*, as a major intellectual defect. James's younger contemporary, Friedrich von Hügel, a scholar of religious experience admired by Adams, voices the same critique of James in a lengthy, unpublished letter dated May 10, 1909, that Adams found in Harvard's Houghton Library, tucked inside James's personal copy of a book by von Hügel.

In addition to this significant literary discovery, Adams reports that he found an unpublished letter from William James to Professor Francis Greenwood Peabody that reflects James's aversion to the group processes which are inevitably involved in social action. Peabody, an early proponent of the Social Gospel, gave one of the first courses on social ethics at Harvard, a course dubbed by students as "Drainage, Delinquency, and Divorce." He at one time invited James to join a new committee on alcoholism. In a typed, undated letter James declines the invitation and gives his reason, asserting that setting a good example would be more effective than the activity of a committee. The letter concludes, "Excuse the appearance of churlishness that this letter wears. I am no man for committees anyhow."

Adams is not anything if he is not a man for committees!

Rudolf Otto, author of the classic study *The Idea of the Holy* and of the work that Adams cites in his interpretation of New Testament eschatology, *Kingdom of God and Son of Man*, became his close friend and confidant in prewar Germany. Adams remembers,

> ...the major thing that happened to me [in my early development] was my experience of Nazism in 1927, 1936, and again in 1938. In connection with the church people and with the Evangelical academies in Germany, my major mentor in those years became Rudolf Otto, a retired professor at Marburg University. In his earlier years Otto had been politically active, even having won election to the *Landtag*. This was striking because I had become aware of the apolitical character of both the religious and the academic leadership in Germany.... I finally decided that the lack of social infrastructures had made even the so-called democratic society of the Weimar Republic ineffectual.

Yet, how different were we in the United States? As an organizer of and activist in the Independent Voters of Illinois, Adams has special scorn for good-hearted but unengaged professors at the University of Chicago:

> I used to get somewhat annoyed when some of my colleagues would come around at election time saying, "Gee, I don't know anything about these candidates, Jim. Tell me who's who." It was only through the grace of God, and the desire at least to get them to vote, that I suppressed prophetic indignation.

Adams notes that, "According to Robert Michel's 'Iron Law of Oligarchy,' in any organization oligarchy tends to set in, because the rank and file members simply do not pay attention; so the eager beavers take over." He also comments that those who stay to the end of a political meeting, no matter how late the hour, exercise the largest influence because that is when the preponderance of decisions are made. Knowing this, the Communists always stayed to the end of meetings.

Adams himself—more than once falsely accused of being a "fellow traveler"—was the sort to stay to the end of the meeting. His energy and activism were legendary. He recalls a conversation with the philosopher Charles Hartshorne, an old friend on the University of Chicago faculty:

> Charles said he'd enjoyed an eleven-hour sleep the night before. I said to him, "Charles, if I slept for eleven hours I'd be uncontrollable." He retorted, "What makes you think you're not already?"

The Human Vocation

Our human vocation is a calling to do justice in effective ways, through religious and civic associations, for a universal good that transcends and forever surpasses us. This is the gospel according to Adams:

> Max Weber once suggested that the Old Testament prophets in their independence and criticism of the monarchy and the society were an anticipation of the modern free press. There is an important difference, however. The prophet presupposes a religious vocation, the demand of the Lord of history for a society of justice and mercy combined with a demand for individual piety—corporate and individual integrity under the Great Taskmaster's eye. The priest maintains the traditional fabric of society; the prophet holds up a higher and universal standard that sanctions dissent looking toward social change.

Adams wrote the following program note for a performance of an oratorio by Felix Mendelssohn at the Arlington Street Church in Boston, where Adams was a member and served, after his retirement from theological teaching, as minister of adult education:

> The text of Felix Mendelssohn's *Elijah* includes the familiar biblical passage about the prophet Elijah's running away

from the Lord's call to prophesy against the wickedness of King Ahab, and then in his flight being confronted in turn by a great wind, an earthquake, a fire, and a tempest. Yet, the Lord was not in these but in a "still small voice." In conventional interpretation, the still small voice has been wrongly associated only with the privatized inner life of the individual, a reduction that amounts to a spiritual lobotomy making possible an easy social and political conscience. In the Biblical narrative it possesses radical political import. Elijah's life was in danger because he had condemned the (false) gods of the authoritarian Baal and also because he opposed the queen Jezebel's attempt to import a totalitarian political system in violation of Judah's more democratic ways. The still small voice was urging him to do his duty as a prophet. [See I Kings 19:12.] Elijah was a worthy, courageous precursor of the great eighth-century prophets of the Covenant.

Adams is highly critical of inward and private conceptions of religion, but he affirms the personal dimension of religion, along with the public and the political dimensions. *Personal* does not mean *private*, since people are necessarily social from birth. He notes that complaints about political theologians go back at least as far as Edmund Burke in England and Lyman Beecher in the United States:

> A biblical conception of vocation is a conception that entails power. That is, it entails participation in those processes that illuminate, criticize, and transform institutions. We see a striking contrast already beginning more than a century ago in American piety. In 1811 in the city of New Haven, Lyman Beecher asserted, "It is not for the Christian citizen to try to think about, to deal with, the issues of politics. What the Christian citizen should do is choose a man who is truly pious and leave it to him to think about the decisions. The task of the Christian is simply to recognize piety and select a man who has the piety." We who live in a modern culture

dominated by the mass media of communications are aware now of the techniques whereby such piety can be promoted.

Nevertheless, Adams believes in the importance of personal spiritual disciplines and in the importance of kindred groups that develop shared disciplines and stimulate or sustain individuals in keeping them. He practiced devotional reading and prayer on a private basis and during at least one period had a spiritual director. Many do this; he asks for something more:

> I now believe that every Christian should be actively and persistently engaged in the work of at least one secular organization which is exercising a positive influence for the sake of peace and justice against the forces of hatred and greed.

Adams helped to form a clergy group called the Brothers of the Way (in a time when he himself did not find it remarkable that there were virtually no women in the ministry), of which he says,

> We worked out personal and interpersonal disciplines that included not only daily prayer and meditation, but also active membership in a voluntary association concerned with controversial issues. It was understood that it did not count if the individual were a member of the Library Board, unless the librarian were under attack as a Communist.

Many people count themselves good because they work hard at their job and they love and take responsibility for their families. What this "private realm goodness" leaves out is the public realm. Their idea of vocation is too small, too impersonal, Adams insists:

> One can find physicians, lawyers, professors, workers who believe that their public responsibilities consist almost entirely in their vocational activity. Many clergy believe that they can be better parish priests if they keep themselves aloof from the controversies of the marketplace and the public forum. The profile of this sort of underling (to use Dostoyevski's term)

appears on a tombstone that Dean Willard Sperry tells us he once saw in Scotland:

> Here lies John MacDonald.
> Born a man.
> Died a grocer.

The story—probably apocryphal—is told that rather than purchase the *Chicago Tribune* (in the days when it was a bastion of reaction), Professor Adams could be found in the early morning hours poking through his neighbors' trash cans in the ally behind the house, looking for a current copy. Adams believes in "the creative uses of controversy":

> To a leader in the movement for better race relations, a real estate promoter in Chicago asked the question, "Are you really happy at home? If you were happy in your home, would you be causing all this disturbance in the community? Aren't you a little neurotic?" This sort of argument can, of course, cut two ways, eliciting the question as to whether the accuser is not becoming neurotic about a certain brand of harmony. Those who speak much about such harmony are seldom eager searchers for facts or remedies of correction.

Adams does not promote controversy or conflict for the sake of winning a battle. He believes that to be creative and not simply destructive, controversy requires personal acquaintance with the situation of others in the controversy. He cites Martin Luther King Jr.'s succinct statement: "We hate each other because we fear each other. We fear each other because we don't know each other, and we don't know each other because we are separated." And he says,

> All of us on all sides of the irrepressible conflicts of our time will be doomed to uncreative and perhaps to violent conflict unless we can, at least at crucial moments, be grasped by the spirit that was in Jesus when he said, "Let whoever is without sin cast the first stone." To the sinner in the dock he said, "Go and sin no more." [See John 8:1-11.] Forgiveness, acceptance.

These are the first prerequisites of creative controversy. These are the antecedents of new beginnings, of constructive innovation, of new creation. However, they mean we must give up something if the new is to come into being.

Adams always sees both, or rather several, sides of any question. He asks us to adopt a holistic vision—a vision that "sees life steadily and sees it whole," as Matthew Arnold says of Shakespeare, and an eschatological vision—a vision of life in its present brokenness and promised healing. The fulfillment of a vision that is both holistic and eschatological requires of us more than lip service; it requires a costing commitment. And yet even moral courage depends upon an underlying faith, a belief that even when we act alone, as finally we all must, we are not ultimately alone but companioned. I call the story that follows, recalled from Adams's last trip to Germany before the war, "You Can't Go There Alone":

> The Gestapo sent two officers with bloodhounds to my boarding house, and the landlady—well, Frau Schild was an outspoken anti-Nazi, popular in the neighborhood, and they weren't able to do anything with her. The Nazi officials had come to her and told her that she had to stop trading at the Jewish grocery store. She practically spat them out of the house. "You aren't going to tell me where to buy my groceries. My husband was killed in the First World War and I got a measly little pension out of that and the only way I could start this boarding house was the Jewish grocer—he was the one who loaned to me the money for two years—and you are not going to tell me I am not going to trade with him and you get out of here!" Can you imagine that—the way she talked back to the Gestapo!
>
> I had collected papers from the underground anti-Nazi churches, the Confessing churches. I cut out stiff cardboard very carefully for each of the drawers of the desk and put some of the secret papers, which I later turned over to the

U.S. War Department, under the card-boards. The papers described the kinds of punishment imposed by the Nazis on
ministers and laymen in the churches. When the officers
came to search while I was out and went through all my
clothes, everything—Frau Schild was standing right there by
them, sputtering. But they didn't see any of those papers.
They were even more stupid than I! They left word that I was
to come immediately upon my return to the Gestapo office.

Well, I had heard many stories about the Gestapo, for example that they did not trust each other, so they didn't share
more information than they had to. I didn't know why they
were after me. I had some close connections with the
Confessing Church group and had been in several situations
where the police were involved. I didn't know how much they
knew. I was smuggling money for a Jewish family who had
been exiled. Frau Schild and I decided that it might be that
the local Gestapo were just following orders and didn't know
why they were after me. So I said to her, I think I will play the
role of a professor. (I was not old enough for that role, to be
sure; I was about 35.) In Germany Herr Professor is one you
click your heels for. I said I will go to a public phone—her
phone might be tapped—and say, "I understand that you
want to see me, Professor Adams, but I have a heavy schedule
today and I won't be able to come today, but I think I could
arrange to come tomorrow." "Well, just a minute." The fellow
came back in a couple of minutes and said, "All right. Eight
o'clock, punctually. *Um ocht Uhr, punkt!*"

This gave me time to talk to various friends, including
Rudolf Bultmann on the faculty, and they all said the same
thing. No telling why they are after you, but you shouldn't go
to the Gestapo headquarters alone. But where was I to find
anyone to go with me? That night I couldn't sleep, and about
5:30 in the morning I heard Frau Schild poking around in the
kitchen. So I got up and started off about an hour before I
was due, *um ocht Uhr, punkt!* I decided not to take the street-
car but to walk to town. On my way, palpitating, I went by the

home of a pastor who had been in jail for political activities, so I decided to stop there. I had met the man once or twice before, because the library didn't have a journal I was looking for, but the librarian said, well there is this learned pastor in town who probably takes that journal. So I have borrowed two issues from him and later returned them. It was probably 7:15 in the morning when I told him what had happened. He whispered, "You can't go there alone." I said, "That's what everybody in town has been telling me. Who's going to go with me?" "You can't go alone," he repeated, "there's no telling what will happen to you. They'll cut your throat and the Berlin officials will apologize and say that their people went beyond instructions. But your throat will be slit." "I promised to be there at 8:00," I said. "Well, let me think."

He paced the floor, and finally he said, "I am going to do something. But I will have to ask you to solemnly swear that you will never tell anyone in Germany what happens from this moment on." "All right," I said. He said, "I have to do something. The mayor of this city is the principle anti-Nazi in this city." "What? I've never seen a larger swastika than the one he wears on his lapel. You can see it a block away." "Never mind," he said, "anti-Nazi. Now I will have to take a chance. I know that my telephone is bugged, so I am going to call him and talk to him in a very oblique fashion. And I hope he will get the point. Remember, you are never going to tell anybody in Germany." "Yeah." So he called the mayor, and before long the mayor was saying, "I live near the city hall, so tell your friend to go there immediately—the offices are not open but I will leave word with the guard to let him enter."

So I went to the city hall and there was the mayor. He said, "I am trying to figure out what to do. You can't go there alone." "I've heard that before!" "Well, I have decided that at five minutes to 8:00 I am going to call the Gestapo on the phone. Now, I will tell you there is nothing a Gestapo hates more than a mayor, because a mayor is a municipal official and the Gestapo is federal. I am going to tell them that you are in my office and I am sending you to their office." "Well," I said, "thank you very much, but just tell me what does that do for me?" He said, "I might as well accompany you. I've told them I know you. That's my way of saying, if anything happens to you, whatever they do, I'll find out about it." So I went to the Gestapo office and they put me through an hour and three-quarters questioning about every place I had been in Germany and that sort of thing, with people taking shorthand notes.

Adams cites G. K. Chesterton's saying that the most important thing to know about your landlady is her "world view." His own *Weltanschaung* includes the principle that when life gets tough, you can't go there alone.

The concept of vocation—our human vocation as our holy work to do—is central to Adams's sense of courageous action in association with others. The German pastor Peter Brunner made an especially deep impact upon him, simply because he lived out his faith, starting with the First Commandment, in a way that risked his own life and well-being. Adams says,

I found myself in Nazi Germany in association with a German Harvard classmate [Peter Brunner] who had just served time in the concentration camp in Dachau. Immediately on release from Dachau he had boldly resumed his leadership in the dangerous anti-Nazi underground movement of the resisting churches. There I came to appreciate at first hand the vocation, the calling, of prophetic religion in its perennial and creative struggle against the false gods of idolatry—racism, classism, and sexism. I learned anew and "existentially" the meaning of the Commandment, "Thou shalt have no other gods before me." I learned that as soon as the universal God is forgotten, false gods rush in to fill the vacuum.

The commitment to confront injustice—violations of God's inclusive covenant wherever they appear—follows from the commandment against giving your devotion to idols, the gods we make rather than the God who makes us. Also, it takes starch.

God, in thy presence we acknowledge ourselves for what we are—creatures of vision, of blindness, and of perverted vision, stumbling creatures of love and fear and hate. We acknowledge that the cleavages and the injustices of our world spring from our own blindness and impotence and irresponsibility. In thy presence we know that nothing can be right for any one of us that is not right for the groups to which we belong, which is our part in the common life and the good of all. In this hour we reaffirm our part in a covenant that embraces our concern for the vitalities of nature within us and around us, a concern for the integrity of the individual mind and conscience, a concern for the viable structures of the societal order and also for the needs of the deprived and the powerless in our nation and of other nations—a covenant that embraces concern for our families, for the family of humankind, and for the ecology of all beings. Amen.

—JLA

Renewing Community:
The Covenant of Being

ERIK ERIKSON IDENTIFIES HOPE AS the first and foundational virtue of human development, rooted in infancy. He defines hope psycho-genetically as the belief that one's "fervent wishes" will not be disappointed but fulfilled. It is natural that we should long to integrate hope into the final stage of life—the distinctive virtue of which Erikson names *wisdom*. The dynamic of theological and ethical reflection, Adams suggests, carries us along a similar trajectory—from the harmonies of the original creation, to the destructive conflicts of human history, to the fulfillment of our deepest moral commitments, fervently hoped for. It is to this third moment—the hope-filled renewal of community and faith—that we turn in the final two chapters of our reflection on the thought of James Luther Adams.

Visions that fit seemingly disparate things together in a single whole fascinate us, perhaps because they are intrinsically hopeful. Perceived patterns of meaning move us to seek out larger patterns of meaning and, by extension, to believe that reality itself is meaningful. This belief may hold even in the face of desperate circumstances, as in the plea of the epileptic boy's father to Jesus: "I believe, help thou mine unbelief!" (Mark 9:24). This seems to me the chief reason for religious belief: We affirm a vision that enables us to make sense of the world, a vision in which all the parts come together, ideally in a seamless whole. Adams finds such a vision in surprising places, as his report on a medieval allegory shows:

> In the Middle Ages one of the most celebrated and influential treatises on the Liberal Arts was *The Marriage of Mercury and Philology*, attributed to Martianus Capella, an African grammarian of the fifth century. Wishing to wed the rigor of the learned disciplines to the beauty and grace of the imagination, Capella introduces his manual with a romance. He imagines that Mercury, having decided to take unto himself a wife, asks the hand of Philology [the love of literature]. In order to fetch home his bride, Mercury appears on the wedding day with a retinue of the Seven Arts. He presents in turn each of these nymphs, and in the presence of the god each gives a discourse on the art she represents.
>
> Two things captured the medieval imagination in this conception presented by Capella. First, the Liberal Arts were held to be in the service of a god, either Philology or Philosophy. Stuart Pratt Sherman's phrase offers us an Americanized formulation of this aspect of the medieval conception. The arts, he says, have "a heart full of service." Second, each of the arts found its proper place in relation to the god and to each other only by virtue of a clearly defined character of its own. Martianus Capella accomplished what greater creative artists came short of. His figures became permanent types, all of them together constituting the pictorial representation of the *Trivium* and the *Quadrivium*, the seven paths of human activity leading to what is possible apart from revelation. Indeed, they were held to be indispensable for the understanding of the Scriptures and of the service of God even in the church. In his finely wrought definitions each of the disciplines of the Liberal Arts found its soul.

Although to modern sensibility the allegory is exceedingly fanciful, it captures the imagination with lasting effect. As in a covenant, each constituent part is distinctive, and each wants to serve the whole; each has its own "soul" and together, all are one "at heart."

In Biblical thought history moves—not inevitably, but with our moral decision and sustained commitment—from the "old covenant" written in stone to the "new covenant" written in the human heart, a symbol of fulfillment and renewal first used by the prophet Jeremiah. The "new birth of freedom" of which Abraham Lincoln speaks in his Gettysburg Address is similarly a symbol of hope and promise. Adams finds a commonality between Doris Humphrey, the master choreographer and modern dance performer, and Jeremiah, the ancient Israelite prophet:

> Miss Humphrey says that the choreographer may wish to express the spirit of this age, the age of the right angle. But she would prefer something different. A dance form, she acknowledges, is logical. It has to have structure, but it comes to life in the realization of feeling, sensitivity, and imagination. These things have been beaten out of modern life, she says, as hindrances to "getting on." But human movements are not made of building blocks, nor of the right angle. Choreography, she says, should be in the search for and the use of the new and elusive relationships.
>
> Jeremiah would have liked what Doris Humphrey says about the right angle and about the use of elusive relationships that constitute the fullness and richness of sensitivity and imagination. Jeremiah says, "Thou shalt again be adorned with thy timbrels and shalt go forth in the dance of them that make merry." Jeremiah is the exponent of what he called a new covenant. He was not satisfied with the covenant of law and judgment, the kind that could be enforced by the king and his lawyers. He says, "Not according to the covenants that I made with their fathers, saith the Lord, but this shall be the covenant that I will make. I will put my law in their inward parts; I will write it in their hearts" (Jeremiah 31:26-31).

As this chapter shows, the idea of covenant serves as a power-ful, integrating concept in Adams's thought, for covenants entail both the voluntary consent of individuals and a shared commit-ment to the well-being of others within a group. Adams notes that, while covenants may stipulate promises or agreements, they are distinct from contracts in that they are are rooted in affection and gratitude; this is the source of the Biblical use of *covenant* to de-scribe the relationship between God and a "people of God." Thus this idea brings together Adams's theological and ethical concerns.

Adams argues that history can be read as the story of the mak-ing, the breaking, and the renewing of covenants. A primary voca-tion of the religious community is to model and work for more inclusive social covenants within the larger community. When Adams speaks of covenant as a creative principle operating in his-tory for the renewal of communities, he articulates the faith that nerves liberalism. Taking a social and historical concept, covenant, as a metaphor for the dynamic and relational character of ulti-mate reality, he speaks of the cosmos and all beings within it as forming a "covenant of being."

The Meaning and the Use of Covenants

The preamble to the Constitution of the United States ("We the people of the United States of America, in order to form a more perfect union...") begins in the classic form of a covenant, that is, a commitment binding those who are party to it to common pur-poses. The specific means to this end, "a more perfect union," fol-low in the body of the document. The idea of covenant and its multiform applications enter powerfully into Adams's mature thought. *Covenant* functions on two levels at once, the historical and the ontological, that is, covenants function both as solemn agreements of particular groups in history and as the basis of such enactments in "being," or the nature of reality.

Shifting from philosophical to religious language, Adams de-scribes *covenant* in both theological and ethical terms—theologically

as a covenant between God and a person or a community, and
ethically as a covenant among persons or human communities.
Both the act of covenanting, which is always an act of faith, and its
outcomes—actual historical covenants that entail moral commitments to the future—can be seen as expressions of human participation in the creative and redemptive power of God. This is the
background of Adams's simplest and most profound definition of
God, "the community-forming power." Thus the idea of covenant
links faith and history, for meaningful history is the story of community-forming power, and faith is the discernment of the working of this power in time. The New Testament asserts, "Now faith
is the substance of things hoped for" (Hebrews 11:1a); covenant
shapes faith in a way that provides hope of reconciliation, fullfil-
ment, or spiritual wholeness.

Reflection on ordinary moral experience generates reflection
on the diverse meanings of the term *covenant*. In various contexts
it can mean promise, agreement, compact, social contract, commitment, or testament. Take *agreement*, a commitment we make
to others to fulfill our part in a joint undertaking, contingent on
their commitment to fulfill their part. We say: "This is the deal."
No sooner do we state the matter than we notice complexities
lurking just under the surface. Thus, a covenant is a kind of
"deal"—Roosevelt had his "New Deal"—and yet a covenant can
never be reduced to a bargain or even to a contract, for it is open-
ended. Thus a marriage is a kind of covenant—a commitment
rooted in affection; a marriage contract is something else—an
agreement regarding the property of the parties to the marriage
covenant, during the marriage or after its dissolution. But
covenants can also be described as agreements, a foundational
term in the thought of Richard Cabot, a distinguished professor of
ethics at Harvard Medical School a generation ago. Adams speaks
of Cabot as "a teacher of uncommon insight and persuasiveness,"
and goes on to say,

> Concerned with the nature of the good life and the
> religious life, [Cabot] proposed an intriguing concep-

tion.... He suggested that our conduct is measured by the agreements we make, both with each other and with ourselves. Whether open or tacit, these agreements determine the quality of our life together. They express our definitions of what we deem to be worthwhile, of what we think we should stand by, of what we believe we should be loyal to.

But not all these agreements, Dr. Cabot pointed out, are worthy.... revision of our understanding of our agreements with each other and with ourselves, he said, is necessary if as individuals we are to grow, and if the groups of which we are members are to grow. He summed up the good life, then, in these three propositions: the good life is to make agreements, to keep agreements, and to revise or improve agreements in view of new situations.

Of course, there are always ambiguities in human history. Not all movements in human history toward "improvement" are true improvements—for instance, some movements achieve order or conformity at the price of freedom and creativity. "The individual," Adams says, "may always say, 'I don't care if your beehive is perfect; I don't like beehives.'"

One sign of the importance to us of freedom, as compared with order, is the fact that we humans have what Kenneth Burke calls "the capacity for symbolic action," and thereby the urge to create, the desire to make something new and unique. At its elemental level the capacity for symbolic action is seen in the urge or the need to name things. According to the Biblical creation story, God names Adam and in turn, Adam names the animals, thus participating in the establishment of a meaningful order of things. Thereby we human beings fulfill something essential to our humanity. We act out the belief that we are made in "the image of God" by becoming creators of meaning ourselves. It is something we cannot *not* do; that is, it is humanly imperative. As Adams tells the story,

Adam and Eve finally sat down in the shade of a tree, think-ing with great satisfaction, "Well, we've named them all," when suddenly something came hopping through the grass which they hadn't seen before. "What's that?" Adam said. "I've never seen that before." Eve—she was the truly creative one—seeing this thing hopping around said, "Ah, ha! It looks like a frog to me." She named it.

In Adams's version both Adam and Eve are involved in the naming; according to the Genesis story, however, Adam alone does the naming, and in this very process learns that "there was not found an help meet for him" (Genesis 2:19-20). So the story con-cerns the kinship of the man and the woman, setting them apart from the other animals. This more complex picture does not con-tradict the point that Adams is making—that the capacity to name things (including unseen realities) is a primary mark of human creativity:

> Human beings, who have to achieve self-understanding and communication, have to name things; so in his command-ment to name things, God was commanding something ab-solutely indispensable to human beings if they were going to be human.

Recalling the fairy tale of the princess and the frog, we may well wonder about the mythic roots of this story. It gives humor-ous reflection to a philosophical puzzle: Which comes first, the name or the thing that we name? And if we never named it, would it exist? Where is God in this mysterious transaction, the giving of names? In his introduction to *The Eclipse of Faith*, Martin Buber responds to a philosopher's impassioned protest against speaking of the "blood-soaked term, God." He says that he could not *not* speak of God, for this was one of those *ur-Worte*, original words, which is necessary and for which there is no substitute.

There may be, nevertheless, ambiguities of language, arbitrary ways in which we label ineluctable reality, as Adams's tale about Englishman and Harvard professor Kirsopp Lake suggests. Adams reports that the classically eccentric Lake once told this story about his sojourn at a major center of Greek Orthodox monasticism:

> While Professor Lake was at Mt. Athos, he was talking with one of the ecclesiastical superiors, called the Metropolitan. Lake was fully conscious that the rule of the monastic order held that no female entity was permitted on the sacred premises. Interrupting the conversation, he pointed to a cat followed by five kittens. The Metropolitan didn't seem the least bit concerned. "Don't you see what I see there, that cat with all those little kittens?" "Why, what's the matter?" "Well, that's a female." "Oh, it's all right." "What do you mean, 'all right'? I thought you had a rule here." "Yes, we do, but that's not a female." "Do you mean to say that all those kittens are following a tomcat?" "Yes." "But how could that be?" "Very simple. It's a miracle."

Following Paul Tillich we may say that an authentic name is not an arbitrarily assigned "sign" but rather a "symbol," something that points beyond itself to the being of its object. What is at issue here is something like the Platonic idea of participation: I am what I am by virtue of my participation in a more complete reality—by my membership in a larger body.

The story of Eve's naming the frog introduces what Adams calls "one of the great namings" in intellectual history, *covenant*. Covenants exemplify the principle of participation; the members of a group have their identity by virtue of their participation in the group, and in turn they constitute it. The point is subtle but all-important. In the act of creating a group by covenanting, the members do not join as if attaching themselves to a preexisting body; rather, they are themselves constituting—or perhaps reconstituting—the body. As in a hologram, each part contains the whole; hence the whole is constituted by, and does not exist apart from, its constituent parts. So covenants are not arbitrary expressions of human wish or will but historical processes through which we discover our authentic identity and our authentic destiny. They render human freedom serious. They render human decision fruitful and fateful in history. They incarnate "the community forming power." Adams goes so far as to say,

> The intimate and the ultimate—indeed all parts of the inter-related world—the individual, middle structures, the government, the society, and the divine creative ground of meaning—are held together by covenant. The bonding and binding quality of covenant, the ordering principle, is the promise. God is the promise-making, promise-keeping reality upon which we ultimately depend as the reliable, creative, sustaining, judging, community-forming and community-transforming power. Wherever these powers are working, the divine is working. The secular-minded person who is alienated from the churches or the theologians, or who for some other reason is not, in Max Weber's phrase, "religiously musical," may find unacceptable any theological formulation. Yet, this promise-making, promise-renewing power is the flywheel of meaningful human existence.

Conceptualizing is naming at a higher level of abstraction. In the theological and social ethical reflections of Adams, *covenant* becomes a key term. He calls attention to the multidimensionality of the concept of covenant several times in his writings: First, it has essentially to do with the human (and the humanizing) capacity to make promises, agreements, and commitments. Second, it locates meaning in social-institutional context, not in psychic or scientific considerations. Third, it points to the inclusion of the weak and the deprived within the community and invites critique of the powerful. Fourth, it speaks to the individual, evoking sensitivity and commitment to the group. Fifth, it is not only social but also ontological; it opens awareness of what we may call "the covenant of being." Sixth, it includes and supports the rule of law as an expression of the social compact. Seventh, however, ultimately it is founded on freely given affection, on love, not on law and not on calculated advantage, individual or mutual. Eighth, it is the basis of prophetic criticism; reformers forever decry the "broken covenant"—the founding agreement and moral ideals—of the community. In short, the idea is multifaceted. It is close kin to the idea of social contract in political theory.

The idea of covenant becomes, in Adams's writings—and increasingly so in his later years—the key constructive principle of his theologically rooted social ethics. The term has secular uses in the realm of law, but due to its significant use to designate the two parts of the Bible—the Old and New Testaments, also known as the old and new covenants—the word has taken on profound and sacred overtones. (*Berith* in Hebrew becomes *diatheke* in Greek translation, and *testamentum* or *pactum* in Latin. *Covenant* in English probably derives from *covenir* in Middle English and Middle French and from *convenire* in Latin, meaning "to agree.") In the ancient world a covenant was a political form, signifying a treaty, pact, or compact, sometimes between a sovereign king and a vassal (hence a radically non-egalitarian relationship, analogous to the relationship between God and a person or a human group). Adams notes,

> The metaphor of covenant is a form of political rhetoric. Like "kingdom of God" and "messiah," it is drawn from the political realm—an example of what Shailer Mathews called "transcencentalized politics." "Our theology is not a system of philosophy, but an extension of forms of social experience to religious belief. It is a sort of parable in whose plot can be read the history of the social experience of centuries."

Adams also asserts a close connection between historical experience and theology, which his revered teacher, Shailer Mathews, also sees as symbolic stories or parables-writ-large. In a letter to me Adams writes, "The function of theology is to explicate the major symbols of a religious tradition in the face of a changing historical situation." The definition (one of several employed by Adams) is formal, not substantive; in consequence it invites (or even requires) us to identify what we say are "the major symbols" of our tradition. (And for some this would bring the question to the fore: What is our tradition?) The symbols—Adam and Eve in Eden is an example—are in one sense changeless and in another sense constantly changed by new historical situations calling for new interpretations.

Like Mathews, Adams is interested in the continuities between ordinary experience and religious experience, or between social ethics and theology. It is a characteristically liberal-theological strategy, for it tends to make sense out of theological ideas for those whom Friedrich Schleiermacher called religion's "cultured despisers." Adams, following Mathews, often points to the social and secular roots of theological and sacred ideas, such as covenant. But dialectical moves follow: The sacred criticizes the secular, and in turn, the theological criticizes the political (or the prophet criticizes the powers that be). The first move is necessary and natural, the second is creative and prophetic, as in the dialogue Adams sets up between two intellectual revolutionaries of the nineteenth century, Kierkegaard and Marx:

> Søren Kierkegaard endeavored to uncover the isolated individual, revealing the person as lonely, anxious, guilty. This solitary individual cannot by any rational or social means find a way out of this condition of isolation or lostness. Such a person does not live from an objective truth, but from an inwardness that is either despair (sometimes under the mask of comfort) or an openness to love. But Kierkegaard came near to repudiating a major concern of Biblical faith, faith as a response to the power of God through the creation of a new community. In his pietistic individualism Kierkegaard was in his way as lopsided as was Karl Marx in his sociologism. In contrast to Kiekegaard, Marx tried to understand history and society purely in terms of social forces and institutions. Thus Kierkegaard and Marx are lopsided in complementary ways. What Marx emphasizes, Kierkegaard almost entirely ignores. What Kierkegaard stresses in terms of individual inwardness and

integrity, Marx ignores. The contrast is between the yogi and the commissar.

Arthur Koestler's typology, "the yogi and the commissar," becomes grist for Adams's dialectical mill. Nevertheless, Adams gives Kierkegaard his due as a creative figure and a founder of existentialist thought, a tradition that Adams in large measure makes his own. A liberalism that does not absorb a large dose of existentialism is apt to remain in what Adams calls "the spectator mode"— not recognizing the existential moment in which a decisive choice comes to the fore and not to decide (perhaps because "all the evidence is not in," as of course it never will be) is to decide.

The central thrust of Biblical faith is existential, in Adams's understanding. That is, it is personal (*not* individual) and social (including interpersonal). Thus he identifies distinctly Biblical faith as "a response to God through the creation of a new community":

> Nothing individual or collective, natural or human, inner or outer, personal or institutional, is excluded from meaning, from potential relatedness, to the divine. This is characteristic of the exclusive monotheism of Israel: "You shall have no other gods before me." The covenanted people are responsible for the character of society as a whole, for institutional as well as individual behavior. Martin Buber calls this idea of covenant "a special kind of politics, theopolitics." Meaning, significant relatedness, points to a holy ground, to an ultimate source and resource.

The First Commandment, cited here and elsewhere by Adams, is foundational: "Thou shalt have no other gods before me" (Exodus 20:3). By asserting a personal relationship, it forms the basis of the idea of a God-given covenant. It also gives the covenant-bound "people of God" a sacral and ethical vocation that extends to all realms of life. It can be read to acknowledge the existence of other divine powers, but it assures their subordination, providing a stricture against idolatry.

Adams regularly employs what I have called "parabolic vision," using a story or an image as a medium of perception. Sometimes it is a kind of double vision, a way of seeing one thing in two ways at the same time. For instance, if we humans are in fundamental ways self-made, as our entire culture attests, then our "original sin" is idolatry, making ourselves in any image other than the image of God. In a sense, you may "play God," but only so long as you remember what you are doing, do not take yourself too seriously, and recognize the kind of god you are—a thoroughly fallible and probably laughable demigod. We are called to make ourselves not with ultimate seriousness but with playfulness. A primary quality of creative freedom, the image in which the Bible first presents God, is playfulness.

If it is in the nature of God to make promises and enter into covenants—if this is our experience of the divine creativity—then this must be our nature as well and part of what it means to be purposeful, social beings. Adams says,

> Human beings, individually and collectively, become human by making commitments, by making promises. The human being as such, as Martin Buber says, is the promise-making, promise-keeping, promise-breaking, promise-renewing creature. The human being is the promise maker, the commitment maker.

Adams notes that Daniel Eleazar points to the analogy that the covenant relationship is to social and political life as Buber's "I-Thou relationship" is to personal life. Buber's fundamental insight is not unlike the central idea of process-relational thought: We are changed by the relationships we enter into and we are morally constituted by the covenants we enter into. The relationship and the covenant are ontologically prior to our individual being.

Adams calls attention to the political roots of covenant (*berith* in Hebrew), a concept drawn from the political realm and applied by analogy to social life and history. By using the ontological term *covenant of being*, he suggests that reality itself is constituted by structures of mutually attractive or persuasive forces, forces that establish relatively stable and therefore enduring relationships. Such relationships are not formed by arbitrary will or external force but require an internal agreement or receptiveness—power that is susceptible to influence as well as influential (see the chapter on "Being Human"). The Biblical poem of creation is often said to depict God as creating "by fiat" and "out of nothing" (*ex nihilo*), an image that may suggest a magical event, like pulling a rabbit out of a hat. In the Genesis account a primordial chaos—an "uncreation," a realm "without form and void"—is present at the outset; the light is created by being "separated" from the darkness. Similarly, the "firmament" (sky) is separated from "the waters," and "dry land" from "the waters under the heavens." Creation, then, means differentiating one element from another and thereby building structures that allow other new things to come into being. Since we can see these ideas functioning in a social context, we may call this a social vision of reality.

In this metaphysical vision the keeping of covenants points to the affirmation of being, to consent to being, to being itself, while the breaking of covenants points to the negation of being, to dissent from being, to nonbeing.

Covenants Constitute History

Human history may be read as the story of the making, the breaking, and the renewal of covenants. History so understood—as Adams understands it, in a long tradition of theological reflection— is a story finally rooted in an original, God-given covenant, "the covenant of being." A fundamental philosophical proposition regarding the relationship of necessary and contingent being underlies this asserton. Failing to understand this, Adams's use of covenant language might be misread as merely metaphorical. The principle of covenant—under this name or another—is inescapable and therefore necessary, but actual, historical covenants are contingent, for they require a freely given act of consent within a particular historical context. Being voluntary, covenants are rooted in freedom; they also actualize freedom by establishing new social orders.

Understanding freedom as self-determined and purposeful action and covenant as a harmonizing structure, we see freedom as created by covenant. (We are never so un-free as we are in a chaotic or anarchic situation.) As the whole is constituted by the parts, so the parts exist only as constituent elements of the whole. The primary source of these reflections is the faith evoked by the central theme of the Bible. Adams seeks to identify that theme:

> What is biblical faith to us? The Bible is most concerned with the resources upon which meaningful human existence ultimately depend, with the resources that give rise to a community of viable justice and righteousness, "a many-flavored compound" elusive of definition. For the Bible human history is the arena of a struggle between the force or capacities that make for the development of individual and social integrity, and the forces that impede that development. But in the Bible the ultimate resource for this fulfillment is not in humanity, though the human being is created in the image of God and is a creative self. Paradoxically, the integrating forces represent at the same time a divine gift and a divinely given task or vocation for persons. The lines of a Michelangelo sonnet express the transcending dimension of this paradox:
>
>> What leads me on
>> Is not in me.
>
> What is biblical faith to us? This is not a question one considers for old times' sake. At bottom it is a question about the meaning of life itself, about the ground and purpose of human fellowship.

The free church ideal—the church standing over against the state and the culture—was born out of the Radical Reformation in continental Europe during the sixteenth century. It arose among men and women who, in fidelity to their understanding of the Gospel, sought to recreate the primitive Christian church as they understood it—a voluntary association among the faithfully committed. Adams tells and retells the story of this historical recovenanting:

> Martin Luther said that all people must do their own believing and their own dying. But Luther did not believe the intention of doing one's own believing could in the slightest degree justify the forming of a religious association or organization independent of "the establishment." For Luther the religious association within which one was to do his believing or her believing was the association sponsored by the Elector. He reasserted the ancient principle *Cujus regio ejus religio*—"the religion of the prince is the religion of the people." Jakob Burckhardt has asserted that the confession prevailing in any territory in the sixteenth century was the religion that possessed the strongest battalions.

In the early nineteenth century William Ellery Channing speaks of the church in idealistic terms. Turning the notion of creedal conformity on its head, he calls the true church "the place of perfect spiritual freedom." Nor is it to be confused, he says, with a congregation or a sect. It is part of the Church Universal from which "no man can be excommunicated, except by the death of goodness in his own breast."

The fact remains that every existing social community, be it a church or a state or family, depends on some forms of coercion, some subtle or overt deprivations of individual freedom. Can a community be powerful and not coerce or dehumanize but remain authentic? This puts the dilemma in highly generalized form; concrete examples of social institutions abound in which it is played out. The negative function of an idealized form like the Church Universal is to maintain a standard against which our actual, historical churches must be judged, or on the positive side, to maintain a larger reality and objective that they must serve. But the meaningfulness of the concept depends on a prior belief, namely in an efficacious transcendent reality. Because issues of freedom and power within a community cannot be answered in the abstract but only in historical experience; the question of renewing community will lead us, finally, to the question of renewing faith.

Political commitments are heavily shaped by fundamental assumptions about human nature and history; an authentic faith, again, does not simply reflect those assumptions, it critically examines and qualifies them. For instance, liberals tend to speak glowingly of change and to idealize the future; conservatives, on the other hand, tend to abhor change and to idealize the past. In the judgment of history, Alexander Hamilton looked backward where Thomas Jefferson looked forward; and yet, in the face of a century of social chaos, Hamilton and other "realists" are heard again. Adams calls attention to their contrasting views:

> Arguing with Thomas Jefferson's confidence in "the people," Alexander Hamilton pounded vigorously on the table and said, "The people! Your people, sir, is a beast!" Here he echoed the word of John Winthrop, the Governor of Massachusetts 150 years before: "The people is a many-headed monster." Responding to these ideas Jefferson had said, "I have always believed that the mass of mankind was not born with saddles on their backs, nor a favored view booted and spurred to ride them legitimately, by the grace of God." The American Constitution that was framed expressed confidence in the people to hold the reins themselves.

We may side with Jefferson, as Adams the civil libertarian does. Still we must ask why Jefferson's optimism has so often been sorely disappointed? Do "we, the people" effectively hold the reins of government in the United States still today, or have we sold our democratic birthright for a mess of prosperity? Corporate economic interests are more powerful today than ever.

Adams holds that without effective social forms, human nature as such is not trustworthy. We must be embedded in the many covenants of humanity to become reliable. A democracy especially depends upon the independence of public-regarding voluntary associations to safeguard human rights and welfare. He often laments the failure of Americans—increasingly, through the decades of the twentieth century—to exercise their simplest democratic right, the right to vote. And much more than a right to vote—a highly individualistic political act—is needed. Many community organizations, he holds, including labor unions and churches committed to the prophetic vision of social justice, are needed to fulfill Jefferson's vision of democracy. Adams returns to one of his favorite exchanges between seventeenth-century Puritans to accent the point:

> "Every English he hath his own contribution to make," said Colonel Rainsborough. "Yes," said another, "if it can be got out of him!" This history of liberal religion has not been content with promoting liberal attitudes. It has sought the kind of organization that elicits tolerance, individual responsibility, and spontaneous cooperation. This organization began with a church meeting. It became what we call congregational polity and then it was taken up by democratic government, democratic education, the democratic family, democratic labor and business organization. In all of these ways the contribution that each man, woman, and child can make is got out of the people. The strong liberal church is the seedbed of democracy.

At this point we need to ask, what social conditions do we need to establish and sustain to bring hopeful assessments of the democratic prospect to fruition? The difficulty we have today in answering this kind of question underlies the challenge to liberalism in all its forms. What is at stake is the renewal of community amid the broken covenants and broken spirits of our time. The question is finally a spiritual question: What will sustain our hope when our optimism has been shattered? Adams observes,

In Massachusetts a new group of mothers organized a march to the State House on Beacon Hill in Boston. Mothers for Adequate Welfare they call themselves: "M.A.W." And what are their demands? They not only request more money for food, housing, and clothing; they also claim the right to know the rules under which society pays them, the right to privacy in discussing their problems with welfare workers.

It requires no fertile imagination to recognize the consequences of such frustrations.... The principal consequences are apathy, cynicism, and despair—the soil of irrationality, criminality, and violence. A sense of inferiority, felt as a consequence of being relatively deprived of rights others enjoy, engenders anger and it turns inward in the form of self-hatred, or of violence against family members and neighbors. The drama...is a tragic one. "The essence of tragedy," as Alfred North Whitehead has observed, "is not unhappiness. It resides in the solemnity of the remorseless working of things."

The remorseless working of things...has produced in the midst of our society a host of exiles...trapped...in the welfare state, exiles from the benefits of dignity and the equal protection of the law. But the remorseless working of things does not end in self-hatred. It can explode outward against the entire system.

...If we see these exiles in their plight, we may be able to hear in a new way the words of St. Paul, that "God hath tempered the body of the community together...that the members should have the same care for one another, whether one member suffer, all the members suffer with it, or one member be honored, all the members rejoice with it" (I Corinthians 12:24-26).

The themes of exile and social body, of broken covenant and new covenant, of alienation and being knit together are parabolic images. They bring transcendental values (sometimes called theological virtues) into the discussion—a discussion that would oth-

erwise remain on a pragmatic or problem-solving level. Often the
theological virtues are precisely named as faith, hope, and love
(see I Corinthians 13:13). On these keystone virtues all other
virtues, such as fortitude, patience, prudence, and temperance, are
said to depend. These value-commitments are rooted in a tradition of faith. If they are to thrive, Adams says, they must be cultivated in a deeply rooted religious community:

> Many a church is mounted by a steeple. Standing high above
> ground, the steeple is subject to wind and storm, to severe
> cold and severe heat. In addition, this steeple points upward.
> The steeple is also grounded by support from below. We
> often hear it said that the roots of a tree reach as deeply into
> the earth as the branches are high. So we might say that the
> spiritual roots of the steeple must go as deeply into the hid-
> den spiritual resources of existence.

Space and time are the physical conditions of our spiritual
existence. A strong sense of place and a strong sense of history are
needed by everyone who would grow into a strong personal identity. Adams says,

> Richard Cabot used to define an idiot as a person without a
> sense of the past. All of the times and places of significant
> memory are a part of us; without them we should not be
> what we are. They are, as Emily Dickinson said, "a single
> hound" pursuing us, the single hound of our own identity.
> We need to strike root into a definite plot of soil. We need
> somehow to find our place in a continuing and promising
> tradition with its sacred books, its communion of saints and
> its disciples. We need the church's community of memory
> and hope through the sharing of which we may in the full-
> ness of time first sense our need for conversion and then
> grow in the grace and knowledge of Christ. In the church we
> accept the truth: *By their fruits shall you know them.* But we
> also accept the truth: *By their roots shall you know them.*
> Where there are no roots, there will be no fruit.

Adams repeats Goethe's maxim often, "A tradition cannot be inherited, it must be earned." You earn a tradition in the process of making it your own. You live with it, argue with it, and restate it in the language of your own experience. The trajectory of Adams's story points to a reappropriation of biblically rooted faith while sustaining the vastly significant contributions of the modern era to human freedom and dignity, in both the personal and social realms of life. It is precisely in this work of reappropriation, while cherishing the humanistic achievements of the modern era, that many have followed the lead of James Luther Adams. However, after a century of horrific violence, we are entirely clear: The attempt to liberate ourselves from all traditions of faith, seeing in them only the dead weight of the past, fails. The Enlightenment project, to build new foundations of civilization and even to understand religion, as Immanuel Kant proposes, "within the limits of reason alone," fails. It cuts the nerve of transcendence and therefore, of the human capacity for self-transcendence. Adams proposes an alternative vision:

> The God of costing love is confronted only when we stand
> as it were at the edge of being and at the edge of our possessions, only when we discover our limits, only when we in
> guilt cry out of the depths for forgiveness, only when we
> stand in the extreme situation, as the existentialists call it.
> T. S. Eliot puts his finger on the inadequacy of the natural
> religion that stands on its own securities:
>
> > In order to possess what you do not possess
> > You must go the way of dispossession.

When Barry Goldwater ran for President, an anonymous wag said, "I always knew that the first Jew to be President would be an Episcopalian." Of Eliot we could say, we always knew that the greatest Unitarian poet of the twentieth century would be a high church Anglican. The joke is pertinent to the broader theme of liberal religion's loss of spiritual and intellectual leadership in the twentieth century, since Eliot, raised within a prominent clan of

Unitarians, is a prime example of return to the basic themes of Christian faith. After discussions with him in the 1930s, Adams comments that Eliot is also personally engaged in the social concerns of his religious community.

"The way of dispossession" means making yourself vulnerable to the claims of others, especially the dispossessed, and living "by faith alone." Every faithful soul must come to terms with dispossession, whether it come by way of chance events or by way of deliberate renunciation. Meeting its truth may come by bitter experience, but we must somehow come to terms with it or die spiritually.

Those who do not hide but reveal their vulnerabilities, their struggles, their doubts—those who acknowledge their common humanity with us—can become what Robert Greenleaf calls "servant leaders." Guiseppi Roncalli understood this principle of spiritual power. Adams tells a story about this extraordinary Pope that comes to him from Etienne Gilson, the distinguished historian under whom he had studied in Paris years before, at the Sorbonne:

> [Etienne] Gilson was a friend of Cardinal Roncalli's, so it was only natural that, after Roncalli became Pope John XXIII, he should visit him at the Vatican. In the course of one of their conversations Gilson finally said, "Well, now, John, how do you like this new job, anyway?" Whereupon the Pope responded, "It's a very interesting job, a fascinating job, but I have my problems." "For example?" said Etienne. "Well, some of those problems are very difficult and some are perhaps a little trivial. You know, Etienne, this is not so important, but it bothers me. One of my favorite relaxations is window-shopping. Wherever I have lived, in Paris or Venice, when I have had free time, the thing I loved most was to go window-shopping. I like to see what the new gadgets are, and I like to see what the new styles are that the ladies are wearing, the hats and shoes and dresses. But now that I have this new job, if I go down in Rome on the streets there is such a tumult of people climbing all over each other—trying to see

what he looks like! They tell me here at the bureaucracy that I can't do it anymore. It's not so important, but by this job I have been deprived of my favorite relaxation. I can't go window-shopping any more."

"What about a more important one?" asked Etienne. "Yes, you know, Etienne, every day I think more and more about the martyrdom of us priests." "Martrydom?" "Yes, it's martrydom, I tell you it's martrydom. You know we priests have to live in singleness all our lives. We can't marry. We're vowed to celibacy. So we can't have any of the joys of family life or conjugal love, or having children and rearing children. I say that's martrydom." And then he said to the professor of medieval philosophy, "You know where we got that, Etienne? You fellows from the Middle Ages imposed it on us. And I can't do anything about it. But worse than that, it isn't in the Bible. It isn't in the Bible."

It is not only the Catholics who suffer the pathos of oppressive theologies from which they cannot liberate themselves but still more the fundamentalist Protestants. The prophetic work of the Universalist church was to challenge fear—ultimately, the fear of hell—as a motivating force of faith. In 1931 Adams heard Jane Addams, the social reformer and founder of Hull House in Chicago, give the Ware Lecture at the May Meetings of the American Unitarian Association:

[Jane Addams] recalled that Horace Greeley, the famous Universalist, when challenged as to the tenets of his church, said, "Yes, it is true that the Unitarians consider themselves too good ever to be sent to hell, whereas the Universalists think God is too good to send anybody there." Miss Addams saw this Universalist view in sharp contrast to that of the pioneer women and men living in the great stretches of the country. Their state of mind, she said, was not unlike that of the vagrant who envied his faithful dog, not only that he grew his own canine clothing and was fashioned to forage easily for his own food, but that his luck was that when he died he would be dead. Here he was unlike his disconsolate master, who said that he "had to go to hell yet."

I heard Adams tell this story in 1986, extemporaneously, fifty-five years after the event. Probably he had told it before, but never in my hearing or reading.

Toward an Inclusive Covenant

A central task of the church is to exemplify and carry forward the quest for more inclusive social covenants in all realms of human existence, overcoming the alienations that breed segregations and the segregations that breed still more rancorous alienations.

Besides the great cultural separations of the modern age, as between religion and science, there are great separations between the religions and a need for extraordinary individuals taking extraordinary steps to overcome them. Enacted parables were used by the Israelite prophets and used again by a prophetic figure of our time, Pope John XXIII, who Adams met as an observer at the Second Vatican Council in 1963. He recalls the scene and the widely admired man:

> After very elaborate preparations, and briefings as to what we Protestant observers were to do in our first audience with the Pope...we arranged ourselves in a circle in the large consistory of the papal palace, the Vatican. At the end of this large room there was a high throne, obviously the place where the Pope normally sits for audiences of this size. At the appointed moment we saw the Pope come in...he sort of toddled or waddled along—with his retinue. He came, shall we say, bouncing in and, looking around, saw us, turned and saw the throne, and immediately began to expostulate. We soon found out that he was saying to the assistants, "I'm not going to sit up there. No, go and get me a chair. I'll sit with my brethren." They had to rearrange everything—pull the

loudspeaker system down from the high throne, bring in a chair—then he sat down among us and proceeded. That's a rather effective way to make friends.

Even if, affirming his separated brothers as brothers, he forgot his separated sisters.

Another symbolic act recalled by Adams demonstrates the Pope's commitment to a more open future for the Roman Catholic Church:

> In the opening ceremony of the Second Vatican Council, the *Kyrie Eleison*, from the opening section of the mass, was the first choral piece that we heard—with the great organ in the Baroque cathedral of St. Peter and the choirboys singing from the cupola.... The sentiment of the *Kyrie Eleison*, "Lord, have mercy upon us," is always pertinent in a worship service but was especially pertinent then, when we consider what has happened as a consequence of the Second Vatican Council. This part of the mass suggests that the first act of the worshipper is to ask for the divine mercy and forgiveness for those alienations, those separations, among us and between ourselves and God.
>
> ... When Pope John XXIII was asked was about the purpose of the Second Vatican Council, he went to the window, opened it, and said to the reporter, "There, perhaps some fresh air will get into the church."

The Pope undertakes this effort to "throw open the windows" because it is necessary, he sees, to the renewal of his faith community. Community is renewed in many ways: by internal self-criticism, by responding to new challenges, and by overcoming alienations, separations, suspicions, and fears—all in the service of a larger vision. Adams says,

> There is one Church that includes all men and women of good will and that points beyond itself to the source and end, to creation and redemption. It is the inheritor of a liv-

ing tradition from Israel and from intellectual traditions of ancient Greece. The Church is bound by something higher than the ideals or accomplishments of its members. It is bound to maintain the spirit of liberty that comes from our being the children of one divine parent.

Adams affirms a concept of the universal church, an "invisible" community of goodwill transcending sectarian and even Christian identifications. The church that understands itself in narrowly sectarian ways, either as "the one true church" or as "we few gathered here," has lost touch with its historical vocation. The renewal of the church depends on our rediscovery of its mission in relation to the contemporary world. It depends on being rooted simultaneously in an ancient tradition of faith and in a sense of the demands of the present world-age. It depends on an egalitarian spirit. Adams calls it *radical laicism*:

> "Gentlemen, let me remind you, Jesus was not a parson." That is, he was from the laity, the people. This salty maxim was a familiar one to theological students at Harvard Divinity School a generation ago from the lectures of Dean William W. Fenn. The word *laity* is one of the most ancient in our heritage. In ancient Athens, "Hear ye people"—*laos* in Greek—was the traditional cry of the herald to introduce his announcements or official declarations. Eventually the word acquired in Greece a note of "archaic solemnity." In ancient Israel the word acquired an explicitly religious meaning in the phrase "the people of God," a people who had received a call, a special vocation: "For thou art a holy people unto the Lord thy God" (Deuteronomy 7:6).

The use of *minister* exclusively in reference to the ordained or the professional minister is a mistake, because ministry is the primary function of the church itself, a calling in which all members—the laity—share. Luther speaks of "the priesthood of all believers" (all are priests to one another); to this Adams adds "the prophethood of all believers" (all are prophets to the world).

The phrase "people of faith" could be substituted for "believers," since it is often felt that *believer* signifies adherence to a particular creed, while *faith* signifies trust and confidence. Of the many distinctions between the two terms, my favorite occurs in a story by Andre Dubus, in which a priest says, "Belief is believing in God. Faith is believing that God believes in you."

Adams does not exalt the preacher as a lone prophetic voice, fundamentally because he believes in the priesthood and the prophethood of *all* believers; *radical laicism* means that the designated preacher is the midwife of a ministry shared with the laity:

> In Herman Melville's novel *Moby Dick*, Father Mapple mounts the pulpit by a rope ladder and for the sake of his independence pulls the rope up after him. The liberty of prophesying about social or institutional evils certainly belongs to the minister. But in radical laicism the trained minister should as it were take the congregation along into the pulpit.

Ministry is the service of the laity, of the professional minister, and of the church body as a whole. Together, these form what Paul Weiss calls "the dedicated community," or in the language of the New Testament, the *koinonia*. The church is renewed, in Adams's vision, through the renewal of its vocation to serve and to befriend one another in community:

> Since the church itself is a ministry, and composed of ministers, the roles of the professional minister must be performed with two presuppositions or goals in mind. First, the church as community and institution is a radically lay apostolate. Only by being such can it offer promise of casting out demons of the mass culture, or (even within the church) of subverting "the iron law of oligarchy." Second, the fructifying locus of the church community is *koinonia*. A transformation of the accommodative, secularizing "denomination" is required. This process can take place not through the revival of sectarianism but through the appearance of the *ecclesiola in ecclesia*.

The small church in the large church—the *ecclesiola in ecclesia*—
can exercise transforming social power. A sect that consciously sep-
arates itself from the larger church gains freedom of action but
loses influence as its members lose any sense of being part of "the
church universal." The small group (*ecclesiola*) that deliberately
stays within and acts upon the larger group (*ecclesia*)—in Edwin
Friedman's terms, "self-differentiated" but remaining "in touch"—
exercises effective leadership within the larger group. Adams says,

> The creation of community is not purely a matter of delib-
> erate contrivance. The process depends also upon the unex-
> pected workings of the divine Spirit, upon tradition, upon a
> sacramental group life. Because of the complexity and sub-
> tlety of the mysterious working of the power of God, the
> agent of healing and renewal must be the *koininia* [commu-
> nity] which nourishes and protects and responds to the di-
> versities of gifts that come from the hand of God.

The complexity and obscurity of the sources of authentic
community is analogous to the complexity and obscurity of profound parables. To tell a parable (and to have the ears to hear it
with comprehension) is to uncover hidden realities. In this sense
a parable can be a mediator of transcendental meaning or, we
could say, an instrument of revelation. In just such terms Adams
conceives the essential task, the ministry and vocation, of the
church, a theme he relates to a painting and a poem that interprets
it. Adams cites "Musée des Beaux-arts," W. H. Auden's poem that
begins, "About suffering they were never wrong The Old Masters,"
and he comments,

> The mythological figure Icarus and his father had been im-
> prisoned on the island of Crete. To enable Icarus to escape,
> his father had made artificial wings that he attached to his
> son with wax. But Icarus flew so close to the sun that the wax
> melted and he fell into the Agean sea. Prominent in the paint-
> ing "The Fall of Icarus," by Pieter Brueghel the Elder, are
> peasants tilling the field, while in the background a beautiful

ship is "sailing calmly on" in the harbor. Icarus, who has fallen into the sea, is almost invisible in the lower corner of the picture, and his cry of distress remains unheeded. Normal life is going on steadily and unwittingly all round while Icarus falls and drowns. Here we find a paradigm of the vocation of the church and the minister—to reveal the hidden, to point to hidden realities of human suffering, and also to point to hidden realities that offer release and surcease.

The world sails by heedless of human suffering; it is the loneliness of pain that makes it so unbearable. It is "hidden" in large part by our willful blindness, our moral unwillingness to see or aid those who suffer. In this light Paul's grand metaphor, the church as "the body of Christ" (Romans 12:4-5), becomes a parable of moral action, for the church embodies the Christ when it perceives and suffers with the sufferings of the world in concrete and costing ways.

We speak in parables—in figures of speech, aphorisms, obscure or surprising tales, oracles, and other rhetorical devices—out of a sense that the deepest meanings of life are hidden from sight and yet revealed by some symbolic action, verbal or gestural. It is the function of the church, Adams says, "to uncover hidden realities." They are hidden because they embarrass us, or they feel morally uncomfortable and we want to keep them out of sight—as Dylan Thomas notes about the way Americans love flashy wealth and fashionable styles, keeping the squalor of poverty hidden away in back streets. This is why liberation theology insists upon the power of the poor to reveal truth. God favors them, according to the prophets, because they make no pretense to self-sufficiency.

Adams speaks of the ministry of the church as one of "acceptance of the unacceptable" and inclusion of the excluded. Its covenant should not be "restricted" but "inclusive." Reflecting on "The Fall of Icarus," he says,

> We are aware of the axiom from the New Testament, "By their fruits you shall know them." Of the believer and of the

congregation we may say also, By their *roots* you shall know them. They are hidden roots to be sure, but roots that ever give life and newness of life to the faithful, to the trans- formed and transforming community of faith, which instead of "sailing calmly on," can hear the call of human need. That need is for the community seeking for mercy and justice.

The endorsement of community is qualified, since commu- nities can also be oppressive and unjust. There is something par- adoxical about Sartre's famous outcry, "Hell is other people," for it is only other people that torment us—unless we torment our- selves. The focus on "other people"—omitting mention of one's self from the picture of Hell—reminds us that ultimately the tor- menters and the tormented are bound together. We torment one another and in our neuroses we also torment ourselves. Sartre is beyond blaming God for the inexplicable pain of the human con- dition. As a professed atheist he would not indulge in God-talk, of course, but as Adams suggests, his existential humanism lies close to an existential theism, a faith that accurately describes the utter absence of God and therefore may imply a "waiting for Godot":

> Jean-Paul Sartre's anti-hero speaks for many when he cries out of his loneliness, "There is no need for hot pokers in this place. Hell is—other people," That is, other people with whom one enjoys nothing significant in common. In the end this sort of isolation leads to the madhouse. Sartre's demand for fellowship is a secularized version of the sovereignty of God. The human being is made for fellowship.

We should note that Adams refuses to make any principle ab- solute, even the positive principles he makes the most of, includ- ing community, fellowship, church, and covenant. He notes, for instance, the use of "restrictive covenants" in real estate to exclude "undesirables." He could also note Isaiah's oracle decrying the Israelite leaders' "covenant with death" (Isaiah 28:15, 18). No reli- gious community, whether it fancies itself progressive or conservative, is immune to the ravages of petty jealousies over leadership and stout resistance to change.

Nevertheless, the positive valuation of community is primary, while the negative as its distortion remains dependent upon it— "as the shadow points round to the sun," in Adams's phrase. He notes,

> The first line of modern "psalm," by English artist and social reformer William Morris, reads, "Fellowship is life; lack of fellowship is death." Authentic and viable fellowship, however, must be fellowship in self-criticism, a harbinger of the fellowship of renewal. The alternative is "fellowship" in routine, that is, in living death. The fellowship that is life is fellowship in growth.

Adams turns Shakespeare's phrase "the uses of adversity" into "the uses of diversity." As the university should be a diverse community in which and through which an underlying unity of purpose is expressed, so should the church be. Such a vision of the church is so far removed from the kind of haven for childish behavior frequently displayed in congregations— mature people sooner or later flee in disillusionment—that it makes us wonder at Adams's idealism. We must say, yes, this is an ideal, a vision that serves as the foundation of a doctrine; if we did not in some sense believe in this ideal we would despair altogether.

In history events do not always turn out as we expect or wish. We are not fully in control of our own destinies. We may be radically disillusioned, painfully disheartened. Blessed are those who expect much and yet learn and grow, and sometimes even rejoice, when their expectations are contradicted, turned around, and sometimes changed for the better. Adams tells this delightful story about finding the unexpected amid the familiar:

> G. K. Chesterton once said that he had toyed with the idea of writing a novel in which a group would undertake an expedition of exploration. They would sail for many months, the voyagers seeking hitherto unknown territory to be declared

a colony for Great Britain. Finally land would be sighted, and they would head for the shore and plant the Union Jack and the flag of St. George, doing all the things necessary to claim the land. Previously they had noticed some barbarous buildings and appurtenances. But now as they advanced they would discover that they had landed on the southern coast of England at the bathing resort of Brighton!

I take it that Chesterton's intention was to remind us of the variety of things, amazing things, that we fall into the habit of taking for granted. The novel would show how different it was and what a great thing it would be to discover England—or even to discover oneself!

The feast of Pentecost (also called Whitsunday, falling fifty days after Easter) is "the birthday of the Church," when the unifying spirit of God descended upon Christians from several different lands (see Acts 2:1-21). Adams suggests that the "birthday" is rendered contemporary by renewals of spiritual freedom, producing a purely voluntary unity:

> The people of Babel were caught up by a demonic suprapersonal power that drove them into blasphemous unity. By way of contrast, the Christian church had its forceful and missionary beginning at Pentecost. The Holy Spirit then raised persons above themselves not into a Procrustean conformity but rather into a community where many languages were heard and yet where everyone heard the others speak in one's own language, where persons retained their own individuality and yet through the Spirit were open to the others, where the common relation to the universal engendered unity in diversity. Here we find the paradigm of diversity as a gift from the divine fecundity. May we not say, accordingly, that the true uses of diversity are in the hands of God, leading us again and again from our pretentious and self-destructive Towers of Babel to ever new Pentecosts, which let "the wind bloweth where it listeth"? (See John 3:8.)

Covenants are solemn commitments, declaring, "This we will do, come what may." One of the basic commitments of a church or other religious community is to venture together into uncharted seas—not just to say "we know" but "we will learn," and not just "we have arrived" but "we will discover." In Adams's words, "The church that is free is a pilgrim church on adventure." In 1975, on the sesquicentennial of the founding of the American Unitarian Association, Adams responded to William Ellery Channing's litany on spiritual freedom, "I call that mind free" (1830), with his own litany, "The Church That Is Free." To Channing's heroic individualism Adams responds in his characteristic accent, namely, the social nature of freedom: We are free when we join with others in voluntary association for ends that transcend us. The highest end and aim of human life, reflected in these words, is a vision of reality in which all beings are reconciled to one another and redeemed from destructive tendencies:

> I call that church free which enters into covenant with the ground of freedom, that sustaining, judging, transforming power not made with human hands. It protests against the idolatry of any human claim to absolute truth or authority. This covenant is the charter and joy of worship in the beauty of holiness....
>
> I call that church free which promotes freedom in fellowship, seeking unity in diversity. This unity is a potential gift, sought through devotion to the transforming power of creative interchange in generous dialogue. But it will remain unity in diversity.
>
> I call that church free which responds in responsibility to "the wind [that] bloweth where it listeth." The tide of the Spirit finds utterance ever and again through a minority. It invites and engenders liberation from repression and exploitation, whether of nation or economic system, of race or sex or class. It bursts through rigid, cramping inheritance, giving rise to new language, to new forms of cooperation, to

new and broader fellowship. The church of the Spirit is a pilgrim church on adventure.

But the church is never wholly free: It tolerates injustice,
special privilege, and indifference to suffering, as though it
were not accountable to a tribunal higher than the world's. It
"passes by on the other side," thus breaking the covenant. In
the midst of this un-freedom the congregation comes together to adore that which is holy, to confess its own brokenness, and to renew the covenant.

Even his ecstatic utterance ends with a warning against ideal-
izing the church or any human community. From the confession
that, like the priest and the Levite in the parable of the Good
Samaritan, it "passes by on the other side" (Luke 10:31), the
church can renew its covenant, its founding charter. Authentic
worship will remind the church itself and not only individuals of
its need for confession and recommitment.

Covenant as Creation in Time

Creation takes place not only in nature but also in human history.
We participate in the creativity of the natural and temporal order
by acting with conscious intent, individually or in groups. But
even when we act individually, we are working with the materials
of the natural and social worlds that are at hand, so when we create we never really "go it alone." The Biblical creation story
(Genesis 1-3, melding two distinct stories) leads up to a series of
covenants that the Creator makes, first with Adam and Eve and
then with succeeding generations, in the form of rules that cir-
cumscribe human freedom of action. "Eat whatever you want, but
don't eat from this particular tree"; thus Genesis provides a mythic
understanding of that which distinguishes our humanity, creative
freedom, "the image of God" in which we humans are (continually) made.

Scholars agree that the creation story in the first chapter of
Genesis was composed much later than the stories of the ancient

Israelite confederation and entry into "the promised land." So it seems likely that, in the historical development of ancient Hebraic thought, the idea of covenant preceded the idea of creation. Thus the Biblical creation story in Genesis 1 is a poem that describes the process of creation by presenting a vision of the beauty and order of "the creation," including human beings. Genesis 2-3 describes the responsibilities that belong to the original man and woman, called Adam and Eve—that is, to human beings as such—in relation to the creation. That they are said to be made "in the image" of the Creator seems to mean that they enjoy a freedom that is analogous to that of God, but with the responsibility to use it for good rather than for bad ends. Thus later commentators have spoken of a "covenant with Adam," as something implied in his special place in the creation. The creation—a great and good gift—is covenantal in that it implies that we cannot blame our pains or our troubles, or even death, on external, malevolent agencies or realities, because these are part of the natural order and the humanly made moral order. The covenant is founded in love and gratitude for the natural order in which our lives are embedded, and the covenant is fulfilled by taking moral responsibility for our deeds, knowing that then we can repent and correct our wrongs.

Consider this analogy: Creation is to nature as covenant is to history. In this sense *covenant* is creation within the history of human societies, and humans participate in "social creation" by acts of covenanting. Adams comments,

> According to Genesis, God looked upon his creation and saw that it is good. *Esse est bonum qua esse.* "Being as such is good." The evil in humanity or in nature does not issue from their materiality. The true destiny of humanity is not to escape from flesh and time. No matter how evil we have become through the abuse of our freedom, our restoration or our fulfillment is held to be a realization that fulfills creation. The ancient doctrine of the resurrection of the body is a mythological expression of this view as is also the doctrine that "the Word became flesh" (John 1:14). Even after the

mythological formulations of the Book of Genesis had been abandoned or "broken," this positive evaluation has remained. In this respect we may say that modern secularism is a Jewish-Christian secularism.

To read a myth, metaphor, aphorism, or parable literally is to misread it; to "break" a myth, then, is not to destroy it but to move beyond naïve realism to critical realism. Kenneth Burke makes this point in his seminal work, *The Rhetoric of Religion*; to understand a metaphor, he says, you must "discount" it. To say that a myth is broken is to say that it cannot be swallowed whole any more; to break it open is to release the insight "bound," as it were, within it—as energy is bound with an atom until it is "broken."

Hence Adams argues that the Resurrection and Incarnation are theological symbols that affirm the value of temporal existence by pointing to an ultimate fulfillment of the creation; theologically, this is a divine promise, a covenant. He is seeking a way beyond rationalistic humanism to what Martin Buber calls *Biblical humanism*:

> Humanistic interpretations of sin and grace and humility seemed to me truncated, only parodies of Christian theology. Humanism envisaged them in too narrow a frame of reference. It reckoned without its host, "our neighbor the universe." Both scientific and literary humanism had done what Millet did when he first painted "The Sower." They and he alike left no room on the canvas for the field into which the sower was casting his seed. Like the Millet of the second (and better-known) painting—also called "The Sower"—I felt that the man should be placed in the larger setting so that there might be two principles rather than one: the man and the earth upon which he is dependent for the growth of the seed.

Adams's attention to history and its struggles, as compared with his relative neglect of nature and its powers, runs parallel to the priority he gives time over space, or more precisely, the ascription of meaning or power to particular spaces, or places, which he calls "spatialization." He notes two reasons for this: "The great achievement of the covenantal religion of Israel was to disengage itself from the cults of fertility of the Caananites and to think of the human being as in this sense overcoming nature." His transformed liberalism is not far removed from Reinhold Niebuhr's neoorthodoxy; both men share the "neo-Reformation" focus on history and God as acting in history.

Nevertheless, Adams seeks a balanced view of history and nature: "In our time Protestant Neo-orthodoxy has tended to overstress the view that God is to be understood not so much as the Creator of nature as the redemptive Lord of history." He reflects on the theological significance of nature in an essay on his student, close friend, and colleague, George H. Williams:

> There is grace from below as well as grace from above. We are both a part of nature and are separated from it. "There is surely a piece of divinity within us," says Sir Thomas Browne, "something that was before the elements and owes no homage to the sun." We come from below in one sense: the very salt solution of our blood corresponds to that of the salt density of the sea. We are nevertheless brought out of the water and the seas and lifted up to be reborn as rational, responsible creatures sustained by grace. But the water and the seas are still a part of us. Indeed, water becomes in baptism a symbol for creation and re-creation, of spiritual birth and regeneration through grace from above. In this sacrament, and also through the elements of the Lord's Supper, nature is brought into the history of salvation in a community of faith. Sight, sound, touch, and the olfactory all belong in the liturgy and the sacraments, that is, in the liturgy and the sacraments that do not submerge us in the subhuman, the biological sphere.

Even here nature is circumscribed by history and by Adams's reflections on the way elements of nature are drawn into the sacramental life of the church, the human and historical sphere.

Consideration of natural and involuntary forms of association moves the discussion from a purely historical and voluntary conception of covenants to an ontological expression, the idea of a *covenant of being.*

Interpersonal relationships in marriage and in the family are highly important sources of meaning in human existence. These relationships are only in part voluntary; in part they are inherited, in part they are socially or biologically impelled. A mixed case is the communal home, such as Gould Farm, in Great Barrington, Massachusetts, where Jim and Margaret Adams built a summer home and for many years took part in its therapeutic community. In 1956 Adams wrote,

> Gould Farm is a fellowship not only for the inner "family" of members who maintain the community. It is open to "outsiders," to people who in distress of mind or spirit wish for a time to participate in a community of affection that gives renewed meaning and depth to life. Gould Farm, in short, is a therapeutic community. It does not live merely for itself, as many intentional communities have done. It is a "self-transcending" community. To all sorts of people it offers healing, the healing that can only emerge as [its founder] William Gould believed and showed, in the atmosphere of harmony and mutual aid that characterizes the true family. The Farm has been a haven not only for those who in sickness of spirit desperately needed the fellowship that is new life but also for those who, like the many refugees from Europe of the past two decades, needed a place in which to get new bearings and a new start in a strange land. Many have come with nothing or little in hand to pay for shelter. For others the maximum weekly fee is a very modest one.

Adams also compares this community to the extended family he remembers from his own childhood:

> In certain respects we can see in Gould Farm and in many intentional communities a revival (and a revision) of the

earlier extended family, where a dispersed cathexis [concentrated psychic energy] obtained and where the channels of affection and the transmission of values were more varied and more effective than in the current urban nuclear family.... What I would like to see is the kind of commune that attempts to combine "separation from the world" and impact upon it through community social action and other kinds of political activity.

For all his emphasis on the role of voluntarism, Adams is fully aware of the background of involuntary associations, especially the family, as primary bearers of grace and judgment in our lives:

The mental and emotional "landscape" within which one lives makes a world of difference. I can recall that when on the farm I was scheduled for punishment for misdemeanors, my grandmother could be depended upon successfully to mitigate the vigor of my father. My grandfather was a delightful raconteur, and I listened to him eagerly while father and mother were busy. My grandmother, in her youth a schoolteacher, was a stickler for grammar, correct spelling, and precise vocabulary and syntax. Besides, she sang old folksongs from the South. "Go tell Aunt Patsie, the old gray goose is dead." And so it went in the extended family. Let us say that Aunt Mary loved poetry, and Uncle George was a Socialist. The father might suggest to the children that George was a crank and should not be taken seriously. But around behind the barn Uncle George expostulated on the evils of capitalism and the "antics" of the revivalist preachers. Aunt Mary in her love of poetry was also not to be taken seriously. "What good was that poetry?" Both the Uncle George and the Aunt Mary of the extended family represented a gentle criticism of (and complement to) the "establishment."

Viewing the situation of the extended family as a whole, we can say that more channels for the transmission of value preferences and cultural sensitivities were immediately available. In the nuclear family these channels of sensitivity and stimulus are radically reduced.

Extended families and communes offer a breadth of experience and thus can vastly enlarge the emotional "landscape" of the child's development—involuntary associations though they be. The marriage covenant, in Adams's view, seems to work in the opposite direction, for it begins as a voluntary commitment and gains its value precisely from the stability of that commitment.

> In a memorable short story, "The Darling," Anton Chekhov depicts a woman who successively becomes the wife of several husbands who, one after the other, die or disappear. One is the manager of an open-air theater, another is a lumber merchant, and still another is a veterinary surgeon. In each of these marriages the woman completely identifies with the interests and also with the vocation of her husband. As a consequence, each of the husbands calls her "a darling." Chekhov, for his part, makes her appear to be a chameleon, possessing no intrinsic mark of her own, though he says also that "she was always fond of some one, and could not exist without loving." After reading the story, Tolstoy wrote a sharp and perceptive criticism of it. Chekhov, he says, completely misses the heart of the matter. He should not have been content to mock at this woman. Indeed, Tolstoy concludes that Chekhov, "like Balaam, intended to curse, but the god of poetry forbade him, and commanded him to bless. And he did bless, and unconsciously clothed this sweet creature in . . . exquisite radiance."

Clearly Adams sides with Tolstoy and his perception of a divine compassion that of necessity overwhelms human ridicule, for those with ears to hear. The covenant binds us to meanings deeper than we consciously know or deliberately decide. Willy-nilly, we serve the gods of poetry, or of love, or of the covenant people of God. Adams notes that the covenant of marriage can lead us into fuller discoveries of our humanity:

The ambiguity of the marriage relationship was stated succinctly by the Britisher who on hearing that large numbers of people in the United States were becoming divorced by reason of incompatibility, exclaimed, "But I thought that was the purpose of marriage!" This comment serves to remind us of an extremely important aspect of marriage and also of friendship—the role of contrast in relations between individuals. Marriage brings together two people possessing special individualities with particular qualities and limitations. Acceptance of the limitations of the self and of the other, besides appreciation of the positive qualities of each, is an implication of the covenant. The vocation, the opportunities and the perils, of the marriage covenant reside in a special way precisely in the particularity and even in the limitations of the covenant.

Adams draws an admittedly imperfect analogy to artists who work with the limitations of their materials and of traditional forms:

William Wordsworth, writing about the sonnet form, sees in its confines something like "the convent's narrow room":

> ...'twas pastime to be bound
> within the Sonnet's scanty plot of ground.

The beauty of a particular poem depends upon the poet's respect for the unique form of the sonnet. Marriage is not different in is opportunities and its demands. It is the enduring occasion, the vocation, to find meaningful and responsible fulfillment in the peculiar, individual qualities and limitations of the other and the self.

According to Harvard Divinity School lore, the faculty entered into a pact. They would preach for the Wednesday noon chapel services on a common theme, the Ten Commandments, each taking the one assigned by the group. We must imagine Adams liking the idea of such a shared discipline and graciously accepting his being assigned the Seventh, "Thou shalt not commit adultery." He says,

> The intercourse that makes two people into one body is im-
> bued with the love of the one for the other. It is without its
> proper meaning unless it consummates love in its various
> dimensions, and unless it expresses the recognition of the
> ontological change in the man and the woman and in their
> relation to each other, a change that gives rise to a special vo-
> cation of togetherness under God. Adultery is a denial of this
> ontological change and a demise of the new vocation. This
> denial can arise from a variety of motives. It can be a form of
> discontent with the self or of discontent with the other. It
> can issue from a chaotic desire for variety. As such it is a
> form of *acedia* similar to the slothfulness of noon day which
> John Cassian [early fourth century] attributed to the monk
> who in a wandering of spirit and in loss of self-discipline
> yearns for a different monastery where, he imagines, true
> piety is properly appreciated.

This sermon elicited a rebuke from fellow theological ethicist Beverly W. Harrison in one particular, namely the suggestion that marriage is ontologically rooted, so that the sexual fidelity one commits oneself to in marriage cannot be violated without violating our "being." Harrison says, "'Thou Shalt Not Commit Adultery' attests Adams's devotion to marriage, but its claim that 'marriage is rooted in the covenant of being itself' is a rare example of ahistorical theological cant and does not answer to the urgent need we have for fresh critical reflection in sexual ethics." Yes, this is a hot-button issue, and yes, Adams does not address the broad range of questions in sexual ethics. But he does not argue that monogamous marriage is an eternally decreed or historically unchangeable form. He presumes that the fact that people have always and everywhere established ethical norms and legal codes regarding the sexual and procreative relations of people of one sort or another suggests that a "covenant of being" is involved—within which, as we have noted, historical covenants can take various forms. These few comments cannot resolve the intricacies of the issue that Professor Harrison raises, but we may note that they are an instance of the unresolved tension that arises for liberalism when it is said that something is historically relative: What sources of ethical norms will liberalism appeal to? If liberals in the face of the contemporary gay marriage controversy assert that "marriage is a human right," they are making a philosophically rooted moral claim about a social form called *marriage* (not *civil union* or some other term that sounds morally neutral).

Adams is a traditionalist in terms of personal morality and never questions traditional norms and institutions of interpersonal sexuality. I do not read his argument so much as a defense of monogamy as a giving to Eros, a god too powerful to be trifled with, his due. I know a woman—a feminist and realist about human nature—who holds a more radical opinion; she says, "There is no such thing as divorce." She is not voicing Roman Catholic doctrine but one of those "lies" that, once qualified, turns out to be true. There is a legal right to divorce, and often divorce is a personal and social necessity; nevertheless, we deceive ourselves if we think there are no lasting psychic effects of important personal commitments, once entered into, even if they prove untenable in time.

This case-in-point may show the inadequacy of a voluntarism that is not ontologically grounded. Adams is aware of the ambiguity in voluntarism: Although we have free will, we are not free to form or dissolve whatever covenants we wish (and trying to do so, we come to grief) but only those that partake of the nature of being, or better, the covenant of being.

The aforementioned Kirsopp Lake, a professor of New Testament and one of Adams's teachers at Harvard, is a favorite subject of his stories:

Kirsopp Lake published a book entitled *Religion Yesterday and Tomorrow*. A reviewer said that its substance could be summarized in the words of Lewis Carroll as "Jam yesterday and jam tomorrow, but no jam today." The notion of no jam today did not, evidently, carry into every arena of Professor Lake's life. There were various stories of his philandering. A professor who was looking for him at Widener Library, where Lake had his office, was unable to find him. He asked an attendant if he had seen him. The fellow said that he had, indeed, seen Professor Lake a little while ago, "declining upstairs." "That's all right," said the inquirer, "just so long as he's not conjugating."

This is Adams's published version. As I recall the oral tradition, the inquirer after Professor Lake was Mrs. Lake. Be that as it may, Adams's own views of the matter are not jaded or moralistic but socially and psychically realistic:

> Marriage is a bond within the context of a larger covenant, a covenant of the community of faith under God. To violate the covenant of marriage through the act of adultery is to break not only a covenant between husband and wife but also their covenant with the community. One cannot consider adultery a merely private action.

A "communitarian" concept of marriage, as distinct from our society's dominant "libertarian" concept—an individualistic concept that denies any wider social consequences of divorce—follows from Adams's "old fashioned" observations. His story of Charles and Dorothy Hartshorne celebrates what Shakespeare calls "the marriage of true minds":

> Dean "Pomp" Colwell told a story at a faculty reception at the University of Chicago about Professor Charles Hartshorne. (Charles was not himself present, but his devoted wife, Dorothy, was there.) At an afternoon affair Charles got into an intense discussion with one of his colleagues. At a certain moment he looked down at his hand to discover a lighted cigarette there, whereupon he said, "My God! What is that lighted cigarette doing in my hand? I don't

smoke!" The laughter was of course hearty, for the group had now heard still another story about the notoriously absent-minded Charles Hartshorne. Then Dorothy Hartshorne, being annoyed, tried to stop the irreverent laughter, but without immediate success. Finally she was able to say with earnest indignation, "But Charles doesn't swear, either!"

Charles Hartshorne, a philosopher who reflects at length on natural and divine processes, told me that when he first came to Austin and was shown around an old residential section near the University of Texas by a real estate broker, Dorothy had not accompanied him. He was choosing a house on his own. When they approached a modest house on Sparks Street with a huge, bifurcated live oak in the front yard, Charles said, "I'll take it." "But don't you want to see what the house is like *inside*?" the broker asked. "That won't be necessary," he replied. He chose the tree, and I am sure that Dorothy Hartshorne fully approved the choice.

Adams's nocturnal habits are legendary. It is said that staff arriving at the Meadville Theological School building in Chicago would not uncommonly find him in his bathrobe, shuffling out of the library stacks, on his way home next door, in hand the open book he'd gone to find in the middle of the night. It may seem odd, then, to hear him praise sleep, or perhaps not, for he could not but be attuned to the restorative and healing powers of sleep:

> Dr. Robert South, the eminent court preacher in London, once interrupted his sermon to awaken the prime minister and warn him that if he did not moderate his snoring, he might awaken his majesty, the king. By way of contrast we recall that in ancient times sleeping in church was a hallowed practice. Indeed, as a form of dream therapy it was given a technical name, "incubation." This word denotes the practice among the Greeks and Romans of sleeping within the precincts of a temple for the purpose of receiving a vision, a portent of the future, or relief from disease or pain. Ancient inscriptions record priestly prayers giving thanks to God

(under countless names) for revealing himself or herself during the sleep of the worshiper. Sleep (with its dreams) has been interpreted under countless names—from a supernatural source of revelation and healing to the work of a demon to a biological-psychological fountain of refreshment—and also of terror. Is it possible to find a religious interpretation of sleep, and even of dreams? Perhaps we should with Robert Frost go out and try "to clear the pasture spring...to rake the leaves away (and wait to watch the water clear, we may)."

Dreams are closely associated with myths. Adams cites Emerson's claim that humanity is "a myth-bearing tree." Gleaning anywhere and everywhere, Adams calls up myths and metaphors that glimpse life, beyond the opaque, illusion-bound surface that life often presents. Even then, many dreams are reflections from that surface, more baffling than enlightening, as Adams notes:

> Human beings are dreaming, myth-bearing creatures, and our myths are our bane as well as our blessing; they are the harbingers of damnation as well as of salvation, of disease as well as of healing, of the demonic as well as of the diamonic, of abject pessimism as well as of indomitable optimism. Every functioning myth is susceptible of these polarities.

All things that partake of time and history are ambiguous, yet this is the condition of all creative endeavor.

Covenant, Grace, and Peace

Adams takes a historical and ethical term, *covenant*, as a root metaphor for existence as a whole, *being*. The term *covenant of being* serves as an eschatological vision of the unity of reality and a reminder that this unity is not a human achievement but a gift of God's grace, a gift given for love's sake alone. He affirms,

> The covenant is a covenant of being. It is a covenant with the creative, sustaining, commanding, judging, transforming

powers, which can be interpreted theistically, non-theistically, humanistically. It is a religious covenant, the orientation to something we cannot control but something upon which we depend, even for our freedom.

When I asked Adams about the origin of the term, he thought it might have come from Jonathan Edwards; subsequently I have found the term used by the philosopher Fritz Kaufmann in a source that Adams was probably familiar with but had forgotten. Professor Kaufmann writes,

> It seems to me the nature of Jewish thought to make the idea of the Covenant an ultimate category of religious metaphysics—not merely penultimate such as it appears in the neo-Platonic tradition and in the interpretation of the Divine from Philo to Schelling and Jaspers. *B'rit* [covenant] and *z'dakah* [righteousness] are keys to the world of the Hebrew language because they mark a correspondence which is not merely one of harmonious proportions but one of true community and communication as the pith and marrow of being.... Human existence as a free and bold enterprise is communication with and communication of the creative impulses that rise from a depth deeper than the depth of the Self which we control, the Self which we can sacrifice by placing ourselves at the disposal of what may ultimately dispose of *us* one way or the other. We sanctify and glorify it by our unconditional accord and cooperation, but also, if need be, by defying and running counter to the currents and prevailing conditions of our time. Through this union and communion with the Highest—not the haughtiest or most clamorous—we become partners—junior partners—in the Covenant of Being.

In a letter to me Adams asserts that *covenant* and *consent* are parallel terms, drawn from theological and philosophical thought, respectively. Jonathan Edwards does use a closely related phrase, *consent to being*, which he calls "dissent from that which dissents from Being." Edwards writes,

> Excellence in and among Spirits is in its prime and proper sense, Being's consent to Being. There is no other proper consent but that of Minds, even of their Will; which, when it is of Minds toward Minds, it is Love, and when of Minds towards other things, it is Choice.... Dissent from such Beings, if that be their fixed nature, is a manifestation of Consent to Being in general; for consent to Being is dissent from that, which dissents from Being. Wherefore all Virtue, which is the Excellency of minds, is resolved into Love of Being....

The phrase *consent to being* implies that participation in Being— the largest imaginable reality—depends upon processes of voluntary consent, a bonding or a covenanting; the alternative, *dissent from being*, implies an unstable state, a state of passing out of existence. Thus an element of freedom is inherent in all existence; a being must "consent," as it were, must devote itself to the whole of its own volition. *Consent to being* combines the sense of necessity, or inescapability, and the sense of voluntary commitment, or acceptance. Adams says,

> The intimate and the ultimate—indeed all parts of the interrelated world—the individual, the middle structures, the government, the society, and the divine creative ground of meaning—are held together by covenant. The bonding and binding quality of covenant, the ordering principle, is "promise." God is the promise-making, promise-keeping reality upon which we ultimately depend as the reliable, creative, sustaining, judging, community-forming, and community-transforming power. Wherever these powers are working, the divine is working. Accordingly, to be human is to be able to make a commitment in response to the divine promise.

Together with his friend Walter Bense, Adams published and commented upon the works of Rudolf Sohm, a German Lutheran jurist and theologian active in the early years of the twentieth century. Sohm sees the deadly connection between authoritarian and legalistic patterns of thought. Arguing that this is an aberration from Luther's original genius, he rejects legalistic definitions of authority in the church in favor of charismatic ideals. Persuasive power, attractive charm—whatever *charisma* is—has been seen as a gift of the gods. Adams finds pagan origins of the word (perhaps its first literary use) in Homer:

> Odysseus, after he was shipwrecked, lands on a small island and is hiding in the rocks, and suddenly overhears the voices of young maidens. Nausicca and some other young ladies of this principality have finished the Monday morning laundry and they start to play softball. The ball is thrown out of bounds and Nausicca herself runs off into the rocks to pick up the ball. There, she suddenly confronts Odysseus, a shipwrecked sailor in his natural costume. And at this moment Athena gave him grace—she surrounded him with an aura of majestic beauty, an aura, a glow of power and attractiveness, beauty. The word used is *charis*. She gave him grace.

Adams refers us to the sixth book of the *Odyssey* for the original story, in which the *charis* that Athena showers on Odysseus is what enables Nausicca to recognize him as a man—and no doubt a handsome fellow—rather than a salt and seaweed–encrusted beast. Adams then turns back to his theological theme, noting that "Sohm selected this word, charisma, to characterize the power that gives life to the religious community and holds it together." Further, he suggests that *charis*, or grace, signifies spiritual freedom, a quality that is the mirror opposite of demonic possession:

> When the gods depart, the half-gods arrive. Nietzsche suggests in psychological terms the tragic nature of the process of fragmentation. In order to become effective in history, he says, a thing must be loved for more than it is worth. Yet it becomes a monstrous *Unding* destroying its own context. Demonic fragmentation substitutes the part for the whole.

A German word like *Unding* is untranslatable. "Nonthing" seems too static; "something negated" is awkward but comes closer.

Adams sees academic specialization as an instance of cultural "fragmentation." He asserts that specialization, while inherent in "the search for reliable knowledge" in the university and the theological school, can have dehumanizing and de-politicizing effects:

> There can be a demonic devotion to isolation from public concerns and accountability, a devotion that tempts us to say that some specialists are more dangerous for their virtues than for their vices. I recall that the day after the atomic bombs were cast upon Hiroshima and Nagasaki, the atomic physicist Leo Szilard, who with Albert Einstein had persuaded President Roosevelt to sponsor the Manhattan Project, came to me and Charles Hartshorne to say that science and religion had been too long separated, that the time had come for them to work together with a new sense of public responsibility for the uses to which their knowledge was put. He acknowledged that he was a little late. We formed an all-University Committee to express protest and penitence. One wonders what might have happened had the cooperation come earlier. As it was, we had traveled what Shakespeare called "the flowery path that leads to the broad gate and the great fire."

All things exist in relationship to each other. To act as if that were not so is an illusion. To will it not to be so is demonic. And to recognize that a falling out of relationship among living beings is inexorable, if any being is to assert itself and become effective in history, is to recognize the tragic dimension of existence. But Adams affirms that, to the person of faith, tragedy is not the last word, for in the end the relatedness is more inevitable and inexorable than its opposite, the constant falling out of relationship:

> How can anything have meaning if everything does not? Or, as Calvin would ask, how can anything be viable if it is not

rooted in "the God who is the fountain of all livingness"—
that is, if it is not rooted in grace?

Grace, then, is a kind of fertile soil, the place of a garden.
There is a dreamlike quality of aspiration, an aspiring to a "state of
grace"—a place kept pristine, beyond the tearing, striving, frag-
menting world that surrounds it and from which it is fenced off,
like the unicorn of medieval myth in his garden. Adams finds
symbols of grace in ecological relationships:

> Strictly speaking a myth is a story about the gods. In Western
> symbolic tradition myth tells of the divine in relation to the
> human, or the whole in relation to the parts. To ignore insti-
> tutional behavior and responsibilities is to ignore the whole.
> It is to imprison the flower within the crannied wall. In the
> poem "Peter Bell" William Wordsworth protests against the
> failure to recognize broader relatedness:
>
> > A primrose by a river's brim,
> > A yellow primrose was to him
> > And it was nothing more.
>
> In the Old Testament the sense of authentic ecology, an ecol-
> ogy of grace, is present in institutions as well as in personal
> experience.

Adams uses the intriguing term *ecology of grace* in another
context as well:

> John Bunyan has epitomized what we may call an ecology of
> grace. "Christians," he says, "are like the several flowers in the
> garden, that have upon each of them the dew of heaven,
> which, being shaken with the wind, they let fall their dew at
> each others roots, whereby they are jointly nourished, and
> become nourished of each other."

Grace, then, is not a substance but a structure, a form of relatedness. Among other notoriously obscure Tillicheanisms, Adams
explicates the term *Gestalt of grace*—grace as embodied in histor-

ical or social form. Here we see that parabolic and paradoxical sensibilities are akin; both set side by side things that are not apparently congruent. Adams says,

> Grace is something present, but not something objective. According to Paul Tillich, "It symbolizes something that transcends existence and spirit, and yet something that is the real meaning, the real significance, of a concrete form." Thus reality can become the bearer of a meaning that unconditionally surpasses or transcends it. Wherever this meaning exists, we have a *Gestalt* of grace, that which supports and gives meaning to existence but not as an object.

So grace is not simply an outward appearance, like Athena's bright shower over Odysseus; it is something that goes before or underlies existence. It is the root of faith, met in "signals of transcendence." Attempts to express the meaning of grace are often paradoxical, as Adams knows.

The most powerful spiritual realities can only be expressed by symbols, such as light, or in parables. Johann Wolfgang von Goethe says, "What is more splendid than gold? Light. And what is more refreshing than light? Conversation." A riddle, too, is a kind of parable. On his deathbed Goethe, as quoted by Adams and others, cried out, *Mehr licht!* "More light!" The story as reported by K. W. Müller is less oracular, more human:

> Towards sunrise—as the doctor had predicted—[Goethe] had got considerably worse, and his strength continued to ebb. The room had been left quite dark, to keep the patient quieter, but he said: "Give me light; it's unpleasant in the dark."

Further on in Müller's notes for March 22, 1832, after rising from his sickbed and going to his study, Goethe complains that someone had left his friend Schiller's correspondence on the floor (Schiller had predeceased him) and calls out, "'Will someone please open the other shutter in this room as well, to let in more light!' These were said to have been his last words."

The term *covenant of being* evokes the sense of reality being knit together in ways that are hidden from our full understanding, ways that allow good things to happen. Adams cites a symbol of transcendence in which all contradictions are overcome:

> Nicholas of Cusa's "icon of God" (1454), an omnivoyant portrait which, regardless of the quarter from which the pilgrim regards it, "Looks upon him as if it looked on no other," each experiencing the directness of its gaze, each being precious in its sight but none claiming to possess the icon as his own prerogative, and each knowing that "it taketh the same most diligent care of the least of creatures as of the greatest, and of the whole universe."

Adams returns several times to this image of mystical union between "the intimate" and "the ultimate," between human particularity and divine omnipresence. The spiritual experience is an event; it is necessarily interactive rather than a property belonging to the icon in itself. The icon becomes a mediator of a meaning contained neither in itself nor in its viewer but in the interaction between them.

Adams similarly finds a symbol of transcendence through transforming relationships in Jesus' parable of "the Prodigal Son." In his interpretation of the familiar story (Luke 15:11ff.), the father is "the icon of God" who steadily reflects back what each son needs to see:

> The parable of the prodigal son is, we might say, a metaphysical parable, a picture of the social cosmos of divinely given community, of the divinely given human freedom, and of the divinely given task to fulfill that freedom in all its venture and risk. In short, this is a parable of the nature of existence and meaning, and of the love of God—of God's love for humanity and of the human response to that love. Its principle religious import lies in the parable as a whole—in its assertion that the total human condition is to be understood as a manifestation of God's love and

that participation in community is our responding to love
for God. Each of the elements of the parable must be understood in this context, the dignity of the creature by
virtue of its participation in the social cosmos, the community of relatedness in freedom ("Give me my portion,"
says the son), the isolation and frustration that issue from
the breaking of fellowship, the possibility of new beginning, the enrichment and fulfillment of community that
comes from reconciliation. And we should add that this
whole picture depicts not only the loss and the regaining
of community on the part of the son; it presents, in the
image of the father, the attitude of love which all must take
toward each other in the re-formation and transformation
of community.

These metaphysical sensibilities underlie and inform the moral
dilemmas and imperatives that present themselves to us in history. Here our covenants, our agreements, are formed, broken,
and reformed.

Adams devises the following allegory of the covenant of
being, which he also calls *shalom*, or peace:

Would it be possible to contrive a visual image, an icon that
projects for us the nature of shalom, of peace and wholeness,
in a way that is appropriate for our religious faith, appropriate for the recognition of individual conscience in an open
and free community? Can we find an image for a community that strives for unity in diversity, a visual image that
takes into account a concern for the powerless in our society,
an image that can communicate to the eye what language
cannot do through the ear?

To my surprise there has come to mind a visual image
from the work of a contemporary American artist,
Alexander Calder, who is famous for his mobiles. How shall
we in words describe a mobile? Everyone has seen one. A
mobile is a light, abstract construction usually suspended

from the ceiling. It is made up of little pieces of metal subtly poised and deployed in space and delicately held in balance by a web of thin wires. The entire mobile is sensitive to gentle breezes that stir it into movement. Each little piece of metal possesses its individuality, sometimes enhanced by color; yet, all of the pieces taken together form a unity, a community, a covenant of being composing a whole. Individuality of the members, relatedness of each to each and to all, organic wholeness, and all in movement and in perfect balance and tension. Why not call it *shalom*? This mobile, we may say, is an artist's ideal image, a composite icon of dynamic fulfillment individual and social—the transcending harmony of the kingdom of God. In this image the powerless have a place in which they possess the power of self-determination in community. Moreover, when you disturb a mobile by touching it, it veers out of balance but then returns to equilibrium drawn thither by gravity, the integrating power of the divine.

I know not what Alexander Calder would have said to my calling one of his mobiles an image of the kingdom of God susceptible to the tides, the winds, of the Spirit. He might have pleaded, "God save me from pulpit homilies." But could not Jeremiah yearning for *shalom*, and Jesus weeping over Jerusalem, see in it an ideal image nourished by hope? The image, to be sure, is an ideal; it is not an image of "the real world." But it suggests how that world lives when it is creating a viable world of wholeness.

꩜ *O Thou whose glory fills all things, whose majesty is beyond our comprehension but richly apprehended, and whose presence we would always seek; we turn to thee in joy and thanksgiving, in joy because thou hast called us to have some part in the creative and redemptive life of the world, in thanksgiving because we*

*have been vouchsafed a cloud of witnesses to thy love.
We pray that thy presence may inform and form our
labors, bringing us toward an ever purer joy and fellowship in obedience to thy commandments. Amen.*

—JLA

Renewing Faith:
Taking Time Seriously

LUDWIG WITTGENSTEIN OFFERS an abstract but precise description of the nature of religious belief. His words provide a template that aids our understanding of the thought of James Luther Adams:

> It strikes me that a religious belief could only be something like a passionate commitment to a system of reference. Hence, although it's a kind of *belief*, it's really a way of living, or a way of assessing life. It's passionately seizing hold of *this* interpretation. Instruction in a religious faith, therefore, would have to take the form of a portrayal, a description, of that system of reference, while at the same time being an appeal to conscience. And this combination would have to result in the pupil himself, of his own accord, passionately taking hold of the system of reference. It would be as though someone were first to let me see the hopelessness of my situation and then show me the means of rescue until, of my own accord, or not at any rate led to it by my *instructor*, I ran to it and grasped it.

The "system of reference" Adams is committed to is, broadly speaking, the sacred tradition that lies at the heart of the Hebrew and Christian scriptures and is extended in the history that follows from it—or more precisely, a selection from this history, ignoring

this and accenting that. The central criterion in this process of selection and interpretation is what Adams calls *prophetic theology*, a
theology that attempts to see all things in relation to the creative,
judging, and re-creative power of God at work in history. Adams
uses the phrase *taking time seriously* to title his autobiographical
essay, written at midlife and announcing the social-ethical seriousness of his lifework. A critique of both individualistic mysticism
and of intellectual distance is more than implied; it is explicit in
Adams's "passionately seized interpretation."

Thus a moral directive and a critical principle ("a way of living" and "a way of assessing life") are entailed in Adams's thought.
Wittgenstein apparently takes for granted what intellectuals often
ignore, namely that "instruction in a religious faith" is a primary
purpose of religion and its institutions, especially congregations
and theological schools. Adams himself does not ignore education
but writes on the nature and importance of liberal arts and professional education, including training for the ministry. In personal terms, he maintains vocational commitments to both the
church and the academy throughout his life.

Wittgenstein also speaks of a portrayal or description of a system of reference as amounting to "an appeal to conscience." In
terms that are parallel to these, Adams says that theology speaks
first in the declarative voice, describing the play of human and divine powers in time and history. In response to these perceptions,
it speaks also in the imperative voice, appealing to our moral sensibilities and social-ethical concerns. The end in view is commitment, as Wittgenstein charmingly accents.

As noted in the Introduction, Adams sees in Jewish and
Christian thought constant variations on the themes of Creation,
the Fall, and Redemption. We see these elements and this pattern
in Adams's own thought, too. Obviously, this pattern is not provided by rational analysis; it is the story line of an ancient myth.
Every theologian, then, will have some notion of the original
goodness of life, of something that has corrupted or twisted or re-
pressed the original goodness, and finally of that which redeems

the situation. The story incorporates a strong element of tragic loss, but it is finally not a tragic but a triumphant story. It is worth recalling, at this point, Adams's formal definition of *theology* as the interpretation of major symbols in the face of the present historical situation. The three symbols in the story are interrelated; thus the last, Redemption, renews the first, Creation, but on a new level. In time and history, of course, the last act is never last but becomes a new first act, beginning a new cycle. Adams is most interested in these symbols of faith in relation to the present historical situation, that is, the social-ethical bearing of this narrative of faith upon contemporary life and history. He is interested in the seasonal relevance of any story, theology, or philosophy. He asks, Does this interpretation of reality "take time seriously"?

The theme that ties these many themes together is the question of authentic faith. Adams speaks of the primacy of the will as "the red thread" running through his thought. The phrase refers not only to his philosophical voluntarism, which he contrasts with intellectualism or rationalism, but also to a religious standpoint, one that sees faith as a personal commitment, or an "original decision." That is, faith is an act of will that orients the heart and the mind to transcendence, a stance from which truer understanding—including reasoned inquiry—can grow. In this way the true, or the authentic, expression of one's will is one's love.

A prophetic theology, in Adams's understanding, observes that having faith in something is a human inevitability. The central theological issue is to distinguish authentic from inauthentic or idolatrous faith. (Adams does not speak of true and false faith, probably because that implies an objective certainty, or knowing, in a realm where the best we can have is meaning.) To recapitulate the argument:

First, an authentic faith focuses our attention on ultimate issues, such as God, human nature, and the meaning of life, but in a way that connects with our immediate, personal, existential life concerns. It links what Adams calls the *intimate* and the *ultimate* dimensions of life.

Second, an authentic faith elicits from us a commitment that is costing in some significant way and degree. *The primacy of the will* means that intellectual understanding follows from the commitment expressed by the original decision in favor of faith and its subsequent life decisions.

Third, an authentic faith wrestles with what St. Paul called "the principalities and powers" (Colossians 2:15) of the world. It takes responsibility for the shape of things to come in the human community. It does not withdraw from the world but even ventures a new beatitude, *Blessed are the powerful*.

Fourth, an authentic faith seeks to incarnate its spiritual and moral value commitments in the community and world about us in social institutions. It cannot do this by labors of individual virtue or piety but only in groups acting together in history. Therefore we may say, *By their groups you shall know them*.

Fifth, an authentic faith takes shape in history through the commitments that we, the promise-making animals, make with others. It is shaped by the historical covenants we form within the context of a sacred, encompassing *covenant of being*.

Sixth, an authentic faith locates itself within the encompassing drama of history. It believes that there is a meaning in history and that the true directive of human life is found in responding faithfully to this meaning. The heart of Adams's thought about the character of faith is that it *takes time seriously*.

The final subject, then, is faith and its renewal. Not a fanaticism masquerading as faith or the stoic reaction, which having seen through the masks of religion vows to live without faith. In the fanatic and the stoic, opposites coincide. Both live by denials of responsiveness and feeling, and we are asked to settle for truncated forms of humanity. What we need is the renewal of an authentic faith, without diminishment and indeed with the enlargement of our humanity. In the prayer at the end of this chapter, Adams voices a prayer for this kind of faith: "Awaken in us the faith to open ourselves to the grace of renewal."

In this chapter, Adams argues that having some faith is un-avoidable; therefore, the distinction between authentic and mis-placed (or idolatrous) faith comes to the fore. In our time "the acids of modernity" have rendered both ancient and modern statements of religious belief problematic; consequently, faith seeks authenticity in paradoxical and imaginative forms of ex-pression, including metaphorical, narrative, and other artistic forms. Adams's own story-telling and other rhetorical inventions exemplify this creative process.

Adams holds that faith is never purely private but is necessar-ily personal and rooted in historical communities. It concerns de-cisions regarding our personal and social existence that cannot be evaded; that is, faith is existential. Adams does not think that faith can be distilled in a changeless creed. It is both stained by history and, if it is powerful, it leaves its indelible mark on history; in his phrase, there is no "immaculate conception of truth." Faith is formed through the historical experience of human communities, and reformed through processes of "deliberation and decision" within those communities. This is the lived meaning of Adams's phrase that best captures his conception of authentic faith, "taking time seriously."

The Inescapability of Faith

Faith is inescapable, for all of us put our faith—our trust and ef-fective life commitment—in something. Therefore, the question is not whether we shall have faith or be persons of faith. The ques-tion is whether our faith will prove to be authentic over time and in the face of the challenges of human existence. In the words of Adams,

> The question concerning faith is not, shall I be a person
> of faith? The proper question is, rather, which faith is
> mine? Or better, which faith should be mine? For whether
> a person craves prestige, wealth, security, or amusement,
> whether a person lives for country, for science, for God, or

for plunder, that person is demonstrating a faith, is showing that he puts confidence in something. He may go to
church regularly, he may profess some denominational af-
filiation, he may repeat his creed regularly, but he may actually give his deepest loyalty to something quite different
from these things and from what they represent. Find out
what that is and you have found his religion. You will have
found his god. It will be the thing he gets most excited
about, the thing that most deeply concerns him. But speak
against it in the pulpit or the Pullman car, and he may forget what he calls his religion or his god and rush "religiously" to the defense of what really concerns him. What
moves him now is more important than his creed or his
atheism; it gives meaning and direction to his life, to his
struggles, and even to his foibles.

Faith as such seems wholly abstract. We want to know what,
in concrete terms, we may place our faith in. To a theist the answer
seems simple. The one, proper object of faith is God, and all other
articles of faith are subsidiary to that. While sounding straightfor-
ward, this is deceptively simple, for the questions quickly follow.
Why believe in God in the first place?

The answer illustrates again the circularity of theology because any lesser faith is a form of idolatry, that is, a trust and belief in something we have created rather than something that
created us. This supposes something more than a mythic or literalist notion of what it means to create. It includes the recognition
that absolute origins are shrouded in mystery, so we are speaking
of a transcendental idea, something indefinable.

A second question follows: What, concretely, is the meaning of
God? As Adam's writings clearly show, the assertion that God is the
one object of faith does not conclude but only begins the adventure of religious reflection. Such an adventure is directed both
outward and inward; it is a quest for firmly anchored meaning and
it is a quest for self-discovery. Tell me about your God and I will
tell you who you are. Adams characteristically speaks of a God

who is the power of true liberation at work in history, who is
known in the experience of personal or communal liberation.
However, in essence the divine Spirit is "free as the wind," as the
Gospel of John suggests, and not to be captured in words or in any
symbol system. Adams says,

> I call that church free which responds in responsibility to the
> Spirit that "bloweth where it listeth" [John 3:8]. The tide of
> the Spirit finds utterance ever and again through a minority.
> It invites and engenders liberation from repression and ex-
> ploitation, whether of nation or economic system, of race or
> sex or class. It burst through rigid, cramping inheritance,
> giving rise to new language, to new forms of cooperation, to
> new and broader fellowship. The church of the Spirit is a pil-
> grim church on adventure.

Adams synthesizes the thought of many others. His predeces-
sor in teaching social ethics at Harvard, Francis Greenwood
Peabody, develops the idea of "the church of the spirit." Alfred
North Whitehead, one of Adams's intellectual mentors, accents
the "adventure of ideas," which is more than an intellectual adventure; it is also a spiritual adventure insofar as it signifies the exercise of human freedom in an open universe. I have spoken of
faith as an *original decision*, but not, as people commonly assume,
to the exclusion of further questions. To the contrary, the original
decision of faith—or as Adams often accents, *authentic faith*—
opens continually outward to new questions.

Too often, what passes for faith is arrested development.
When people say they have outgrown their childhood faith, they
are speaking of faith as a static thing, a given set of beliefs now
seen as childish. Mature people recognize that their childhood experience, ideas, and beliefs enter into their adult self-awareness,
and they would not have it otherwise. We see the transformation
of religious awareness ("emotion passed through the fire of
thought," as Emerson says) in the many stories Adams draws from
his childhood and youth.

The mature faith Adams seeks for himself and commends to others is not only a passionately embraced faith, it is a critical, self-questioning faith, "an examined faith." In a personal tribute to his teacher Irving Babbitt, Adams cites Friedrich von Hügel's praise of Ernst Troeltsch and reflects on his own ideal and method of education.

> Surely...the most ready, yet also the most costly method of learning deeply, that is, of growing in our very questions and in our whole temper of mind, is to learn in admiration of some other living fellow man, recognized as more gifted, or more trained, or more experienced than ourselves.

Here is a philosophy of education in a nutshell: We learn by inspiring personal exemplars, and we learn by "growing in our very questions." Answers always beget further inquiry, new and larger questions, as Adams sees in his intellectual mentors, including Babbitt, von Hügel, and Troeltsch.

We are often reluctant to make judgments about the faith of others, and rightly so. That is why we need the principle of discernment: "By their fruits you shall know them." "Fruits"—just deeds, truthful words, a spirit of goodwill—are one test of authenticity. Another is self-criticism and openness to reform.

Adams's story of how his undergraduate speech professor administered a "shock of recognition" to him, namely the recognition of his vocational passion—"You're going to be a preacher!"—is cited in the first chapter. He says he went "to talk to this strange counselor by night," a reference to the Biblical story of Nicodemus who went by night, sight unseen, to Jesus and asked him, "How can a man be born when he is old?" As a later re-telling of the story makes clear, it was only symbolically "by night" that he went to talk with the professor, Frank Rarig. What is notable about their conference, as Adams remembered and reported many years later, was its significant duration and its apparent recognition of the student's seriousness. The professor offered an incisive and memorable criterion distinguishing a liberal religion:

By appointment I went to his office on a Saturday morning, and we talked for three and a half hours. He told me that I was provincial and naïve, that I apparently had never encountered a self-critical religion, and that this was the reason for my blanket hostility. He went on, however, to say that obviously my most passionate interest was religion.

An authentic faith is not a "blind" but an "examined" faith, Adams says. Its integrity depends on its ability to maintain a self-critical rather than a dogmatic or unquestioning stance.

It is of course natural to resist criticism, and when it comes to matters of personal devotion, in which an emotional investment has been made, it is even more natural to resist self-criticism. While all religious traditions teach humility before the transcendent, many regularly violate the principle of humility, especially with respect to their own brand of religion.

Many people will remain reluctant to accept the implications of the inescapability of faith. They believe that they know the meaning of "God" in popular or common-sense usage. The only remaining question is whether or not such a divine being exists. This attitude is a setup for either dogmatic belief or dogmatic atheism. The principle of humility ("This I believe, but I may be mistaken") is foreign to them, because they've staked their identity on their belief or unbelief. But people who are spiritually aware or self-aware are likely to approach the question of God differently. Adams says,

> We might say that there are two quite different ways to discuss theology. One may start with a definition of God—as the Creator of the world, for instance—and then try to prove that this Creator exists; or one may start with some other conception of God and try to prove that such a God exists. On the other hand, one may identify known realities or tendencies that are worthy of loyalty, or that we can rely upon— realities that are ultimately a gift to us, that are viewed as sacred and sovereign, that are inescapable if life is to have

meaning. If we speak of a reality as ultimately reliable, as dependable, as sovereign, as sacred, we are speaking of the divine, whether we use the word "God" or not.

We may say that naming God is necessary and unavoidable if we are not to surrender what is essential to our humanity, namely, living for ends and by standards that transcend us. The basic conflict is not, as we commonly suppose, between belief and unbelief, but between authentic and distorted, truncated, or otherwise inauthentic faith. The issue is not atheism but idolatry. Rationalists have been slow to recognize the shift to existential and historical forms of consciousness and have continued fighting the intellectual battles of earlier generations—reason and science versus superstition and dogma. This is not a new story. From the 1930s on Adams decried religious liberals' obliviousness to this shift. They were, he said, "caught in a cultural lag."

Much of what passes for intellectually grounded atheism is tainted with anti-intellectual attitudes toward religion. Popular or common-sense atheism—"God-talk doesn't make sense"—tends to close off theological discussion and resists attempts to reopen it. But to Adams,

> The supposition is that the unexamined life is not worth living, or as one of our colleagues used to say, "An unexamined faith is not worth 'faithing.'" This signifies the soul of learning and religion.

What Adams calls "an examined faith," I have called "critical theism," a theism that has passed through the fire of doubt and self-reflection. It is a strategy for opening the subject to intellectual inquiry through empirical research, conceptualization, dialogue, and consensus formation. By these processes people in community gain distinctive character and gain a sense of shared purpose in history. This outlook has practical consequences. As Adams approvingly notes, the educational ideals established in the last century by Unitarians at the Meadville Theological School, then in Meadville, Pennsylvania, draw upon "the broadest range of disciplines, of scholars and their traditions out of Athens, Sinai, and Galilee, indeed also out of Benares and Peking and Cairo."

Theological education so conceived is not apart from a liberal education but is virtually an extension of it. My great grandfather, John Boughton Beach, graduated from Oberlin College, married Celestia Ann Holbrook (one of the first women to graduate from Oberlin, the first undergraduate college in the world to admit women), and went on to graduate in 1861 from the Meadville Theological School. Oberlin, founded by Congregationalists, was a hotbed of evangelical Christianity and abolitionism, precisely the mix of reformism and faith that Adams identifies with. He says,

> The free person does not live by an unexamined faith. To do so is to worship an idol whittled out and made into a fetish. The free person believes with Socrates that the true can be separated from the false only through observation and rational discussion. In this view the faith that cannot be discussed is a form of tyranny. An unexamined faith is not worth having, for it can only be true by accident. A faith worth having is a faith worth discussing and testing.

From its origins, religious liberalism has been virtually defined by openness to rationalist and historicist perspectives. But in Adams we also see the shift from liberal modernism to the postmodern outlook of liberation theology, in which all perspectives are colored by the social position, whether privileged or marginalized, of the individual. Rather than seeking to escape time and embrace an inward spirituality, such a theology "takes time seriously," that is, it seeks historical awareness and engagement in current issues of social justice.

Religious liberals typically have difficulty recognizing that their own belief or unbelief, faith or faithlessness, and not somebody else's, are implicated in this liberationist perspective. They are not accustomed to starting from the supposition of voluntarism—the primacy of the will also means the primacy of commitment—

but have been satisfied to have reason and common sense liberate them from some brand of fundamentalism, or perhaps from some brand of cynicism toward organized religion. Often, they still want to believe that there is an objective, ahistorical viewpoint, perhaps a rational or scientific viewpoint, from which we can be the sovereign judges of the truth or falsity or the meaning or meaninglessness of any claims of faith or faithfulness. Adams seeks to awaken liberals from this dogmatic slumber. Without this awakening there is no renewal of faith in the sense that Adams advocates:

> Let me repeal reticence so far as to say that the experience of Nazism induced in me a kind of conversion. I recall a conversation with Karl Jaspers at his home one day in Heidelberg in 1936. I asked him what he deemed to be the contemporary significance of liberal Christianity. He replied with unwonted vehemence, "Religious liberalism has no significance. It is *Zwang*—no costing commitment." He was thinking of the liberals who had become "German Christians" (Nazis), the while overlooking the impotence and silence of orthodoxy and neoorthodoxy in the burgeoning period of Nazism, overlooking also the collaboration of the Catholic Center Party and the Vatican with Fascism and Nazism—a collaboration that is now at last receiving candid discussion precisely in Catholic circles in Germany. So Jaspers now offered me some advice. "If I were a young man of liberal preferences today, I would return to the most orthodox branch of my heritage." Immediately I asked him if he planned to do this himself. He flushed, he blushed, and replied, "I am not making a personal confession. I am giving you a sociological judgment." So spoke the pupil of Max Weber!

Nevertheless, Adams's respect for Jaspers runs deep. His thought is characteristic of the turn of European intellectuals from liberalism to existentialism in the last century. Like many other theologians of his generation, Adams followed the path they marked out. In one of the films that he made in Nazi Germany during this time, we see Karl Jaspers and his wife, who was Jewish. Adams comments on the grave difficulties the philosopher underwent to protect her—successfully, in the end—from the Nazis.

Movement in the direction of religious liberalism is often seen as a temporizing or weakening of a literalist view. But when strong faith commitments apparently lead the believer to withdraw from the world into pristine spirituality, moving toward religious liberalism can mean the opposite—a strengthening of faith. At the same time, this means that religious liberals must learn once again to take theological language seriously. Those who have thought to leave God-talk behind forever find, under Adams's tutelage, that they must reconsider the strong theological language of incarnation and eschatology, doctrines that speak of the embodiment of faith in human existence and of the directive of history toward transformation and fulfillment. Adams comments,

> In the tonic words of Walter Bagehot, "Strong beliefs win strong men, and make them stronger." But this strength is ultimately not our own. It is a gift that awaits the taking—and the sharing.

The "strong beliefs" of the Puritans and other movements to revive Augustinian Christianity have won strong men and women. Calvinist Puritanism especially has shaped the modern world, with its science and technology, democratic ideals, and economic triumphs—along with the cultural and ecological disasters associated with these same achievements. By insisting that the strength lent by strong beliefs "is not our own," Adams recalls the central religious concepts of faith and of grace. Indeed, he calls himself "a theologian of grace." To move beyond the failures and depredations of the modern age, the period in which liberalism has been the dominant cultural force, we must seek an equally strong sense of grace, a way of confessing a strength "not our own." Grace is the gift of God that is offered not as a reward for good behavior but for love's sake alone. In Adams's words it only "awaits the taking—

and the sharing." Faith is an act of trust and consent, an inclination of the heart and orientation to the whole of life. He expresses his liberal Christian orientation quite simply and clearly:

> The liberal Christian outlook is directed to a Power that is living, that is active in a love seeking concrete manifestation, and that finds decisive response in the living posture and gesture of Jesus of Nazareth. In a world that has with some conscientiousness turned against this kind of witness and its vocabulary, the effect of this witness will in a special way depend upon the quality of its costingness in concrete action and upon its relevance to the history that is in the making.

In two sentences Adams says virtually all that needs be said, first about theology, classically defined as "faith seeking understanding," and then about ethics, which he defines as "faith seeking understanding in the realm of action." True to his dialectical sensibility, the first sentence is modified by the second, leaving it to his readers to synthesize the two. We need to hear both sentences, the one about the Christian story, the other about the fate of this story in our time. When a sacred story becomes an idol, then nonbelievers (who even without knowing it may be persons of authentic faith) will turn against it with "some conscientiousness." Hypocrisy is devastating. So the problem is not rational doubt, it is inauthentic faith—in Adams's words, "faith that is not the sister of justice."

Paradoxical Faith

Faith depends on discernment of what is worthy of our devotion, loyalty, and confidence. But in our time relativism, scientism, skepticism, nihilism, and various sorts of ideological radicalism have rendered traditional expressions of faith problematic. Authentic faith does not depend on having the right words, even the word *God*, for this word too becomes an empty idol when you assume you have captured it in a definition or, as more commonly happens, a cliché. Then faith may take refuge in oblique, satirical, and even grotesque forms. Acts of reverence can become just "acts." Adams reports,

> In Paris there is a *cabaret philosophique* called *Le Neant* ("Nothingness"), which for a certain kind of playful grotesquerie is probably unmatched in the world. Everything in this cabaret is designed to remind the customers of death, including their own. They sit at coffins instead of tables in a palatial room hung with skeletal remains and with various texts on the nature of death. A master of ceremonies dressed as a priest makes the rounds, reminding the customers individually about the ominous pallor of their complexions. One customer is usually persuaded to get into a coffin and be wrapped up to the neck in a shroud. What fun for the affluent society!

The grotesque, whether playfully or painfully handled, is significant as a reflection of the dark side of human existence, a side that has grown ominously large in our time, an age of incongruities. Adams is interested in "the grotesque" in the arts as a deeply felt, and therefore deeply motivating, moral judgment:

> Dylan Thomas, taking a close-up view and writing from America to his wife, epitomized this grotesquerie in a homely way: "The food shops knock you down. All the women are smart, slick and groomed, as in the magazines— I mean in the main streets; behind lie the eternal poor, beaten, robbed, humiliated, spat upon, done to death."

The age itself is grotesque and incongruous and often evokes moral revulsion and various forms of "acting out." The alternative response, psychic numbing and social withdrawal, is also common. Either way, Adams says, our humanity is under stress:

> We live in a world of terrorism, holocausts, nuclear weaponry, and indifference to poverty and hunger. How shall we not

feel what Wilfrid Gibson in the poem "Lament" calls "the heart-break in the heart of things"? A hand is laid upon us.

Ours is the age of anguish, of irony, of paradox, of acerbic observation and satiric humor. Such parabolic forms may serve to spark theological insight and perhaps even faith itself. Adams appeals again to his familiar partners in dialogue:

> Ernst Troeltsch, by including chance among the concepts of historical study, does not overlook Pascal's dictum, "If the nose of Cleopatra had been shorter, the whole face of the earth would have been changed." One recalls Pascal's speaking of the contradiction: That which is just on the west side of the Pyrenees is unjust on the east side.

Blaise Pascal is a harbinger of our age in that he sees with full clarity the contingencies of history and the resulting arbitrariness of human claims to truth and justice.

Once asked if he were a Tillichean or a Whiteheadean, Adams responded, "There is always Troeltsch." While Adams draws deeply on the thought of Paul Tillich and Alfred North Whitehead, in numerous writings he also interprets the work of the less well-known scholar, social historian, philosopher, and liberal theologian Ernst Troeltsch. Reflecting on Troeltsch's attempts to overcome historical relativism—the recognition that history does not support absolute judgments of truth or morality—Adams says,

> How, then, can history be overcome by history? Certainly not by forgetting it. Rather, by facing the new historical situation with its evils and its possibilities, individuals and groups may give new application to the value insights of the heritage. Ernst Troeltsch viewed history as providing the matrix out of which treasures both new and old are born, but only through sharp criticism and re-conception in the face of new situations. If liberal Christianity cannot deliberately participate in this process, it is not to remain viable, for it

cannot assist the person of today to achieve an identity or individuality that overcomes history with history.

Speaking of orthodoxy's bifurcation of history into sacred and secular—into the dogmatic realm of miracle and
the realm of the history of culture—Troeltsch characterized
the contemporary religious "dogmatists" as those "who believe that they are able to pluck fruit without having a tree,
or those who, after cutting a small, dry twig from an old
trunk, expect fruit to grow from this twig." On the other
hand, religious liberals who have desisted from reflection on
the pregnant past have for their part attached themselves to
a small, dry twig of contemporaneity, expecting fruit to grow
from this twig alone. Noting the similarity between this kind
of orthodoxy and a converse type of religious liberalism, one
may say with Sainte-Beuve, "Nothing is so much like a hole
as a swelling."

Troeltsch's magisterial work *The Social Teachings of the
Christian Churches* correlates types of religious thought with types
of religious organization—the church, sect, and mystical types. In
Troeltsch Adams finds his intellectual and spiritual soul-mate.

Troeltsch wrestles repeatedly with the questions of historicism,
that is, the way all modern knowledge is tinged with consciousness
of historical change, leaving no certainties in its wake. This is especially unsettling to historical religions, like Christianity, which are
built on a sacred history of divine revelation. But pressed to the extreme, historicism may be said to transcend itself: Seen through the
lens of historicism, all things are seen in their uniqueness. Adams
comments,

> In a 1923 lecture, never delivered on account of his untimely
> death, Troeltsch says that he has been "more forcibly" im-
> pressed every day by the significance for history of the con-
> cept of individuality. He therefore comes to hold that what is
> "nobly common to mankind and universally valid...is at

bottom exceedingly little." Here he seems to push the "uniq-
uity" of historical phenomena to the extreme. Nevertheless
he retains the conviction that standards of truth and value in
the various high religions are valid for them, and that the
Christian standards are "valid for us." "Each of the faiths," he
says, "may experience its contact with the divine life."

This position has been called nominalistic, unlimited
relativism. It has also been called a form of henotheism. It is
neither of these.... Troeltsch asks, "Who will presume to
make a really final pronouncement?" And he replies, "Only
God himself, who has determined their differences, can do
that." Thus he combines an acute relativism with a sense of
the transcendent meaning of the relative. He says, "A truth
which, in the first instance, is a truth for us does not cease
thereby to be the very truth and life." On the religious level he
maintained a tension within his mind, asserting on the one
hand that "the divine life is not one but many" and on the
other that "to apprehend the One in the many constitutes the
special character of love."

Thus the idea of the One speaking distinctly and with equal validity to all who gaze devoutly upon it, an essentially mystical parable, is said to resolve the problem of historical relativity. With such
parabolic faith the problem of acting with confidence and moral
integrity seems, in principle, soluble.

It remains that we live and act amid the ambiguities of existence, and we must take "the courage to be" upon ourselves, recognizing that often we will be in the wrong and in profound need
of forgiveness. Just this brings us back to the crux of faith. It remains that "history is not the place of human happiness," as Hegel
says, but the place where we travel with Death and the Devil at our
sides. And just this reminds us that faith is the first, the foundational, theological virtue. Adams quotes Paul Tillich:

It has rightly been said that Albrecht Dürer's master engrav-
ing, "Knight, Death, and the Devil," is a classic expression of

the Lutheran Reformation and—it might be added—Martin Luther's courage of confidence, his form of the courage to be. A knight in full armor is riding through a valley, accompanied by the figure of death on the one side, the devil on the other. Fearlessly, concentrated and confident, he looks ahead. He is alone but he is not lonely. In his solitude he participates in the power which gives him the courage to affirm himself in spite of the presence of the negativities of existence. This new confidence is the consequence of the forgiveness of separation from God, the consequence of the person's accepting that one is accepted.

Here Adams seems to adopt Tillich's concept of faith as "the courage to be," a courage rooted in the experience of forgiveness, the liberating and renewing act of "accepting that one is accepted."

A religion that does not touch the depths of human despair and personal failure, a religion that substitutes talk about religion for existential experience and self-expression, a religion that does not offer forgiveness (accepting that "you are accepted" thanks to an unaccountable grace), the religion that is oblivious to divine love—that religion will fade from human hearts. Adams notes,

> Paul Tillich restates Martin Luther's doctrine of justification by faith by adopting the existentialist concept of the "boundary situation." He uses this concept to expose the spurious search of the individual for security in terms of one's own resources; he applies it also to the church's claim to have something securely in its possession. Both the individual and the church (and also the culture) must be driven to the "boundary" where human possibility reaches its limit. Luther, he said, "stood in the depth of the boundary-situation and dared to reject all safeguards that piety and the church wished to extend to him."

This is the original radicalism from which Luther's Reformation sprang, restated in the language of contemporary existentialism (especially its accents on particularity and contingency), and Marxism (especially the idea of unmasking ideologies as false securities). Tillich describes "the boundary situation" as the most propitious position from which to describe a culture. On the boundary one is neither purely insider nor outsider.

We may wonder: Where does Paul Tillich's thought end and Adams's thought begin? That seems impossible to say, except in those instances where Adams explicitly dissents from Tillich. Of all his partners in theological dialogue, he is closest to Tillich and transmits his ideas directly:

> Faith is "receiving and nothing but receiving." It is a channel and not a cause. It is to be distinguished from *fides historica*, the acknowledgment of historical facts. It brings forgiveness and new beginnings. It engenders confidence that the unacceptable is accepted. It accepts the unjust person as just, and transforms the person in terms of anticipation. It creates personal courage in the face of temptation, anxiety and despair. It brings participation in a divine reality, the ultimate center, which is the ground of the person and of the good and the true. It gives rise to the trans-moral conscience—the joyful conscience—that in turn establishes morality from a point above morality. It brings victory over law, guilt, and death. In short, faith is the accepting of the power itself out of which we come and to which we go.

Personal confession can be a parable, a revelation of otherwise hidden meanings of wide and even universal significance. Lest faith be reduced to one more good work, its dialectical negation, doubt, must also be brought into play, especially in the face of contemporary culture's hyperreligious cultural soup. Adams explains,

> When believing the unbelievable appears to be demanded as a work of piety, then faith comes to be identified with the repression of doubt. Over against this kind of "piety" Paul Tillich sees a positive religious significance to doubt itself. Precisely when the unbeliever is seriously concerned to maintain intellectual integrity to the point of radical doubt,

divine grace is present. Doubt can be the reception of meaning in the very midst of meaninglessness. Thus the doubter
is "justified." Doubting is participation in truth. Here one is
reminded of Augustine's insight, "I doubt, therefore I am."

Doubt is the *No* that is rooted in an underlying, if still unrecognized, *Yes*. Paradoxically, doubt purifies and renews faith. Tillich
reaffirms Luther's conviction that faith alone, faith in God's grace,
justifies us before God. Does Adams, for all his Puritan moral athleticism, take this view as his own? Apparently he does, since he
nowhere distances himself from it and seems, by his eloquent re-
iteration of the doctrine, to make it his own. Does this mean he
does *not* think—as religious liberals generally accent—that "faith
without works is dead" (James 2:26)? No, he thinks that while
faith can hardly be authentic if no acts of courage and goodwill
flow from it, it is only faith that sees the utter inadequacy and even
the smug self-righteousness of its presumptive good works; therefore it is only faith that enables us to cross over into what Dante
calls "the new life." Moralism by itself knows nothing of this
boundary situation and even blinds us to it.

Meaning in History

Faith seeks meaning in history—in the temporal experience of the
person, the tribe, the civilization, or the world itself. Formative
events (such as an exodus, a revolution, or the appearance of a
mahatma) become symbols of meaning in history. Passionate belief attaches to them. The process is anything but immaculate.
Rather, it is dialectical and riddled with ambiguities, for faith is
shaped by history and, in turn, shapes history. At the same time,
movements of faith are stained by history and also leave their indelible mark on it.

> The basic image of the Old Testament is that of a people
> being led by God into ever new situations, journeying
> through the wilderness into a Promised Land. The exodus
> from Egypt was viewed as a divinely given liberation from

bondage and as a thrust toward fulfillment, under covenant with the Lord of history. As John Donne would say, this people of God was on pilgrimage; it had made a future engagement with its higher self.

Biblical faith comes packaged in stories that have some kind of historical locale; particularity is more prominent than universality. The stories that are not patently fictions—for instance, the story of Jonah—are presumably true in the sense that they, or something very like them, actually happened. Nevertheless, they also take on symbolic overtones, becoming types for interpreting other persons and events. In some sense we believe in these stories, these histories-become-parables, and this belief shapes our actions. Our actions, in turn, influence the stories we select and the features of the stories we accent. Religious conservatives will readily agree that our actions are, or should be, shaped by our faith. But will our experience and the choices we make enter into and reform our faith? In turn, will our faith be motivated by ideal ends we have dreamed, such as working for the fulfillment of our common humanity? It is this latter accent that makes Adams a religious liberal, one who sees history as a creative process in which we can play a creative role.

Adams returns several times to Percy Shelley's dictum that "the poets are the unacknowledged legislators of the world," for he sees in the long, historical sweep of religion a process of selecting basic images, myths, and metaphors that govern our ways of seeing the world. He speaks in particular of "root metaphors" generated by religious traditions—metaphors that lie at the root of basic patterns of thinking:

> Root metaphors such as the covenant with God or the kingdom of God may not have been devised by people whom we call poets. Yet, these and similar images are manifestations of *poiesis*, that is, of "making"—of creative imagination. In Greek the word "poet" literally means "maker."
>
> The root metaphors of the Bible or of early religious symbolism are not poetic in the ordinary sense. As

Kierkegaard would put the matter, they come not from the genius who proudly displays his own creations but from the apostle who points beyond himself. That is, they are kerygmatic [proclaiming the word of God] in intention; they are the saving word, the sacred word, for the religious community.... Unlike poetic images (which "supervene on life"), the root metaphors "intervene" in life—they *aim* to affect behavior (Santayana). Hence, the "makers" of these metaphors are in a sense to be counted among the unacknowledged legislators of the world.

The root metaphors that most interest Adams are those that concern the shape and direction of history. St. Augustine becomes for Adams a fabulous case in point, one in whom we see the theologian as poet, as a "maker" of history through the making of metaphors that enable us to understand our personal experience on the largest scale:

> [Augustine] lived in a time of historical crisis when Rome, the capitol of the Empire, was sacked by Alaric and his Goths and "when fugitives from Rome came flying to Carthage in the wake of the news." People were asking, was the fall of Rome, "the eternal city," the result of abandoning the old civic gods? Was the fall due to the victory of Christianity, the new faith? In the teeth of this historical situation Augustine ventured boldly to offer an answer.
>
> ...he adapted old and familiar concepts, the concept of drama and the concept of the City, in order to interpret the meaning of history.... The concept of the City was a thousand years old as a cosmic symbol, but it had lost much of its power. Augustine gave it new birth in the conception of the Two Cities, the heavenly and the earthly. In speaking of *two* Cities he recaptured the metaphor in a special way by uniting it with another metaphor.
>
> In the years before his conversion Augustine had been a professor of rhetoric. In this profession he had devoted his attention to analyzing the *poiesis*, the "making," of the pagan

dramatists. When he came to formulate a new theology of history he drew upon these poets. In the Greek and Roman tragedy he had found a protagonist and an antagonist. Accordingly, he now interprets human history as the perennial drama of Two Cities; thus he combines the literary metaphor of *drama* with the political metaphor of *the city*. The Two Cities are the City of God and the City of Earth, the "heavenly city" of *sojourners* in the world and the city of those who are "at home" in this world and wish to live after the flesh. These two Cities are in dramatic conflict. In this dichotomy faith and unfaith become the organizing principles. In terms of this drama he sketched out a philosophy of history, past, present, and future, a drama in seven acts or great periods.

Adams calls special attention to the fact that Augustine draws on not only Jewish and Christian traditions but on pagan sources as well, especially for the idea of dramatic conflict. A *myth*, precisely defined, is an ancient story of the conflict of the gods. In the Jewish scriptures there are no gods to be in conflict; angels and demons take adversarial roles, but in the last analysis they are creatures of the one God. In consequence, the drama of history is moralized, that is, it becomes a story of *human* conflicts.

In some respects this represents a gain, in others, a loss. An ethical criterion enters the religious equation, but the tendency to reductive moralizing represents a loss. The good are supposed to prosper, eventually, and the evil to suffer, eventually. The Book of Job wrestles with the fact that our experience of life is radically different from this.

In the case of Augustine, the moralizing trend is reversed by a new infusion of pagan sensibility: The gods of the Two Cities are in combat to the end of time; God transcends and indeed creates time. Adams asks,

> How do I understand myself in the context of American culture and in light of the fact that I was reared a . . . Plymouth Brethren fundamentalist? It has been interesting for me to try

to assess this because of the radical rejection of culture by the Brethren. The strong eschatological element in this group— "Jesus Christ is coming at any moment," they would say—has had some effect on me. I remember from my earliest years a map of the history of salvation, from the Creation right through to the Last Judgment, on the wall of a Presbyterian church sanctuary. Also I had the *Scofield Reference Bible*, with its copious footnotes and with a whole philosophy of history—a periodization of history.

Years later, when I started reading Troeltsch and found him saying that the problem for the philosophy is the periodization of history, I said, "I learned that already from my fundamentalist map of eschatology!"

Paul Tillich gave lectures at Harvard University in which he divided the ancient history of the West into periods of four hundred years, working forward and backward from the year 100 B.C.E. Thus, for instance, the high classical age of Greek culture falls roughly 400 years earlier, and the beginning of the Constantinian age of Christianity falls roughly four hundred years after. The undergraduate students who filled the lecture hall gave Tillich a standing ovation after each of these twice-weekly performances. One suspects they had never in all their days at skeptical, iconoclastic Harvard heard a professor make such grandiose and erudite speculative claims. In one bold stroke he characterized the transition from the archaic to the classical period in ancient Greek culture, between the sixth and the fifth centuries B.C.E. The stone figures of the earlier period, Tillich says, display the distinctive "archaic smile" (a half smile, seen also in representations of the Buddha) "in anticipation of the dawning of a great classical period," when the face and the form of the figure become idealized and naturalistic, in accord with the emergent ideals of Greek classicism. Adams reports,

> Someone pointed out to Georg Wilhelm Friedrich Hegel that the facts of actual history of the United States did not fit into his philosophy of history. Hegel replied, "So much the worse for the facts."

Philosophies of history are grand schemes, even "belief systems," that shape our understanding of the facts and resist alteration even in the face of contradictory evidence. In this way they are more like religion than empirical science. Sometimes they will seem forced, biased, or stereotypical, but they persist and are continually reinvented. Adams often speaks of the periodization of history and the identification of major epochs:

> Already in the twelfth century an anticipation of the modern spirit appears in the revolutionary vision of the Cistercian abbot Joachim of Fiore. He was the first Christian to make a slogan of the word *reformare*. In protest against the hierarchical domination and sacramental system of the medieval church, Joachim appealed to what he called the Eternal Gospel. He demanded a reform that would emancipate the Christian community from the conservative Augustinian philosophy of the church that had prevailed for over half a millennium. The Augustinians had deprived the primitive Christian eschatology of its power, by affirming in effect that the kingdom of God was already present in the church. Joachim, whose ideas were taken up by the Spiritual Franciscans, revived the ancient yearning for a new age; he proposed a new theory of the periods or dispensations of history. For Augustine, humanity was living in the last age of history, which had begun with Christ. For Joachim, a new, third era was to come. The age of the Father was from the beginning to Christ; the age of the Son was from Christ down to the appearance of a new monastic order that would introduce new life into the church and society. In the coming, third era, the age of the Holy Spirit, there would be no need for authority of the priests; the Spirit would be given to everybody. The Gospel of Christ would be replaced by the Eternal Gospel; filial obedience would issue in a new spiritual freedom.

I have argued elsewhere that the idea of spiritual freedom— the inward, creative, divine image in which the person is made—

is the essence of liberal Christian faith; its pedigree runs from Jeremiah to Paul to Joachim to Channing. For each, there is an historical period of renewal, a new covenant that is present and/or yet to come, a potential if not a realized eschatology. Joachim's idea of the Eternal Gospel is reminiscent of Schleiermacher's term *eternal covenant*. Both are universalizing interpretations of Biblical terms, in the same way that liberal Christianity humanizes Jesus in order to find the potential Christ in every person.

Adams cites Friedrich Schleiermacher's manifesto: "The Reformation must go on." Schleiermacher writes,

> If the Reformation which produced our community of faith does not have as its goal the creation of an eternal covenant between the living Christian faith and an independent and freely working science, a covenant by the terms of which science is not hindered and faith is not excluded, then that Reformation cannot do justice to the need of our time, and we need a new Reformation, no matter how hard we will have to struggle for it....

Schleiermacher's "third age" is now in the making.

Adams develops a trinitarian periodization of the history of religious liberalism in his essay "The Ages of Liberalism"—but not in the usual order of the three personas of God. Briefly stated, he says that religious liberalism was born amid the revolutionary and Holy Spirit-filled era of the Reformation and the Renaissance (the sixteenth and seventeenth centuries); it flourished in the rationalistic and universalizing era, accenting the benevolence of God the Father, in the Enlightenment and Romantic periods (the eighteenth and nineteenth centuries); and now it comes of age, or comes into its age of absolute crisis when it will either re-vision and transform itself or else die (the twentieth and twenty-first centuries). Adams originally calls these the ages of the Spirit, the Father, and the Son (in that order). In contemporary gender-neutral language, we can call these the ages of the Spirit, the Creator, and the Mediator. Contemporary theology reflects a Christological interest in its preoccupation with modes of inter-

pretation, for the person and story of Jesus are central to the
process by which meaning is symbolized. Adams says,

> Jesus—in his inwardness, in his love of persons, in the au-
> dacity of his liberation from the bondage of mere tradition,
> in his confidence in the Kingdom that grows of itself in re-
> action to the human response, in his faithfulness to his
> unique mission, in his eliciting a new community in the
> world but not of it (a community above nation and race and
> class, embracing the humble and the wise), in his trust in the
> mysterious mercy of God—has made and makes more read-
> ily known and available to us the powers that can release us
> from self-worship and give us constant renewal of life and
> love. So persuasively and costingly has he made these powers
> available that we can understand why most of his followers
> through the ages have given him a special place and function
> within the order of being.

Jesus, then, comes to be seen as the embodiment or the incarnation of the Christ (Messiah), the anointed ruler (Lord), and the
divine *Logos* (word), the principle and agency of creation. Adams
reflects on the portraits of the historical Jesus found in the Gospels,
but he recognizes that idolatry of Jesus is not a viable theological
stance. A Christology, that is, a conception of the theological meaning of Jesus, is needed. To speak of Christology in functional terms
is to understand the Christ as the principle of mediation or interpretation. The Christ is, then, the principle that underlies the various means by which what is sacred and beyond form can
nevertheless be recognized and communicated. Whatever is
known, whatever is historically effective, is given form and substance in history by such artful forms of interpretation as images,
metaphors, myths, stories, and parables. Jesus as the Christ represents this mediating power, which we ourselves are called to incarnate in our humanity; although our humanity be partial and
broken, by grace it is healed and made whole again. The full image
of our humanity can be seen only in this both/and way.

Sometimes Adams seeks to recall religious liberals to the genius of the sixteenth-century Radical Reformation, their original Age of the Spirit; sometimes (especially in his earlier writings) he sounds like a classical Unitarian Christian, devoted to the one Creator and championing the great progeny of the age of reason, liberal democracy. It may astonish us that this protean man could also imagine Christology taking a central place in emergent liberal religious thought. But just so, he identifies the present age as an Age of the Mediator, the age when meaning is mediated by metaphor and parable and by social institutions and voluntary associations. Whatever incarnates the original impulse of a liberating faith, the Spirit of God, in the present history and renders it available within the covenant of being is functionally Christological.

The content of Jesus' preaching is eschatological; "the kingdom of God" that he calls people to recognize is both present and yet to come. This is not a contradiction. Peter Steinke notes that while *eschatology* refers to "last things," it does not come last in theological reflection. It comes first, for *eschatos* refers to the promises of God affecting us in the present. In this sense liberation theology speaks of "the pull of the future." Faith is "inviting the day to come" and worship celebrates "the future present," in the phrase of Marianne Micks. All of these examples reflect the "eschatological consciousness" that Adams lifts up and celebrates:

> Thomas Hobbes said that the Roman Catholic Church is the ghost of the Roman Empire sitting at its grave. Rudolph Sohm, a Lutheran jurist of half a century ago, would agree with Hobbes that a political form of organization was adopted by the Roman church, and herein he sees the "fall" of the church from its proper order. In his *Kirchenrecht* (1892) Sohm argues that the primitive Christian *Ecclesia*, described by St. Paul as the body of Christ, was an organism ruled spontaneously by the Holy Spirit, that is by charismatic authority. The *Ecclesia* was changed and corrupted into the Roman church when it adopted an alien principle, the principle of law, an authority that belongs to the political order. Thus the

Ecclesia "fell" from grace into law, from pneumatocracy into bureaucracy. Max Weber considered the process described by Sohm's concept of charismatic authority and then character-ized the bureaucratization of authority as "the routinization of charisma," a process to be observed in non-ecclesiastical as well as in ecclesiastical institutions.

The recovery of spirit, of charisma, of grace, must wait for the *kairos*, the Greek term meaning the "fulfilled," "right," or "ripe" time. Adams takes everything that swirls around this Biblical term as his lifelong preoccupation:

> Tillich intends to "present a summons to a consciousness of history, a demand for a consciousness of the present and for action in the present in the spirit of *kairos*." His conception of the *kairos* was born out of an attempt to capture the sense of promise and at the same time to warn against the dangers of utopianism. *Kairos*, meaning "the fullness of time," is drawn from the New Testament and connotes all that is dis-tinctive in the Christian conception of time: that time may be invaded by eternity, that it has a direction, that it has a center and therefore a periodization based on qualitative dif-ferences, and yet that in time itself the human being may never achieve the fullness of the eternal.

The *kairos* is not discernable by one who is not involved in history, one who stands apart and renders supposedly objective judgment. Here again we see the divide between modern and postmodern, objective and engaged social science. Adams's long friendship with the distinguished church historian George Huntston Williams provides occasion for him to reflect on the vo-cation of "the historian who lives within a community of faith" and whose very intellectual integrity depends on it:

> The church historian ... recognizes with Goethe that a tradi-tion cannot be inherited, it must be earned. That is, once the main ingredients of a tradition have been discovered, only

the words of the historian as artist can give it tangible form by bringing it into focus. Once this happens, it then has the impact of an emblem on the society or the community of faith.

... The historian who lives within a community of faith does not sit on a pedestal outside history. He shares the agonies, the frustrations, and the sense of promise in history. Like the jurist, he is aware of precedents of the past which are pregnant with new relevance, new life. Therefore, also in order to take time by the forelock, the historian must participate with a sense of social responsibility in the processes that define current conflicts and policies. The church historian accordingly writes of the past not merely for the past itself, but also for its impact on the present.

Adams once noted that "the idiom, 'to take time by the forelock'—to take Father Time by the little tuft of hair on his balding head—is attributed to the first Greek philosopher, Thales." Thales himself takes time by the forelock when he repudiates the inherited myths of his culture in favor of what he believes to be a purely rational principle, although as Adams observes, it is in fact a new myth:

Thales, perhaps the first man of science in the West, rejected the traditional myths, the stories about anthropomorphic gods. These stories could no longer explain existence or reliably direct commitment; they were losing their symbolic power, their numinous quality, their reference to the ultimate. But when Thales asserted that water is the first principle of all things, he was opening the way to a new myth; for him, water was probably a numinous reality, possessing the power, the sovereignty, of a god .... So also modern secularism in its conflict with or its indifference to religion does not eliminate myth; it struggles for a new myth. All such struggles are concerned with the question of what is, or should be, sovereign in human existence. The standards, the motives,

the ends that give content to the successive myths constitute
what Whitehead called "the driving force of ideas in the history of mankind."

The Personalization of Faith

The coming of the kingdom of God and Christ's sacrifice on the
Cross are central symbols of Christian faith. They effect a personalization of faith. Before faith is formulated in doctrine or expli-
cated and preached, such symbols of faith elicit a response that is
primarily emotional. They speak to us, individually and collectively, at the psychic level, lending confidence and commitment.
To pray "Thy kingdom come" is to invite the future with confident
hope, whatever it may bring. To add "Thy will be done" is to subject one's own will to the divine will and recalls Jesus' prayer in
Gethsemane (Matthew 26:39). Adams explains his understanding
of prayer:

> One of my teachers at Marburg University, Friedrich Heiler,
> drew a distinction between mystical prayer—a sense of com-
> munion—and prophetic prayer. Prayer that is prophetic is
> prayer that aims to share, in a congregation, the sense of re-
> sponsibility. Prayer, then, is a discipline whereby one offers
> oneself and the community to the Ultimate for the sake of,
> for the nourishment of, for the establishment of, authentic
> community.... We need to develop an alternative to the pri-
> vatization of piety—a personalization of piety that gives
> people the joy of commitment, a "costing" commitment.

Because Adams makes so much of the public realm and our responsibilities as citizens and as persons of faith in it, and because
he so mercilessly derides pietism as a privatization of faith, we may
miss the deeply personal character of his own piety. He distinguishes between the personalization of faith, which he calls for, and
its privatization, which he excoriates. The personal is in fact an im-

portant aspect of his thought. For instance, he insists that when you begin with an impersonal concept of God, you are likely to end up with a subpersonal idea of God, a God that is something less than our ultimate concern as persons, because "it" does not relate to us at the personal level of our existence. Adams's religious language is thoroughly personalist. Thus, discussing the conjunction between the intimate and the ultimate, he cites Samuel Miller's words on "the inner church of the friends of God" and its entranceway, marked by the saying of the Quaker founder, George Fox: "The light that shows us our sins is the light that heals us."

Light—that which we not so much see as see by—often serves as a symbol of God, as in the words of Simone Weil, cited by Dean Miller: "It is only from the light that streams constantly from heaven that a tree can derive the energy to strike its roots deep into the soil. The tree is in fact rooted in the sky." We, no less than the tree, are rooted in and draw our sustenance and strength from a transcendent source, the sky. The sky and the light that come from it are not material realities, in the parabolic way of speaking, but images of what T. S. Eliot calls "the uncreated light." In the words of a prayer by Adams, "We sense a presence we inherit not from the sun." He elaborates:

> According to an ancient fable...the phoenix was supposed to live for five hundred years and then consume himself and his nest with fire, only to rise out of the ashes to new life. A more widely prevalent version of the fable is repeated in Clement's First Epistle to the Corinthians. This bird, according to him, "when it reaches the time of it dissolution, maketh for itself a coffin of frankincense and myrrh and other spices, into which in the fullness of time it entereth, and so it dieth. But as the flesh rotteth, a certain worm is engendered, which is nurtured from the moisture of the dead creature, and putteth forth wings." For Clement the death and rebirth of the phoenix, like the decay and growth of seed in the earth, are a symbol—and indeed, also evidence—of

God's power to raise mortal flesh up through death to newness of life.

What accounts for the ascendancy of Christianity in the ancient pagan world? I believe it was the inward turn of thought—
the personalization of faith—that had been effected by prophetic
Judaism and was enshrined in the Hebrew Scriptures and by the
closely related moral seriousness and spiritual power of the
Christian story. These are things to which many people today
seem tone-deaf. Adams says,

> This sense of the co-suffering of God is explicit in the idea of
> the Crucifixion. It has been set forth in memorable fashion by
> the German poet Heinrich Heine in his *Pictures of Travel*.
> After describing in vivid fashion the enjoyment of the Greek
> gods and goddesses on Mount Olympus with their wine and
> song, he continues: "Suddenly there came gasping towards
> them a pale Jew, dripping with blood, a crown of thorns on
> his head, bearing a great cross of wood on his shoulder, and
> he cast the cross on the high table of the gods, so that the
> golden goblets trembled and fell, and the gods grew dumb
> and pale, and even paler, till they melted in utter mist.... Was
> it perhaps necessary for miserable and oppressed humanity?
> He who sees his God suffer bears more easily his own
> afflictions.... Of all the gods who were loved in the olden
> time, Christ is the one who has been the most loved."

Adams counts himself among the countless grateful students
of Archibald Davidson who had sung under his direction. He
notes that Davidson had said, after years of playing for services at
the Harvard chapel, "he was always struck by the discrepancy between the theology contained in the sermon and that belonging to
the anthems and the hymns." (Apparently he had not encountered
a "politically correct" hymnal!) Adams comments,

> Something of Dr. Davidson's theological outlook is indi-
> cated by his statement that, on the theme of the salvation

of the world through the death of Jesus Christ, "it is no exaggeration to say that probably not less than eighty percent of the greatest church music centers about his theme upon which, incidentally, I have not heard a sermon preached in years." I recall his once saying that a test of one type of church music is that it expresses a sense of the cross, an aloofness from secularity. Christianity for him was compounded of mystery and renunciation, as well as of affirmation. In his own words, "Music, like religion, is fundamentally a mystery."

A mystery is something known by participation and reenactment, insofar as it is known or understood at all. The interest in renunciation, alluded to as "an aloofness from secularity," is striking perhaps only because it has become so rare today, when being "up front" and "in your face" is in vogue. But surely, if we want to recover a genuine spirituality, we shall have to recover a sense of the sacred as a realm of being set apart, unworldly if not otherworldly, not surrendered to the world and its imperious and profane ways. Perhaps this is why the cross remains a powerful symbol. It signifies the presence of God where there is suffering and death and therefore the presence of God with us when we are present with others in their sufferings and their deaths. It is a mystery play in which God takes on the *persona*, the mask, of the Christ, as they who wear the masks and enact the play in everyday life come to know. Adams says,

> By this name [Christ] we refer to the reality that manifested itself in the person and work of Jesus and in the new community which was formed in loyalty to him and to the power of which he spoke with authority. In prayer, we, in fellowship with our Elder Brother, seek again this spirit and this power unto salvation.

When Adams was asked to speak at the memorial service for Paul Nathaniel Carnes, he asked me about Paul, under whose tute-

lage I had ministered in Buffalo some years before. I told him that
Paul had once said we Unitarian Universalists "ought to get over
our argument with my namesake, St. Paul." That impressed
Adams, who then quoted Dr. Carnes (who like his namesake knew
what it meant to be no saint but justified, nevertheless, by faith in
the grace of God) in his address. Carnes says,

> What we need is simply to take the time to "see." I am aware
> of this when I look out of my office window. Cast against the
> sky on the one side and a high-rise apartment on the other
> is a scraggy tree whose mutilated trunk sends out its limbs—
> limbs that form interesting traceries against the ambiguous
> background. It is now winter's tree. In summer it will all but
> camouflage the high rise and let through only the blue of the
> sky. When autumn comes it will be as if all the heat of the
> summer is concentrated in the leaves, and they will burst
> forth in the familiar yellows and oranges mixed with linger-
> ing touches of green. And I shall watch that tree for the first
> signs of spring. I confess I am a child of today. I am moved
> by all of this, but I am not cast down. I find this in my
> human relationships. Here is where my battles are fought. It
> is, however, a saving knowledge that above this battle the
> scraggy tree outside my window goes its preordained way.

Paul Carnes died of cancer in 1979 while serving as president
of the Unitarian Universalist Association. His words reminded
Adams of the story commented on in the Introduction, about
what Martin Luther said he would do if he knew the world were
about to end: "I would go out and plant a tree."

Eschatology is not only a cosmic or historical issue but also a
personal issue. This is not surprising since the stories we tell about
the universe, which we know hardly at all, are very likely to be like
the stories of our own lives, which we know somewhat. The story
that follows links Adams's memory of a boyhood challenge, a
complex psychic need, and his anticipation of life's final challenge,
one's mortality:

One of the more vivid recollections of my youth was a railway trestle that spanned a deep gorge near my boyhood home. The boys of the town agreed it was a sign of manliness and bravery to walk that long trestle, which had no plank walk but only railway ties. It was always a major event when still another boy would announce, with dependable witnesses, that he had crossed the trestle. Because our parents knew that we were under a perpetual dare, they warned us repeatedly of the extreme danger. What if we should get to the middle and become dizzy and be unable to continue or to return? What if an unexpected freight train should happen to come? If these warnings were not enough, we got some sense of the height of the trestle by looking up to it from the valley below. Then, too, there was the fearful sign at each end of the bridge: NO THOROUGHFARE. PEDESTRIANS CROSS AT THEIR OWN RISK. What then about the bridge that leads across the valley of the shadow of death?

We may answer that what is yet unknown will probably bear the same quality as the known. The fact that we are children of the universe and heirs to all its glories is trustworthy. The bridge to the unknown is a bridge in which we may have some confidence. The possibilities of the universe are not exhausted. Thornton Wilder expressed this conviction in these words: "We ourselves shall be loved for a while and forgotten. But the love will be enough; all those impulses of love return to the love that made them. Even memory is not necessary for love. There is a land of the living and a land of the dead, and the bridge is love, the only survival, the only meaning."

Thornton Wilder was the brother of Adams's good friend and colleague, Amos Wilder—my own first teacher of New Testament at Harvard Divinity School. Adams once notes that the story of "the woman taken in adultery," alluded to in the passage that follows, is the most famous and loved story in the New Testament.

Now recognized as a late addition to the Gospel of John's text (John 8:1-11), we read it, as Adams does, as pure parable:

> All of us on all sides of the irrepressible conflicts of our time will be doomed to uncreative and perhaps to violent conflict unless we can, at least in crucial moments, be grasped by the spirit that was in Jesus when he said, "Let whoever is without sin cast the first stone." To the sinner in the dock he said, "Go and sin no more." Forgiveness, acceptance: these are the antecedents of new beginnings, of constructive innovation, of new creation.

Sometimes it is said that God in the Old Testament is harsh and judgmental, while God in the New Testament is kind and loving. Adams recognizes, rather, the continuity between the two Testaments; founding covenants are forever in need of renewal, and yet new covenants always stand on the foundation of the old:

> Hosea, apparently considering the emphasis on God's wrath and God's judgment set forth in Amos, decided that if we are all to be understood only in terms of that judgment, we're all lost. And then he presented that remarkable parable—one of the outstanding ideas in the history of thought, especially when you contrast it with the Greek sense of Nemesis, according to which the wrath of the gods continues through the generations. But Hosea says that Yahweh, in the face of the faithless Israel, pursues Israel, and pleads, "I care not what you have done. Know you not that I love you? Come back. Come back for new beginnings." And so for me, this is a basic element of faith—in the face of despair regarding our own accomplishments or that which is going on around us. We can hear the plea, "Come back. There are always new beginnings."

The book of the prophet Hosea is notoriously obscure, in part because the text seems to have been corrupted in its long transmission (from the eighth century B.C.E.). Adams often refers to the foregoing story, told in its opening chapters. In another remarkable passage Hosea catalogs the moral virtues—named by various Biblical prophets in various places—that constitute Israel's covenant with Yahweh:

> And in that day will I make a covenant for them with the beasts of the field, and with the fowls of heaven, and with the creeping things of the ground: and I will break the bow and the sword and the battle out of the earth, and will make them to lie down safely. And I will betroth thee unto me for ever; yea, I will betroth thee unto me in righteousness, and in judgment, and in loving-kindness, and in mercies. I will even betroth thee unto me in faithfulness; and thou shalt know the Lord (Hosea 2:18-20).

Here mercy, justice, steadfast love, righteousness, and faithfulness are named; also peace is implied within the prophet's eschatological picture of "the peaceable kingdom." The prophets' oracles are also parables, stories of what the people do or fail to do and what God faithfully has done and will do. Adams comments,

> The close association between religion and conflict...is a commentary not only on the nature of religion but also on human nature. "To fight," says George Santayana, "is a radical instinct; if men have nothing else to fight over, they will fight over words, fancies, or women, or because they dislike each other's looks, or because they have met walking in opposite directions." One is reminded of the two Maori tribes, one of which sent a message to the other in the middle of a battle: "We have no more ammunition. Unless you will send us some, we shall have to stop fighting"—a request that was promptly granted.

What is the answer to this absurd predicament? Perhaps satire—like looking in the mirror and seeing the "angry ape" that

Shakespeare says "makes the angels weep, who, with our spleens, would all laugh mortal." Adams tells the story:

> As a student I got my dental work done for nothing by going to the dental school. I had only to pay for materials. But there were some long waits. The student would grind a while and then have to wait for the professor to come by and approve and tell him where to grind next. I took something with me to read for those long waits, and one Saturday I took Charles Eliot Norton's prose translation of *The Divine Comedy*. While I was sitting there the book fell open and the only word on the page was "Hell." Usually the Italian term "Inferno" is used, but Norton used the literal English word, "Hell." The student asked, "Are you a student?" "Yes." "Well, where do you study?" "The Divinity School." "Oh, I see," he replied. "You have to study that kind of stuff there?" I tried to explain to him that this was a great renaissance epic by Dante. "Oh yes," he said. "He wrote *The Three Muskateers*, didn't he?" I tried to explain the difference to him. He looked down at the open book and saw at the top of the page "Canto Four." "Oh, I know who you mean. The German philosopher Kanto."

Besides laughter, what is there but forgiveness—to forgive "as we would be forgiven"? Adams retells this story:

> ...during the years of his exile, Dante was once apprehended in a small village through which he was wandering and was hailed into a convent court as a vagrant. When the officer of the court asked him what he was looking for, he replied in a wistful tone of voice, *La pace*—peace. In speaking this word, Dante expressed the aspiration of the saints and the prophets of the ages who, recognizing humanity's exile into a far country, have longed to be at one with God and with humanity. To Dante himself the word "peace" was no accidental or whimsical reply. It is the word that appears in the memorable line of *The Divine Comedy* which Matthew

Arnold singled out as one of the touchstones of great poetry: "In His will is our peace."

We could make of this a mantra: "In Your will is our peace." Another affecting mantra, also from Dante (in Charles Eliot Norton's translation) is this:

> Give us this day the daily manna
> without which in this rough desert
> they backward go who toil most to go on.

These few lines are also replete with parables: The manna that feeds the children of Israel during their forty years in the wilderness, the angelic food that sustains Jesus during his forty days in the wilderness, and "the daily bread" for which he teaches us to pray—which is to say, the acknowledgment that we live always by the grace of God. Adams says,

> The great and original people of history have brought upon the stage the old process of sorrows, passions, and delights. They loved life for its own sake and sought to live life at its best. Consider Dante's expression at the end of *The New Life*: "A wonderful vision appeared to me, in which I saw things which made me resolve to speak no more of this blessed one (Beatrice) until I could more worthily treat of her. To attain this I study to the utmost of my power, as she truly knows. If it shall please God through whom all things live that my life be prolonged for some years, I hope to say of her what was never said of any woman." Dante did not set out to write a new kind of book, for women had been praised before, as he implied, and there had been poems of vision and pilgrimage through hell. His hope was to excel. Originality is not so much the creation of something wholly new but the revival of something old. We are most truly individual when we build upon what is common to us and to our kind. Our purpose is not that we should express ourselves but that life should be expressed through us. We must lose ourselves in a greater, higher life. That is what religion means.

Redeeming Time

Adams quotes Andrew Marvel's opening lines of "To His Coy Mistress"—"At my back I always hear Time's winged chariot hurrying near...," and comments,

> The poet reminds his beloved that "had we but world enough and time," her reluctance to respond to him would not be a serious matter. But they are finite beings subject to Time, and there is no time for tarrying. Indulging the poetic license of religious allegory, we may say that every person, from childhood onward, is in pursuit of a "coy mistress." Her name is "the meaning of life." Decision regarding this meaning is ultimately a religious decision. Time is always hurrying near, leaping beside and past us, and one must try to take its meaning by the forelock.

He goes on to justify his taking poetic license by citing Pascal, who "reminded us that imagination is the mistress of humanity." The arts—music, painting, dance, literature—and ethics are closely linked in his thought and feed his theological imagination.

Authentic faith is personally affirmed and reexamined and communally formed and reformed. It issues in action on the stage of history. It takes time seriously. Adams tells the story of how he came to this recognition during the early period of his ministry:

> I did in those days recover a sense of the centrality of the Bible and of the decisive role in history of both the sacramental and the prophetic elements. I mention only in passing here the influence of Christian art, and especially of Bach, upon me. In addition I pressed upon myself the question, "If Fascism should arise in the States, what in your past performance would constitute a pattern or framework of resistance?" I could give only a feeble answer to the question. My principal political activities had been the reading of the newspaper and voting. I had preached sermons on the depression or in defense of strikers. Occasionally, I uttered

protests against censorship in Boston. But I had no adequate conception of citizen participation.

The passage indicates the close connection between spiritual and moral development and the experience of *metanoia* (a radical change of heart and mind) in Adams's reflection. The story of his personal transformation under the pressures of the social and intellectual crises of liberal democracies is intimately related to the transformed liberal religion that he seeks:

Many of Adams's stories are recollections from childhood and bear upon his sense of identity-formation. His father, James Carey Adams, was a powerful figure in his life and apparently a man of fixed, fundamentalist religious views. We can infer his overbearing manner and effect on his son from Adams's many stories about him; there are comparatively few stories about his mother. But Adams never speaks critically about either of his parents in written or spoken word. He holds his father in awe, even while throwing over the narrow literalism and otherworldliness of his father's faith and going his own way. The following story shows young Adams learning that his father is a man of principle:

> When I was about ten years old [my father] took me with him to attend a revivalist service in a neighboring rural church where the evangelist was supervising seizures of the Spirit which brought converts to roll on the floor. In pens in back of the church others groaned and travailed as they waited for seizure. Inside the church in the midst of the service, indeed at its height, my father, standing up in front of the pulpit, interrupted the service and warned the ecstatic congregation against the preacher, in stentorian tones reminding them that the way of salvation is not through emotional seizures but alone through belief in the vicarious sacrifice of Christ on Golgotha. Having given his warning, he seized me by the hand, and (shaking the heretical dust from our feet) we marched out of the church, departing from that astonished congregation. Several members of the group followed us out.

The son's admiration of his father is palpable in this story of courageously standing up for one's convictions. That his father speaks in the name of an evangelical Christian faith may be surprising if we think of this faith not as principled but as rooted in emotional needs. As an adult Adams does not hesitate to administer such surprises; he defends politically radical evangelicalism and criticizes liberals who fail to distinguish between them and the reactionary evangelicals and fundamentalists.

Unbending convictions give one power, the kind of power that others experience as intimidating or as provoking resistance. It commands respect, but it is not endearing. Adams reports that it was said during the protectorate of Oliver Cromwell: "There is nothing so dangerous as a Presbyterian just off his knees."

His father was unwilling to compromise with or accommodate to the world because he thought that true faith demanded endless renunciations of worldly pleasures and powers. Max Weber called it "Protestant asceticism." As a result he developed what his son concludes is an utterly otherworldly faith, a faith that is unwilling to engage the principalities and powers of this world or to enjoy its pleasures. That is, if you put your trust in this entire way of thinking, it will lead you into the dead end of a joyless and loveless, perhaps even an unfaithful, existence.

Adams tells us that, in midlife, he concluded:

> One who takes time seriously must do more than talk about it. He must learn somehow to take time by the forelock. He must learn to act as a Christian and as a citizen through socially effective institutions, to do what E. C. Lindeman has called the humdrum work of democracy. I for one now believe that every Christian should be actively and persistently engaged in the work of at least one secular organization that is exercising a positive influence for the sake of peace and justice against the forces of hate and greed. But even this is, of course, not enough. Christianity is no longer an optional luxury for me. Salvation does not come through worship

and prayer alone, nor through private virtues that camou-
flage public indolence. Time and history are fraught with
judgment and fulfillment. We are in "the valley of decision."
But there is reason for hope, for God will make all his mountains a way.

Echoes like this one from the Biblical prophets are often heard
in Adams's words. He sees God working not in the priestly cult or
the congregation but in history itself. For instance, the prophet
Micah depicts Yahweh as pleading with Israel and calling her to remember how they came to be the people of God that they are.

> O my people, what have I done unto you? In what have I
> wearied you? Answer me! For I brought you from the land of
> Egypt, and redeemed you from the house of bondage; and I
> sent before thee Moses, Aaron, and Miriam. O my people, re-
> member now what Balak king of Moab devised, and what
> Balaam the son of Beor answered him, and what happened
> from Shittim to Gilgal, that you may know the saving acts of
> the Lord. (Micah 6: 3-5)

The passage follows in which Micah also names the central
covenantal virtues in his famous words, "What does the Lord require of you but to do justice and to love kindness, and to walk
humbly with your God?" The words conclude an oracle that tells
a story about the divinely given directive of history and the imperative to renew faith, which follows from it. Adams's phrase *taking time seriously* expresses a consciousness steeped in the Bible:

> But I have been a pastor, and from time to time became
> aware of the limitations of the endurance of the people in
> the pews. I can remember when I used to preach occasion-
> ally as a visitor in the Danvers [Unitarian] church. There was
> a clock at the other end of the sanctuary, and around the
> clock was the legend: Redeem the Time. [see Colossians 4:5]

Eschatology, the faith that time will be redeemed even though
we have not taken time seriously, is finally personal. Returning to

the place where we began, we may say that eschatology is intimate as well as ultimate. After Adams published a book in his nineties, Ronald Thiemann, the dean of Harvard Divinity School, asked him, "How do you do it?" Without missing a beat Adams replied, "Well Dean, I've heard it's 'publish or perish.'" He was still working with the optimism of one dubbed "the smiling prophet." Having witnessed his constant engagement with other people in the late years of his life, I want to correct the old academic adage. I would say, "It's keep up lively dialogue—or perish." Adams says,

> God moves in mysterious ways his wonders to perform: *Deus absconditus* [the hidden God] is often present in the very rejection of "God." God may be present in the rejection of a semantic convention, and absent in the acceptance of it: not everyone who says "God is dead" really believes his unbelief, and not everyone who defends the name of God knows God. "The Spirit bloweth where it listeth" and faith lives on—in the optative mood.

True witnesses have always known the utter unpredictability of God.

The optative mood is the wishful mood, the desiring mood, the fulfillment-seeking mood, for instance Emily Dickinson's fabulous ejaculation, "Prove true, imagination, O, prove true!" We may understand Jesus' first recorded parable, "The kingdom of God is at hand," as spoken in the optative mood, for it is an invocation of what is eminently longed for, virtually willing it into reality. This is what Adams means by "taking time by the forelock":

> The primary question is not whether one believes the "deity" is encapsulated in this or that formulary. It is rather, *does history have a meaning and a demanded direction?* This is the issue that cuts through all others, the ranks of those who believe in God and the ranks of the unbelievers. The affirmative answer of prophetic religion, heard in the midst of the doom which threatens like thunder, is that history is a struggle in dead earnest between justice and injustice, looking to-

ward the victory of the good in the promise and the fulfillment of grace. Anyone who does not with the affirmation of love and beauty enter into that struggle misses the mark and thwarts creation as well as self-creation. The deepest positive meaning of Unitarian Christianity is found in the golden thread of a directive in time. Eschatology runs through its thought and its history. What we need today is a searching common inquiry into the structures and forces of history which thwart and which fulfill a meaningful destiny. For this inquiry the optative mood alone offers only a truncated and in the end frustrated conjugation. The full paradigm demands the penitential and the imperative moods, and it demands the declarative mood that speaks of the resources of fulfillment.

If the social-ethical voice, the voice of social justice, is characteristically heard in the imperative mood, the theological voice—the voice of faith—is heard in the declarative mood. In the declarative voice the kingdom of God is already present and yet waiting for us to grasp it. Here Adams cites a memorable and enlightening re-translation of Jesus' words:

In our megapolitan, technological society, with its nuclear power, mass media of communication, military-industrial complex, powerful special interest economic and political pressure groups, widespread poverty and dehumanization, both individual and corporate responsibilities must be reconceived if religion is to fulfill its vocation—to promote the kind of participation that possesses the wisdom, the audacity and power to risk new social decision. Both present and future are at stake. Indeed we are already living in the future in the sense that what we do or fail to do will affect the future. Authentic religion, relevant concern for meaning, demands eschatological orientation. But hope, alas, can become a form of cheap grace, unless we recognize that we live in the valley of decision that extracts the high price of sacrificial participation. To be sure, the final ends of humanity are hidden. Yet, the Kingdom of God is always at hand—in the translation of Joel Cadbury, "it is always available."

If this kingdom or realm of God is "at hand" and waits only for us actively and courageously to appropriate it, then it is a reality equally available to us in any age and in any place. Who is to say whether Jesus of Nazareth is "mistaken" in expecting God to institute his realm imminently? Spiritually, as Adams affirms, Jesus is our contemporary. The historical question fades into the background once the spiritual question, the question of present meaning and power, comes to the fore.

In many respects, Adams was like the English poet John Milton—religiously, politically, in his "moral athleticism," and in his imaginative prose. According to Cleanth Brooks, "Milton is constantly thinking in concrete particulars. His prose is fundamentally metaphorical." In *Areopagitica* Milton writes,

> It was from out the rind of one apple tasted, that the knowledge of good and evil as two twins cleaving together leaped forth into the world. And perhaps this is the doom which Adam fell into of knowing good and evil, that is to say of knowing good by evil. As therefore the state of man now is, what wisdom can there be to choose, what continence to forebear without the knowledge of evil? He that can apprehend and consider vice with all her baits and seeming pleasures, and yet abstain, and yet distinguish, and yet prefer that which is truly better, he is the true wayfaring Christian.

Therefore, we must be free to sort out good from evil in whatever is published. So Milton argues, announcing the classic civil libertarian argument. Adam is the generic human being, one of us. Like him we are doomed to be free, or as Adams says, "we are fated to be free." Moral knowledge is thus paradoxical, like Milton's "two twins" who both cleave together and are also cleaved apart as they "leaped forth into the world." Such is the ambiguous world of moral experience. To work and act for the good is not to stand apart and keep one's hands clean, but to be involved in the world where good and evil are forever in contest.

This is the world of moral reflection and action to which Adams invites us. It is a world rooted in a faith that transcends morality and therefore, by overcoming the ambiguities of moral assertion, makes truly moral action possible. Adams cites the words of Milton that follow those cited above and extend the thought:

> The meaning of life is fulfilled only by those who enter the struggle for justice in history and community. Any other way is the way of loneliness, of alienation from each other, and it leads to the feeling that "hell is other people," knowing the while that it is in ourselves. Let us then invoke the spirit of John Milton when he said: "I cannot praise a fugitive and cloistered virtue, unexercised and unbreathed, that never sallies forth and sees her adversary, but slinks out of the race, where that immortal garland is to be run for, not without dust and heat. That virtue therefore which is but a youngling in the contemplation of evil, and knows not the utmost that vice promises to her followers, and rejects it, is but a blank virtue, not a pure."

Adams adopted the phrase "not without dust and heat" for the title of his autobiography, published in 1995, the year after his death. Milton's words, from a pamphlet protesting against state censorship in publishing, evokes the radical political stance that characterizes the English Puritans and Adams himself. He is no "youngling in the contemplation of evil," nor does he always keep hands and heart pure and clean. He says,

> Humanity can surpass itself only by surpassing itself. Do we as religious liberals have access to the religious resources for this surpassing of the present? If not, the time will come when others will have to say to us what Henry IV said to the

tardy Crillion after victory had been won: "Hang yourself, brave Crillion! We fought at Arques, and you were not there."

Such words we do not forget. Again and again Adams elicits our "involuntary attention" with stories and aphorisms, with prophetic utterances and metaphors. Laurel Hallman retells the story of the Hasidic rabbi in Poland who sees a steam engine for the first time. He reports to his community what he sees, "one hot one pulling many cold ones." Adams is himself a "hot one," pulling behind him a whole train of "cold ones." How many non-joiners, aloof anti-institutionalists, ex-churchgoers out jogging, should hear King Henry's hot words!

William Crout reports that "when T. S. Eliot was the Charles Eliot Norton lecturer at Harvard (1932–1933) and in residence at Eliot House, a reading of his poetry was attended by the young James Luther Adams," who told this story about the event:

> Following Eliot's reading of one of his poems, an under-graduate asked, "Mr. Eliot, would you tell us what it means?" Eliot asked in turn, "Did you hear me read it?" "Yes, sir," was the reply. "Then be grateful, be grateful," Eliot replied.

Adams likewise rarely pauses to tell what his stories mean but usually lets them speak for themselves. They enter into his rhetoric of authentic faith. No doubt others will have their own reflections in response to this rhetoric or may even, in Wittgenstein's dramatic imagery, cited at the beginning of this chapter, "run to it and grasp it." In any event, to be grateful will suffice.

The rhetoric of persuasion is a conscious strategy in Adams's speaking and his writing and a long-practiced art:

> When I was teaching in the department of English I warned a student that if, in his next theme, he did not include an integrative metaphor, or a clinching incident from history or fiction, he could expect his theme to be returned without a grade. He turned in a theme on thrift, concluding with the

sentence: "And so we see that a young man in his youth should save his money in order to have a nest egg to fall back on in his old age." I wrote in the margin at this point, "I hope that the egg will be a Chinese Egg, in order to avoid a colorful splash."

Adams responded to several of us who spoke at the Arlington Street Church on the occasion of his eighty-fifth birthday, a time when "time's winged chariot drawing near" was almost audible, with these words, warning us that they were *not* his last words:

> As a former instructor in English composition at Boston University, I want to make a correction. The item here assigned [to me] is entitled: "The Last Word." I would like to correct that. What is meant is, *the latest*.
>
> Now, finally, I want to read to you a favorite set of lines by Carl Sandburg: "I am riding on the limited express, on one of the crack trains of the nation. Hurtling across the prairie in the blue haze of the dark air go fifteen all-steel coaches holding a thousand people. All the coaches shall be scrap and rust, and all the men and women laughing in the diners and sleepers shall pass to ashes. I ask the man in the smoker where he is going, and he answers, 'Omaha, I hope.'"
>
> So here we are, as pilgrims—friends here together today, as a part of our pilgrimage, the pilgrimage in which we have been learning who we are, and, sometimes, whither we are bound. It is that fellowship and that pilgrimage that has provided the strength of our lives, and the sense of our destiny.

Adams's apparently extemporized response, published under the title "The Latest Word," does not lack an "integrative metaphor." It is his parable of what life is like, drawn from his early experience working on the Union Pacific Railroad in its glory days. Carl Sandburg's evocation of a crowded, racing passenger train on the midwestern prairie becomes his image of the intimate and ultimate pilgrimage in which we find ourselves thrown together with humanity in all its diversity. To what destination is such a restless life drawn? Sandburg is often sardonic, and that is probably the way to read the story's punch-line: "Omaha, I hope." But some of us taking part in Adams's birthday celebration thought we heard him say, rather poignantly, not "Omaha" but "home"—"Home, I hope." Augustine's prayer, "And restless is our heart until it comes to rest in Thee," is apt for such a life.

Jim Adams's restless and richly imaged life is itself a parable, a story that tells exactly what a life uniquely embodied and passionately engaged in one's own time and place is like. His story frees us and impels us *not* to imitate him in thought or deed, but rather to "go and do likewise," precisely as Jesus frees and impells his auditors, following his most famous parable, the story of the good Samaritan.

> *O thou ancient of days who art higher than our highest thought, thou has gathered us into a community, a church of freedom in fellowship, inspiriting us together to search and proclaim a knowledge of thee and of thy truth, and to enter into a covenant of fidelity and to that truth and its responsibilities. We are grateful for the heritage that is upon us, and for the spirit which we have known and may share with thy servant Jesus of Nazareth, a spirit transcending the demonic idolatries of sex and race and nation. We lift our hearts in joy and thanksgiving. But we also bow our heads in penitence. We confess the distressed confusion of the common life. As in times past, the nations are in carrion struggle, and we are aware of a savage destruction we may yet bring upon ourselves. Awaken in us the faith to open ourselves to the grace of renewal. We seek thy blessings in the name of the divine love that will not let us go. Amen.*

—JLA

Endnotes

Introduction

p.vii ... *of moral and intellectual passion*, letter from James M. Gustafson, professor of theological ethics at University of Chicago Divinity School, to Caroline L. Birdsall, senior editor at Beacon Press, March 12, 1986.

p.viii ... *in the company of such artist-teachers*, Karen Smith, "James Luther Adams —Artist Teacher," *Cross-Currents*, vol. 37 (Spring, 1987), p. 122.

p.ix ... *his generosity and personal interest*, For essays on Adams by George H. Williams and Walter George Muelder, see *Andover Newton Quarterly*, vol. 17, no. 3 (January, 1977); by Donald W. Shriver Jr., Max L. Stackhouse, David Little, M. Gregor Goethals, and Theodore M. Steeman, see *Union Seminary Quarterly Review*, vol. 37, no. 3 (1982); by Frederick S. Carney, see *Perkins Journal*, Fall, 1972; by Walter G. Muelder and Ralph B. Potter, see *Religious Studies Review*, vol. 3, no. 2 (April, 1977).

p.ix ... *however fragmentarily, in a human being*, Paul Tillich, "Foreword," *Voluntary Associations: A Study of Groups in Free Societies, Essays in Honor of James Luther Adams*, edited by D. B. Robertson (Richmond, Virginia: John Knox Press, 1966), p. 5.

p.x ... *genuine freedom is persuasive*, Walter George Muelder, "James Luther Adams as Theological Ethicist," *Andover Newton Quarterly*, vol. 17, no. 3 (January, 1977), p. 192.

p.xi ... *freedom and equality around the world*, David Little, "Liberalism and World Order: The Thought of James Luther Adams," *Harvard Divinity Bulletin*, vol. 31, no. 3 (Summer, 2003), p. 7.

p.xi ... *are essential to religion*, Paul Tillich, *op. cit.*, p. 5. For Adams's comments on "the mystical element in religion," see James Luther Adams, *The Prophethood of All Believers*, ed. George K. Beach (Boston: Beacon Press, 1986), p. 70.

p.xi ... *ground of all meaningful existence*, James Luther Adams, *The Prophethood of All Believers*, ed. George K. Beach (Boston: Beacon Press, 1986), p. 41.

p.xii ... *takes time seriously, Ibid.*

p.xii ... *has 'mere God,'* James Luther Adams, *An Examined Faith: Social Context and Religious Commitment*, ed. George K. Beach (Boston: Beacon Press, 1991), p. 305.

p.xiv ... *is theologically significant, The Prophethood of All Believers, op. cit.*, p.57.

p.xv ... *the nerve of prophetic faith, An Examined Faith, op. cit.*, p. 148.

p.xv ... *men and women find themselves, Ibid.*, p. 148.

p.xvi ... *the transforming power of love,* The full text of the Principles and Purposes statement, see *Unitarian Universalist Association Directory 2003–2004* (25 Beacon St., Boston, MA 02108), p. 6. Adams's role in proposing language for the statement was stated in a letter to the author by Walter Royal Jones, chair of the commission that developed the text for the revision of the Principles and Purposes.

p.xix ... *Shady Hill estate in Cambridge, Massachusetts,* For more detailed information on the life and work of Adams, see "Memorial Minute: James Luther Adams," by George Kimmich Beach, *Harvard University Gazette* XCVI: 7 (November 2, 2000), p. 11; online at www.news.harvard.eu.

p.xx ... *dangers are threatening today,* "Why Liberal?" and "The Liberalism That Is Dead" appeared in *The Journal of Liberal Religion,* vol. 1, no. 2 (Autumn, 1939) and vol. 2, no. 1 (Winter, 1940).

p.xxi ... *Long live liberalism!* James Luther Adams, "The Liberalism That Is Dead," *The Journal of Liberal Religion* vol. 2, no. 1 (Winter, 1940), pp. 38, 42.

p.xxiii ... *the contemporary relevance of Adams's thought,* A number of Adams's essays address aspects of his concern for a transformed liberalism. The two essays on liberalism cited in the text, "Why Liberal?" and "The Liberalism That Is Dead," are partly incorporated in "Guiding Principles for a Free Faith," *On Being Human Religiously,* edited by Max L. Stackhouse. See also "Changing Frontiers of Liberal Religion," "Natural Law and the Doctrine of Human Being," "The Need for a New Language," and "The Church That Is Free," in *The Prophethood of All Believers,* edited by George K. Beach. See also "Prophetic Theology: Interrupting the Meeting," "The Liberal Christian Holds Up the Mirror," "Liberals and Evangelicals," "Liberal Religion and the Phoenix," and "The Ages of Liberalism," in *An Examined Faith,* edited by George K. Beach. See also "The Changing Reputation of Human Nature" and "Taking Time Seriously," in *The Essential James Luther Adams,* edited by George Kimmich Beach.

p.xxv ... *recipient of many surprises, An Examined Faith, op. cit.*, p. 55.

p.xxv ... *with the historical alternatives,* Max L. Stackhouse, "James Luther Adams: A Biographical and Intellectual Sketch," *Voluntary Associations, op. cit.*, p. 334. This commentary and Stackhouse's subsequent essay, "Truth Befriended: James Luther Adams as a Teacher," *Union Seminary Quarterly Review*, XXXVI: 3 (1982), pp. 205ff., are excellent intellectual portraits of Adams.

p.xxvi ... *and even in Marxism, The Prophethood of All Believers, op. cit.*, p. 235.

p. 32 ... *my doctoral field would be Christian ethics,* Frederick S. Carney, "James Luther Adams: The Christian Actionist as a Man of Culture," *Perkins Review,* Fall, 1972, p. 15.

Being Religious: The Intimate and the Ultimate

p.1 ...*divine imminence and divine transcendence*, James Luther Adams, *An Examined Faith: Social Context and Religious Commitment*, ed. George K. Beach (Boston: Beacon Press, 1991), p. 20.

p.1 ...*operate in mutuality*, James Luther Adams, *The Essential James Luther Adams*, ed. George Kimmich Beach (Boston: Skinner House Books, 1998), p. 218.

p.3 ...*something implicit in every story*, See Frank Kermode, *The Sense of an Ending: Studies in the Theory of Fiction* (London: Oxford University Press, 1966), pp. 66ff.

p.3 ...*need not be anxious about the next hour*, Peter Steinke, lecture on "Healthy Congregations" to North Florida Ministers' Association, Gainesville, Florida, February, 2000.

p.4 ...*in praise to God forevermore. Amen!* See *Hymns of the Spirit* (Boston: Beacon Press, 1937), hymn 486, melody and text by Philipp Nicolai, translated by Paul English, harmonized by J. S. Bach.

p.5 ...*for the Second Coming*, James Luther Adams, *The Prophethood of All Believers*, ed. George K. Beach (Boston: Beacon Press, 1986), p. 33.

p.6 ...*Its own identity*, "This consciousness that is aware" is poem number 822 in the listing of *The Poems of Emily Dickinson*, edited by Thomas H. Johnson (Cambridge, Mass.: Harvard University Press, 1958), vol. 2, pp. 622-623.

p.6 ...*sums up the whole work*, Kenneth Burke, *The Rhetoric of Religion* (Boston: Beacon Press, 1961), pp. 24-27.

p.7 ...*the meaning of our very existence*, An Examined Faith, op. cit., p. 20.

p.8 ...*fellowship in growth*, James Luther Adams, "Fellowship Is Life," unpublished manuscript of statement at New Harmony, Indiana, October 13, 1983.

p.9 ...*chief expression of his intellectual creativity*, See James Luther Adams, "The Need for a New Language," *The Prophethood of All Believers, op. cit.*, pp. 212-227.

p.10 ...*way to becoming human*, An Examined Faith, op. cit., p. 20.

p.12 ...*beneath and beyond ourselves*, James Luther Adams, "Bright Shoots of Everlastingness," *Andover Newton Quarterly* (September, 1969) vol. 10, no. 1, pp. 12ff.

p.12 ...*thrust of grace towards wholeness and action, Ibid.*

p.13 ...*pearl of great price sought by a merchant, The Prophethood of All Believers, op. cit.*, p. 90.

p.13 ...*enciphering a script*, See "Runes," first stanza, in Howard Nemerov, *New and Selected Poems* (Chicago: University of Chicago Press, 1963), p. 4.

p.14 ... *"In the beginning is the word," An Examined Faith, op. cit.*, pp. 365-366.

p.15 ...*other symbol systems, for instance, money*, Kenneth Burke, "Above the Over-towering Babel," *Michigan Quarterly Review* (Winter, 1976), pp. 88-102.

p.15 ...*a creature who is free to turn against God, The Prophethood of All Believers, op. cit.*, p. 288.

p.17 ... *Tell all the Truth but tell it Slant,* is the first line of poem number 1129 in *The Collected Poems of Emily Dickinson, op. cit.*

p.17 ... *an otherwise hidden truth,* See George Kimmich Beach, *Questions for the Religious Journey* (Boston: Skinner House Books, 2002), pp. 165-166.

p.17 ... *in the declarative mood,* An Examined Faith, *op. cit.,* p. 21.

p.18 ... *a nightmare from which I am trying to awake,* Words of the character, Stephen Daedalus, James Joyce's classic novel, *Ulysses* (1922).

p.19 ... *the Biblical myth of creation, fall, and redemption,* The Prophethood of All Believers, *op. cit.,* p. 234.

p.19 ... *the support of being,* Ibid., pp. 234-235.

p.20 ... *realities that oftentimes may destroy our own makings,* James Luther Adams, "Three Lectures," transcribed by Alice Wesley (Chicago: Meadville-Lombard Theological School, 1977), p. 11.

p.21 ... *knowledge born of religious love,* Bernard J. F. Lonergan, *Method in Theology* (New York: Herder and Herder, 1972), p. 115.

p.21 ... *the ethical standards rooted in it are operative,* James Luther Adams, *The Essential James Luther Adams,* ed. George Kimmich Beach (Boston: Skinner House Books, 1998), pp. 76-77.

p.22 ... *in the light of the changing historical situation,* From a letter to the author dated June 8, 1988.

p.22 ... *the reality we confront, and the reality we are,* An Examined Faith, *op. cit.,* p. 62.

p.24 ... *to glorify God and to enjoy him forever,* Ibid., pp. 192-193.

p.25 ... *the isolated individual and God,* Ibid., p. 174.

p.25 ... *ever increasing mutuality and creativity,* Ibid., pp. 193-194.

p.26 ... *can only result in organized religious illiteracy,* Ibid., p. 319.

p.28 ... *the focal point of his concept of God,* Max Stackhouse, "Introduction," in James Luther Adams, *On Being Human Religiously* (Boston: Beacon Press, 1957), p. xxviii.

p.28 ... *There must be a doctrine and a discipline,* James Luther Adams, "The Religious Content of Liberalism: Some Practical Applications," Unitarian Ministers' Institute, September 11, 1934, pp. 47-48.

p.29 ... *so we finally voted him in!* An Examined Faith, *op. cit.,* pp. 22-23.

p.30 ... *I cannot tell them apart,* James Luther Adams, "The Minister With Two Occupations," *The Christian Register,* September 17, 1931, p. 713.

p.30 ... *I think at Meadville they do it in less,* James Luther Adams, "Unitarian Philosophies of History," mimeographed reprint from *The Journal of Liberal Religion,* vol. 7 (Autumn, 1945), p. 4.

p.31 ... *between the yogi and the commissar,* The Prophethood of All Believers, *op. cit.,* p. 80.

p.32 ... *all you have is* mere *God!* An Examined Faith, *op. cit.,* p. 305.

p.32 ... *before the facts of life,* The Prophethood of All Believers, *op. cit.,* p. 314.

p.33 ...*indeed, it is* very good *to be good,* Cited in Beach, *Questions for the Religious Journey, op. cit.,* p. 174.

p.33 ...*only secondarily with ought-ness,* An Examined Faith, *op. cit.,* p. 306.

p.34 ...*It sounds rather fusty somehow to me, The Prophethood of All Believers, op. cit.,* p. 63.

p.35 ...*it is* ultimate, *An Examined Faith, op. cit.,* p. 47.

p.36 ...*twentieth-century liberal religion,* David Robinson, *The Unitarians and the Universalists* (Westport, CT: Greenwood, 1985), p. 211.

p.36 ...*the intellectual, the moral, and the religious levels,* See Bernard Lonergan, *Method in Theology, op. cit.,* pp. 237ff.

p.37 ...*were raised in the Baptist fold, The Prophethood of All Believers, op. cit.,* p. 131.

p.38 ...*the anti-Rotarianism of H. L. Mencken, Ibid.,* pp. 33-34.

p.38 ...*Harvard Divinity School, Ibid.,* p. 34.

p.39 ...*first prize among the cats, Ibid.,* p. 61.

p.40 ...*infallible in order to recognize it,* James Luther Adams, *On Being Human Religiously,* ed. Max L. Stackhouse (Boston: Beacon, 1977), p. 24.

p.40 ...*new life and power,* James Luther Adams, "Introduction," in Ernst Troeltsch, *The Absoluteness of Christianity and the History of Religions* (Richmond, VA: John Knox Press, 1971), pp. 19-20.

p.41 ...*both history and synthesis,* Donald Shriver, "Truth Befriended: James Luther Adams as Teacher," *Union Seminary Quarterly Review,* vol. 37, no. 3 (November 3, 1982) pp. 197, 201-202.

p.42 ...*We are beginning to specialize, you see, Ibid.,* p. 202.

p.42 ...*age already foreseen by Jeremiah,* "The Ages of Liberalism," *An Examined Faith, op. cit.,* pp. 337ff. *Reason and the Prophethood of All Believers, op. cit.,* pp. 112ff.

p.44 ...*the skill of a great artist,* Colleen Griffith, "Aesthetical Musings: Interviews with Amos Niven Wilder and James Luther Adams," *Religious Education,* vol. 76, no. 1 (January-February, 1987), p. 23.

p.45 ...*pinned wriggling on the wall,* James Luther Adams, "The Good Samaritan," *Faith and Freedom,* vol. 42, no. 124 (Spring, 1989), pp. 31-32.

p.46 ...*the good life which no coming time will transcend,* James Luther Adams and James Bissett Pratt, "The Congregational Idea," unpublished manuscript, 1932.

p.46 ...*God's almighty force of love,* From Adams's unpublished sermon for the ordination of the Rev. Marta Flanagan at the First Universalist Church, Salem, Massachusetts, on November 15, 1987.

p.47 ...*how can that be perfect bliss for you? The Prophethood of All Believers, op. cit.,* pp. 13-14.

p.48 ...*his early "religious socialist" and "depth sociology" writings,* Adams was a leading translator and interpreter of Paul Tillich's thought, from the time that

Tillich came to Union Theological Seminary in New York in 1933. See *The Prophethood of All Believers, op. cit.*, p. 222.

p.49 ... *it contributes only to the surface of things, The Prophethood of All Believers, op. cit.*, p. 222.

p.50 ... *the coincidence of opposites, An Examined Faith, op. cit.*, p. 134.

p.51 ... *Let us not to the marriage of true members admit impediments, The Prophethood of All Believers, op. cit.*, p. 70.

p.51 ... *Prospero answers, "Both, both, my girl!"* See William Shakespeare, *The Tempest*, Act I, Scene 2. I am indebted to Clarke Dewey Wells for reminding me of this passage in his book of poems titled *Both, Both, My Girl* (independently published, 1975).

p.51 ... *some eternal greatness incarnate in the passage of temporal fact*, James Luther Adams, "Man in the Light of the War," *The Christian Century*, vol. 60, no. 9 (March 3, 1943), p. 259.

p.51 ... *unconditional power into our contemporaneity, The Prophethood of All Believers, op. cit.*, p. 219.

p.52 ... *the paradoxical immanence of the transcendent*, James Luther Adams, "Introduction," in Paul Tillich, *What Is Religion?* (New York: Harper and Row, 1973), pp. 14-15.

p.53 ... *and in historical situations, An Examined Faith, op. cit.*, p. 182.

p.54 ... *And this after we have drunk only one flask of wine! The Prophethood of All Believers, op. cit.*, pp. 165-166.

p.54 ... *between the necessary and the contingent, An Examined Faith, op. cit.*, p. 182.

p.55 ... *before it will abandon false gods*, James Luther Adams, "Man in the Light of the War," *op. cit.*, p. 259.

p.55 ... *The Storms of Our Times and* Starry Night, Adams's essay on Tillich was originally published in James Luther Adams, Wilhelm Pauck, and Roger L. Shinn, eds., *The Thought of Paul Tillich* (New York: Harper and Row, 1985). Tillich's essay was published in *The Protestant Era*, tr. James Luther Adams (Chicago: University of Chicago Press, 1948).

p.56 ... *as a "belief-ful realism," An Examined Faith, op. cit.*, pp. 154, 156.

p.56 ... *Leave them out, Ibid.*, pp. 158-159.

p.57 ... *that in which we should place our confidence, The Prophethood of All Believers, op. cit.*, p. 49.

p.58 ... *individual and social health will be impaired, Ibid.*

p.58 ... *He cannot be comprehended by anyone*, James Luther Adams, "Tillich on Luther," in *Interpreters of Luther: Essays in Honor of Wilhelm Pauck*, ed. Jaroslav Pelikan (Philadelphia: Fortress Press, 1968), p. 319.

p.59 ... *earliest tradition of intimacy and ultimacy, An Examined Faith, op. cit.*, pp. 41-42.

p.60 ... *the might of atoms. Amen., The Prophethood of All Believers, op. cit.*, p. 249.

Being Human: The Primacy of the Will

p.61 ... *In the beginning was the deed,* Johann Wolfgang von Goethe, *Faust: A Tragedy,* Part 1, lines 1236–37; edition annotated by F. H. Hedge, translated by Miss Swanwick (New York: Thomas Y. Crowell & Co., publication undated), p. 59. These seminal lines are variously translated from the original German (*Mir luft der Geist! Auf einmal seh' ich Rat / Und schreibe getrost: Im anfang war die Tat!*), but comparisons lead me to judge this version clearly superior. I am indebted to Spencer Lavan, a biographer of the Unitarian divine, Frederick Henry Hedge, for identifying the translator, who was English and deserves a first name: Anna Swanwick (1831–1889).

p.62 ... *Dare to think!* James Luther Adams, *The Prophethood of All Believers,* ed. George K. Beach (Boston: Beacon Press, 1986), p. 67.

p.63 ... *rather than dialectically about God,* Marjorie O'Rourke Boyle, "Rhetorical Theology: Charity Seeking Charity," *Rhetorical Invention and Religious Inquiry,* edited by Walter Jost and Wendy Olmsted (New Haven: Yale University Press, 2000), pp. 89-90.

p.64 ... *on the theme of "conversion,"* The Prophethood of All Believers, op. cit., p. 20.

p.65 ... *commitment, humility, boldness, and affection,* Ibid., p. 120.

p.65 ... *some precision of definition,* James Luther Adams, *Taking Time Seriously* (Glencoe, IL: Free Press, 1957), p. 26.

p.66 ... *name would smell as sweet,* Romeo and Juliet, II, ii, 43.

p.67 ... *the secret police,* The Prophethood of All Believers, op. cit., p. 88.

p.68 ... *that is faith, Joseph praise,* Joseph here refers to the adoptive father of Jesus. See "For the Time Being: A Christmas Oratorio," *Religious Drama I: Five Plays,* edited by Marvin Halverson (New York: Living Age Books, 1957), pp. 30, 51.

p.68 ... *pure and rightful lover of wisdom,* Plato, *Sophist 253 D-E*; translation and commentary by Francis M. Cornford, *Plato's Theory of Knowledge* (New York: Library of Liberal Arts, 1957), pp. 262-263.

p.69 ... *even as in those of a god,* Plato, *Phaedrus,* 266b.

p.69 ... *paves the way for Aristotle's empirical and rational thought,* See Francis M. Cornford, *From Religion to Philosophy* (New York: Harper Torchbook, 1957), pp. 254-261.

p.70 ... *And even into the face of God,* James Luther Adams, "The Law of Nature: Some General Considerations," *Journal of Religion,* vol. 25, no. 2 (April, 1945), pp. 1, 9.

p.70 ... *not to recognize the limits of rationalism is unreasonable,* Bernard Lonergan, *Method in Theology* (New York: Herder and Herder, 1972), p. 20.

p.71 ... *in the belly of man,* James Luther Adams, *An Examined Faith: Social Context and Religious Commitment,* ed. George K. Beach (Boston: Beacon Press, 1991), p. 106.

p.71 ... *Mephistopheles said of Margaret, "She is not the first,"* Johann Wolfgang von Goethe, quoted by James Luther Adams in "The Law of Nature," op. cit., p. 9.

p.72 ...*two wills struggling with one another, An Examined Faith, op. cit.*, p. 162.

p.72 ...*humanity and history, Ibid.*, p. 176.

p.73 ...*what one gives attention to, Ibid.*, p. 38.

p.73 ...*central role of will in his thought*, See James Luther Adams, "The Storms of Our Times and *Starry Night*," in *ibid*, pp. 153-172.

p.74 ...*substance in everything that is, An Examined Faith, op. cit.*, pp. 156, 160.

p.75 ...*whole of our conception of the object*, James Luther Adams, *On Being Human Religiously*, ed. Max L. Stackhouse (Boston: Beacon Press, 1977), p. 121.

p.76 ...*ethical ideas that flowed from them*, Ernst Troeltsch, *The Social Teachings of the Christian Churches*, tr. Olive Wyon (London: Allen and Unwin, 1931); originally published in 2 volumes in 1912.

p.76 ...*pragmatic theory of meaning, On Being Human Religiously, op. cit.*, p. 125.

p.77 ...*the next temptation comes, The Unitarian Universalist Christian: James Luther Adams Papers*, ed. Herbert F. Vetter, vol. 48, nos. 3-4 (Fall/Winter, 1993), p. 31.

p.77 ...*even to destroy ourselves and our fellows*, James Luther Adams, "Man in the Light of War," *Christian Century*, vol. 60, no. 9 (March 3, 1943), p. 257.

p.78 ...*A purely spurious religion, The Prophethood of All Believers, op. cit.*, p. 175.

p.79 ...*creates and molds, Ibid.*, p. 52.

p.79 ...*principally by catchwords*, Robert Louis Stevenson, *Virginibus Puerisque*, (1881), I, ch.1.

p.80 ...*some day you will be able to tax it, On Being Human Religiously, op. cit.*, pp. 23-24.

p.80 ...*passionate, irrational* Dionysian, *The Prophethood of All Believers, op. cit.*, pp. 51-53.

p.80 ...*a variety of implications or connotations, On Being Human Religiously, op. cit.*, p. 127.

p.81 ...*the consequences of religious belief are not in our hands, Ibid.*, pp. 137-138.

p.82 ...*the graceless voice of the right angle, An Examined Faith, op. cit.*, p. 363.

p.82 ...*creation comes from conflict, Ibid.*, p. 363.

p.82 ...*sentimental glow of indiscriminate indulgence, The Unitarian Universalist Christian: James Luther Adams Papers*, ed. Herbert F. Vetter, vol. 48, nos. 3-4 (Fall/Winter, 1993), p. 30.

p.83 ...*it is good because he wills it,* James Luther Adams, "Paul Tillich on Luther," in *Interpreters of Luther: Essays in Honor of Wilhelm Pauck* (Philadelphia: Fortress Press, 1968), p. 321.

p.83 ...*although they destroy, Ibid.*, p. 322.

p.84 ...*for the most part cast up again without effect*, James Luther Adams, "Religion in the State University," in *Religion in the State University: An Initial Exploration*, ed. Henry E. Allen (Minneapolis, MN: publisher unknown, cited from a mimeographed, undated reprint, p. 1).

p.85 ... *The Methodist lost the bet, The Prophethood of All Believers, op. cit.,* p. 129.

p.86 ... *the lack of a neat and tidy system, An Examined Faith, op. cit.,* pp. 172-173.

p.87 ... *lives with other members of the same species, The Prophethood of All Believers, op. cit.,* p. 176.

p.88 ... *will end only in becoming a brute, Ibid.,* p. 175.

p.88 ... *its sense of meaninglessness and despair,* James Luther Adams, "Introduction," in Paul Tillich, *Political Expectation* (New York: Harper and Row, 1971), p. ix.

p.89 ... *a standpoint, that is, of bourgeois society, Ibid.,* p. x.

p.90 ... *that sort of mutuality which can organize the power to check it,* "Man in the Light of War," *op. cit.,* p. 257.

p.90 ... *we participate in the divine creativity,* James Luther Adams, *The Essential James Luther Adams: Social Context and Religious Commitment,* ed. George K. Beach (Boston: Beacon Press, 1991), pp. 64-65.

p.91 ... *the sort of hyperbole that lies without deceiving,* "Man in the Light of War," *op. cit.,* pp. 257-258.

p.92 ... *what his own hand is to a man, Ibid.,* pp. 257, 259.

p.93 ... *its manifestation is the question,* Michael Novak, *Belief and Unbelief* (New York: Macmillan, 1965), p. 108.

p.93 ... *a great deal of suffering before it will abandon false gods,* "Man in the Light of War," *op. cit.,* p. 259.

p.94 ... *which they must expiate by their own destruction,* James Luther Adams, *Voluntary Associations: Socio-cultural Analyses and Theological Interpretation,* ed. J. Ronald Engel (Chicago: Exploration Press, 1986), p. 25.

p.95 ... *this man "secretes his own void,"* Joseph Williamson, "The Christian Life: An Interview with James Luther Adams," *Colloquy,* vol. 5, no. 9 (October, 1972), p. 13.

p.96 ... *a boundary between East and West Berlin,* James Luther Adams, "Introduction," in *Political Expectation, op. cit.,* p. vii.

p.96 ... *just the opposite of what I think I am! The Prophethood of All Believers, op. cit.,* p. 277.

p.97 ... *one of the most destructive forces in the whole of human history, The Essential James Luther Adams, op. cit.,* p. 67.

p.97 ... *the dictatorship of the bureaucrats, On Being Human Religiously, op. cit.,* p. 181.

p.97 ... *less ambiguous outcome of this movement—popular democracy,* See James Luther Adams, "The Protestant Ethic with Fewer Tears," in *Voluntary Associations: Socio-cultural Analyses and Theological Interpretation,* ed. J. Ronald Engel (Chicago: Exploration Press, 1986), pp. 103-119.

p.98 ... *un-freedom, irrationality, and meaninglessness, On Being Human Religiously, op. cit.,* p. 181.

p.99 ...*a level of civilization never before achieved, Ibid.,* pp. 181-182.

p.100 ...*necessary for salvation, The Essential James Luther Adams, op. cit.,* p. 76.

p.101 ...*Mass in B Minor,* See the "Introduction," by George K. Beach in James Luther Adams's *The Prophethood of All Believers, op. cit.,* p. 14. This is the author's interpretation. Adams read this introduction and commented that his sister, Ella Adams, called the essay the best writing on his life and thought that she had seen.

p.102 ...*those who think they have found security, The Essential James Luther Adams, op. cit.,* pp. 77-78.

p.103 ...*the world is not as bad as it seems,* See Vladimir Nabokov, "Speak, Memory," in *The New Yorker,* January 4, 1999, p. 126.

p.103 ...*under his auspices, An Examined Faith, op. cit.,* p. 39.

p.104 ...*the establishment of, authentic community, Ibid.,* p. 33.

p.105 ...*it is always "available," The Prophethood of All Believers, op. cit.,* p. 242.

p.106 ...*get hold of people like me and change them,* James Luther Adams, "The New Narcissism," in "Three Lectures," transcribed by Alice Wesley (Chicago: Meadville-Lombard Theological School, 1977), p. 33.

p.106 ...*regarding themselves and each other, The Prophethood of All Believers, op. cit.,* pp. 275-276.

p.107 ...*remember that you may be mistaken! Ibid.,* p. 95.

p.107 ...*You can be a Unitarian without knowing it, An Examined Faith, op. cit.,* pp. 32-33.

p.108 ...*bringing forth new life, The Essential James Luther Adams, op. cit.,* p. 78.

p.108 ...*a self-identified "come-outer," An Examined Faith, op. cit.,* p. 164.

p.109 ...*as he tells the story,* Story cited and discussed by George K. Beach, editor, in the Introduction to James Luther Adams, *The Essential James Luther Adams, op. cit.,* pp. 1ff.

p.109 ...*a long and hard way,* James Luther Adams, "Man in the Light of War," *op. cit.,* p. 259. On "achieving self-identity" as a life task in Adams's own experience, with commentary on his story of attempting to become a proficient violinist, see the "Introduction" by George K. Beach to *The Essential James Luther Adams, op. cit.,* pp. 1-5.

p.110 ...*the single hound of our identity, The Unitarian Universalist Christian, op. cit.,* p. 44.

p.110 ...*a step toward self-definition,* See George K. Beach, *Questions for the Religious Journey, op. cit.,* pp. 7-8, for fuller development of the concept of existential decision.

p.111 ...*the grace and knowledge of Christ, The Unitarian Universalist Christian, op. cit.,* p. 47.

p.112 ...*talk back to the boss the way you did!* Transcribed from videotape, "Adams at Home: Six Conversations," produced by George K. Beach (The Unitarian Universalist Church of Arlington, Virginia, 1988).

p.112 ...*a world in which novelty occurs, The Prophethood of All Believers, op. cit.,* p. 186.

p.113 ...*only the people who have many other things to do write letters,* James Luther Adams, "Dedicatory Letter to Professor Jerome Hall," *Hastings Law Review*, vol. 32, no. 6 (July, 1981), p. 133.

p.113 ...*from fundamentalism to liberal Christianity, An Examined Faith, op. cit.,* p. 323.

p.114 ...*If the spirit is greater than the letter, yes, The Prophethood of All Believers, op. cit.,* pp. 129-130.

p.115 ...*the spirit dies, Ibid.,* p. 68.

p.115 ...*reads sense into the absurd, On Being Human Religiously, op. cit.,* pp. 163-164.

p.116 ...*I think that's why I'm a Catholic! The Prophethood of All Believers, op. cit.,* p. 2.

p.117 ...*the basis of his analysis of Isaiah 6,* See Von Ogden Vogt, "The Mysticism of the Prophet Isaiah," in *Art and Religion* (Boston: Beacon Press, 1957).

p.118 ...*Whoever has wholly forgotten Christianity will hear it here again, The Prophethood of All Believers, op. cit.,* pp. 36-37.

p.118 ...*an optional luxury for me, Ibid.,* p. 42.

p.118 ...*heart and soul and strength. Amen , Ibid.,* p. 249.

Confronting the Demonic: Blessed Are the Powerful

p.122 ...*the remaining sessions of the conference,* James Luther Adams, *An Examined Faith: Social Context and Religious Commitment,* ed. George K. Beach (Boston: Beacon Press, 1991), p. 145.

p.122 ...*any other philosophical foundation,* See *Ibid.,* pp. 188ff.

p.122 ...*if not already dead, moribund,* James Luther Adams, "The Liberalism that is Dead," *Journal of Liberal Religion,* vol. 1, no. 3 (Winter, 1940), pp. 38-42.

p.123 ...*to fulfill our destiny,* James Luther Adams, *The Essential James Luther Adams,* ed. George Kimmich Beach (Boston: Skinner House Books, 1998), pp. 51-52.

p.124 ...*the organization of power,* James Luther Adams, *Taking Time Seriously* (Glencoe, IL: Free Press, 1957), pp. 48-52.

p.124 ...*primacy of the will,* Adams's essay on Irving Babbitt with reference to the concept of "the primacy of the will" is found in *An Examined Faith, op. cit.,* pp. 67ff. On Babbitt's thought on Buddhism, see his translation and commentary, *The Dhammapada* (New York: New Directions Books, 1965).

p.125 ...*the strongest battalions, The Prophethood of All Believers, op. cit.,* pp. 267-268.

p.126 ...*without exercising human freedom, human power, The Essential James Luther Adams, op. cit.,* p. 197.

p.126 ...*a response which is both individual and institutional, Ibid.,* pp. 195-196.

p.127 ... *goodness, wisdom, justice and power in the world,* Joseph A. Bassett, *Theology for Pulpit and Pew: The Everlasting Song* (Shippensburg, PA: Ragged Edge Press, 1996), p. 15.

p.128 ... *the capacity* to be influenced, *The Essential James Luther Adams, op. cit.,* p. 199.

p.128 ... *by the effects it produces or suffers,* Francis M. Cornford, *Plato's Theory of Knowledge: The Theatetus and the Sophist of Plato translated and with a running commentary* (New York: Liberal Arts Press, 1957), p. 237. See also Cornford's comments on Jowett's and his own translations of this very passage, in his "Preface," p. v.

p.129 ... *something you have to take away from others,* James Luther Adams, *The Prophethood of All Believers,* ed. George K. Beach (Boston: Beacon Press, 1986), p. 268.

p.129 ... *on the human family than all others,* William Ellery Channing, "Introductory Remarks," *The Works of William Ellery Channing* (Boston: American Unitarian Association, 1895), p. 8.

p.130 ... *hardening of the heart, The Prophethood of All Believers, op. cit.,* pp. 271-272.

p.130 ... *a manifestation of divine power,* Richard R. Niebuhr, "Religion Within Limits," *Harvard Divinity School Bulletin,* vol. 1, no. 2, 1968, pp. 2, 6.

p.131 ... *power engenders conflict, The Unitarian Universalist Christian: Special Issues, James Luther Adams at 75,* ed. Herbert F. Vetter, vol. 32, nos. 1-2 (Spring/Summer, 1977), pp. 32, 34-35.

p.131 ... *this grace of freedom, The Prophethood of All Believers, op. cit.,* p. 268.

p.131 ... *and a moral covenant,* See George Kimmich Beach, "The Moral Covenant," in *Questions for the Religious Quest: Finding Your Own Path* (Boston: Skinner House Books, 2002), pp. 91ff.

p.133 ... *sustaining quality present in whatever is, The Prophethood of All Believers, op. cit.,* p. 59.

p.134 ... *a new human type which we call genius,* Erwin Panovsky, *Albrecht Dürer* (Princeton, NJ: Princeton University Press, 1943) vol. I, p. 235 and vol. II, plate 295.

p.134 ... *this present darkness, The Prophethood of All Believers, op. cit.,* p. 167.

p.135 ... *eat up himself,* William Shakespeare, *Troilus and Cressida,* act I, scene iii.

p.135 ... *to the totalitarian state, The Prophethood of All Believers, op. cit.,* p. 169.

p.136 ... *one long bargain counter, Ibid.,* p. 169.

p.136 ... *the religion of the West, Ibid.,* p. 170.

p.137 ... *divine sanction for the autocratic monarch!* From a letter Adams wrote to friends, dated March 16, 1988. On the basilica at Daphni, see F. Perila, *Daphni: Aquarelles, Xylographies, Photographies de l'Auteur* (Athens, Greece: Editions Perilla, 1942).

p.138 ... *like movie stars, perfect and untouchable,* John Updike, "Singular in Everything," in *The New York Review of Books* (November 6, 2003), p. 18.

p.138 ... *the faith of the Nazis! The Prophethood of All Believers, op. cit.*, p. 44.

p.139 ... *who believes in action and acts*, James Luther Adams, "Frontiers of Freedom," radio broadcast, NBC Blue Network, October 26, 1941.

p.140 ... *a theological interpretation, The Prophethood of All Believers, op. cit.*, p. 86.

p.141 ... *the tragic destiny of humankind—and of God, Ibid.* p. 87.

p.142 ... *in the manner of* A Clockwork Orange, *Ibid.*, p. 87.

p.142 ... *(Now is the appointed time)*, W. H. Auden, *The Dyer's Hand and Other Essays* (New York: Vintage Books, 1948), p. 430.

p.142 ... *the "natural" religion of humanity is polytheism, The Unitarian Universalist Christian, op. cit.*, p. 15.

p.143 ... *future engagement with its higher self, The Prophethood of All Believers, op. cit.*, p. 71.

p.144 ... *they adopt self-worship, Ibid.*

p.144 ... *not to be confined to a particular space, An Examined Faith, op. cit.*, p. 45.

p.144 ... *Will Ye Speak Falsely for God?* Frank M. Cross Jr. was a professor of Old Testament and an authority on the Dead Sea Scrolls. His convocation address, "Will Ye Speak Falsely for God?" was published in *Contemporary Accents in Liberal Religion*, ed. Bradford T. Gale (Boston: Beacon Press, 1960), pp. 92-105.

p.145 ... *informs and overcomes space, An Examined Faith, op. cit.*, p. 45.

p.145 ... *ethical issues and responsibilities,* The contemporary theological revaluation of nature and "space" is discussed in Walter Brueggemann, "The Loss and Recovery of Creation in Old Testament Theology," *Theology Today*, 53:2 (July, 1996), pp. 177ff.

p.147 ... *The gods of the time were territorial gods, An Examined Faith, op. cit.*, pp. 272-273.

p.147 ... *define what the public wants, Ibid.*, p. 277.

p.148 ... *wrapping the flag around it, Ibid.*, pp. 279-280.

p.148 ... *whereupon the conversation ended! Ibid.*, p. 49.

p.149 ... *which he exemplified in his own habits*, Max L. Stackhouse, "A Puritan's Pilgrimage: Beyond the Iron Cage," *Union Seminary Quarterly Review*, vol. 37, no. 3, p. 206.

p.149 ... *we're just people with bad taste*, James Luther Adams, unpublished sermon manuscript.

p.150 ... *over against you and your group*, Joseph Barth, *Toward a Doctrine of the Liberal Church* (Boston: Minns Lectureship Committee, 1956).

p.150 ... *God is in us! The Unitarian Universalist Christian, op. cit.*, p. 13.

p.151 ... *a sanction for a culture-religion, An Examined Faith, op. cit.*, p. 148.

p.152 ... *I cannot believe in such a God, Ibid.*, p. 151.

p.153 ... *scientifically objective and verifiable*, Owen Barfield, *Saving the Appearances: A Study in Idolatry* (New York: Harcourt, Brace and World, undated), p. 111.

p.153 ...*an anti-theological or secular humanism*, I am indebted to John Buehrens for bringing to my attention Martin Buber's use of the term "Biblical humanism." The argument that humanistic commitments are rooted in Biblical beliefs and values is developed in George Kimmich Beach, *Questions for the Religious Journey* (Boston: Skinner House Books, 2002), pp. 102–108.

p.154 ...*an authority higher than that of Caesar and the territory*, An Examined Faith, *op. cit.*, pp. 272-273.

p.154 ...*his disease became endemic*, The Prophethood of All Believers, *op. cit.*, p. 151.

p.155 ...*I must be different from the way I have been*, An Examined Faith, *op. cit.*, p. 33.

p.155 ...*self-differentiation requires constant, conscious effort*, Edwin Friedman, *Generation to Generation* (New York: Guilford Press, 1985), pp. 228-230.

p.156 ...*no transcendent dimension to bring judgment*, James Luther Adams, "Congregational Polity and the Covenant," in "Three Lectures," transcribed by Alice Wesley (Chicago: Meadville-Lombard Theological School, 1977), p. 57.

p.157 ...*evident in the churches*, James Luther Adams, "The Marxist-Christian Dialogue," *The Unitarian Universalist Christian*, vol. 26, nos. 3-4 (Autumn/Winter, 1971), p. 3.

p.158 ...*the composer pipes to their tune*, The Prophethood of All Believers, *op. cit.*, p. 104.

p.159 ...*the discussion of human rights*, Ibid., pp. 106-107.

p.160 ...*a symbol of a lost humankind*, Ibid., p. 83.

p.160 ...*a part of the total community*, James Luther Adams, *Voluntary Associations: Socio-cultural Analyses and Theological Interpretation*, ed. J. Ronald Engel (Chicago: Exploration Press, 1986), p. 277.

p.161 ...*my father was a man of principle*, The Prophethood of All Believers, *op. cit.*, p. 33.

p.162 ...*some kind of compromise*, An Examined Faith, *op. cit.*, p. 27.

p.162 ...*it requires love*, The Prophethood of All Believers, *op. cit.*, p. 273.

p.163 ...*let my people go!* Ibid.

p.163 ...*they have will be taken away*, Ibid.

p.164 ...*the performance of binding obligations*, Ibid.

p.164 ...*faith and fortitude on both sides*, Ibid., pp. 127-128.

p.165 ...*their unexpected American guest in astonishment*, The Essential James Luther Adams, *op. cit.*, pp. 179-181.

p.167 ...*you don't have to send in your spies!* Transcribed from videotape, "Adams at Home: Six Conversations," produced by George K. Beach (Arlington, Virginia, 1988).

p.168 ...*out of the house within a minute*, James Luther Adams, *Not Without Dust and Heat* (Chicago: Exploration Press, 1995), p. 191.

p.169 ...*the paradox of justification*, James Luther Adams, "Paul Tillich on Luther," *Interpretations of Luther: Essays in Honor of Wilhelm Pauck*, ed. Jaroslav Pelikan (Philadelphia: Fortress Press, 1968), pp. 311-312.

p.169 ... *is peculiarly significant*, James Luther Adams, "Is Marx's Thought Relevant to the Christian? A Protestant View," *Marx and the Modern World*, ed. Nicholas Lobkowicz (London: University of Notre Dame Press, 2003), p. 382.

p.169 ... *the abyss in one's own heart*, *The Prophethood of All Believers*, *op. cit.*, p. 8.

p.171 ... *the least of these my brethren*, *Ibid.*, p. 206.

p.172 ... *now is the time for me to say* "Nichts!" *[Nothing]*, *An Examined Faith*, *op. cit.*, pp. 45-46.

p.172 ... *one must remain silent*, Rudiger Safranski cites Wittgenstein's statement and relates it to Arthur Schopenhauer's reflections on the "meaning" of music; see *Schopenhauer and the Wild Years of Philosophy* (Cambridge, MA: Harvard University Press, 1991), pp. 197, 343.

p.173 ... *our common responsibility. Amen*, James Luther Adams, unpublished manuscript.

Confronting Injustice: By Their Groups You Shall Know Them

p.175 ... *Laodicean lack of commitment*, James Luther Adams, *On Being Human Religiously*, ed. Max L. Stackhouse (Boston: Beacon Press, 1957), p. 25.

p.177 ... *By their groups you shall know them*, James Luther Adams, *The Prophethood of All Believers*, ed. George K. Beach (Boston: Beacon Press, 1986), p. 24.

p.178 ... *It's that we don't stay mad!* James Luther Adams, "Introduction," in Paul Tillich, *Political Expectation* (New York: Harper and Row, 1971), p. xx.

p.178 ... *dread of the civil power*, *The Works of William Ellery Channing* (Boston: American Unitarian Association, 1895), p. 7.

p.179 ... *established moral and spiritual order*, Paul Ricouer, *The Symbolism of Evil* (Boston: Beacon Press, 1969), p. 55.

p.180 ... *the altars of some churches*, *The Prophethood of All Believers*, *op. cit.*, pp. 304-305.

p.181 ... *By their fruits you shall know them*, James Luther Adams, *An Examined Faith: Social Context and Religious Commitment*, ed. George K. Beach (Boston: Beacon Press, 1991), p. 309.

p.183 ... *community seeking for mercy and justice*, *The Prophethood of All Believers*, *op. cit.*, p. 85.

p.183 ... *religious liberalism that they represent*, see *An Examined Faith*, *op. cit.*, pp. 337ff.

p.183 ... *major stages of development*, On "epochal thinking," see *The Prophethood of All Believers*, *op. cit.*, pp. 99ff. On Adams's periodization of modern, Western history, see *An Examined Faith*, *op. cit.*, pp. 337f.

p.184 ... *prophets' demand for justice*, *Ibid.*, p. 19.

p.185 ... *mend our common ways*, *The Prophethood of All Believers*, *op. cit.*, pp. 102-103.

p.186 ... *swift to do righteousness*, *An Examined Faith*, *op. cit.*, pp. 263-264.

p.187 ...*Amos, Hosea, Micah, and Joel,* For fuller development of these ideas see George K. Beach, "Covenantal Ethics," in *The Life of Choice,* ed. Clark Kucheman (Boston: Beacon Press, 1978), pp. 107-125.

p.188 ...*our committed relationships,* Charles Hartshorne, *The Divine Relativity* (New Haven: Yale University Press, 1948), pp. 65ff. See also George Kimmich Beach, "James Luther Adams's 'Covenant of Being' and Charles Hartshorne's 'Divine Relativity,'" *The Unitarian Universalist Christian,* vol. 58 (2003), pp. 57-70.

p.189 ...*A prophet is one who proclaims doom, The Prophethood of All Believers, op. cit.,* p. 57.

p.190 ...*See in order to foresee, Ibid.,* p. 101.

p.190 ...*the right deed for the wrong reason,* T. S. Eliot, *Murder in the Cathedral,* Part I in *The Collected Poems and Plays of T. S. Eliot,* (New York: Harcourt, Brace, and Co., 1954), p. 196.

p.191 ...*in other social spheres, The Prophethood of All Believers, op. cit.,* p. 313.

p.192 ...*you can start again, Ibid.,* pp. 59-60.

p.192 ...*the meaning of forgiveness, Ibid.,* p. 60.

p.193 ...*the creative maintenance of justice, Ibid.*

p.193 ...*salvation is for time and history, Ibid.,* pp. 74-75.

p.193 ...*only through time time is conquered,* T. S. Eliot, "Burnt Norton," "The Four Quartets," *The Collected Poems and Plays of T. S. Eliot, op. cit.,* p. 120.

p.194 ...*by prophet bards foretold, The Prophethood of All Believers, op. cit.,* p. 99.

p.195 ... *"the haves" and "the have-nots,"* James Luther Adams, "The Liberal Churches and Community Organization," unpublished manuscript, 1968.

p.195 ...*the first generation raised without religion,* Douglass Coupland, *Life without God* (New York: Pocket Books, 1994), p. 161.

p.196 ...*I just love the liturgy, An Examined Faith, op. cit.,* p. 32.

p.196 ...*you'll see what it's all about,* James Luther Adams, "Three Lectures," transcribed by Alice Wesley (Chicago: Meadville-Lombard Theological School, 1977), p. 2.

p.197 ...*our conception of responsibility,* James Luther Adams, "You Can't Escape History: A Christian Theory of Political Vocation" (Theta Chi Beta Address, Syracuse, NY, May 8, 1964), unpublished, p. 10.

p.198 ...*culturally created over centuries, An Examined Faith, op. cit.,* pp. 31-32.

p.198 ...*the role of the prophet, Ibid.,* p. 26.

p.199 ...*You're just a very well-paid prostitute! The Prophethood of All Believers, op. cit.,* p. 18.

p.199 ...*the historical context of the time,* James Luther Adams, *Voluntary Associations, op. cit.,* p. 226.

p.200 ...*Amos and the prophets and Jesus,* James Luther Adams, "George Huntston Williams: A Portrait," *Continuity and Discontinuity in Church History,* ed. Forrester Church and Timothy George (Leiden: E. J. Brill, 1979), pp. 8-9.

p.201 ... *William Ellery Channing calls "spiritual freedom,"* See Paul's Letter to the Galatians, 5: 1ff, and Channing's 1830 election sermon, "Spiritual Freedom," in *Collected Works of William Ellery Channing* (Boston: American Unitarian Association, 1895), pp. 172-186.

p.201 ... *the transcendent and the individual,* James Luther Adams, *Voluntary Associations, op. cit.,* p. 228.

p.202 ... *the church universal, catholic and invisible, The Prophethood of All Believers, op. cit.,* p. 314.

p.203 ... *fellow's claim to be a radical individualist, Ibid.,* p. 251.

p.203 ... *Protest in the economic sphere also soon appeared, An Examined Faith, op. cit.,* p. 308.

p.204 ... *there is no beginning, Voluntary Associations, op. cit.,* p. 399.

p.204 ... *deeper than reason—intuition and feeling, An Examined Faith, op. cit.,* pp. 308-309.

p.204 ... *freedom of association is exercised,* James Luther Adams, "Is Marx's Thought Relevant to the Modern World?" *Marx and the Modern World,* ed. Nicholas Lobkowicz (London: University of Notre Dame Press, 2003), p. 32.

p.205 ... *tried to smother freedom of association, The Prophethood of All Believers, op. cit.,* p. 256.

p.205 ... *His prediction was correct, Ibid.,* p. 244.

p.206 ... *the Lord Coke perceiving fell flat on all four, An Examined Faith, op. cit.,* p. 266.

p.206 ... *were of their doing, Ibid.*

p.206 ... *above the assembly of the Lord? Ibid.,* p. 264.

p.207 ... *the majority opinion of another,* James Luther Adams, "Three Lectures," *op. cit.,* p. 52.

p.207 ... *were brought to book, The Prophethood of All Believers, op. cit.,* p. 110.

p.208 ... *This practice obtained for almost 1,500 years, The Prophethood of All Believers, op. cit.,* p. 265.

p.209 ... *want the people who believe in it to pay for it,* James Luther Adams, "Three Lectures," *op. cit.,* pp. 44-45.

p.209 ... *I do not think the church could challenge even a rabbit,* James Luther Adams, "Where the Spirit of the Lord Is, There Is Liberty," unpublished sermon.

p.210 ... *how they snuggle up to those sermons!* James Luther Adams, "You Cannot Escape History," *op. cit.,* pp. 8-9.

p.210 ... *I am going into the study of Africa, Ibid.,* pp. 15-16.

p.211 ... *also to listen to the minority,* James Luther Adams, "Transactional Analysis: Psychotherapy and Social Responsibility," unpublished lecture.

p.212 ... *carried through by "outsiders,"* James Williamson, "An Interview with James Luther Adams," "The Christian Life," *Colloquy,* vol. 5, no. 9 (October, 1972), p. 17.

p.212 ...*subject to change under law*, James Luther Adams, "The Creative Thrust of Conflict," address at the General Assembly of the Unitarian Universalist Association, Hollywood, Florida, May 17, 1966.

p.213 ...*no personal problem that is not also a social problem*, James Luther Adams, *Not Without Dust and Heat: A Memoir* (Chicago: Exploration Press, 1995), p. 128.

p.213 ...*By their groups you shall know them*, The Prophethood of All Believers, *op. cit.*, p. 263.

p.214 ...*it will remain unity in diversity*, Ibid., p. 313.

p.214 ...*laws unto themselves*, The Rev. John Buehrens is a former President of the Unitarian Universalist Association. The Rev. Henry Whitney Bellows was a prominent Unitarian clergyman and a denominational organizer in the nineteenth century.

p.215 ...*with the assistance of the other professions*, An Examined Faith, *op. cit.*, p. 53.

p.215 ...*participating in social decisions*, James Luther Adams, *Voluntary Associations, op. cit.*, pp. 95-96.

p.215 ...*what makes us a people*, James Luther Adams, "Why I Oppose the 'Freedom of Conscience' Resolution," unpublished manuscript, 1981.

p.216 ...*a strong bond of union*, James Luther Adams, "Three Lectures," *op. cit.*, p. 7.

p.217 ...*is still going strong*, An Examined Faith, *op. cit.*, pp. 40-41.

p.217 ...*draining off the national energy into "warbling,"* James Luther Adams, *On Being Human Religiously*, ed. Max L. Stackhouse (Boston: Beacon Press, 1977), p. 186.

p.217 ...*what does the theologian say?* An Examined Faith, *op. cit.*, p. 42.

p.218 ...*That's an aspect of power*, Ibid., p. 43.

p.218 ...*the destructive use of atomic energy*, Not Without Dust and Heat, *op. cit.*, p. 286.

p.219 ...*an international nuclear arms race*, For the text of this letter, see *The Prophethood of All Believers, op. cit.*, p. 262.

p.219 ...*no man for committees anyhow*, On Adams's discovery of von Hügel's letter to James, and James's letter to Peabody, see *An Examined Faith, op. cit.*, pp. 83ff. James's statement about his being "no man for committees anyhow" is on p. 88.

p.220 ...*of the Weimar Republic ineffectual*, Ibid., p. 34.

p.220 ...*I suppressed prophetic indignation*, James Luther Adams, "You Cannot Escape History," *op. cit.*, pp. 13-14.

p.220 ...*the eager heavens take over*, The Prophethood of All Believers, *op. cit.*, p. 19. See also page 260.

p.221 ...*What makes you think you're not already?*, Ibid., p. 20.

p.221 ...*looking toward social change*, Ibid., p. 243.

p.222 ...*eighth-century prophets of the Covenant*, Ibid., pp. 6-7.

p.223 ... *such piety can be promoted,* Quoted by Thomas Mickelson in "*On Being Human Religiously,*" sermon, March 20, 1988.

p.223 ... *forces of hatred and greed, The Prophethood of All Believers, op. cit.,* pp. 41-42.

p.223 ... *under attack as a Communist, Ibid.,* p. 15.

p.224 ... *Died a grocer, Ibid.,* p. 152.

p.224 ... *facts or remedies of correction, The Unitarian Universalist Christian: James Luther Adams Papers,* ed. Herbert F. Vetter, vol. 48, nos. 3-4 (Fall/Winter, 1993), pp. 35-36.

p.224 ... *because we are separated, Ibid.,* p. 36.

p.225 ... *if the new is to come into being, Ibid.,* p. 37.

p.228 ... *with people taking shorthand notes,* Transcribed from "Adams at Home: A Conversation in Six Parts," a videotape produced by George K. Beach (Unitarian Church of Arlington, Virginia, 1988).

p.228 ... *false gods rush in to fill the vacuum, An Examined Faith, op. cit.,* pp. 18-19.

p.229 ... *for the ecology of all beings. Amen,* James Luther Adams, unpublished manuscript.

Renewing Community: The Covenant of Being

p.231 ... *of which Erikson names wisdom,* Erik H. Erikson, *Identity: Youth and Crisis* (New York: W. W. Norton & Co., 1968), p. 233. Erikson's scheme of eight stages, running from "basic trust" and "hope" in infancy to "integrity" and "wisdom" in old age, is diagramed on p. 94. These themes are also developed in his book, *Insight and Responsibility* (New York: Norton, 1964).

p.232 ... *the Liberal Arts found its soul,* James Luther Adams, *Voluntary Associations: Socio-cultural Analyses and Theological Interpretation,* ed. J. Ronald Engel (Chicago: Exploration Press, 1986), pp. 261-262.

p.233 ... *I will write it in their hearts,* James Luther Adams, *An Examined Faith: Social Context and Religious Commitment,* ed. George K. Beach (Boston: Beacon Press, 1991), pp. 363-364.

p.236 ... *in view of new situations, Ibid.,* p. 359.

p.236 ... *I don't like beehives, Ibid.,* p. 197.

p.237 ... *She named it,* James Luther Adams, *The Prophethood of All Believers,* ed. George K. Beach (Boston: Beacon Press, 1986), p. 4.

p.237 ... *if they were going to be human, Ibid.*

p.238 ... *It's a miracle,* James Luther Adams, *Not Without Dust and Heat: A Memoir* (Chicago: Exploration Press, 1995), pp. 74-75.

p.239 ... *flywheel of meaningful human existence, Voluntary Associations, op. cit.,* p. 243.

p.240 ... *moral ideals—of the community,* See *An Examined Faith, op. cit.,* pp. 139-240, and *The Prophethood of All Believers, op. cit.,* pp. 137-138.

p.240 ... *the social experience of centuries, Voluntary Associations, op. cit.,* pp. 392, 403.

p.242 ... *the yogi and the commissar, The Prophethood of All Believers, op. cit.,* pp. 79-80.

p.242 ... *an ultimate source and resource, Voluntary Associations, op. cit.,* p. 392.

p.243 ... *image as a medium of perception,* George Kimmich Beach, *Questions for the Religious Journey* (Boston: Skinner House Books, 2002); see "Parabolic Vision," pp. 151-172.

p.243 ... *the promise maker, the commitment maker, The Prophethood of All Believers, op. cit.,* pp. 136-137.

p.245 ... *ground and purpose of human fellowship, Ibid.,* pp. 74-75.

p.246 ... *religion that possessed the strongest battalions,* James Luther Adams, "Historical Perspectives on the Pluralistic Society," address at Loyola University, Chicago, June 7, 1974, unpublished manuscript, p. 2.

p.247 ... *to hold the reins themselves,* James Luther Adams, "Where the Spirit of the Lord Is, There Is Liberty" (2 Cor. 3: 17), unpublished sermon manuscript.

p.248 ... *the seedbed of democracy, Ibid.,* p. 10.

p.249 ... *all the members rejoice with it, An Examined Faith, op. cit.,* pp. 270-272.

p.250 ... *the hidden spiritual resources of existence, The Prophethood of All Believers, op. cit.,* p. 85.

p.250 ... *there will be no fruit, The Unitarian Universalist Christian: James Luther Adams Papers,* ed. Herbert F. Vetter, vol. 48, nos. 3-4 (Fall/Winter, 1993), p. 44.

p.251 ... *go the way of dispossession, The Prophethood of All Believers, op. cit.,* p. 125.

p.252 ... *the social concerns of his religious community,* See *An Examined Faith, op. cit.,* p. 35.

p.253 ... *It isn't in the Bible, Ibid.,* p. 121.

p.254 ... *he "had to go to hell yet," Ibid.,* p. 10.

p.255 ... *effective way to make friends, Ibid.,* pp. 120-121.

p.255 ... *fresh air will get into the church, Ibid.,* p. 121.

p.256 ... *the children of one divine parent,* James Luther Adams, "Crystalizing Unitarian Beliefs," in "Lecture VI, The Nature and Function of the Church," unpublished manuscript.

p.256 ... *a holy people unto the Lord thy God, The Prophethood of All Believers, op. cit.,* p. 93.

p.257 ... *believing that God believes in you,* Andre Dubus, "A Father's Story," *God: Stories,* ed. C. Michael Curtis (Boston: Houghton Mifflin Co., 1998), p. 40.

p.257 ... *along into the pulpit, The Prophethood of All Believers, op. cit.,* p. 94.

p.257 ... *the appearance of the* ecclesiola in ecclesia, James Luther Adams, "Changing role of the Ministry Today: Sociological Factors and Theological Implications," unpublished manuscript, p. 11.

p.258 ...*come from the hand of God, Ibid.*, p. 11.

p.259 ...*hidden realities that offer release and surcease, The Prophethood of All Believers, op. cit.*, p. 82.

p.260 ...*seeking for mercy and justice, Ibid.*, p. 85.

p.260 ...*The human being is made for fellowship, An Examined Faith, op. cit.*, p. 186.

p.261 ...*life is fellowship in growth*, James Luther Adams, "Fellowship Is Life," unpublished manuscript, October 1983.

p.262 ...*or even to discover oneself! An Examined Faith, op. cit.*, pp. 19-20.

p.262 ...*the wind bloweth where it listeth? Ibid.*, p. 300.

p.264 ...*to renew the covenant, The Prophethood of All Believers, op. cit.*, p. 314.

p.266 ...*we may say that modern secularism is a Jewish-Christian secularism*, James Luther Adams, "Is Marx's Thought Relevant to the Christian?: A Protestant View," *Marx and the Western World*, ed. Nicholas Lobkowicz (London: University of Notre Dame Press, 2003), p. 373.

p.266 ...*you must "discount" it*, Kenneth Burke, *The Rhetoric of Religion* (Boston: Beacon Press, 1961), p. 18.

p.266 ...*for the growth of the seed, The Prophethood of All Believers, op. cit.*, p. 36.

p.267 ...*God as acting in history, Not Without Dust and Heat, op. cit.*, p. 139.

p.267 ...*the redemptive Lord of history, An Examined Faith, op. cit.*, p. 104.

p.267 ...*the sub-human, the biological sphere, An Examined Faith, op. cit.*, pp. 104-105. Professor George H. Williams was the author of, among other works, *Wilderness and Paradise in Christian Thought* (New York: Harper and Row, 1962).

p.268 ...*the maximum weekly fee is a very modest one, Voluntary Associations, op. cit.*, p. 255.

p.269 ...*other kinds of political activity*, Joseph Williamson, "The Christian Life: An Interview with James Luther Adams," *Colloquy*, vol. 5, no. 9 (October, 1972), p. 16.

p.270 ...*channels of sensitivity and stimulus are radically reduced, The Prophethood of All Believers, op. cit.*, pp. 286-287.

p.270 ...*this sweet creature in...exquisite radiance, Ibid.*, p. 295.

p.271 ...*the limitations of the covenant, Ibid.*, p. 300.

p.271 ...*the other and the self, Ibid.*

p.272 ...*true piety is properly appreciated, Ibid.*, pp. 299-300.

p.272 ...*critical reflection in sexual ethics*, Beverly W. Harrison, "Vintage Adams" (review of *The Prophethood of All Believers*), *The World Journal of the Unitarian Universalist Association*, January/February 1988 (vol. II, no. 1).

p.274 ...*just so long as he's not conjugating, Not Without Dust and Heat*, p. 75.

p.274 ...*consider adultery a merely private action, The Prophethood of All Believers, op. cit.*, p. 301.

p.275 ... *Charles doesn't swear, either! Ibid.*, p. 128.

p.276 ... *wait to watch the water clear, we may, Ibid.*, p. 233.

p.276 ... *Every functioning myth is susceptible of these polarities, Ibid.*, p. 228.

p.277 ... *even for our freedom, Ibid.*, p. 137.

p.277 ... *the Covenant of Being*, Fritz Kaufmann, "On the Covenant of Being," *Journal of the Liberal Ministry*, III:3 (Fall, 1963), pp. 154-157.

p.278 ... *resolved into Love of Being*, Jonathan Edwards, "Notes on the Mind," *Jonathan Edwards: Representative Selections*, edited by Clarence H. Faust and Thomas H. Johnson (New York: American Book Company, 1935), pp. 35, 37.

p.278 ... *in response to the divine promise, Voluntary Associations, op. cit.*, p. 243.

p.279 ... *She gave him grace*, James Luther Adams, lectures on Rudolf Sohm, undated, unpublished manuscript. An essay by Adams, "Law and the Religious Spirit," is found in James Luther Adams, *On Being Human Religiously, op. cit.*, pp. 188ff.

p.279 ... *substitutes the part for the whole, The Prophethood of All Believers, op. cit.*, p. 228.

p.280 ... *the flowery path that leads to the broad gate and the great fire, The Unitarian Universalist Christian: Special Issue: James Luther Adams at 75*, ed. Herbert F. Vetter, vol. 32, nos. 1-2 (Spring-Summer, 1977), p. 77.

p.281 ... *if it is not rooted in grace?, The Prophethood of All Believers, op. cit.*, p. 228.

p.281 ... *as well as in personal experience, Voluntary Associations, op. cit.*, p. 390.

p.281 ... *become nourished of each other, The Prophethood of All Believers, op. cit.*, p. 231.

p.282 ... *gives meaning to existence but not as an object*, James Luther Adams, "Paul Tillich on Luther," *Interpreters of Luther*, ed. Jaroslav Pelikan (Philadelphia: Fortress Press, 1968), p. 313.

p.282 ... *These were said to have been his last words, Goethe: Conversations and Encounters*, eds. David Luke and Robert Pick (Chicago: Henry Regnery Company, 1966), pp. 247-248.

p.283 ... *of the greatest, and of the whole universe, An Examined Faith, op. cit.*, pp. 105-106.

p.284 ... *re-formation and transformation of community*, James Luther Adams, *On Being Human Religiously*, ed. Max L. Stackhouse (Boston: Beacon Press, 1977), p. 97.

p.285 ... *a viable world of wholeness, The Prophethood of All Believers, op. cit.*, pp. 308-310.

p.286 ... *in obedience to thy commandments. Amen*, James Luther Adams, unpublished manuscript.

Renewing Faith: Taking Time Seriously

p.287 ... *I ran to it and grasped it*, Ludwig Wittgenstein, *Culture and Value*, ed. G. H. von Wright, tr. Peter Winch (Chicago: University of Chicago Press, 1980), p. 64e; italics in original.

p.292 ... *even to his foibles*, James Luther Adams, *The Prophethood of All Believers*, ed. George K. Beach (Boston: Beacon Press, 1986), pp. 46-47.

p.293 ... *a pilgrim church on adventure, Ibid.,* p. 313.

p.293 ... *idea of "the church of the spirit,"* Francis Greenwood Peabody, *The Church of the Spirit* (New York: Macmillan, 1925).

p.293 ... *human freedom in an open universe, The Prophethood of All Believers, op. cit.,* pp. 194-196.

p.294 ... *more experienced than ourselves*, James Luther Adams, *An Examined Faith: Social Context and Religious Commitment*, ed. George K. Beach (Boston: Beacon Press, 1991), p. 58.

p.295 ... *my most passionate interest was religion, Ibid.,* p. 17.

p.296 ... *whether we use the word "God" or not, Ibid.,* p. 361.

p.296 ... *the soul of learning and religion, The Unitarian Universalist Christian: Special Issue, James Luther Adams at 75,* ed. Herbert F. Vetter, vol. 32, nos. 1-2 (Spring/Summer, 1977), p. 77.

p.296 ... *a faith worth discussing and testing, The Prophethood of All Believers, op. cit.,* p. 48.

p.298 ... *So spoke the pupil of Max Weber!* James Luther Adams, *The Essential James Luther Adams. Social Context and Religious Commitment,* ed. George K. Beach (Boston: Beacon Press, 1991), p. 126.

p.299 ... *a gift that awaits the taking—and the sharing*, James Luther Adams, *Unitarian Universalist Register-Leader*, 1968, page number unknown.

p.300 ... *the history that is in the making, An Examined Faith, op. cit.,* p. 307.

p.301 ... *oblique, satirical, and even grotesque forms, The Grotesque in Art and Literature* , eds. James Luther Adams and Wilson Yeats (Grand Rapids, MI: William B. Eerdsman Publishing Co., 1977), pp. 69-74.

p.301 ... *What fun for the affluent society! An Examined Faith, op. cit.,* p. 354.

p.301 ... *spat upon, done to death, Ibid.,* p. 356.

p.302 ... *A hand is laid upon us, The Prophethood of All Believers, op. cit.,* p. 95.

p.302 ... *unjust on the east side*, James Luther Adams, "Foreword," in Ernst Troeltsch, *The Crisis on Consciousness*, unpublished manuscript.

p.303 ... *Nothing so much like a hole as a swelling, The Prophethood of All Believers, op. cit.,* p. 147. Charles Augustin Saint-Beuve was an influential literary critic and writer in nineteenth-century France.

p.304 ... *the special character of love,* "Introduction," in Ernst Troeltsch, *The Absoluteness of Christianity and the History of Religions* (Richmond, VA: John Knox Press, n.d.), pp. 17-19.

p.305 ... *the consequence of the person's accepting that one is accepted*, James Luther Adams, "Paul Tillich on Luther," *Interpreters of Luther*, ed. Jaroslav Pelikan (Philadelphia: Fortress Press, 1968), p. 326.

p.305 ... *the church wished to extend to him, Ibid.,* p. 311.

p.306 ... *out of which we come and to which we go, Ibid.,* pp. 314-315.

p.307 ... *I doubt, therefore I am, Ibid.,* p. 316.

p.308 ... *future engagement with its higher self, The Prophethood of All Believers,* op. cit., p. 71.

p.309 ... *unacknowledged legislators of the world, Ibid.,* p. 243.

p.310 ... *seven acts or great periods, Ibid.,* pp. 244-245.

p.311 ... *my fundamentalist map of eschatology! Ibid.,* p. 38.

p.311 ... *So much the worse for the facts, The Prophethood of All Believers,* op. cit., p. 291.

p.312 ... *filial obedience would issue in a new spiritual freedom, Ibid.,* pp. 113-114.

p.313 ... *from Jeremiah to Paul to Joachim to Channing,* George Kimmich Beach, "The Covenant of Spiritual Freedom," in *Redeeming Time,* ed. Walter P. Herz (Boston: Skinner House Books, 1998), pp. 99-106.

p.313 ... *no matter how hard we will have to struggle for it,* Gerhard Spiegler, *The Eternal Covenant: Schleiermacher's Experiment in Cultural Theology* (New York: Harper and Row, 1967), p. 23.

p.314 ... *a special place and function within the order of being, The Prophethood of All Believers,* op. cit., p. 75.

p.315 ... *both present and yet to come,* Members of the Jesus Seminar have argued for a wholly non-eschatological message of Jesus. For a contrary view, see E. P. Sanders's scathing review of *Excavating Jesus: Beneath the Stones, Behind the Texts,* by John Dominic Crossan and Jonathan L. Reed (HarperSanFrancisco, 2002), in *The New York Review of Books* (April 10, 2003), pp. 49-51.

p.315 ... *in the phrase of Marianne Micks,* Marianne H. Micks, *The Future Present: The Phenomenon of Christian Worship* (New York: The Seabury Press, 1970).

p.316 ... *non-ecclesiastical as well as in ecclesiastical institutions,* James Luther Adams, "Some Uses of Analogy in Religious Social Thought," *Proceedings of the IXth International Congress of the History of Religions* (Tokyo: Maruzni, 1960), pp. 470-471.

p.316 ... *the fullness of the eternal,* James Luther Adams, "Tillich's Interpretation of History," *The Theology of Paul Tillich,* ed. Charles W. Kegley (New York: Pilgrim Press, 1982), pp. 330, 342.

p.317 ... *its impact on the present, An Examined Faith,* op. cit., pp. 95-96.

p.318 ... *the driving force of ideas in the history of mankind, The Prophethood of All Believers,* op. cit., pp. 112-113.

p.318 ... *the joy of commitment, a "costing" commitment, An Examined Faith,* op. cit., p. 33.

p.319 ... *the light that heals us,* James Luther Adams, "Bright Shoots of Everlastingness," *Andover Newton Quarterly,* September 1969, p. 16.

p.319 ... *The tree is in fact rooted in the sky, Ibid.,* p. 17.

p.320 ... *up through death to newness of life, An Examined Faith,* op. cit., p. 332.

p.320 ... *the one who has been most loved, Ibid.,* p. 205.

p.321 ... *Music, like religion, is fundamentally a mystery, The Unitarian Universalist Christian,* op. cit., p. 62.

p.322 ...*seek again this spirit and this power unto salvation*, An Examined Faith, op. cit., p. 212.

p.322 ...*the scraggy tree outside my window goes its preordained way*, The quotation is from the memorial address by Adams in March, 1979; an unpublished manuscript.

p.323 ...*the only survival, the only meaning*, The Unitarian Universalist Christian, op. cit., pp. 72-73.

p.324 ...*of constructive innovation, of new creation*, Ibid., pp. 37-38.

p.324 ...*There are always new beginnings*, An Examined Faith, op. cit., p. 56.

p.325 ...*a request that was promptly granted*, Ibid., pp. 281-282.

p.326 ...*I know who you mean. The German philosopher Kanto*, Transcribed from the videotape, "Adams at Home: Conversations with James Luther Adams," produced by George K. Beach, Arlington, Virginia, 1988.

p.327 ...*In His will is our peace*, An Examined Faith, op. cit., p. 281.

p.327 ...*they backward go who toil most to go on*, Dante Alighieri, Purgatorio, Canto xi, verse 1.13.

p.327 ...*That is what religion means*, The Unitarian Universalist Christian, op. cit., p. 15.

p.328 ...*one must try to take its meaning by the forelock*, The Prophethood of All Believers, op. cit., p. 281.

p.329 ...*no adequate conception of citizen participation*, The Essential James Luther Adams, op. cit., p. 127.

p.329 ...*Several members of the group followed us out*, An Examined Faith, op. cit., p. 324.

p.330 ...*the reactionary evangelicals and fundamentalists*, See ibid, pp. 323ff.

p.331 ...*God will make all his mountains a way*, The Prophethood of All Believers, op. cit., pp. 41-42.

p.331 ...*Redeem the Time*, An Examined Faith, op. cit., p. 55.

p.332 ...*Well Dean, I've heard it's "publish or perish,"* For the report of this story I am indebted to my colleague, Rev. Kenneth Torquil MacLean.

p.332 ...*faith lives on—in the optative mood*, James Luther Adams, "Unitarian Philosophies of History," The Journal of Liberal Religion, vol. 7 (Autumn, 1945), p. 13.

p.332 ...*O, prove true!*, Emily Dickinson, quoted by Harold C. Goddard, The Meaning of Shakespeare (Chicago: The University of Chicago Press, 1951), p. 552.

p.333 ...*speaks of the resources of fulfillment*, "Unitarian Philosophies of History," op. cit., p. 13.

p.334 ...*it is always available*, The Prophethood of All Believers, op. cit., p. 242.

p.334 ...*the true wayfaring Christian*, See John Milton, Areopagitica: A Speech for the Liberty of Unlicensed Publishing, in The Complete Poetry and Selected Prose of John Milton, edited by Cleanth Brooks (New York: The Modern

Library, 1950), pp. 691ff. The preceding citation is from Brooks's "Introduction," p. xi.

p.335 ...*a blank virtue, not a pure, The Prophethood of All Believers, op. cit.*, p. 181.

p.336 ...*and you were not there, Ibid.*, p. 103.

p.336 ... *"Then be grateful, be grateful," Eliot replied,* William Crout, "Letters to the Editor," *The New York Times* (January, 2001); I thank Katherine Converse for sending me this clipping.

p.337 ...*to avoid a colorful splash, The Prophethood of All Believers, op. cit.*, p. 88.

p.337 ...*the sense of our destiny, An Examined Faith, op. cit.*, p. 55.

p.338 ...*until it come to rest in Thee, Augustine: Confessions and Enchiridion, Library of Christian Classic, Vol. VII, translated and edited by Albert C. Outler* (Philadelphia: The Westminster Press, MCMLV), p. 31.

p.339 ...*divine love that will not let us go. Amen.* James Luther Adams, unpublished manuscript.

Acknowledgments

THIS BOOK IS A SIGNIFICANTLY ENLARGED and revised version of the Minns Lectures for 1999 presented under the title, "The Parables of James Luther Adams," in Cambridge, Massachusetts, Chicago, and Berkeley, and in several subsequent continuing education programs for clergy in Florida, Massachusetts, Illinois, and North Carolina. The questions and observations that came with these discussions have greatly benefited me as I reworked the text for publication. The Minns Lectureship Committee of King's Chapel and First and Second Church of Boston, chaired by Dianne Arakawa, sponsored the original lectures and the Committee and its current chairperson, Jeffrey Barz-Snell, provided funds to help underwrite this publication. Thanks to all.

Mary Benard, Editor of Skinner House Books, provided expert editorial advice throughout the publication process. The critical reading and suggestions of Paul Rasor, Dean of Pendle Hill, Wallingford, Pennsylvania, helped me clarify the text at many points. I want to express my deep appreciation to them.

Especially I want to thank Barbara Kres Beach, my wife. She shares my admiration, appreciation, and love for Jim and Margaret Adams, and has had a special part in the making of this book.

G. K. B.
Campicello, Madison County, Virginia
May 25, 2004

Index